# International Political Economy in the 21st Century

Understanding of the theories that underpin international political economy (IPE), and their practical applications, is crucial to the study of international relations, politics, development and economics.

This is a comprehensive and accessible introduction to the field, with an engaging and coherent foundation to the subject. It considers traditional and alternative approaches to IPE, and in doing so elucidates key concepts, assumptions and the intellectual and historical context in which they arose and developed. At all times, it makes clear their relevance to issues from trade, finance and government, to environment, technology, health, labour, security, migration, development and culture. The book encourages independent reflection and critical thinking through a range of in-text guiding features. In addition, each chapter presents theoretical analysis alongside contemporary issues, helping the reader to relate to the real world of IPE and to better understand how theory helps inform interpretation of it.

New to this edition:

- comprehensively updated to include key coverage of the post-2015 framework of the Sustainable Development Goals, the financial crisis and international government responses – successful or otherwise – to recent challenges;
- fully updated data, reflective questions, recommended readings, concept and example boxes, and illustrations;
- new chapters on health, migration and labour;
- additional coverage of trade theories and key contemporary issues, such as national versus human security, economic versus human development and illegal networks in global trade.

**Roy Smith** is Principal Lecturer and Programme Leader for the MA in International Development at Nottingham Trent University, UK.

**Imad El-Anis** is Senior Lecturer and Programme Leader for the MA in International Relations at Nottingham Trent University, UK.

**Christopher Farrands** is Principal Lecturer in Global Studies at Nottingham Trent University, UK.

# International Political Economy in the 21st Century

## Contemporary Issues and Analyses

### Second Edition

Roy Smith, Imad El-Anis and Christopher Farrands

Routledge
Taylor & Francis Group

LONDON AND NEW YORK

Second edition published 2017
by Routledge
2 Park Square, Milton Park, Abingdon, Oxon OX14 4RN

and by Routledge
711 Third Avenue, New York, NY 10017

*Routledge is an imprint of the Taylor & Francis Group, an informa business*

First edition published by Pearson Education Limited 2011; Routledge 2013

**British Library Cataloguing in Publication Data**
A catalogue record for this book is available from the British Library

**Library of Congress Cataloging in Publication Data**
Names: Smith, Roy H. author. | El-Anis, Imad, author. | Farrands, Chris, author.
Title: International political economy in the 21st century : contemporary issues and analyses / Roy Smith, Imad El-Anis and Christopher Farrands.
Description: Second edition. | Milton Park, Abingdon, Oxon ; New York, NY : Routledge, 2017. | Includes bibliographical references and index.
Identifiers: LCCN 2016037518| ISBN 9781138808409 (hardback) | ISBN 9781138808416 (pbk.) | ISBN 9781315750637 (ebook)
Subjects: LCSH: International relations--History--21st century. | Globalization. | International economic relations.
Classification: LCC JZ1318 .S625 2017 | DDC 337--dc23
LC record available at https://lccn.loc.gov/2016037518

ISBN: 978-1-138-80840-9 (hbk)
ISBN: 978-1-138-80841-6 (pbk)
ISBN: 978-1-315-75063-7 (ebk)

Typeset in Bembo
by Servis Filmsetting Ltd, Stockport, Cheshire

# Contents

# 5 National, international, regional and global governance 123

# 6 Trade 143

# 7 Global finance 165

## 8 Development 185

## 9 Environment 205

## 10 Technology in the global political economy 225

## 11  Culture                                                                    249

## 12  Security                                                                   265

## 13  Migration and labour                                                       281

# Illustrations

## Figures

## Tables

# Preface

This textbook is intended as an aid to study for those looking at IPE as a discrete discipline, or as a part of a broader politics, international relations or global studies degree programme. It can be read as an introductory text, or as a supplement to prior reading in related fields. For example, most universities offer IPE as a second-year optional module, which will build on first-year foundations that introduce concepts of power, wealth distribution and the respective roles of governments, non-governmental organisations and market forces.

IPE is a field of study that has increasing significance in relation to 'everyday' life. Processes of globalisation are both widening and deepening and are impacted upon by a range of events and related processes which are beyond the control of most individuals and even their national governments.

The manner in which this book is structured is designed to enable students to gain an initial understanding of the historical and philosophical foundations of various approaches to the study of IPE. This is then followed by a closer look at what might be described as the mainstream approaches. However, one of the appealing aspects of this discipline is the diversity of approaches that it encompasses, and we then go on to look at a number of alternative approaches. It is not suggested that this is a fully exhaustive list of such approaches but it does include a representative range.

Between the theory section and the issues section there is a linking chapter that discusses processes of globalisation and how these are represented and analysed by various schools of thought. There is quite a broad spectrum of attitudes towards the scale and importance of globalisation. For some authors these processes are at the heart of IPE and cannot be underestimated in terms of their impacts in shaping the contemporary world. They apply at the political, cultural and socio-economic levels, and also have huge environmental impacts. Others have a more sceptical approach and refer back to international trading patterns that have developed over several centuries. Although the scale and speed of transport and communication systems may have advanced significantly over time, the fundamental trade and other international relationships have not changed that dramatically. It remains a largely state-centric and competitive world. Finally, there are those who inhabit the middle ground between these two extreme positions. They recognise the importance of new technologies and that issues of scale and speed do have an impact on relationships, but they also note the ongoing relevance of the state as a political unit and the lack of meaningful global governance.

The final section looks at a number of issue areas identified as relevant to the study of IPE. By definition there is a certain element of selectivity taking place here in determining which issues are deemed 'worthy' of a chapter. Health is clearly a major issue and has its own chapter as well as being raised in other parts of the book, such as in the chapter on development. Similarly, the role of the media plays a crucial part in how processes of globalisation are understood. Indeed, media organisations are active players and key drivers in many aspects of these processes. This point is referred to in the chapter on technology and elsewhere in the book. Hopefully the reader should see that the issue areas intersect with each other and are only a sample of the myriad examples that could have been included. If you notice a particular 'gap' it would be worthwhile reflecting on why it is that you feel that a particular issue area has not received due attention. That may also indicate what type of theoretical approach you may feel most at ease with. We all have preferences in terms of how we view the world. One of the purposes of this book is to draw attention to both the range of issues that IPE is concerned with studying and the fact that there are many differing ways in which to study them.

## Advice to readers in Europe and North America

This book has been designed by the authors and the publishers to be used in teaching international political economy wherever you are in the world. We offer a range of examples and illustrations from around the world. Students, instructors and lecturers may want to think about the language we use, and we are well aware that American English is sometimes very different from English used in the UK or Ireland, or in much of Europe. This is not really a problem in terms of spelling, although we apologise if spelling and grammar here irritates some readers used to other conventions. It is more of a problem in political language. There are plenty of examples, but 'liberal' is probably the trickiest, since in the US it can be used rhetorically to mean anyone to the left of the speaker who the speaker doesn't like. In Europe, 'liberal' *can* include a loose inclination to the left rather than the right, but it also includes quite fundamentalist right wing politics: in countries such as Denmark, liberal political parties are well to the right of the mainstream conservatives. This is not just a confusion of language; it reflects important differences of political practice and social history. In the US, libertarianism is a more mainstream position on the right than it is in (Western) Europe; in continental Europe, anarchism is a well-founded and important political tradition with important economic policy implications, even though it is generally the object of fear and suspicion in North America and the UK. 'Conservative' means different things in different contexts too.

Our solution to these difficulties is to explain what we mean by key words as they arise, and the first two chapters spend some time explaining language that we have used, which we hope helps. There is also a glossary of terms that will help you, but this is more concerned with the technical language of IPE. The most problematic issue in this context may be the differences between what have been called 'communism', Leninism, Marxism and variations of Marxisms, which are sometimes referred to as 'Marxian', essentially a watered down Marxism. We have used Leninism and Marxism; we have avoided 'communism' because we don't think it has anything to contribute to an initial study of IPE, and we have avoided Marxian because it is a milk-and-water word that says nothing useful. We have also warned readers to beware of their own preconceptions about political language, and we have aimed to be open about our own. We hope to have been consistent, and we have reflected our experience teaching in both North America and the UK as well as continental Europe in our practice.

But there is a separate problem for the authors: IPE is taught differently in different institutions. This is well known, and has been characterised as a difference between 'European' and 'American' teaching and learning. It is actually more complicated than that, and in any case some US colleagues share a 'European' understanding of IPE and some European academics, especially those in Business School contexts, teach the subject very similarly to many US schools. So we have listened closely to US consumers who complained that the first edition was 'too British', and taken the advice also of anonymous US colleagues who acted as referees to the second edition proposal.

This inevitably leads to compromises. It also explains the greater length of the text. But we have done our best to accommodate the interests of users, students and lecturers, who work in different contexts, and we encourage users to adapt the text as they wish to meet their own curriculum needs. That will include the ongoing debate about whether and how far IPE can be 'scientific', which runs right through the text.

*Roy Smith,*
*Imad El-Anis and*
*Christopher Farrands*

# Acknowledgements

The authors would like to thank the editorial team at Routledge who have been involved during the preparation of this manuscript, in particular Andrew Taylor, Charlotte Endersby and Sophie Iddamalgoda.

*Roy Smith*
*Imad El-Anis*
*Christopher Farrands*

# Abbreviations

| | |
|---|---|
| ACP | African, Caribbean and Pacific |
| ADHD | attention deficit hyperactivity disorder |
| AOSIS | Alliance of Small Island States |
| APEC | Asia-Pacific Economic Council |
| ARV | anti-retroviral |
| ASEAN | Association of South East Asian Nations |
| BIS | Bank for International Settlements |
| BMI | body mass index |
| CDOs | collateralised debt obligations |
| CoP | Conference of the Parties |
| CRAs | Credit rating agencies |
| CSR | Corporate social responsibility |
| ERTMS | The European Rail Traffic Management System |
| EU | European Union |
| FDI | Foreign direct investment |
| FTA | Free trade agreement |
| GAFTA | Greater Arab free trade area |
| GATS | General Agreement on Trade in Services |
| GATT | General Agreement on Tariffs and Trade |
| GCC | Gulf Cooperation Council |
| GDP | gross domestic product |
| GNI | gross national income |
| GNP | gross national product |
| GPE | global political economy |
| G7 | group of seven |
| G8 | group of eight |
| G20 | group of twenty |
| HGP | The Human Genome Project |
| HST | Hegemonic stability theory |
| IBRD | International Bank for Reconstruction and Development |
| ICBMs | intercontinental ballistic missiles |
| ICC | International Criminal Court |
| IGF | Internet Governance Forum |
| IGOs | Intergovernmental organisations |
| IMC | Independent Media Centre |
| IMF | International Monetary Fund |
| INGOs | International non-governmental organisations |

| | |
|---|---|
| INSTRAW | International Research and Training Institute for the Advancement of Women |
| IOM | International Organization for Migration |
| IPCC | Intergovernmental Panel on Climate Change |
| IPE | International political economy |
| IPRs | intellectual property rights |
| IR | international relations |
| ISIS | Islamic State |
| ITU | International Telecommunications Union |
| IUCN | International Union for Conservation of Nature |
| KBI | knowledge-based industry |
| LDCs | least/lesser developed countries |
| LLR | lender of last resort |
| LoN | League of Nations |
| M & As | mergers and acquisitions |
| MAD | mutually assured destruction |
| MBA | Masters in Business Administration |
| MDGs | Millennium Development Goals |
| MFN | most favoured nation |
| MNCs | multinational corporations |
| NAFTA | North American Free Trade Area |
| NATO | North Atlantic Treaty Organization |
| NCDs | non-communicable diseases |
| NGOs | non-governmental organisations |
| NPT | Nuclear Non-Proliferation Treaty |
| NTBs | non-tariff barriers |
| OECD | Organisation for Economic Cooperation and Development |
| OPEC | Organization of Petroleum Exporting Countries |
| PHM | People's Health Movement |
| PPP | purchasing power parity |
| R & D | research and development |
| RMA | revolution in military affairs |
| SAPs | structural adjustment programmes |
| SCP | structure–conduct–performance |
| SDGs | Sustainable Development Goals |
| START | Strategic Arms Reduction Treaty |
| TRIMs | trade-related investment measures |
| TRIPs | trade-related aspects of intellectual property rights |
| TTIP | Trans-Atlantic Trade and Investment Partnership |
| UAE | United Arab Emirates |
| UN | United Nations |
| UNESCO | UN Educational, Scientific and Cultural Organization |
| UNFCCC | UN Framework Convention on Climate Change |
| UNICEF | United Nations Children's Fund |
| UNIFEM | UN Development Fund for Women |
| WB | World Bank |
| WBCSD | World Business Council for Sustainable Development |
| WEF | World Economic Forum |
| WHO | World Health Organization |
| WIPO | World Intellectual Property Organization |

| WMDs | weapons of mass destruction |
| WSF | World Social Forum |
| WSIS | World Summit on the Information Society |
| WST | world system theory |
| WTO | World Trade Organization |

# Introduction

One of the key characteristics of life in the twenty-first century is the importance of political and economic relationships both within and between states. Governments and citizens are increasingly affected by structures and processes beyond their immediate locality and control. These changes in the nature of world politics can initially appear overwhelmingly incomprehensible. Such phenomena are at the heart of contemporary debates within the discipline of International Political Economy (IPE).

The first part of the book is designed to introduce you to the evolution of IPE as a distinct discipline. We also provide a summary of the theoretical tools that have emerged to help make sense of the increasingly complex contemporary world. The second part of the book considers a range of issues and trends pertinent to the study of IPE. Reference will be made to challenges to state sovereignty, the increased interconnectedness between national economies and the growing number of issues that are most appropriately understood within the context of either sub-national or international/global frameworks of analysis.

What we also intend to do throughout this book in each of the areas we look at, including finance, the environment, globalisation and trade as well as other central issues, is to keep reminding the reader of the relationship between theory and practice in IPE. IPE emerged in universities in the late 1960s and early 1970s because of the growing weakness of the world economy, because of the decline in the power of the US dollar, because of the failure of established institutions to cope with trade conflicts and monetary disputes, and because of the emerging power of global corporations and financial trading which individual governments found they could no longer control. How were these changes (and many others) to be explained? The established theory in international relations failed to answer the questions, and often did not even think it important to address them. Economists had some answers, but they were highly contested and the apparent consensus among both policy makers and academics of the 1950s and 1960s eroded rapidly. IPE was the answer to practical as well as theoretical problems, and has continued to try (not always successfully!) to cover both agendas.

Finally, we have tried to ask who are the key actors in IPE? How have they changed? What are the main coalitions of interests and ideas in IPE, and how do they work? How have changes in the main actors and processes (most obviously the 'rise of China' but there are plenty of others) reshaped the world political economy, and what challenges does this pose for theory and for academic critique?

IPE draws on a multidisciplinary basis. This is exciting, but also takes patience to grasp. Established ideas in IPE draw on politics, sociology, business studies, philosophy, economics and psychology. IPE all the same forms a distinctive field of study with its own questions and its own methods. But these are 'distinctive', not sealed off from the other social and human sciences. So IPE borrows from and influences other ways of thinking about social life all the time. In particular, the main questions that IPE has asked form what we will call the 'traditional' agenda. Especially in the last thirty years or so, many scholars have criticised these ways of asking about and finding understanding about IPE, and we look at those important critiques that have pushed the subject further.

We can sum up this discussion by identifying the main themes that run right through this book, and form the main questions we shall ask, once we have got some purchase on the key theoretical questions, which we do in Chapters 1, 2 and 3. These main themes are:

1   The *actors and processes question*: what are the main actors, processes, structures and patterns of behaviour in IPE? How do the different theoretical approaches answer these questions differently (when they do)?

2   The *theory and practice question*: how can we understand the ways in which theory and practice have interacted in the development of academic IPE?

3   The *power question*: how does power work in the global political economy, how has that changed, and what specific different forms does power adopt?

4   The *history/present question*: how does the past impact on the present when we try to study specific issue areas such as finance, the environment and trade?

5   The *change and the future question*: how is the global political economy changing, how far are these *fundamental* or relatively *superficial* changes, and what are the consequences of these changes for geopolitics, for the future development of the world economy, for the production of inequality, for the emergence of new actors, processes and behaviour in the future?

You will be guided through the key concepts and issues in a structured manner using reflective exercises. The book is designed with boxes highlighting key authors, concepts and issues and at the end of each chapter further reading is indicated.

## So what is IPE?

The relationship between the political and economic spheres can be traced back to the earliest times of human interaction. Social anthropologists would recognise the questions of 'who gets what, when, where and how?' as having relevance to all societies at all times. Political decision-making is influenced by what is economically viable. This may seem an obvious point. A more subtle observation is the recognition that the economic values assigned to all manner of goods, services and general resources are politically determined.

What is notable about the contemporary world is the growing complexity of the relationships and processes that relate to these questions. In particular it is increasingly problematic to answer such questions purely in terms of local interactions. Over time we have witnessed the spread and dominance of cash-based economies, as opposed to subsistence-based. Linked to an international system of exchange of goods and services, this means that a greater degree of contextual understanding and analysis is required to fully grasp what is happening. In part this can be seen as the impetus for the emergence of IPE as a distinct discipline. Neither political studies nor simply economics-focused approaches offer a complete picture.

The discipline of International Relations (IR) originated post-First World War with a focus on issues of war and peace, commonly known as 'high politics'. During the 1960s and 1970s there were those who thought that international relations were being not just under-theorised but fundamentally misunderstood. For example, the increasing significance of multinational corporations (MNCs) and natural commodities (especially oil), previously thought of as 'low politics', moved towards centre stage both within the practice and analysis of IR. This shift in focus led to an emerging school of thought that would become known as IPE. Susan Strange's work is widely recognised as being at the forefront of this new approach. She was controversial in her argument that rather than IPE emerging as a sub-discipline within the subject of IR the reverse was the case. Strange's view was that the discipline of IR, particularly those approaches that continued to highlight the centrality of the nation state, was misguided if it failed to take into account both macro and micro issues, processes and trends that resulted from the intertwining of the political and economic spheres. Moreover, Strange and a growing number of other writers argued that it was impossible to usefully separate these two areas.

One of the key elements of IPE is the relationship between the political and the economic. This informs all theoretical approaches, although some more than others, such as structuralism. It is also one of the defining characteristics of how a government operates in terms of the level of intervention it attempts to implement in relation to the operations of the so-called free market. As such, the relationship between state governments and the market economy is central to the study of IPE.

Recent decades have seen what has been termed the 'triumph of liberalism'. Historically this refers to the end of the Cold War period and the collapse of the Soviet Union. More broadly it is an assessment of the expansion of neo-liberal economics and a relative withdrawal of government intervention policies. China is probably the best example of the move away from a command economy, while still maintaining a communist political regime. Beyond this example though there is a more general sense of all governments finding it increasingly difficult to maintain political control over economic issues. This is not such a recent phenomenon as interdependence between economies is something that has evolved over an extended period. What is of increasing significance though is that the free flow of capital and, in some cases, unequal exchange and terms of trade can seriously threaten a state's fiscal policies and financial stability.

The relationship between governments and the free market was severely tested by the mortgage lending and subsequent banking crisis of 2009. Despite the dominant ethos of neo-liberalism the governments of the United States and Western Europe found themselves in a position of having to intervene on a massive scale to 'bail out' failing banks and other companies. The implications of not doing so could have led to an even more severe crisis and economic downturn to the point of recession and mass unemployment. This example demonstrates that despite the rhetoric of neo-liberal policies there remains a close connection between the operations of the market and a degree of government oversight, at both the national and international level.

Analyses of political economy reflect an attempt to make sense of a matrix of actors, issues and processes. As mentioned above, this complexity is evolving over time and greater emphasis on interconnections on a global scale adds to the need to check and reassess one's view of the world. The apparent rise of a global civil society, the ongoing power plays between nation states and the increased significance of free-market liberal economic policies, both in terms of the role of MNCs and the aim of sustainable development, are all factors that feed into the multi-faceted contemporary world. The following chapters will look at how various theoretical approaches have attempted to order the world and make sense of it. This will also involve our own review of what we believe to be the most relevant and significant trends in the world with regard to processes of globalisation. This will recognise that there will be disagreements among analysts not only over what is happening, but also what various identifiable trends might mean, or if they should be welcomed or actively resisted. It is acknowledged that such disagreements are inherent within any exploration of social trends. Differing analysts will have varied worldviews or moral frameworks. Political ideology permeates all aspects of academic study and it would be wrong to suggest that pure objectivity can be found in any of the approaches under review here, including our own. Similarly, you will also form your own opinions on the issues under consideration here.

In addition, this book provides a sense of how the discipline of IPE has developed over time and how relevant some of the antecedents of the discipline remain today. For example, do the writings of Adam Smith, David Ricardo, Karl Marx, Antonio Gramsci or John Maynard Keynes offer useful insights into the politics and economics of the twenty-first century? Or are they simply historical figures that went some way towards developing our understanding of the evolution and diversity of political and economic thought, yet provide little in the way of insightfulness with regard to contemporary affairs? Has the world changed so much in relation to technological innovation and social transformations that newer, more relevant approaches are required? If so, what might these approaches comprise, which actors are seen as key and how are their interactions best represented and understood? Piecing together the 'jigsaw' is a common analogy for gaining an insight into how complex mechanisms operate. As an introduction to how this book is structured it is useful to spend some time looking at how such an analogy might be applied in relation to IPE.

## The global jigsaw

All theoretical approaches can be seen as trying to create a 'picture' from an array of initial beliefs, apparently supported by empirical evidence. However, the basic principle of creating a worldview from a range of evidence-based pieces to form a coherent and understandable whole is a broadly common theme in both the social and physical sciences. How then might this be applied to our understanding of a rapidly changing and complex international political economy?

First of all, do we have a picture on our box of jigsaw pieces to act as a guide that we can follow? For normative theorists, who talk of how the world should be rather than how it is, there can be a sense of a picture of a world to which they aspire. Unfortunately they may not be able to find the pieces with the correct patterns or shapes to fit together to create such a world-picture. The more optimistic of such theorists may still cling to the belief that all the pieces are there but some are face down and not recognised or there are reasons why the piecing together is not progressing as well or as quickly as they would hope. Perhaps some of the pieces are being withheld or there is some form of breakdown in the communication between the various players responsible for fitting the pieces together. The added complication of a changing world means that the picture on the box itself may need to alter as different shapes and patterns of pieces evolve as the puzzle is still being put together. If there is a single theme that reflects the character of globalisation it is that of change. A second theme would be adaptation and the levels of speed and success with which actors and environments can accommodate various changes.

The jigsaw analogy has within it several common assumptions that any theorist or scholar needs to reflect upon. How can we be sure that we have a correct set of the necessary pieces required to arrive at a complete picture? In terms of competing analyses this may be thought of in terms of two different puzzles being mixed together. Both may make coherent pictures but a certain level of skill and discernment is necessary to separate them out, or see how they relate to each other. Marx and Smith were creating pictures with similar actors and similar issues and processes. However, the style and emphasis of both pictures were significantly different, as we will see. Note here that despite having different views both writers were able to piece together coherent pictures using similar pieces. To take this analogy a step further this can be thought of as a puzzle where the pieces have images on both sides. Depending on which side one views a different picture emerges. Imagine a discipline where the pieces are not flat with only two distinct planes. Rather they are cubes, or many-more-sided geometric shapes, with each plane representing a competing worldview. This gives some sense of the enormity of the task involved in determining how the kaleidoscope of pieces that make up the contemporary world are best ordered and understood.

Despite the scale of the undertaking to order, analyse and explain the world in relation to varying IPE theories we need to begin somewhere. If we continue our jigsaw analogy for a little longer, let us assume that we are dealing with a traditional rectangular shape. Therefore, we can deduce that this will have four corner pieces from which we can arrive at a framework within which our remaining pieces should fit together to provide a coherent picture. No doubt from the potential problems alluded to above it is clear that what is being described is an 'ideal' jigsaw and that what we have here is a rather loose analogy that should be seen as a guiding strategy to map our way through the review of the historical development of IPE as a distinct discipline. Now imagine that this rectangle has what we will call a political axis running up the left-hand side and an economic axis running along the bottom. From this would it be possible to begin to map where and how certain writers or issues relate to each other? For example, one would imagine that the free-market school of thought would be well to the right on the economic axis but relatively low on the political axis. In contrast those advocating command economies would score higher on the political axis than on the economic axis. As a simple graph this could tell us something in very general terms about where the emphasis is placed by various writers in relation to the politics/economics spectrum.

Yet before such plotting can take place one needs to consider what factors are in play to pull the subject under consideration towards the political or economic poles. Strange and other writers that will be discussed below would baulk at the idea that these poles can be so easily disaggregated. A defining characteristic of many IPE writers of more recent times has been their desire to highlight the connections between economics and politics. Rather than a mechanistic plotting of a single point on a graph they would create a more complex picture. Here the jigsaw analogy becomes insufficient, as what is being described now is more akin to a moving picture. Shades of colour could become important, representing the emphasis on particular issues. A familiar example could be the depth of green associated with various environmental groups or red for socialist-type policies. The movement in the picture would be a reflection of the dynamics of the processes that see a continual shift in the dominance of certain ideas and capabilities over time. So, although the jigsaw analogy remains a useful starting point, we need to move beyond this to help us order and understand a world most aptly characterised by change.

At the risk of taking our use of analogies too far we suggest that rather than a jigsaw, what we are now looking at is a picture more closely related to that of a television screen. In order to receive a clear picture one needs to be 'tuned in' to the relevant signals. Of course, there are myriad signals to pick up and viewers have a range of channels that they may receive. This channel selection or preference can be seen as relying on one's dominant beliefs and prejudices. The signals may be the same, but various viewers may see and understand things differently. Numerous signals and receivers are in operation around the world. This is not a simple one-way broadcasting process. In this book you will see that there have been a wide range of views formed and promoted. In looking at how such views are formed we will also be asking questions regarding what elements of various schools of thought retain contemporary relevance.

## Structure of the book

The book is structured in line with the above analogies in that the first part introduces various theoretical positions and the 'pieces' that they identify and put together. After identifying these foundations the second part of the book looks at an array of actors, and the third part considers relevant issues and trends that reflect the main aspects of the contemporary world.

Chapter 1 introduces the reader to the theoretical foundations that underpin the study of IPE: realism, liberalism and Marxism. The emphasis here is on the key distinctions between these approaches and their historical evolution. Key historical figures are highlighted by the use of author boxes and although the major focus of the chapter is the development of theoretical approaches, you will be prompted to consider the relevance of each approach to the real world. Having established the theoretical foundations of the discipline, this chapter then assesses the impact of IPE scholars since the early 1970s when many turned their attention to what had been perceived as 'low politics'. It focuses on the growth of different strands of thought within the neo-realist, neo-liberal and structural approaches.

Chapter 2 introduces the most significant alternative theoretical approaches that have developed in response to the 'orthodoxy' described in Chapter 1. You will be introduced here to Critical Theory, constructivism, feminist, Gramscianism, green, regulation theory and postmodern/poststructural approaches.

Building on the theoretically focused discussions in the preceding chapters, Chapter 3 explores business theories and global business behaviours. It explains how the complexity of multinational enterprise behaviour and strategies contribute to the complexity of IPE.

Having introduced a broad range of theoretical perspectives, Chapter 4 begins to develop an understanding of how these relate to 'real world' experiences. The degree and significance of processes of globalisation (itself a contested concept within IPE) is the subject of varying interpretations. Here we ask you to consider the salient points of the globalisation debate. This chapter links the perspectives discussed earlier in the book to the more specialised issue-based chapters.

The second part of the book focuses on actors and issues within IPE. We begin with Chapter 5, which considers governance at the national, international, regional and global levels. After an overview of the origins and development of the Bretton Woods Institutions the attention shifts to more contemporary debates. The number of international organisations at the end of the 1990s was over 2,500, as compared with around 30 that existed at the start of the twentieth century. Their role has become more complicated as the transnational flows that these institutions are attempting to regulate become larger and harder to control. The role and significance of the major 'private' political economy actor will also be described. Here, issues as to how and in what ways MNCs are seen as both the drivers and victims of global changes are highlighted. In what ways and forms are they reflectors of a political–economic ethos, and by which routes and methods do they lobby for a political environment that reflects the current dominance of neo-liberalism? How and to what extent do they interface with both states and civil society? Finally, the role of civil society in increasing the representative nature of global governance institutions is focused upon in more detail.

Chapter 6 considers world trade and the development of the international trade system after 1945. Particular attention is paid to the management of this system. Pertinent issues in world trade are discussed, including the position of developing countries and the 'free trade versus fair trade' debate.

Chapter 7 analyses the development of a global financial system and the impact this has had on actors within the world economy. The demise of the post-war system of fixed exchange rates, the wave of market-oriented reform in domestic financial markets and the rapid integration of many once-national capital markets across political and regulatory boundaries provide the focus of the discussion. The chapter concludes with a focus on the impact of financial crises and the stability of the contemporary financial system.

Chapter 8 considers the position of development issues and strategies in the world economy. The contested nature of the term is highlighted and the historical understandings are outlined in the first section. The shift towards a neo-liberal orthodoxy in development is discussed and the impact of salient issues such as foreign aid and the debt crisis is highlighted.

Chapter 9 addresses the diversity of opinion and debate in relation to environmental ramifications of current and proposed future practices of production. At one end of the debate 'deep ecologists' question the wisdom of exclusively human-centred development policies; while other commentators ('environmentalists' in varying shades of 'green') prefer to emphasise conservationism and the utilisation of natural resources. Climate change, potential rises in sea levels, acid rain, deforestation and loss of other habitats resulting in decreasing biodiversity are among the issues that will be discussed. The range of responses from the various parties, both private and public, will be illustrated and explained.

Chapter 10 considers the paradoxical role technological developments have in many aspects of IPE. On the one hand, they may be seen as the means by which the neo-liberal project has been advanced and come to dominate much of the world. On the other, they offer potential solutions to many pressing global problems, both in logistical and coordinating capacities. Debates over access to technology and the significance of English as the leading medium of international discourse will be considered. Comparative advantages within the international trading system and the entrenchment of divisions of wealth are a direct result of the ownership of relevant resources and application of technical expertise.

Chapter 11 looks at cultural issues as another significant factor in relation to globalisation. It has even been suggested that the seeds of a global monoculture have already been sown. This chapter considers this proposition in the light of the issue areas discussed above and related theoretical debates. The potential impact of the spread of a dominant system of production, and the possibility that a common set of intrinsic values necessarily follows, will be critically presented. The emphasis here will be on the promotion of certain types of 'knowledge', values, norms and 'rights'. Huntington's 'Clash of Civilisations' thesis has attracted renewed attention with regard to competing value systems. The ongoing debate surrounding cultural relativism and/or universality will be reviewed. In particular this chapter discusses the possible relationship between a near-universal trading system and a concomitant system of assumptions and values.

Chapter 12 is designed to relate to all of the above issues and trends in the context of a dynamic, contentious and evolving set of security agendas. Whereas many IR textbooks will focus on state- and military-centric security, the distinctive nature of IPE approaches, as opposed to IR, tend to adopt a broader interpretation and analysis of security issues.

Chapter 13 explores two increasingly controversial issues: migration and labour. The chapter explains the relationships between migration on the one hand, and economic, political and physical security on the other. It also discusses the key driving forces behind contemporary migration trends and the global division of labour.

Chapter 14 is the final substantive chapter of the book and considers health. The chapter explains the demographic shifts leading to a so-called 'health transition' and examines the emergence of lifestyle-related non-communicable diseases. It also critically reflects on the policies of major non-state actors such as the World Health Organization.

The conclusion reviews salient aspects of processes of globalisation and the relative values and explanatory powers of the competing analytical perspectives. These aspects include: which ones are actors focused upon, what are the constraints within which they operate, and how do they relate to each other? This book does not claim to offer a full explanation for all contemporary phenomena. However, it does provide you with an introduction to the various IPE schools of thought and their relevance to a number of selected issues. In doing so, insights into how the world is evolving in response to aspects of globalisation will be demonstrated. It will become clear that in reading this book students of IPE will gain not only enhanced knowledge of the discipline, but also of the world around them and their place within it.

# 1 The origins and core ideas of international political economy

## Chapter learning outcomes

The main aims of this chapter are to enable the reader to:

- Give a brief account of the origins of international political economy (IPE) and its changing identity as an academic field of endeavour.
- Explain why the roots of IPE in International Relations are significant for its current agenda and strengths, but also its weaknesses, of the field as it has evolved.
- Make sense of how IPE evolved as a critique of IR.
- Suggest how IPE was then reintegrated with political economy, economics and economic history, as well as business studies, and with what effects.
- Explore the core contemporary theories of mainstream IPE, the most influential ideas from neo-liberalism and neo-realism, as well as from classical liberal and neo-liberal economics from classical Marxism and theories of trade and economic growth.

In doing these tasks, you will find it helpful to remember that later chapters will also develop the core theories as we go along.

## Introduction

In this chapter, the sources of IPE are examined, a brief history of the field is offered, and the main theories that have shaped contemporary mainstream IPE are outlined and explained. Because these were rooted in the academic study of International Relations (IR), we look very briefly at the IR theories that shaped the origins of IPE, but the reader is asked to remember that this is an IPE text and that to get a fuller picture of IR as a subject of study they need to look at an IR text. Some readers will be studying IR as well as IPE, or as an overall framework for the analysis of IPE, but others will not; and we hope readers will allow us to engage with both groups of users of this text. This chapter goes on to examine the leading conventional theories in IPE, meaning those that reflect both dominant ways of teaching the subject and those that have most claim on the research literature in the field. The chapter does not examine more critical ideas of IPE, although some of these have become widely used and so could also be described as 'mainstream', because they are the subject of Chapter 2. This distinction between 'mainstream' and 'critical' literatures will seem unnatural to some readers because there is some overlap between the two, and because it seems to arbitrarily force a distinction on those entering a complex field of study. But it makes sense in so far as: (i) it is how the subject is often taught; and (ii) it is helpful as you begin a study – and this is an introductory text – to break the field down into manageable elements, even if you subsequently bring these elements together in a different way when you have started to get a more sophisticated understanding.

Before we get into the theory, it would be good just to indicate the basic scope of the world economy, how large it is and which are the key actors. If you use this text sometime after the

**Table 1.1** Basic information on the world economy 2016 (all figures in $US at purchasing power parity)

| | All money values in $US tr. at purchasing power parity | Notes |
|---|---|---|
| No. of UN member states | 198 | Depending on definitions, there are a number of states not in the UN and the European Union is a key actor in the world economy but not a state |
| Size of the world economy (world GDP) | 79.8 tr. | |
| Size of global finance transactions | 180tr. (approx.) | This is harder to assess and more controversial than world GDP |
| Largest actors by GNP | China 19.5 tr. European Union 19.1 tr. United States 17.9 tr. India 8.0 tr. Japan 4.7 tr. | |
| Largest actors – finance | United States European Union Germany Japan UK China | |
| Largest external debtors | United States 17.2 tr. European Union 13 tr. UK 9.2 tr. Germany 5.6 tr. France 5.5 tr. Japan 5.2 tr. | |
| Largest global South economies (by GNP) | | Developed in Chapter 8 |
| Largest multinational companies (MNCs) (by turnover) | | Developed in Chapter 3 |

*Source*: IMF World Economic Outlook, 2016; CIA World Factbook 2016; MNC data from Forbes online.

following information was published, it will be easy to check and update these figures for yourself, and to see how much has changed. As you probably realise, a trillion (tr.) is a number with twelve noughts after it – a thousand billion.

You probably have a good sense of how diverse the world economy is, and also of how many non-state actors – banks, multinational companies, lobbies, environmental groups, international institutions and so on – have power and leverage within the world economy alongside states. So throughout this text, we are talking about a world that has not just many actors, but *many types* of actors. You probably also have a sense that power is distributed among these actors very unevenly. Apple, Google, the leading world banks, the leading oil corporations, hyper-rich individuals, owners of media corporations, owners of patents and copyright all have power beyond the wildest dreams of the smaller states in the world system. They may also often vie with the largest state actors for influence. But remember too that power takes many forms – it is not just, or even primarily, the capacity to force others to do what you want. It may be more persuasive rather than forceful or violent; it may be a psychological relationship, a battle of wills rather than resources; power relates to legal capacity or legal authority, although they are not direct equivalents; and power also lies deeply in key structures of relationships, including structures of domination and structures of interdependence. This last kind of power, usually known as 'structural power', is a key to the understanding of IPE. All this is to say that IPE is interesting and exciting because it tries to make sense of a diverse and complex world.

## The sources of IPE

As just noted, International Political Economy has its main origins as *an academic field* in a series of difficulties in international relations in the 1960s. Perhaps it *ought* to have had its roots in political economy, or in economics. But that was not what happened. As a result, IPE owes many of its methods, key questions and theoretical approaches – and some of its limitations – to IR. What happened next was that scholars in the field, such as Razeen Sally and Justin Rosenberg at the London School of Economics, Robert Gilpin and Craig Murphy in the United States, A. Claire Cutler in Canada and many others, tried to correct some of the distortions produced through IPE's origins in IR. They drew on resources in politics, political sociology, global history, as well as from classical political economy and international economics. Philosophical debates about methods and approaches in social understanding have also shaped IPE throughout its history. Business history and business studies too have shaped the evolving field of IPE (see Chapter 3), and IPE specialists who ignore the role of firms and the experiences of managers run the risk of losing touch with some of the most important realities shaping global relations. This 'correction' against the initial dominance of an IR agenda has been an ongoing process. Some colleagues might say it is still incomplete; or that it has not gone far enough. But these concerns undoubtedly shaped and continue to shape the agendas and theoretical foci of IPE.

So although 'political economy' had been a key area of enquiry and policy debate since at least the early eighteenth century in many countries, IPE began in the form we now understand it at the end of the 1960s, when a group of scholars, mainly in the US and UK, but also in France and in the global South, found the US-dominated mainstream approaches in current academic international relations inadequate. 'Inadequate' precisely because it seemed to so underestimate the importance of trade, finance and exchange as well as work and labour and development alongside the more traditional diplomatic and military agendas of IR. Whether we like it or not, IPE has its origins in a critique of IR. Equally, though, it also has its origins in a series of practical concerns shared by many policy makers as well as academics, not only in the developed Western countries, but perhaps even more in the global South. In this section, we look first at the theoretical issues between IR and IPE. We then explain how much of the substance of IR remained in much IPE. Only then do we explain the policy debates that helped to give a compelling impetus to IPE as it emerged in the English-speaking world and elsewhere. But this is at least as important as the other sources. Susan Strange, one of the founders of IPE, always argued that IPE should be an 'eclectic' field, drawing its examples as well as its theoretical approaches from as wide a range of sources and examples as possible. This diversity of approach as well as of subject matter is worth remembering. Strange's contribution is outlined in more detail later. Along with Strange, key figures in the emergence of IPE at the time included Joan Edelman Spero (author of the first widely used text in the field), Robert Gilpin (the most influential writer from a liberal perspective in the United States), Raymond Vernon (author of one of the most influential studies of the rise of the global multinational firm) and Robert Cox (Canadian scholar who reshaped IPE through a systematic adaptation of the ideas of the scholar and activist

Antonio Gramsci to IR and IPE after leaving a long career as an international civil servant which influenced his theoretical ideas).

Influential economists equally significantly shaped IPE as it emerged. Discussions of trade, finance and investment, as well as the growth of advanced technology industries and the main patterns of globalisation have naturally been dominated by international economic political and social relations. But many more recent economists have had a number of reasons for a relative neglect of political economy. Like mainstream IR scholars, many economists have struggled to sustain the argument that economics is a separate independent subject, a 'true discipline' not dependent on others. Economists – or some of them at least – have retreated into a world of mathematical modelling and mathematic proof, which has made the field more difficult to relate to people's everyday experience of life; they have done this not out of perversity, but in pursuit of a particularly rigorous kind of quasi-scientific knowledge. Reliable knowledge claims, they argued, could only be built on methods similar to those used by 'natural sciences' such as physics. These scholars held that to question the bases of economics as a 'positivist' field was to betray it. Political economy, they suggested, was less rigorous because it tried to be inclusive of economic, social, political and cultural realities. They believed that the more economists could cut out any significant 'exogenous factors' and concentrate on giving complete explanations of economic phenomena in terms of economic factors that could be quantified, the stronger their knowledge claims would be. Political economists have always made the opposite claim; that sound explanations had to rest on taking all the relevant issues and factors into account and that explanations and understandings of IPE had to be more broadly based – politics, sociology, anthropology, statistics, ethics and economics must find a common space if the subject is to fulfil its promise. This argument is separate from the question of whether IPE can be more 'scientific' or whether it might draw more on a range of methods and ideas. This is not an argument to take on right at the start of the subject, but you will find that it runs through many of the debates that we elaborate throughout this book. It is also a debate to be wary of in so far as you may, depending perhaps on what you have already studied, have an instant reaction to support one side or another. But you would be well-advised to keep a more open mind: this is a philosophical argument to which there is no single 'right answer'.

Scholars from economics, which was after all originally called 'political economy', have therefore shaped IPE equally significantly. Historically-minded colleagues continue to draw on their work in a critical evaluation of where IPE is to this day. So the work of Mandeville (late seventeenth century; the creator of what came to be called the theory of the 'hidden hand' in economics, where individuals' pursuit of their own interests could have the overall effect of promoting a general good), Adam Ferguson (mid-eighteenth century; creator of the concept of civil society), Ricardo (early nineteenth century; trade theory and the mechanics of market behaviour), Malthus (early nineteenth century; economics as the 'gloomy science' especially with respect to population and the exhaustion over time of available resources) were among the most important economic theorists. They looked back to earlier thinkers who would not have described themselves as 'political economists', but whose ideas shaped the field. These included (a short selection of a potentially long list) Aristotle, who coined the Greek word from which we take the word 'economics' and who saw economic management as a form of practical knowledge akin to furniture making or shipbuilding, complex, skilled, but capable of being passed on and subject to rational analysis and judgment. It also includes the medieval Islamic scholars Ibn Battuta and Ibn Khaldun, usually described as geographers, but political scientists and historians too. The two Arab scholars travelled widely and established an agenda of comparative recording as accurately as they could of what they observed in economy, agriculture, state finance and debt management as well as trade and the exchange of ideas as well as services. One could add many classical observers to this list, as well as leading political philosophers such as Locke and Hobbes, but the most influential scholar, who has some claim to be the effective founder of modern economics, is the Edinburgh polymath Adam Smith, whose *The Wealth of Nations* (1776) not only dominated the agendas of economic thinking, but also identified trade and international exchange as key elements in all economic relations. Smith developed the idea of the division of labour, the way the structures of production shape the efficiency (or inefficiency) of economic activity and the ways in which changes in technology and labour processes feed into the profitability of both agriculture and industry. Smith may indeed have been the first to try to treat agriculture and industrial production as susceptible to the same kinds of analysis and explanation in detail; he certainly made a considerable contribution to the methodologies of economics, including quantitative work, as well as to its more general ideas.

There is no better illustration of Smith's enormous influence than the first volume of Marx's *Capital* (1861), which is intended to be a critique of then conventional economic thinking, taking Smith to task in particular. But it is impossible to read Marx without also recognising that he pays enormous tribute to Smith as the most profound thinker and the most careful analyst of global economic behaviour before him. It has often been said that all subsequent political economy is a dialogue with the ghosts of Smith and Marx, which does not, of course, imply by 'dialogue' a high level of agreement. Later economists have kept a dialogue between economic analysis and international political economy open, and the most influential of these are discussed throughout this study. As IPE has evolved, its scholars have found resources in the writing of these older scholars, and sometimes turned to ideas once rejected as incoherent or unusable to explain more recent events or crises. Smith's contribution will be more fully examined shortly.

## IPE as a critique of IR

If IPE emerged as a critique of IR, as has just been suggested, it is important to briefly outline the state of play in International Relations theory at the time that it emerged. Before the mid-twentieth century, IR was rarely taught as a distinctive subject in its own right with its own agenda, intellectual boundaries and theories; more usually, it was understood as a branch of politics (or political science), drawing on the theories of politics, including the classical Greek and Renaissance writers as well as more contemporary theorists. But the case was regularly made that politics and IR formed a distinctive discipline with their own methods and methodologies, owing little or nothing to psychology, sociology or cultural studies and only a little to economics. The workings of international business were little considered. At a leading institution in the field, the first anywhere to have a recognised Professor of IR, 'international politics' was taught at the University of Aberystwyth into the 1970s dominated by military concerns, security studies and strategy, although there was also some emphasis on institutions. At Cambridge (UK) until quite recently, IR was taught as part of a history sub-faculty, and the syllabus was largely controlled by historians. It is fair to add that no study of IR *or* IPE makes very much sense without a serious consideration of relevant history and the history of ideas; but to allow historians to dominate the field was simply perverse (and Cambridge has acquired a distinguished IR team including some IPE specialists since the shackles of the historians were thrown off). In many countries, IR consisted largely of the teaching of history and institutions, or of institutions and law: most French and Italian universities continue to follow this pattern, although much has changed in Germany and Scandinavia, and a few French and Italian universities buck this trend and offer programmes and undertake research that reflect a much broader approach including IPE. Thus the problem was that the conventional agenda of IR was limited and failed to recognise the actual changes taking place in the world system from the 1950s onwards (or, arguably, from much earlier, especially in finance). The structure of university bureaucracy and the lines drawn between fields and departments and their power bases was one element in this institutional bias against what became the core elements of IPE. But it was not the only factor. Creating a genuine synthesis of politics, economics, history, social studies and law always proved difficult. But it has been crucial to the emergence of IPE today. It is also only fair to add that IR has changed very significantly since the 1970s in most but not all universities, becoming a diverse, vibrant and multi-disciplined field of study in close dialogue with other social science areas of study. And in the meantime, distinctive agendas of IPE have been set by universities in India, Brazil and South Africa, as well as in the University of the West Indies, in Canada and Mexico, agendas which have stepped outside or beyond those conventionally set in the usually dominant academy in the US and Europe.

## Realist IR and IPE

The label 'realism' in International Relations theory usually refers to a school of writers and practitioners who think that politics is a struggle for power unrestrained by other human institutions, by morality or by law – 'This is just how it *really* is!' But many realists qualify that position and realism is a good deal more carefully thought through than its critics – or some of its cruder adherents – suggest. The origins of realism are often seen in the historian Thucydides' famous classical Greek account of a war between Athens and Sparta and their allies at the end of the fifth century BCE, *The Peloponnesian War*. Thucydides tries to understand a desperate war fought across the Greek world (the whole eastern Mediterranean, not just what is Greece today), the debates, resources, alliances and betrayals in order to understand how his own city, Athens, suffered such a critical defeat. He has a restrained pessimism about human motives and a willingness to recognise the frailty of institutions and agreements. But at the same time, Thucydides was trying to write history, not theory, and although he has furnished material for many later writers, one might want to be wary of drawing generalisations from his very specific account. Realism in IR has many other sources, including the writing of Renaissance scholars and diplomats such as Niccolo Machiavelli and Thomas Hobbes and the emergence of a conservative counter to political liberalism after the Renaissance. But Thucydides was in effect the grandfather of realism even if 'reading him as a realist' is something of a distortion. This gifted IR its agenda of the study of diplomacy, war, the balance of power and the struggle for supremacy among great powers where 'the strong do what they can and the weak suffer what they must'.

While classical realist IR theory tended to ignore, or at least downgrade, questions of political economy, there were exceptions. The downgrading was not purely a mistake in passing. Nineteenth-century scholars across what would later be called a 'realist-liberal spectrum' saw politics as primarily rooted in constitutions and sovereignty. A raft of issues followed on from the determination of the nature of the constitution and the fundamental law-making functions in relations between states as in relationships within them. It follows from this argument that all economic questions are secondary, however important they may appear to be, since the forms and underlying ideas of politics must always have primacy over the 'mere' appearances of the everyday. Despite this approach (which derives from Plato's philosophy reinforced by Immanuel Kant's writing), some scholars did consider questions of political economy. Of the 'realist' writers who saw political economy as more significant, none is more important than E. H. Carr. An enigmatic figure who taught IR at Aberystwyth and later at Cambridge, Carr made his mark as author of reports in 1939 and 1946 for the London think tank Chatham House. which later became central texts of realism. Carr was at once one of the sternest critics of the then (1930s) commonly held liberal idealism. His view that liberal failures and ignorance of real power relations had produced what he called *The Twenty Years' Crisis* after 1919 led directly to the coming of the Second World

War. But Carr was also a convinced, rather secret, fairly orthodox Marxist. He recognised the power of economic interests and imperial motivations and argued that liberal idealism acted as a cloak for imperial ambitions for all the great powers in the 1930s. Most realists since Carr have accepted his broad analysis of the failure of the balance of power and of the League of Nations between the world wars, whether or not they accepted his account of imperialism. Carr was almost alone before the 1970s in the field in making no distinction between IR and IPE.

The economic theory most associated with mainstream realist arguments had been loosely expressed by political leaders from the Roman Empire onwards. But it was more formally articulated in the seventeenth century: mercantilism. Mercantilism argues that the main aims of international economic activity are to build a stock of assets: trade is valuable because it brings in gold; empire building enables the search for stocks of gold and silver through trade, but also through direct conquest. Power is identified with stocks of assets such as gold. A 'balance of trade' is not enough; countries and their rulers should aim at gains. And although it was not a phrase used until the 1950s, the advice of mercantilist writers was that trade and economic activity was, like war and conquest, a 'zero-sum game', where one side could only gain where the others lost. Trade agreements might enhance the opportunity to build a stock of assets; war was the opportunity to seize them. Mercantile theory is thus consistent with the view of international relations as an endless power competition. It is a form of economic nationalism. Each international actor had to pursue their own interests because no other actor would protect them, because their survival depended on it, and because there were plenty of examples of once-powerful states, which had declined and failed in this life-or-death competition. Economic interests were central to these struggles partly because most armies at the time were mercenary forces who had to be paid regularly, and also because larger states with larger populations, such as the leading power of the day, France, could draw on their populations to dominate or defeat rivals. Agriculture was seen as the cornerstone of economic activity. Although there were industrial centres across both Europe and the New World, they were small, and the industrial revolution was not to occur for another century. The liberal ideas of greater efficiency of the use of resources through competition and mutual exchange was not yet born. Companies formed in this period such as the great Dutch East India Company and its later and eventually even more powerful British namesake aimed to accrue gold and silver assets and redistribute them to stockholders and the state. States such as France and Spain were deeply engaged in economic activity and would have thought the notion of the state not involving itself in markets where they had the capability of doing so ridiculous if it had been proposed. Political ideas that centred on the importance of trade protection survived long into the nineteenth century. They were given a further impetus by the publication of Friedrich List's *The National System of Political Economy* (1841).

List is the leading thinker of a more modern mercantilism, which would not only pursue stocks of gold and recognised that states relied on credit and on sophisticated corporate power, as well as on holdings of cash, gold and silver. But the main aims of state policy remained the pursuit of national influence and national interest. List was a Prussian scholar writing as Germany was unifying, but his ideas had a global influence throughout the century after his book was published. In the 1930s nearly every government including the United States, Turkey, Japan, France and Italy were thinking on lines shaped by List's ideas. Indeed, to a large extent List was codifying and formalising ideas which were widely shared, and that would have seemed to be just common sense to Americans such as Alexander Hamilton, as to nationalists and national rulers across Europe. China in the eighteenth and nineteenth century followed roughly similar policies of economic nationalism and autarky until it was undermined by imperial intervention. The only exception to the dominant strain of economic nationalism was Britain, and that only after the 1840s; even in the UK, List's ideas had a considerable resonance despite the much greater impact of more liberal ideas there.

It used to be said among IPE theorists that mercantilism was purely a doctrine of the past, that liberal ideas of free trade and open markets had so triumphed in the twentieth century that only nationalist fantasists such as Hitler and Mussolini would ever have considered 'going back' to these policies. Economic debates were to be conducted between liberals and Marxists, and most of all between advocates of different versions of liberalism. But this is a mistaken account of the past and an illusory idea of the present. Ideas of trade protection and economic nationalism have always flourished in recessions among those who benefitted less from unlimited free trade (often farmers, but also other groups of industrial workers). In the US Presidential elections of 2016, four main candidates vied to articulate economic nationalism, with only one (the Democrat Hillary Clinton) accepting a basic framework of free trade, even though she criticised free trade agreements reached by the previous Obama Administration. Her democrat rival, Sanders, attacked free trade and the globalisation of both finance and industrial production, and called for the repatriation to the US of manufacturing jobs lost to China and elsewhere almost as loudly as his Republican rivals. The two leading Republican candidates, Trump and Cruz, attacked free trade and globalisation in speeches designed to appeal to blue collar workers who had benefitted less well from them, even though the 'establishment' of the Republican party had for a century seen themselves as the 'party of business'. Anti-free trade ideas have been pressed with equal ferocity on the left and the right in many developed countries alongside a rising tide of nationalist suspicion of the global institutions that have managed the world economy since 1945. It is worth adding that many of the most successful emerging economies of the twentieth century, including all the east Asian 'tigers' (such as Taiwan and South Korea), but also China and Indonesia, emerged as leading economies in their region under military governments with tight internal control, protected manufacturing industries and controlled external trade policies led by government-favoured, 'national champion' corporations. The majority of policy leaders would favour broadly free trade policies, but there have always been plenty of exceptions. It is also fair to add that economic nationalist ideas and practices have become linked to suspicion of globalisation in all its forms in the last twenty years; that argument is one this text returns to in Chapter 4, as well as in the chapter on trade later.

Leading 'classical realist' writers include Arnold Wolfers and Hans J. Morganthau, who both recognised the importance of political economy only as a source of the resource base of states alongside population, geography, geology and so forth. Morganthau's text was widely used in IR for thirty years, and (whatever its other theoretical merits) helped to constrain the growth of IPE until it was superseded. The Australian scholar Hedley Bull provided the most sophisticated version of classical realism in his *The Anarchical Society* (1977), which argued that while the realist image of a world society of conflict, violence and struggle for the balance of power was mainly sound, the interactions of states themselves produced a level of cooperation and mutual exchange that many realists had not acknowledged or predicted. Bull is the author of an account that suggests that a relatively high level of cooperation is possible in the global political economy, conditional on there first being a form of political settlement between great powers without which major wars will persist. He preferred the label 'grotian' for this approach to 'realist' (from the leading legal scholar Hugo Grotius), and in some ways he does straddle realism and liberalism, albeit with a firm leaning in the realist direction.

# Liberal IPE

All liberals hold to some basic ideas about human nature, which shape their views of international relations and equally of economic activity and of IPE. These include the view that individuals and their rights are of central importance to a civilised society. Liberals also hold, perhaps to varying degrees, that ideas are important causes of events and of social change, and that law and institutions can be harnessed to make a free society work effectively. Liberals are (again, some more than others) optimistic about the future of human society and the possibilities of rational change and rational understanding of that society. In International Relations, this means that most liberals believe in the possibility of a rational ordering of international relations. Indeed, it was liberal idealism before and after the First World War, which gave rise to the academic study of International Relations as we now understand it. Liberal idealists believed that international law and international institutions can make a real difference to the effective management of relations so as to avoid or control conflicts. They accept that some of the attempts to manage the world through law and institutions, such as the 1919–1939 League of Nations, failed. But they will point to the many successful institutions of the post-1945 world and the institutionally managed agendas of development, the control of trade wars and the development of effective global financial institutions to justify they claims. In IR and IPE, these arguments shaped the understanding of the 'rise of interdependence' in the 1970s as the most important feature of contemporary international relations, a view that translated easily into enthusiasm for globalisation in the 1990s and 2000s.

Liberal scholars – and liberal politicians – also hold to the view most fully established by Smith that free trade is beneficial to all participants: even if the benefits of trade are not spread equally, all benefit sufficiently to have a rational self interest in taking part. This makes an important point: liberalism is not really founded on a blind 'idealism' at all. It argues, and most liberals have always argued, that a rational approach to self-interest would lead to cooperation rather than to struggles for power. Norman Angell cogently argued shortly before the First World War in *The Great Illusion* (1911) that such a war ought to be impossible because the world economy was already so interdependent that any major conflict would wreck the system of trade finance and investment and impoverish the world. He was in a sense absolutely right, for that war did have devastating effects on the world economy in addition to its human costs. But he was wrong in so far as the nationalism and identity politics of the day, together with the weight of alliance commitments and an ideology that saw war as a dramatic heroic arena rather than one of devastation, all caused calls for rational restraint to be ignored in 1914. Today, liberal authors insist, the world is even more interdependent and even more held together by mutually beneficial networks and connections, and so war (major conflicts at least) that threatens this fabric of shared well-being is a challenge to be avoided at almost any cost. Smith, Ricardo, Mill and their liberal successors intended that liberal trade theory would end the hold of mercantilist or economic nationalist ideas in IPE, but also in policy practice. It is fair to say that they succeeded in reshaping political economy as a field of intellectual endeavour, but that their ideas were not so fully successful in economic policy, especially outside the US and UK, until the mid-twentieth century.

Why then is free trade and its accompanying ideas of open competition and open markets so central to liberal economic thought? From Smith, Ricardo, J.S. Mill and others onward, it was claimed that free trade is the *most efficient* way of managing international economic relations and that the freer trade is the more participants will benefit. It was also claimed by all liberal political economists that this 'most efficient' system would produce both ethically justified and politically sound arrangements. The assumption was also that the state would play a limited role in economic activity, although how 'limited' has always been subject to debate. In this framework, each person and each company would produce benefits for the whole economy if they simply pursued their own interests as they saw them without government interference: 'whoever governs best who governs least' (the source of the quotation is disputed between Thomas Jefferson and several others). The reason for this can be summarised as resting on the *theory of comparative advantage*. If two countries both produce two commodities (say corn and manufactured iron), it makes sense for the one with a greater advantage in corn to grow and trade that, and to import iron from the other. Smith and Ricardo showed that this system of exchange produced net gains to both participants. Even if one country has an advantage in both products, it will have a *relatively* greater advantage in producing one, and it will gain more if it specialises in that product and imports from the other country. If one country tries to produce and export both, the other country will in any case have no export earnings to buy what the other produces. This very simple example can be extended from a two-country, two-product example to multilateral trade in a wide range of products. It is the underlying theory that has shaped the growth of free trade agreements and the reduction of tariffs, which, it is generally argued, produced the rapid international economic growth after 1945. One part of this view is that world trade grew significantly faster than world production in this period, and it can be argued that trade growth carried global production and so contributed to global welfare (meaning growth in income, investment and job creation). But notice that liberals claimed that this was the most efficient form of economic management, and not necessarily the fairest. They also took no account of the steady accumulation of power as well as wealth that some would acquire, which might then enable them to dominate society and economy over time.

Liberal economics also stressed the importance of competition. Adam Smith recognised from early in his great work that businessmen would form cartels and combine against the interests of their purchasers, as well as against a general public interest, if they had the chance. Smith would certainly have been in favour of anti-cartel (anti-trust) laws, and he would be suspicious of the lobbying power of major businesses close to government today. We know this because he says so directly of the growth of corporate and cartel power in the capitalist economy of his own day. But he was a staunch defender of capitalism all the same. The market theory that economists use derives from Smith with refinements from others (Mill, Marshall, Walras) along the way. The ideal model of a competitive market is one where there are many buyers and many sellers interacting together. To work, competition in this model is not based on numbers alone. Buyers and sellers must have information about the relative quality of products on offer, and they must have knowledge of the prices paid and the quantity of goods sold. In this way, supply and demand can meet on equal terms. And from this, we have a theory of how 'perfect competition' can produce optimal benefits for both buyers and sellers, and so more widely (through the operation of the 'hidden hand') to society as a whole. To work in this fashion, participants in a market must have a modicum of mutual trust. They should also have a legal framework where contracts are enforced and property is protected (for many reasons, but not least so that buyers and sellers are protected from deceit). Markets therefore require a degree of sociability, of social cohesion, as well as a degree of protection, which can only come from powerful authority (the state or some equivalent). Deal making also requires the existence of a stable medium of exchange, meaning that the value of money should be stable, known and reliable. Again, this last has nearly always been the province of government action. Broadly, then, perfect competition is an 'ideal type' of exchange that depends both on social and on political arrangements as well as on economic exchange. In the real world, there are very few approximations of a perfect market, but it is at least a useful analytic tool to start to think about what makes liberal economic theory powerful. Much economic theory has been devoted to exploring the exceptions and variations of this starting point.

It is not a repudiation of liberal economic theory to say that perfect competition exists very rarely – maybe in an early morning wholesale big city fruit market, or in some examples of online trading, for example. But in international trade, perfect markets are unheard of, and nearly all trade is done by powerful sellers (powerful because of their technology as well as their information) and powerful buyers (probably knowing that they can buy almost anything from a wide range of sources around the world). In most actually traded products in the world market, there are a few buyers or a few sellers or a few of both. For example, in the global energy market, a small cadre of oil and gas companies are both buying and selling at the same time. And in some cases there is a great disparity of information as well as financial resources between buyers and sellers. From these we might say (as many Marxists have) that international trade in goods and services is all about monopolies and cartels. But we might also observe (as many Marxists do not) that even in these markets, there is much more competition between the few players than one might expect, and that although there is quite often behaviour that looks like cartel management or what lawyers call 'the abuse of a dominant position' in international trade, firms rise and fall, failure is possible, and investors are canny and very quick to move their money to the next generation of possible 'winners'. All these ideas are developed later in the chapters on business (Chapter 3) and trade (Chapter 6).

Liberal political economy has always provided a forum for debates about the state. Many nineteenth-century British liberals favoured a growing amount of state intervention, if not in the economy then in infrastructure (e.g. railways, posts, communications) as well as in legal support for the economy. They also came to favour a greater role for the state in education, including technical education. And in the later part of the century, they led an extension of the state's role into education, social welfare, research and development. They also began the encouragement of cooperation between firms where it served state interests (for example in military technologies). J.S. Mill disagreed with his father James, who held a more limited view of the state's role. Marshall extended the idea of the state's role to protect infant industries and the national research base, ideas taken as much from List as from earlier liberal writers. Marshall's ideas led to the growth of government protection for research intensive industries in many countries, as well as for specific regions or cities that promoted their growth (sometimes called the 'third Italy' or 'industrial districts' argument). John Maynard Keynes held relatively orthodox views of the monetary role of the state when he wrote about money in the 1920s. But by 1933, he was arguing that the state could and should have a more fundamental role in managing the overall level of demand in the economy ('aggregate demand') so as to produce a balance of total supply and demand for goods and service at a level that was capable of producing full employment (however that was to be defined). Keynes' arguments shaped the future of economic management in the more advanced economies, although they were not fully adopted anywhere until after 1945, and they were never fully adopted in a number of countries (including Japan and the US). These arguments continue to divide economists and political economy as they continue to form one of the main political cleavages in many countries.

The four key planks of liberal economic thought are therefore: the importance of individuals; the importance of the separation between the state and the civil society of individuals, families and companies; the benefits of trade through the working of relative competitive advantage; and the importance of competition, which should be as close to a 'perfect competition' model as possible, but that will inevitably fall short and may fall a long way short of the ideal. Framed in the context of laws, private property, money credit and debt, and a system of incentives based on profits won through entrepreneurship, these form the bedrock of what is now called contemporary capitalism. And whether or not specific countries conform in practice to this model very closely (many do not), these ideas form the dominant ideology of the global economy today.

## Marxist IPE

Marxism has never been a mainstream force in either IR or IPE, but it has always been present, and it has always had significant influence. However, there has no more been a single Marxist approach than there has been a single liberal view in IPE. Marx's own view of international relations was limited, even though he commented on international issues, including among others the US Civil War, the unification of Italy and the rise of European empires in Africa and Asia. To fill the 'gap' left by Marx's theories, a number of writers contributed different approaches. Of these, the most influential was Hobson's theory of imperialism, on which Lenin drew extensively in his *Imperialism: the Highest State of Capitalism* (1916). Lenin argued that just as industrial capitalism had separated from the earlier forms of mercantile capitalism in the industrial revolution, so now a new form of capitalism was emerging, finance capitalism, which demanded the extension of capitalist modes of production from the more developed economies to others through imperialism. The mechanism here was partly about the falling rates of profit in the most developed economies as they reached maturity, but it was also a result of the conflict between the interests and needs of industrial and finance capital and the coming of the domination of finance. So while a different Marxist theorist, Kautsky, had argued that the growth of a world capitalist economy would produce a form of integration between global monopolies against which working class interests would have to struggle at a global level, Lenin suggested that integration would be undermined by the competition of national interests and financial empires. The result would be global conflict between large bloc imperial interests and the states that represented them. But this global conflict would provide the context in which effective revolutionary action would become possible. Imperialism was the 'highest' stage of capitalism because, Lenin claimed, it would be its last. Lenin's argument seemed to many readers to be open to much criticism, including its close derivation from the writing of the liberal John Hobson, and its relatively crude account of both international economics and international politics (Lenin was a very hasty theorist). But Lenin's view became a rigidly established orthodoxy in the USSR and then after 1945 in the Russian dominated communist world. As a result it became ossified and poorly related to real experience; it was for scholars outside the soviet world to develop Marxism as a powerful way of understanding IPE. Three strands of this tradition are discussed here (while developments of them figure in the next chapter), dependency theory, world systems theory and historical sociology. These three approaches intertwine and share something of a common intellectual history. Each derives directly from a non-Leninist (or Western Marxist) tradition as well as from Marx and Lenin. Each evolved in response to the evolution of realism and liberalism in the 1960s and 1970s as well as responding to currents within Marxism. Each is still influential in studies of IPE.

Dependency theory points to the parallel between a Marxian account of a two-class society (a capitalist class and a working class or proletariat) *within* the developed industrial world and a 'two-class' global society between states and economies. But at a global level the two 'classes' were on the one hand developed capitalist economies, which held structural advantages and the capacity to dictate the rules of the global system, as well as to dominate through their financial, military and corporate activity, and on the other hand dependent societies, poorer and weaker whatever their size, which were highly penetrated by 'advanced' country interests, which mostly had a legacy of colonial influence and which had ruling elites that were, whether through corruption or more open processes, more prepared to represent rich countries' interests than to protect their own people. This model was sometimes advanced rather crudely, and just as few sociologists would accept a crude two-class account of national societies, so it is recognised that there are both genuinely developing countries and non-developing countries in the global South. There are more independent economies alongside more dependent ones and while some societies and economies have shown very little development in the last fifty years, others have achieved very impressive growth and the creation of a much wider distribution of income and wealth. In some of these cases, foreign aid has measurably contributed to growth, while in others foreign aid has if anything been a significant hindrance and has also fostered corruption. In some cases conflict and civil war has undermined development, while in others civil conflict has been absent and in yet others civil conflict has provided the ruling elite with an excuse to maintain its own power provision at the expense of both opposition parties and ordinary citizens. The global South is both more diverse and more difficult to theorise than the basic ideas of dependency theory outlined in the 1960s suggested. But it has been put in much more sophisticated terms.

Raul Prebisch (1901–1986) played an important part in the development of dependency theory as an economic understanding of development. Prebisch, an Argentinian economist who worked in various United Nations' institutions, formed a theory published in the 1950s and was widely admired, which suggested that the 'normal' conditions of trade and finance that liberal economists believe shape competitive advantage do not really apply to weaker countries in the world system. These ideas were of intellectual interest; but they took time to become more widely accepted. It was widely believed in international organisations, in the global South, and in developed societies, that as countries decolonised after 1945 and found their feet as independent states, they would succeed in rapid development on a path towards the status of the most advanced countries. When this did not happen, which was clear by the mid 1960s, the UN established a Commission through the World Bank to report on prospects for future development, chaired by the former Canadian Prime Minister Lester Pearson. The resulting Pearson Report (1969), although primarily liberal in approach, took account of many of Prebisch's arguments, aiming to explain why development had become much more difficult than previously anticipated, and proposing measures to speed growth in the global South. In turn, this initiated a series of debates that continue to shape the international development literature, including whether liberal development policies can work, whether countries develop despite rather than because of foreign aid, whether global aid organisations can effectively represent the global South or only represent a hegemony of dominant voices, and what development really is. All these questions are developed further in later chapters.

The label 'structuralism' is often used when discussing dependency theory because it points to the structural disadvantage of countries in the global South, a disadvantage which it is said no particular policies would be powerful enough to overcome. Structural power here means power derived from one's position in a given structure. Structural power is deeply embedded in institutions, relationships and political practice. It may not be immediately obvious, but it can be identified and measured and evaluated through detailed quantitative analysis if one wishes. For structuralist scholars in IPE, the most compelling evidence of the existence of global structures of power is the difficulty of 'development' in the face of embedded inequalities in the world system. Indeed, they would say that the disadvantage of marginalised countries may be deepened through interaction with the global system as a whole. A different way to put this is that countries do not have the same advantages, that inequalities reproduce themselves over time and that there is no 'level playing field' in international competition. The most widely used development of dependency theory is Immanuel Wallerstein's world system theory, briefly explained here. Wallerstein's colleague, Giovanni Arrighi, has developed a historical account of the recent evolution on the world system in his *The Long Twentieth Century* (1994), influential for its scholarship for non-Marxist writers as well as Marxists. The policy corollary of these arguments is that countries in the global South might be far better off pursuing their own autonomous or 'autarkic' policies rather than integrating ever closer to the world economy. This has, however, not proved a widely possible option despite some countries such as Venezuela attempting it – the exception, the great success story of independent autarky, might be seen as China, but the Chinese economy is a very distinctive case: most specialists would agree that China developed much more rapidly only after it began to integrate with the world economy after 1979. Structuralism might appear to be a very compelling critical analysis; it might also appear to be a much less persuasive set of policy recommendations.

What exactly is the 'structure' in this kind of structuralism? It is understood as a structure of dominance and dependence where one group of countries form a 'core' of powerful actors, holding the financial and trade strings, but also forming the base for dominant corporations and dominant institutions and networks. The majority of countries, and the majority of world population, occupy a 'periphery', a fringe that depends on imports of high-value goods and services from the core, which imports capital and owes debts, which sells mainly primary products (minerals, energy, agricultural products, low value manufactures) on world markets. These peripheral countries are dominated by an elite, who are highly 'penetrated' by core values and core education so that they act as a subaltern class representing core interests rather than those of their own people. Peripheral countries are ruled through violence whether or not they appear to be democracies and they are ruled through corruption. But neither violence nor corruption is as powerful in shaping their lack of control over their own destiny as their lack of ability to shape the rules of international economic and political and cultural relations. This 'core-periphery model' of two kinds of international actor (which mimicked the Marxist 'two-class' model of capitalist society) was fairly quickly modified by the addition of a third group of actors, the semi-periphery states and societies that had some measure of influence, which enjoyed higher GDP and more widely spread wealth than the poorer countries, but that were still essentially peripheral in their ability to shape global markets and political outcomes, and that were often dependent on major core players for their geostrategic security as well as their investment and financial stability. Mexico, Turkey, Romania and Argentina have all been seen as semi-peripheral countries. This structural model remains powerful, especially in the global South, where many academics and many politicians and policy advisors hold either a precise or a roughly formed version of the model (which dominates the teaching of IPE in India, for example). There have obviously been difficulties in holding on to this approach as some developing countries have rapidly developed (where does one fit Singapore or Dubai into this analysis?) and as some, including India, China, Indonesia and Brazil, have become major actors in geopolitics and immensely significant economic powers. But authors such as Wallerstein continue to modify the detail while holding to the main lines of this approach, which has remained one of the most important approaches to IPE.

Historical sociology is the third and final strand of Marxist writing to be considered here. Historical sociology explores the growth of the state and the relations between state and society drawing on conceptual tools that combine the insights of liberal sociology and history – most especially the writing of the German sociologist Max Weber – with Marxist thinking about the relationship between politics and economics in the historical evolution of society. The work of Talcott Parsons on social structure, of anthropologists such as Margaret Mead and Marc Augé, of non-Marxist structuralists including especially Emile Durkheim, and of a range of historians also shapes the field. Perhaps the most influential historian in this context is the French scholar Fernand Braudel. Braudel tried to escape from the narrow confines of detailed historical work arguing that it was also possible to construct a long-term history of societies and economies using evidence in rigorous but different ways to traditional history. Braudel's notion of 'history in a long-term framework ('*longue durée*') shaped much of the work of contemporary scholars on the evolution of relations between state and society. It produced important comparative work on the nature, impacts and significance of revolutions. It also influenced recent work on globalisation by a variety of scholars, some closer to Weber's liberalism and some closer to a Marxian tradition (further discussed in Chapter 4). Contemporary historical sociology reminds one that there is an interesting and significant overlap between (some) liberal and (some) Marxist thinking and research practice in IPE, and that the dialogue between them is often fruitful.

In general the mainstream Marxist approaches are all relatively pessimistic about the possibility of change and tend to see the structures of dominant power as well-established and resistant to strategies or moves to undermine them. Lenin called the often romantic idea of early revolution 'left-wing infantilism'. Chase Dunn more recently anticipated eventual change in the structures of world power but suggested they might come no earlier than one or two thousand years. It is the more radical variants of Marxism discussed in Chapter 2 that challenge these ideas.

# Criticising the mainstream IR approaches

The critique of these IR-derived approaches revolved around six main conceptual issues. First of all, the actors: as noted already, to focus solely on states as actors in IPE is blind not only to the importance of the capacities of many non-state actors, but also to the authority they have often come to wield. That includes institutions such as credit rating agencies, international banking bodies such as the Bank for International Settlements (BIS), trade associations, and non-government organisations and charities delivering aid and development programmes. One also needs to recognise the importance that networks between key actors have, whether they be states or non-state actors or combinations of the two. In particular, leading firms have complex networks of supply chains and complex relations with partners through joint ventures and collaborations on research. The study of these networks leads to very different and much more nuanced understanding of IPE than an approach that only looks at states or market behaviours, or even at international institutions such as the IMF and World Bank.

Second, structure: classic IR theory tended to neglect the importance of structural forces unless they could be pointed to and measured directly. Traditional Marxism, which did give an account of structure as a key factor in its view of IR, nevertheless tended to focus only on three structures (global monopoly finance; class; and the hegemonic power of imperialism) at the expense of any others. It was for later Marxist writers (the 'structuralist' or 'world systems' theorists) to find more sophisticated ideas of structure, often prompted by non-Marxist critiques of Leninist ideas. But liberalism and realism in IR alike neglected structure, and sometimes still do, whereas in IPE they cannot and do not do so. But the label 'structuralist' is also ambiguous in so far as, while there are plenty of Marxist minded structuralist scholars in IPE, there are also at least as many non-Marxist structuralists (often influenced most importantly by a line of theory derived from the sociologist Emile Durkheim), not a few of whom would describe themselves as liberal or realist, as will be explained shortly.

Third, the agenda of the field: scholars in IPE have from the beginning sought to widen the agenda of what counts as important. To give a few examples, they shifted attention from the policy concerns of the largest actors, not just looking at the global South, but also at the situation of women in development or world labour markets, at the relationship between culture and economic growth (or failure of growth), at poverty and debt, and at the importance of informal networks. Thus, arguably, the agenda of IPE is much broader than that of IR even as IR has been re-thought in the last twenty years.

Fourth, many classical IR scholars and teachers held a notion of economics as being essentially about resources available to the state, a view that economists of all schools would reject as hopelessly simplistic. To give examples, Napoleon was able to mobilise resources in this and that way; the British defeated him when they were able to mobilise more and more powerful resources, especially through their use of financial markets to subsidise countries such as Russia, Prussia and Austria against the French. But IPE is concerned with much more than state resources, as many of the examples in this chapter attest. The emphasis on different forms of market behaviour and different and more complex relations such as complex supply chains and the impact of technical innovation on both politics and economics are important illustrations of the point.

Fifth, the conception of power embodied in these approaches is transformed. As Stephen Lukes pointed out, classic IR, like traditional political theory, tended to see power as one of two or at most three kinds. The first was the capacity of brute domination; the second was the capability granted by resources of all kinds; the third was 'psychological' power, or what was often called the capacity to exercise will against a more physically powerful opponent. By neglecting structures, traditionalists neglected most forms of structural power. Beyond these first 'three faces'

(Lukes) of power, IPE must recognise that power lies in language, in the ways that words are used, and in the underlying discourses and structures of speech and action. If it is possible to say a range of things but impossible to say others because it is either inconceivable or because it 'defies common sense' to say them, then one might want to examine what counts as sayable, what the idea of 'common sense' conceals. This kind of discourse analysis (which owes a good deal to the philosopher Michel Foucault) has become one of the main ways of penetrating visions of power, and might be described as a 'fourth face' of power. We might find a 'fifth face' in patterns of relations of trust, which include networks (already discussed, and further developed in Chapter 3). But these forms of 'social capital' rest on distinctions that create structures of influence and ideas, which come to dominate others. These weak links that nonetheless have considerable strength and staying power shape the ways in which global trade is done between firms that have a lot of knowledge of each other, as it shapes negotiations on everything from banking to telecommunications regulation. The most important sources of these ideas lie in business networking theory (developed in Chapter 3), but also in the careful detailed social analysis of Pierre Bourdieu and Bruno Latour, a neat example of how a debate in anthropology and sociology has helped to refine discussion in contemporary IPE.

Susan Strange drew on these critical points, but made a larger one that has continued to shape IPE across the board. She argued that while academic International Relations was too narrowly conceived, it was not enough to bring a study of markets into play. Market behaviour mattered, she held, as did state power and state behaviour. But a 'states and markets' approach to IPE, although an improvement, was still too narrow. IPE needed not only a broader view of who the actors were, what the core structures were, and what values were at issue in any analysis, it also needed to explore how these separate elements interacted and shaped each other, and how the position of academic analysts shaped their own collective understandings. In doing this, IPE might shade into other fields, including business and cultural studies as well as regional analysis. Strange was a *Financial Times* journalist and consultant for the Economist Intelligence Unit before she became Professor of International Relations at the London School of Economics; she was recognised in the US as by far the most influential European scholar in the field. She claimed not to be very interested in theory, although she was very good at it; she rejected many of the boundaries and limitations of individual theories outlined in this chapter, hoping to encourage students towards a more open-minded and self-critical approach to theory, while always testing how good theory might be through assessing its applicability to specific real-world cases. More than most other scholars, she was also open to ideas and possibilities in a range of arguments from Marx, Schumpeter and Keynes through varieties of liberalism to some of the (less radical) versions of feminism and postmodern scholarship. However, she sometimes said that her favourite theorist was Voltaire, a recommendation of engaged scepticism rather than of any specific approach to IPE, and a view that the beginning student might find welcome.

## The practical concerns shaping the evolution of IPE

The emergence of IPE happened at a particular moment in time, which shaped its emergence as much as the history of IR or economic theory. At the end of the 1960s, American domination in the world economy seemed to be beginning to decline; the institutional and financial arrangements founded at the end of the Second World War seemed equally to be crumbling. The growth of other economies (especially Germany and Japan, but later China and Brazil as well as some of the major oil producer economies) weakened the ability of the US to dominate patterns of trade and in turn weakened the US capacity to make the rules of the global economy. This was signalled first of all by a series of crises in the dollar's leadership of international monetary arrangements between 1969 and 1971, when the world economy ceased to rely on fixed exchange rates linked to the value of the dollar. It was further accentuated by the 1973–1974 Oil Crisis and the financial and trade disturbances that followed it in the mid-1970s, including a period of high inflation among developed economies and rapidly growing debt among the less developed economies. The 1960s and 1970s also saw the emergence of larger global companies across many economic sectors; while global firms were not new (banks had been in effect globalised since the late nineteenth century), the range of firms, their varied nationalities and the volume of their activities all looked new. The growth of unregulated international activity outside the apparent reach of governments also caused some concern. The earliest agenda of IPE as it emerged in the early 1970s included the question of economic sovereignty, the structure of the world economy as new actors emerged, the power of multinationals and the inequalities of power and capability between the global South and the larger developed economies. Stability and insecurity in the global political economy pushed these questions to the front of the agenda in academic and policy concerns. This development also included the analysis of individual sectors and individual firms' performance, and it quickly came to include the future of work and the future of workers within this nascent global system.

The most publicised theoretical debate among economists of the 1960s, whether Keynesian economic management inherited from the post-war years could continue, did not touch IPE for some time. One reason for this was that looked at globally, many countries never actually practised Keynesian economic policies. The replacement theory, broadly labelled 'monetarism' (a form of what is also called neo-liberal economics, explained below) did come to affect debate in IPE, but only in the 1980s, when financial regulation changed. The impact of monetarism was also to question what the state could and should do in economic management both at a national and an international level, and this fundamental question crept onto the IPE agenda in the 1980s and has remained central ever since. The question of how growth among 'developing' countries might be possible, and, indeed, whether it was possible at all in terms of 'catching up' with those who had developed earlier was put on the IPE agenda as much by institutions such as the World Bank and the UN Conference on Trade and Development (UNCTAD), as well as by campaigning development research institutes and NGOs, motivated by the apparent growth of international inequalities, as it was by academics. All these issues involved questions of the extent of the role of the state both within and beyond its own boundaries. It also asked whether, when states could not manage their own economies and societies alone successfully, international cooperation through one or another institutional framework might substitute for domestic or internal action, a question that has ramifications in detail but that is ultimately also one of fundamental security or state survival.

We can now summarise some of the main points of the different theories discussed so far before we move to more contemporary versions of them (see Table 1.2).

## Refinements of the traditional theories

One can still find examples of those older (mid-twentieth century) traditions of thinking in IPE without difficulty. But more refined versions that take account both of changes in the world political economy and in the reach and nature of the state affect the theories now most widely in use in IPE. Here, we look first at the evolution of economic theories of growth, which derive from basic arguments within classical economics. We then explore two important derivatives from classical IR theory that have dominated IPE literature in the last thirty years in the Anglo-Saxon world at least; neo-liberalism and neo-realism (or structural realism). We do not develop more recent arguments from Marxist or dependency theory or structuralist approaches because those

**Table 1.2** Summary: mainstream theories of international relations and economics influential in IPE

| | Role of the state? | Role of International Institutions? | Nature of global relations? | Nature of power? | Firms and markets? |
|---|---|---|---|---|---|
| Political liberalism | Important in managing money and contracts and safeguarding basic freedoms | Very important as managers of interdependence and cooperation | Mixture of conflict and cooperation + globalisation | Power conflicts exist but can be managed through cooperation at home and globally | Open markets best guarantee of both growth and moral exchanges |
| Economic liberalism | Limited to legal management of currency and contracts ideally | International institutions tend like the state to produce unnecessary regulation, but needed to provide minimum standards of exchange | Market competition added to conflict of state interests | Power comes from economic strength through the freest possible market activity | Key actors that produce wealth and trade freely |
| Realism | The only key actor, especially great powers' | Only important to extent backed by great powers | Anarchy of conflict; balance of power politics | Military and diplomatic | Secondary – but provide resources for states |
| Economic nationalism (mercantilism) | States and key firms and banks cooperate to compete in int. arena | As for economic liberalism – not to be trusted | Competition for market power, market share and technology leadership added to anarchy of conflict | Military diplomatic finance and trade competition – a struggle for survival | Major actors especially where firms are 'national champions' leading in world competition |
| Leninism | Struggle for power among key interests and firms where states have a major role in imperial and military struggle | A front for state interests especially of the great powers | Changes in historic context – in highest stage of capitalism an all out conflict of imperial powers and monopoly firms | Power derives from position in structure of capitalist and class power, but expressed by firms, lobbies and states | Monopoly capitalist firms in imperial competition |
| Dependency theory | Global structures of dominance and dependence within which states and MNCs have equally important places | International institutions generally represent dominant interests and power groupings | Conflict of interests and powers within a structure, which most dependency theorists see as deeply resistant to change or revolution | Power is both economic and military and legal; power rooted in established structures is the most important source of resistance to change | Firms and markets operate freely within global structures and over time reinforce dominant structures. |

are examined more fully in Chapter 2. These bodies of theory and debate, all of which have been widespread in IR curriculums since the 1970s, form the foundation of much of the subject today, although they are also widely critiqued, as Chapter 2 will show.

---

**EXAMPLE BOX**

# Theories of economic growth

One way to get further under the skin of core economic theories and how they matter in IPE is to ask what causes economic growth. There are two kinds of answer. The first is reviewed briefly here – growth in established capitalist economies; the second, usually called 'development', meaning the growth and development of less developed or emerging economies and societies in the global South, is in some ways a completely distinct body of argument.

Economists will suggest that economic activity results from the interaction of four main 'factors of production': land, labour, capital and entrepreneurship. Land is deployed in exchange for rent; in general the stock of land is fixed in all developed economies and it is difficult to bring more land into production, but there are variations on this. Labour is variable, since it is always possible to dismiss workers or put them on shorter hours; but the stock of labour is difficult to increase beyond a certain level without large scale migration and labour laws make varying the stock of labour more difficult. Capital is money invested for a return. The reward of capital is profit. Capital may in practice mean a given level of technology or a particular kind of machinery. It is possible to vary the quality of both labour (through education, training and skills development) and capital (through investment in new machinery or more advanced technologies). Theories of growth have therefore tended to revolve around ways of varying the mix of labour and capital, with or without external forces intervening. Mistakenly, they often tended to assume a fixed stock of knowledge, although changes in knowledge, skills and technology have been significant sources of growth over at least the last 200 years of global capitalism. Entrepreneurship is management. Some theories have assumed that since management would always perform to the maximum it could not easily (or at all) be changed. More recent theories of management have stressed (and perhaps over-estimated) the capacity of managements to change and evolve in response to changes in business environment and competition. These are discussed further in Chapter 3. Changes in government policy may bring pressures to accelerate growth, although some economists (and many business people) would argue that unstable rapid changes in government policy are disincentives to growth whatever their intentions, and more stability would be welcomed. Liberal economic theories have generally argued that the economy tends towards a balance in specific markets and in overall performance, and so explaining real growth (however defined) is a major problem. The origins of this idea were formulated by the French economist and follower of Adam Smith, J.B. Say, at the end of the eighteenth century. 'Say's Law' proposes that supply and demand will naturally balance each other in a given market. From Malthus to Keynes and since, this has been a key debate in political economy since if it holds, less government intervention is necessary, where if natural balance in markets is illusory, as Keynes and many others have replied, there may be more occasions when the state is justified in intervention. From all this, a variety of economic growth theories have been proposed. Among them have been the following (nearly all developed by pairs of economists, hence their names):

*Ricardian*: Ricardo understood labour as the most important variable input into economic activity; he developed the theory of comparative advantage and suggested that trade would be a key source of economic growth overall. He also wrote extensively on the theory of rent, and his arguments on rent, money and growing capital stocks influenced both Marx and twentieth-century writers on 'exogenous' growth (i.e. growth caused by factors outside the market arrangements of a single country).

*Malthusian*: a broadly pessimistic model developed in the early nineteenth century by Malthus, which assumes that over time the population will rise faster than resources, and that economic growth is eventually limited by population growth and increasingly scarce resources as well as limited returns to scale on investment. Since the 1970s, many environmentalist critics of theories of unlimited global growth have been collectively named 'neo–Malthusian'.

*Harrod-Domar model*: first derived in the 1930s, a Keynesian model that suggests that growth is possible by managing productivity and overall demand, but rejecting the assumption of a natural balance of supply and demand in the economy.

*Hechscher-Ohlin model*: originating in the 1930s and still significant, an expansion of Ricardo's model of global trade, which predicts that trade will grow and produce a growing pattern of international economic integration on the basis of improved quality of inputs as well as on the 'natural' benefits of trade which follow from comparative advantage.

*Solow-Swan*: a neo-classical model designed to refute Harrod-Domar, which pointed to the impact of increases in productivity and resources as sources of growth. The model predicts that given the right conditions, which policy can create, including improvements in education and technology, economic growth can be achieved effectively. Technology and population growth together with development in the quality of work lead to long-term, real improvements in GDP. This model, which originated in 1956, has been much developed by more recent writers, including influentially Aghion and Hewitt, into the 2000s. These models deny that economies will 'naturally' develop without management of technology and innovation as well as labour market improvement and recognise that markets do not 'naturally' balance out in growth. They have also been important because they have lent themselves to detailed quantitative work due to their sophisticated mathematics.

More than anything else, these theories demonstrate the importance of academic debate in detailed discussion in high-quality journals as a source of the evolution of knowledge in the field. They represent a series of arguments about market interactions, the impact of innovation, the debate between exogenous and endogenous growth models and the relationship between trade and growth, which will no doubt continue.

## Neo-realism

Neo-realism has its roots in a reassertion of realism in the face of theories from liberalism that emphasised the power of international organisations and the nature of the complex interdependence between major actors in the global system. By the mid-1970s, authors such as Keohane and Nye and Raymond Vernon pointed to the emergence of ever-greater strands of interdependence between states, multinational corporations and financial empires. John Burton modelled this as a system of networks akin to cobwebs. Realists replied that cobwebs were easily torn open in a crisis. Keohane and Nye and colleagues did not pretend that power did not matter. They suggested that the nature of power was changing, and realists could not say why or how. They also pointed to the emergence of underpinning structures of power in the nexus of interdependent relationships across technologies, firms, governments and financial systems as new frameworks of power. Liberal rejections of the notion that states and state power predominated over other processes and structures met staunch criticisms from realists that states and state power did indeed still matter. Sources such as Fred Northedge's *The International Political System* (1976) argued that interdependence theory was merely 'an American illusion' and that realism demonstrated the importance of the enduring factors of international politics as explanations of both IR and IPE.

It was Kenneth Waltz's *Theory of International Politics* (1979) that really established neo-realism as the dominant position in both IR and IPE in the 1980s and that continues to exert a very considerable influence even now. This is in some ways surprising: Waltz wanted to focus on international politics, political relations among states. He adopted a particular structural approach, which assumed that politics was an autonomous sphere of human activity. Within the international political realm, it was the structure of relations between the main actors, which, for Waltz, determined the nature of politics, the agenda of conflict and cooperation, the behaviour of individual actors and the outcomes. By the 'structure of relations', Waltz meant how those key actors organised and understood their interests in conflict – for Waltz as for classic realists, IR is a field of conflicts of interest and perpetual struggles for power. But in that structure, what mattered was essentially rather straightforward, at least at first sight: whether there was one main dominant actor ('unipolarity'); whether there were two main dominant actors or blocs of actors ('bipolarity'); whether there were three or more main actors ('multipolarity'); and if so how the actors organised themselves in alliance blocs or as a qualified anarchy of competing individuals. Waltz always argued that as a matter of fact the key actors were states, but that his theory would be equally valid if the key actors were other kinds of competing entities (empires, theological powers, tribes, banks, oligopoly firms or some kind of mixed actor system). Waltz's first concern was to critique what he saw (perhaps quite rightly) as the soggy methodologies used by liberal writers in the 1970s about interdependence. He sought to establish a much more rigorous scientific basis for his own theories. This view had a particular attraction in graduate schools and Waltz's approach was taken up as an allegedly more 'scientific' source by many scholars. This approach has remained one of the most used and discussed approaches in the field ever since.

But Waltz did not talk very much about IPE and when challenged about the relevance of his arguments to an understanding of the global economy always responded by saying, first, that he did not know very much about economics (which one was wise not to believe), and, second, that his account was an attempt to theorise international politics. His arguments might well hold in IPE, he agreed, but he did not claim that they would certainly do so, and he had done no work to show that they could. He would add that the global economy was not so interesting to him, and it was for others to develop appropriate theories there, so long as they could meet the same criteria of scientific rigour as he claimed. Others took this argument forward, most notably Stephen Krasner and the editors of the journal *International Organization* in the 1980s. Krasner and a group of fellow scholars and research students took the core insights of Waltz's landmark book and drew a body of IPE theories from them, which remain some of the most influential work in the field. They also borrowed extensively on a much earlier, and previously neglected, study, Albert Hirschman's 1945 thesis *National Power and the Structure of Foreign Trade*. Hirschman, drawing on extensive historical research, provided empirical evidence to suggest that the global trading system was and would be relatively stable if and only if there was an organising key actor or centre of power, a hegemon. That key actor would hold the hegemony over the system. In exchange for providing stability and the possibility of trading efficiently at as great an equilibrium of international trade as possible, the hegemon would gain extra benefits in terms of jobs and leadership and power. Other actors would concede power to that hegemonic actor not only because of its domination and power, but also – and often primarily – because it would be in their own interests to do so since they gained from the stability and possibilities for trade. Shared rules benefitted everyone, whoever wrote them; a lack of rules meant anarchic competition. That anarchy was much more likely to be characterised by generalised warfare, as in the first halves of both the seventeenth and twentieth centuries. This theory of hegemonic stability (HST) is the most important successor to Waltz's work in IPE. What this argument also suggested was that trade and economic stability depended, not just on the relative competitive advantage of producer firms and economies (as liberals argued), but on a prior set of political conditions. Without those conditions, trade would be suboptimal if not impossible. Where there was no dominant hegemonic actor or source of power, an international anarchy would obtain in which life could easily become, as Hobbes had in a different context suggested, nasty, brutish and short. It would be one in which actors would struggle for domination to the detriment of investment and stable trade; conflict to be the controller and author of international economic rules would produce a systemic absence of rules, where competition would be framed by neo-mercantilist struggles.

This account both explained mercantilism and justified a kind of neo-mercantilism. Competition unrestrained by a hegemon was most likely to lead to war, as well as to the failure of systems of international finance, regularised payments between economies, and to tariff wars. Examples of stability were primarily the period when Britain dominated trade, payments and finance, setting the rules and paying some of the costs of managing them. Nascent systems had emerged before with some elements of this stability, especially when France preceded Britain as the dominant power, but neither France nor (before it) Holland and Spain had enjoyed sufficient power for long enough to make for a stable embedded system of hegemony. Hirschman could then point to the long nineteenth century as a period of stable growth under a hegemon, Great Britain. The 1930s then formed another period of contested domination where, in the absence of clear rule-setting, economic nationalism and military conflict had linked the First World War to the Second. For Hirschman, and even more for those who used his work in the 1980s, after 1945 there was a choice. Either there was to be a further period of conflict and disorder, almost certainly leading to another global war, or there was to be the establishment of a single global centre of power, which naturally would have to be based on the United States and on US hegemonic power. After all, in 1945, the US was by far the largest economy, with the largest productive potential for the future, and which held control of the international monetary order through the dominance of US holdings of foreign debt as well as through the power of the dollar. Hirschman's argument suggested that whatever specific roles the US took in a future world economy, it could not retreat into isolation as it had after 1918 without great cost to itself as well as to the world economic order. The theory these scholars developed had immediate policy implications. These may have justified US hegemony in the world economy; but they also asked questions about the implications of a US decline and the potential emergence of successor hegemonic power. These arguments also enabled scholars to find a framework for much more specific forms of analysis, including the analysis of particular sectors and realms of activity (finance, technology, intellectual property, the working of global institutions). Neo-realism, or structural realism retain a compelling place in IPE theory, although of course they are also widely critiqued. These arguments retain their power in academic debates today, especially in those about the 'rise of China' as a serious challenge to US hegemony.

One way to think about neo-realist arguments is to think how a basic analysis of the 'structure of global political economy' would look. Table 1.3 gives some information that is relevant, although you will see that it is very much simplified. It demonstrates the continuing dominant position of the US; the US *has* 'declined' in the sense that it has lost a great deal of *relative* power, but it remains a key actor by any measure. The table does not recognise the substantial gap between the US and the others in 1980, which had almost disappeared by 2015; nor does it recognise the rise of the European Union, which as a whole is now equal to the US when it can

**Table 1.3**   Changing relative size of largest economies (ranked by nominal $US values)

|    | 1980 | 1990 | 2000 | 2005 | 2015 | 2020 (estimated) |
|----|------|------|------|------|------|------------------|
| 1  | US | US | US | US | US | US |
| 2  | USSR | Japan | Japan | Japan | China | China |
| 3  | Japan | USSR | Germany | Germany | Japan | Japan |
| 4  | West Germany | West Germany | UK | UK | Germany | Germany |
| 5  | France | France | France | China | UK | UK |
| 6  | UK | Italy | China | France | France | India |
| 7  | Italy | UK | Italy | Italy | India | France |
| 8  | China | Canada | Canada | Canada | Italy | Italy |
| 9  | Canada | Iran | Mexico | Spain | Brazil | Brazil |
| 10 | Argentina | Spain | Brazil | South Korea | Canada | Canada |

*Source*: International Monetary Fund, 2016.
*Note*: The European Union as a whole would stand at least second in the list for each year over the whole period. It is excluded not because it is not important, but because of its changing membership and impact, expanding from 9 to 28 members, since 1980, which make the comparison dangerous.

act as a whole (which is not always the case). It recognises not just the rise of China (predicted to be the largest economy by a time between 2020 and 2030), but also the rapid recent growth of Brazil and India. The table would provide a valuable basis for class discussion, but as you think about it, ask whether this is the most useful way of presenting this information too.

# Neo-liberalism

'Neo-liberalism' is a nuisance word. It covers at least two arguments, which it is important to distinguish and that may at least sometimes be completely at odds. But we have to live with the vocabulary we have inherited, at least when we start the subject. The reader is simply cautioned to try to be clear what a text they are reading actually means by neo-liberalism, and even more to be cautious and to define terms clearly when she or he writes. 'Neo-liberalism' means, first, a *refinement* of liberal theory in international relations. This is sometimes also called 'neo-liberal institutionalism', a specific theory associated with particular authors and debates, which has considerable explanatory force in both IR and IPE, which we shall explore below. Second, 'neo-liberalism' means a *theory that challenges liberalism from an economic viewpoint*, reflecting a debate within liberalism about the right understanding of the relations between economics and politics within IPE, as well as offering a distinctive idea of policy and what works. This is also how the term is most often used in political and everyday debate in the UK and Europe.

Neo-liberal institutionalism (sometimes just 'liberal institutionalism', but this label does not capture what is distinctive here) emerged as a critique of neo-realism in the 1990s after neo-realism had dominated much of the academic literature (especially in the US) on IPE in the 1980s. A group of scholars, including Judith Goldstein, Helen Milner, Robert Keohane and Katheryn Sikkink (all themselves American) asked how well neo-realism explained more detailed and technical issues. Was it a theory with real explanatory power, as its proponents claimed? Goldstein and Milner focussed on US trade policy. This is a complex subject, but it is hardly unrepresentative of central issues in global political economy today. US trade policy is not made by the White House or President, although they try to manage it. Policy is made primarily in Congress, by the

US Trade Commission, by competing lobby groups, and by the political interactions between them and the government. The federal government has leverage, and is sometimes able to get what it wants. But its position is also qualified by the complex processes of external bargaining necessary to achieve any major trade agreement. Other actors matter, especially China, Japan and the European Union. But each of these also has complex and arcane domestic arrangements for trade policy management. Goldstein and Milner hypothesised that a neo-realist account in terms of hegemony and rule-making dominance would not give more than a crude explanation of these kinds of politics. They suggested a refinement of an old liberal idea. Yes, they agreed, ideas and institutions and norm-building mattered, along with complex interactions and complex negotiation. But *how* did ideas and institutions matter? They suggested that ideas 'worked' in complex diplomatic contexts when they became embedded in institutions. Ideas became embedded in domestic political and economic institutions through a complex and often highly competitive process. But ideas also became embedded in international institutions such as the World Bank and the United Nations' key agencies. It was not any old ideas that counted, that explained events and outcomes. It was those specific ideas that were successfully embedded in the practices and procedures of the institutions concerned. They were able to marshal an impressive array of evidence in support of their case. In trade terms, it was the complex institutional context within the US, dominated by Congressional bodies, and those within the global polity, most importantly the framework and often convoluted processes of the World Trade Organization, which together explained both the making and the management of US trade policy. An analysis of these factors also explained how particular trade agreements were made, and how sometimes trade talks failed. Sikkink extended these ideas in studies of Latin American development and then later in studies of human rights agreements. Keohane developed the notion of embeddedness in other studies of US foreign and domestic policy. Others have used the same theoretical framework to look more closely at political mechanisms dealing with external economic policies in the EU, as well as at multilateral arms control talks. Neo-liberal institutionalism remains an important component in the understanding of IPE and still has most significance in the study of institutions and institutional negotiations.

Neo-liberalism in the second sense argues that liberalism as it has often been proposed is outmoded or just wrong. Markets have, or should have, priority over any political considerations. Concerns of welfare or social effect should not bother economic analysis. The state and political system should stand back from the market. If the market is allowed to operate freely, it can not only produce efficiency, but also meet individuals' needs most effectively. Benefits from free market activity should go to those who earn them, but more than that, if working in a free economic context, those benefits will naturally 'trickle down' from the main gainers to others in society through employment or the spending of the most profitable businesses. Free markets are a moral as well as an economic obligation, and minimum government allows a more moral people. Government intervention encourages free riders at least and generalised corruption at worst. That is true, neo-liberals hold, not least because many of them suspect the legitimacy of taxation: the government has no right to take money from citizens, which they have not agreed to, unless there is some powerful overriding need (such as national defence) for it. The leading British neo-liberal politician Margaret Thatcher asserted that 'there is no such thing as society', thereby implying that political action justified by many liberals as 'socially necessary' was a nonsense. Neo-liberalism in IPE argues, for example, that foreign aid (a key liberal project intervening between richer and poorer states) for the development of the global South is at once wasteful, corrupt and inefficient, but also unjustified since more open economic activity will create better results in the longer run (see Chapter 8 on development for a discussion of this).

What is called neo-liberalism is for more traditional liberals a surrender to blind market forces, a denial of the validity of government engagement in the economy. But more than that, it is a denial of the role that liberalism always stressed for government as the defender of weak or under-represented interests in economic policy management. Thus British liberals supported the abolition of the slave trade and the intervention of government in the Irish famines of the 1840s; neo-liberals opposed the abolition of slavery as an intervention in private property rights, and rejected the intervention in Ireland as interference in a free market, which would in time balance out. Traditional liberals have always agreed that if the way the economy worked (at national or international level) produced inequalities, it was not a problem (it was inevitable), *so long as* there were limits to those inequalities so as not to cause substantial injustice. At the point where major injustices arose, intervention was necessary and justified. If liberalism has a moral basis (as Smith, Ferguson, Mill, Bentham and Keynes had all insisted), it had to be framed so as to protect the weakest in society. It also had to protect smaller producers and buyers against monopolies and cartels, and to vigorously protect real competitive markets. It was for this reason that liberal governments in many countries introduced trade union rights, votes as well as employment rights for women, old age pensions and public health and education systems. 'Big government', as it is called in the United States, did not evolve only when the Roosevelt administration of the 1930s intervened in the economy to try to mitigate the effects of the Great Depression: it had its roots in the origins of liberalism itself. But the counter position, which in more radical forms is sometimes called libertarianism, is also a widely defended theoretical and practical position, associated with a radical right especially in the US, and with writers such as Ayn Rand as well as many on the far right in Congress. These are not always opposite positions, although they can be represented as such; they can also, however, be seen as forming a range along a spectrum of different versions of liberalism. Each position along the spectrum has implications for the understanding of IPE.

## A neo-neo synthesis?

Looking at questions of security and alliance cohesion as well as the question of how to understand the end of the Cold War in 1989–1991, a wide range of scholars since the 1990s have wondered if neo-realism and neo-liberalism did not have more in common than their apparent antagonism might suggest. Keohane, already cited several times, was one such scholar. David Baldwin also questioned the possibility of a synthesis between some versions of neo-liberalism and some versions of neo-realism. Some critics who rejected both debates also agreed that the two positions shared more in their assumptions, and especially in their methodologies, than the apparent opposition between them might suggest (e.g. Richard Ashley and R.B.J. Walker). Was a neo-neo synthesis possible, which took what the two had in common and built on the level of agreement that emerged? Could a neo-neo synthesis be deployed to undermine the then (1990s) rising tide of postmodern thinking in IR and IPE because among other shared assumptions both argued for a more methodologically rigorous attempt to be scientific against what proponents of both saw as the 'irrationalism' of postmodernism? These questions dominated academic conference papers in the United States, as well as some of the main journals for a time. The answer would not still matter very much if it had been limited to straight 'yes' and 'no' answers. But some of the most interesting responses to these questions have mixed arguments in ways that have sometimes been illuminating and productive; but they may have lost intellectual coherence in the process. The most important advocates of a neo-neo synthesis have included many constructivists (discussed in Chapter 2), who have initiated a research agenda that asks questions to which neo-liberals and neo-realists might both agree. But the overlap is rather false: constructivists have generally tended, while sometimes combining 'the two neos', to draw importantly also on postmodern and critical ideas. And many constructivists have, while making some use of a synthesis, nearly always fallen back into a position of being either primarily liberal or primarily realist. Constructivism is explained in the next chapter in more detail because its main drivers and leading scholars are for the most part critical of the mainstream ideas of both IR and IPE. For ease of organisation, we have explored constructivism in one place in this study, Chapter 2.

## Neo-Marxist theories

We should note finally here that a wide variety of approaches and authors have developed the Marxist theories considered earlier in both IR and IPE in the last fifty years. Like realism and liberalism, they have spawned their own 'neo' versions. But these mostly reflect challenges to orthodoxy in contemporary IR and IPE theory, and to avoid duplication they are considered in various forms in the next chapter: Critical Theory, Gramscian approaches to IR, Marxian feminism and regulation theory all owe elements to Marxist theory in IR, although their diversity shows both the richness and the fragmentation of Marxian approaches to IPE.

## Summary

This chapter has outlined the main sources and history of the recent academic study of IPE. In the process, it has explored some of the main theories in IR, which have shaped it. It has explained how IPE emerged in the late 1960s and early 1970s as a critique of IR, but how it has also retained close ties and dialogue with IR. It has also outlined its relationship to political economy. It has explained some of the practical concerns that also helped put IPE on the academic agenda: the insecurities and conflicts of the 1970s and onwards have shaped the scope, methods and debates in IPE and they continue to do so, as we will examine further throughout this text. All of these theoretical and practical concerns will continue to shape the later discussion, but in summarising some of the key ideas here, we can usefully deploy a summary table (see Table 1.4), which can form the basis of further study and further reflection. All three positions outlined here have been claimed to be rigorously 'scientific' by some of their exponents and criticised for that claim by some opponents; but others have also always not made this claim for them.

## Reflective questions

1   How did IPE emerge, and why did it emerge at the time that it did?
2   How might you contrast the views of 'established' mainstream IR theories of IPE?
3   How have neo-realism and neo-liberalism respectively offered understandings of the contemporary world political economy?
4   How far is the idea of a 'neo-neo synthesis' a convincing way forward for contemporary IPE studies?
5   What are the strengths and weaknesses of the theories offered in this chapter and the criticisms outlined of each?

**Table 1.4** Chapter summary

| | Role/nature of the state as actor | Role of international institutions | How 'power' is defined | Nature of international society | Role of non-state institutions |
|---|---|---|---|---|---|
| Neo-liberal Institutionalism | States seen as central but not sole actors. The state acts as a policy coordinator not as mechanical dominator of political economy | Important for stability and policy management; diverse and include civil society as well as economic interests and state established bodies | Power derives from effective cooperation and sharing of sovereignty in many instances although state retains some unique power features | A pluralist interdependent or global arena where complex policy management demands complex institutions | Critical participants in that international society; diverse; necessary and in state interests to encourage effective non-state bodies to participate |
| Neo-liberalism/ Market liberalism | Limited but important; managing stable money values; managing security and contracts; states often tend to try to do too much | OK where they have a limited role to manage 'level playing field' of rules; dangerous and intrusive if they try to go beyond that (which they often do) | Power derives from effective competition through market interactions; winners deserve the power they achieve | Primarily a market arena where 'whoever governs best governs least'; it is dangerous to think of 'society' as justifying state intervention | Private economic actors including firms, banks and others are key actors but non-state political actors and networks may be dangerous if they encourage state intervention |
| Neo realism (structural realism) | Primary actors; but neo-realists do not deny the complexity of actors in IR or IPE | Of limited value and tend to be worthless unless reflecting interests of dominant states where they can agree | Power for neo-realists is more rooted in structure than for classic realists; it is both military and economic; power will differ depending on whether there is a dominant hegemon or a lack of hegemony | A complex balance of power system and an anarchy in which there is no effective overall government (a more sophisticated version of classic realism on this point) | There are many non-state institutions, but they have and can only have limited impact. They mostly either lack the ability to shape the system or reflect the interests of the main great powers and then may have some structural impact |

## Suggestions for further reading

Wise students of IPE will try to combine reading from a range of sources including 'practical' sources (*Wall Street Journal*, *Financial Times*, *Economist* and so on), more critical thinking, and mainstream academic sources. This reading list is very short and very selective, but enables you to build on a reading of the chapter.

### Classical realisms and liberalisms

Angell, N. (1913) [1911] *The Great Illusion: A Study of the Relation of Military Power to National Advantage*, London: Read Books.
Bull, H. (1977) *The Anarchical Society*, London: Macmillan.
Jackson, R. (2005) *Classical and Modern Thought on International Relations*, Basingstoke: Palgrave Macmillan.
Spero, J.E. and Hart, J. (2013) *The Politics of International Economic Relations*, 5th revised edn, London: St Martin's Press.
Vasquez, John A. (1999) *The Power of Power Politics: From Classical Realism to Neotraditionalism*, Cambridge: Cambridge University Press.
Waltz, K. (2001) *Man, the State and War*, 2nd revised edn, New York: Columbia University Press.
Wolfers, A. (1962) *Discord and Collaboration: Essays on International Politics*, Baltimore, MD: Johns Hopkins University Press.

### Economic theories and IPE

Durlauf, S. and Blume, L. (eds) (2009) *Economic Growth*, Basingstoke: Palgrave.
List, F. (2013) [1841] *The National System of Political Economy*, Wilmington, NC: Vernon Press.
Magnussen, L. (2010) *Mercantilism: The Shaping of an Economic Language*, London: Routledge.
Ormrod, D. (2008) *The Rise of Commercial Empires: England and the Netherlands in the Age of Mercantilism 1650–1770*, Cambridge: Cambridge University Press.
Smith, A. (1982) [1776], *The Wealth of Nations* (2 vols, ed. Andrew Skinner), Harmondsworth: Penguin Classics.
Stiglitz, Joseph A. (2003) *Globalization and Its Discontents*, New York: W.W. Norton.
Strange, S. (2015) [1994] *States and Markets*, new edn, London: Bloomsbury Academic.

### Neo-realism and neo-liberalism

Baldwin, D. (ed.) (1993) *Neorealism and Neoliberalism: The Contemporary Debate*, New York: Columbia University Press.
Cerny, P.G. (2010) *Rethinking World Politics: A Theory of Transnational Neopluralism*, Oxford: Oxford University Press.
Gilpin, R. with Gilpin, Jean M. (2001) *Global Political Economy: Understanding the International Economic Order*, Princeton, NJ: Princeton University Press.
Keohane, Robert O. (ed.) (1986) *Neorealism and Its Critics*, New York: Columbia University Press.
Keohane, Robert O. (2005) *After Hegemony: Cooperation and Discord in the World Political Economy*, Princeton, NJ: Princeton University Press.
Krasner, Stephen D. (2009) *Power, the State and Sovereignty: Essays in International Relations*, London: Routledge.
Mearsheimer, John J. (1994) 'The false promise of international institutions', *International Security* 19(3): 5–49.
Northedge, F. (1976) *The International Political System*, London: Faber & Faber.
*Stanford Encyclopedia of Philosophy*, entry on 'Political realism' (available online).

Waltz, K. (1979) *Theory of International Politics*, London: McGraw-Hill.
Williams, Michael C. (2005) *The Realist Tradition and the Limits of International Relations*, Cambridge: Cambridge University Press.

## Marxism and dependency theory

Arrighi, G. (2010) [1994] *The Long Twentieth Century*, new revised edn, London: Verso Books.
Bukharin, N. and Lenin, V.I. (1929) *Imperialism and World Economy*, New York: Monthly Review Press.
Kolakovsky, L. (2008) *Main Currents of Marxism: The Founders, the Golden Age, the Breakdown*, New York: W.W. Norton.
Kubalkkova, V. and Cruickshank, A.A. (1989) *Marxism and International Relations*, Oxford: Oxford University Press.
Lenin, V.I. (2010) [1916] *Imperialism: The Highest Stage of Capitalism*, Harmondsworth: Penguin Classics.
Marx, K. (2008) [1861] *Capital*, Oxford: Oxford University Press.
Wallerstein, I. (2004) *World-Systems Analysis: An Introduction*, Durham, NC: Duke University Press.

# 2 Critical approaches to IPE

## Chapter learning outcomes

After reading this chapter students should be able to:

- Understand and summarise the assumptions and theories of the eight alternative approaches considered in this chapter.
- Cite the work of one or more key author(s) associated with each approach.
- Recognise how these approaches emerge out of a broad critique of traditional approaches.
- Explain how changes in the 'real world' since the late twentieth century and early twenty-first century have shaped the development of these theoretical approaches.
- Demonstrate a critical awareness of the broad strengths and weaknesses of each approach.
- Understand the criticisms of each approach.
- Be able to use these approaches in the study of international political economy.

This chapter is long because we have chosen to present a wide variety of alternatives to mainstream approaches. Students and teachers may want to focus on a selection of particular approaches depending on their interests and curriculum. But attentive readers should explore the whole range of theories discussed here – even if they then specialise in a few – in order to understand the evolution and diversity of contemporary IPE.

## Introduction

This chapter introduces the most significant alternative theoretical approaches that have developed in response to the 'orthodoxy' described in the previous chapter. Here you are introduced to a group of important theoretical perspectives in IPE: critical theory, constructivism, feminism, postmodern approaches, Gramscian approaches, networking theories from the 'new institutional economics', regulation theory, and green thought. Each of these eight approaches have drawn on a range of disciplines not traditionally associated with mainstream IR, and IPE theory. For example, feminism has close associations with both sociology and cultural anthropology in terms of concepts and the issues addressed. Each section also highlights the historical development of each of these approaches and the manner in which they are currently being applied.

As we consider the following alternative approaches you should see how each of them, albeit in markedly different ways, relates to the study of IPE. As with all theoretical approaches, the underlying assumptions have a significant impact upon the focus of any analysis and subsequent conclusions drawn. Critical theory highlights inequalities between people at both national and international levels and it calls for these inequalities to be addressed. It also highlights the structural dimensions of the global system in perpetuating these inequalities, for example, unequal terms of trade. Critical theorists have in common the question of how power and the uses of that power can be understood, taking a wide-ranging conception of 'power' including power 'in the academy', in the world of academic debate, as well as in the world of policy and action. Critical theory is considered in this chapter first because all the other fields of analysis considered here owe something to it, as well as having specific dimensions and questions of their own. Constructivists focus on social structures and dynamics and the way in which they are interpreted, and potentially misinterpreted by the actors involved. Therefore, a constructivist approach could be applied to analysing issues such as trade relations between certain states. For example, why does the United States have a free trade agreement with Jordan but not Syria? Feminist theory has its focus at the level of the individuals as well as looking at structures of power including patriarchy and at the working of institutions. As such, this immediately sets feminist approaches apart from many other theories. Issues of equality, distributive justice and emancipation are all key concerns of this approach. Feminists tend to focus on analysing issues such as human trafficking, prostitution, modern-day slave labour, child soldiers, the availability of maternal healthcare and the roles of women in governance. But, as the reader will see, feminist critics of IPE offer ideas, resources and arguments that are valuable for all students of the field, most importantly in the methods they suggest the field should use. Postmodern approaches question truth claims and argue that all positions and arguments are necessarily open to question, that claims of 'objectivity' collapse on closer scrutiny. Arguably then, this is the most encompassing of all approaches, since it makes a very broad critique of many other approaches. Although it applies to all IPE issues, disputes over truth claims are more apparent in some areas than in others. The dynamics of religious disputes, claims for human rights and other aspects of cultural relativism all involve competing world views. Specific examples include the discourse on 'the war on terror', what constitutes sustainable development, and what strategies and policies should be applied in dealing with these issues. Postmodern scholars have been involved in significant debates among feminist IPE scholars and about the effectiveness and focus of international institutions such as the World Bank and IMF. Green theorists would also see all aspects of IPE through the lens of environmental issues. This can include protection of the world's biodiversity, the manner and level of resource exploitation and how the international trading system operates. Green theorists have shaped innovative theories to combat global warming; but innovative business practices have also been used by green practitioners to develop technologies and corporate interventions to achieve practical results. With regard to international trade, green theorists would highlight the fact that the majority of this trade undervalues environmental protection. Two theories from what is sometimes called heterodox (i.e. non-orthodox) economics are also explained here; networking theory, which explains the behaviour of firms but also other actors in terms of the qualities and management of the networked connections within which they operate; and regulation theory, which argues that the kinds of regulation, and in some cases the failure or lack of regulation, help to explain both behaviour and outcomes in IPE.

As you read the following pages you should be able to see how each of the approaches outlined has its own discrete worldview. That said, you should also notice that there are some important elements of overlap between both the approaches and the issues they consider. One question in common across all the approaches considered in this chapter is the debate whether or not IPE can be in some senses 'scientific'. Part of this debate revolves around the question of what counts as a 'science'. Is IPE only scientific if it uses all the methods and assumptions of a natural science such as physics or chemistry, if it is able to accurately predict events, if it is 'objective' in the sense of value neutral and not dependent on the position or values of the researcher or the researched? Is it scientific if it is more cautiously positivist but does not try to ape the very specific grand claims of natural science? Most approaches outlined in this chapter claim to produce reliable checkable knowledge according to an agreed procedure and agreed conventions of research. But they all reject the claim to be scientific and thus like physics, and they argue that to claim to be is a mistaken understanding of social studies, which aim to understand and interpret human relations but not to be able to predict the future in any detail. Some of them reject any policy relevance, claiming that all one can do is to critique existing power structures, but others firmly claim to be policy relevant even though they are rooted in a critique of existing practices of knowledge production. This complex and important debate will be reflected through the chapter and in all the chapters that follow.

## Critical theory

## Historical development

Critical Theory is largely seen to have its roots in early Marxist thought and as such reflects some of the theoretical traits found in Marxism/structuralism. Like other theoretical approaches, Critical Theory is not an exclusively IPE approach. Instead it has developed as part of the broader social sciences and humanities. During the 1920s and 1930s a group of scholars based at the University of Frankfurt in Germany formed what came to be known as the Frankfurt School. This school focused on critical analysis of the contemporary world system and international relations. Karl Marx, Friedrich Engels, Immanuel Kant, Georg Hegel and Max Weber were all key influences on the Frankfurt School, as can be seen by the attention paid to critiques of capitalism, positivist methodologies and materialism. Critical theorists added several new dimensions to established liberal (radical liberal) and Marxist approaches. First of all, they drew extensively on their understanding of psychoanalysis, which suggested that individuals behaved in ways that the economic focus of both liberalism and earlier Marxism might have misunderstood. The subconscious of individuals and the subconscious motives engaged in social movements including both revolutions and social conformity had to be understood. Second, and partly following from this suspicion of 'economism' (the reduction of everything to be explained in economic and social life to a narrowly defined focus on economic behaviour to the neglect of both politics and culture and belief), critical theorists gave much greater attention to culture and cultures. Drawing on anthropology and sociology as well as cultural studies, they enlarged both the agenda and the focus of critique in IPE. They also share a concern for the ways in which power assumes different forms, and the ways in which language is used, very often as a vehicle for particular articulations of power. Third, critical theory was suspicious of the assumptions of rationality in liberal and realist thought in both politics and economics, most importantly in Adorno and Horkheimer's *Dialectic of Enlightenment* (1944). Individuals might believe that they were trying to 'maximise their gains' in any situation, but their view of what maximisation might be was both changeable and not necessarily coldly rational, especially when identity politics or religious belief were at issue, or when a traditional but strongly held set of values were under threat, rationality often went out of the window. This suspicion of the rationality that many scholars in the nineteenth century had taken to be sacred was doubled by *the very fact* that it was treated as sacred and not itself subject to scrutiny. And the European experience of the Holocaust was a powerful historical event in which industrial management, rationality of ends and means and calculations of planning and strategy were combined for a barbarous purpose. How, asked critical theorists (and many others) could we continue to trust the rational apparent objectivity of science and social understanding when it can be used to push a genocidal agenda? This was not necessarily to reject rationality altogether; but it did call for a wholesale re-evaluation, which critical theorists have been evolving ever since 1944. These factors combined to produce a new critique of industrial society and the industrial increasingly international economy, which moved some way from conventional Marxism.

**AUTHOR BOX**

# Max Horkheimer

Horkheimer was born in Stuttgart, Germany in 1895. In 1930 he was appointed Director of the Institute of Social Research, which was the base for the so-called Frankfurt School. With the rise of the Nazi Party in Germany, Horkheimer emigrated, initially to Switzerland and then on to the United States. For many years he was a close collaborator with Thomas Adorno. He died in 1973.

Horkheimer (1982) was one of the leading early Critical Theorists. He was interested in the historical transition from feudalism to limited capitalism to the emergence of the global capitalist system. The experiences of urbanisation, industrialisation and mechanisation combined with enduring poverty, inequality and widening divisions of wealth between rich and poor across Europe led Critical Theorists to study the structural causes of human suffering. They also began to consider the value of dominant methodologies in order to re-evaluate what IR and IPE understand 'knowledge' to be. They argue that many forms of knowledge serve to prop up established patterns of power both in academic work and in the wider world. Some critical theorists have suggested that only critical forms of knowledge that undermine any kind of practical policy response to the world have validity; but many others argue that a critical understanding of the world and of established power patterns can provide a starting point for more effective policy, by supporting the disadvantaged or excluded as well as building institutions which reflect values that question the status quo. In this second sense, critical theorists have been influential in studies of international institutions, global hegemony and the balance of power, trade development, the place of women in development policy, historical sociology, and in the analysis of global environmental outcomes, among others. Critical theory broadly described has been the most influential intellectual movement in IR and IPE in the last thirty years or so. But it has taken different forms, and influenced all of the alternative approaches to the mainstream 'orthodoxies' described in the previous chapter. Critical theory has been more influential in political science and political sociology than in economics, but there are all the same plenty of economists who also claim a debt to it.

Theodor Adorno (1997), for example, argued that there are knowledge structures that are created by social and political processes. This phase of Critical Theory's development saw a broader critique of not only capitalism or social science methodologies but also of Western civilisation as a whole and the move towards supposed scientific, rational and triumphant knowledge production. In this way, this approach shares some of the core theoretical arguments or assumptions of postmodernism in its critique of modernity. Following the end of the Cold War and the 'triumph' of liberal capitalism as a world system and ideology, Critical Theorists have developed their critique of capitalism and modernity to include broad criticism of inequality and injustice in the world. In many ways, Critical Theory has increasingly been informed by a desire not only to understand the world but also to change it – again, a reference to the early Marxist thought that influenced the early Frankfurt School.

## Central arguments

- The contemporary world system is characterised by inequalities between people.
- There are global structures in place that rely upon and perpetuate inequalities between people. These structures and these inequalities are not random; they are susceptible to careful analysis

and open to change. Critical knowledge – knowledge through critique and reflection – is the main tool of analysis to understand this; forms of knowledge that fail to develop critique reinforce the existing status quo.

■ Change is necessary in the global system in order to remove structural impediments to equality.

■ There is no real distinction between relations in the national and international realms – the two are interdependent and interconnected.

■ Key to change in both realms is the possibility of new critical knowledge on which radical change is possible; knowledge is always a reflection of interests and interpretations and power position until it is critical and capable of criticising itself as well as the knowledge claims of others. The task of critical theory is to do this criticism so as to make change and a shifting of power structures possible. Without critique, no change is possible; but the aim of critique is not merely to make observations from a distance – critical theory aims to change the inequalities and injustices it observes.

## Specific theories

Robert Cox (1987: 207) has claimed that all 'theory is *for* someone and *for* some purpose'. Critical Theory argues that there are processes of theory-creation in the social sciences that are all influenced by subjective values. This is a direct critique of the positivism of realism, which claims that the social world can be observed in an objective and empirical manner, allowing for the creation of 'scientific' theories. This position relies on the assumption of the existence of objective facts that cannot be interpreted in different ways and so are not influenced by any subjective agendas. Critical Theorists, on the other hand, suggest that knowledge is never entirely objective and we cannot observe the social world in an empirical manner without interpreting what we observe and its meaning in different ways. The reflexivity of human minds along with the variance in values, beliefs, perceptions and so on mean that the same social phenomena can be observed and interpreted in different ways. At the same time both 'knowledge' and theories are created by people, and so are inherently subjective (not in the sense that they are arbitrary or purely individual but in the sense that the context of individuals cannot be ignored in understanding them). They vary from other forms created by other people. This leads Critical Theorists to question how knowledge has been constructed and received, and also their own place in knowledge construction. Questions about the origin, purpose and value of different forms of theoretical approaches are also raised.

Many other approaches such as realism, liberalism and structuralism look at structure in the global system as an important element in determining international relations. Critical Theory also looks at a structural determinant in the form of capitalism. Here, Critical Theorists argue that capitalism is inherently founded on competition and accumulation and this has led to global divisions of labour, wealth, resources, power and control between the two classes: the bourgeoisie and the proletariat. In order for industrial development, economic growth and prosperity the bourgeoisie must exploit the mass of workers and accumulate profits. This structure is seen as very negative and damaging to the vast majority of the global population. Furthermore, capitalism and its structures of exploitation and competition is the primary cause of both domestic and international conflict. While liberals would point to the value of international institutions in preventing conflict and aiding the development of the poor, Critical Theory argues that these institutions are established and controlled by powerful elites and therefore serve the purpose of the bourgeoisie. Instead of relying on contemporary international institutions, Critical Theorists suggest that peace and stability can only be achieved on a global scale when the proletariat are no longer exploited.

## Unequal exchange and terms of trade

For the critical theorist (of whatever specific kind), exploitation is a fundamental aspect of the contemporary capitalist global economy. It is the basis by which the core economies and rich elite classes both maintain their position of dominance and prevent the dominated from significantly improving their own position. Critical theorists emphasise the negative factors associated with an international trading system, whereby one party to an exchange benefits a great deal more than the other. This can be represented in many sectors across the global economy. This is of course a direct attack on the liberal belief that free trade benefits all participants even if it may not benefit them all equally.

Many examples of unequal exchange have their roots in imperial history. Even post-independence, the economic structures that characterised the colonial era can remain very similar. Often this involves the developing countries continuing to exploit its primary resources, such as minerals or timber, for a relatively low market value. The value of such commodities is often determined by world markets rather than by the exporters. There can be a stark contrast between these low-value exports and the often high value of imported, manufactured goods, especially when local purchasing power is taken into account. Another dimension of inequality, despite the rhetoric of free-marketeering, is the disadvantages faced by the exporters of agricultural produce from the developing world when many developed states, notably those in the EU, create an unfair advantage for their own farmers by heavily subsidising this sector.

While in the modern era we have known the 'state' as the main unit of societal organisation in international relations, 'states' (that is, the modern state) are in fact a relatively new form of political unit. Furthermore, the idea that every geographical territory and every people are divided up into specific states is also a new concept. Many states have existed as modern states in their current form for only a few decades. Even the oldest states do not go back very far in terms of the entirety of human history. Critical Theory claims that the state as a unit or political and economic entity in which people are grouped and to which they 'belong' is a result of the capitalist system formed in the last 500 years out of the need to organise and control the masses. State creation is done much the same way as knowledge creation, as discussed above. States are created and maintained through knowledge, which is created and perpetuated to generate timeless 'truths' about the state – or what can be seen in a critical sense as national myths. Ideas of the state aim to conceal the basic fact that all states are founded on violence rather than on some eternal principle of legitimacy. This is at least as true of the liberal democratic state as it is of others, it is argued by critical theorists (including Cox and Marcuse, but especially Giorgio Agamben). Critical Theorists, therefore, acknowledge the importance in studying states as actors in international relations, but in the sense of how they maintain the capitalist system and how they perpetuate inequalities and class divisions. A reorientation of how the 'state' is perceived is seen as necessary if change and emancipation are to be achieved.

## Criticisms

Critical Theorists argue that there is much inequality and injustice in the world and that this needs to be changed in order to attain a fairer system. However, critics argue that Critical

Theory's own critique of dominant forms of knowledge as being subjective and as privileging some over others can be used against its own call for a universalistic human condition. As highlighted above, and especially in the case of Gramscian forms of Critical Theory, hegemonic forms of knowledge and theory as well as overarching universal claims are invalid and undesirable. It does seem somewhat strange, then, that Critical Theorists themselves claim that there is *a* problem with the world system and that there is *a* desirable condition that should be aspired to. This can be seen to defeat the whole point of critiquing knowledge claims which are tautological.

There has been criticism of earlier work done by Critical Theorists, which emphasised class conflict as the main characteristic of world politics and economics. Realists, for example, see weaknesses in any analysis that fails to acknowledge the contrasts between the same social class in different states. The elite or bourgeoisie is seen by Critical Theorists to be the dominant class in control of state and private sector policy and resources. However, this does not explain why states often go to war with each other, thus pitting bourgeoisie against bourgeoisie and proletariat against proletariat. Of course, the Critical Theory response to this critique is to suggest that the proletariat class is deceived and manipulated into fighting on behalf of *their* state by hegemonic forms of knowledge. Furthermore, conflict can often be profitable and beneficial to the bourgeoisie. Nevertheless, realists would still question why the bourgeoisie would engage in conflict. The two World Wars are used as examples of when conflict between states could not be seen to have benefited the bourgeoisie.

In terms of the methodology of Critical Theory, positivists argue that without following a rigorous and scientific methodology no solid conclusions can be formed from any study. Critical Theory is, therefore, unable to produce convincing conclusions and unable to solidly predict or prescribe in international relations. The rejection of positivist forms of study and the advocacy of more subjective and interpretive methods means that the conclusions that Critical Theory produces are not infallible. This is especially problematic as one of the core aims of this approach is to highlight problems with the global system and call for change in it. Critics simply ask how Critical Theory can highlight problems as true and prescribe courses of action in order to achieve a better world when knowledge and theory are said to be subjective and for someone and some purpose.

# Constructivism

## Historical development

The majority of theoretical approaches in IPE offer varying and often contradictory assumptions and explanations for social phenomena. Constructivism also offers different positions on international political economy and international relations from, say, liberalism and realism. However, constructivism can also be set apart to an extent as unique in IPE theory as a school of thought that allows for the synthesis of elements of other approaches. Constructivism has emerged as one of the more recent (post-1990s) theoretical approaches in IPE and seems in many ways to sidestep some of the key theoretical debates. While realism and liberalism seem endlessly engaged in critique of each other, constructivism has developed in a manner that allows for the rebuttal of common critiques because it has an inclusive nature. So while advocates of realism and liberalism debate the suitability of state-centrism and pluralism, constructivism offers an approach which can adopt either state-centrism or pluralism at varying times. Constructivists come in different varieties depending on the main questions they ask, including those about subjectivity, identity, structure and agency, perceptions and metaphysical considerations.

Through the 1990s, constructivism as an approach to understanding international relations was developed by a range of scholars; but Nicholas Onuf (1997) is often cited as key in its emergence. In many ways this approach developed as a response to what was seen as a common flaw on both realist and liberal perspectives. This was that international relations were being studied in a manner that was only concerned with the tangible and material elements of the social world. Scholars like John Ruggie (1998) and Richard Ashley (1988) shared Onuf's ideas that intangible features of human relations such as beliefs, perceptions and understanding are also important. The constructivist approach gained in influence and theoretical complexity through the 1990s and is now a major alternative approach within the study of international political economy. Constructivists drew on liberal institutionalism ('ideas embedded in institutions and social practices') to explain international behaviour and outcomes – see Chapter 1.

## Central arguments

■ Subjectivity is the key to understanding agency and actor behaviour at the domestic and international levels.

■ Identity is an important element in the creation of coherent actors and helps to determine how other actors are perceived.

■ Perceptions of other actors, issues and processes are more important than structures, institutions and regimes in determining international relations.

■ All types of state and non-state actors can be important and worthy of study in varying situations; in exploring the range of types of actors we need to take account of the interaction of structures *and* agency rather than relying on explanation in terms of *either* structure *or* agency to the exclusion of the other, and constructivist approaches enable one to do this coherently.

■ All types of issues including, among others, war, cooperation, trade, development, labour rights, financial flows and environmental change are important and worthy of study in IPE.

## Specific theories

At the heart of constructivism are assumptions about the importance of subjectivity and inter-subjectivity in all domestic and international relations. For constructivists, phenomena in both the human and natural worlds do not have any relevance until we ascribe some form of meaning to them. Furthermore, the meaning and interpretations of phenomena will determine how they impact on us and our relations with each other. Metaphysical debates are thus of prime importance to the constructivist. How a given phenomenon is observed and interpreted can and will vary from one person to another and from one collective group of people to another. The differences in the ways in which events, issues, processes, actors and so on are viewed and interpreted are the determining factors in actor behaviour. For example, constructivists agree with realists (and some liberals) that the global system is one of domestic governance but international anarchy. However, the relevance of the lack of existence of a global governing authority and the existence of anarchy in the international arena do not necessarily mean conflict is inevitable – which is exactly what the liberal counter-argument to the realist assumption of the effects of anarchy claims.

**AUTHOR BOX**

# Alexander Wendt

Born in 1958 in Mainz, West Germany, Wendt is one of the leading scholars in the field of social constructivism. He has held positions in several US universities including Yale, Chicago and Ohio State, where he is the Ralph D. Mershon Professor of International Security.

Wendt claims that 'anarchy is what states make of it' (1999), denoting different possible outcomes of the existence of anarchy. A group of teenage friends may exist in an anarchic environment (in other words they may have no authoritative figure watching over them) yet they remain friends. A group of rival teenagers may exist in an anarchic environment and engage in hostilities. The key for constructivists is not whether or not there is anarchy but how actors perceive this anarchy and each other.

Constructivists claim that cooperation is possible between states or peoples in the international arena (and indeed between people in the domestic arena), but not simply because institutions and regimes are created to control actor behaviour, as liberals claim. Instead, the perception of international institutions and regimes as being beneficial and perceptions of other actors as friends, partners or even collaborators leads to cooperation. If a state, for example, sees an international institution, such as the World Intellectual Property Organization (WIPO), as actually infringing on its sovereignty and damaging its economic interests then it may not cooperate with other states via this organisation. On the other hand, if a state perceives an organisation or other external actor as good and useful to work with then it probably will cooperate. The very fact that institutions and regimes exist does not guarantee cooperation.

While Marxian analysis focuses on economic materialism as a key factor in driving world history and international relations, constructivism also sees social relationships as key drivers. The existence of economic materialism and material capabilities are acknowledged by constructivists as being important. But social relationships between individuals or groups of individuals are seen as playing very significant roles in determining international relations. When we discuss 'international relations', constructivists say we must remember that we are discussing human relationships as acted out by individual humans and so the personalities, characteristics, beliefs, values and relationships of individuals must be seen as important. For example, the personal friendship between the late King Hussein of Jordan and the late former Prime Minister of Israel, Yitzhak Rabin, was pivotal in the signing of a treaty of peace between the former enemies in 1994. Israel and Jordan had been in a state of war since 1948 and conventional understandings of the international relations of the Middle East at the time suggested peace and a normalisation of relations between the two states would not be likely. The long friendship and mutual respect the two leaders had for each other allowed an agreement to be made. Constructivism claims we should examine this factor.

In order to possess a measure of agency in international relations an actor usually has to have a relatively large and capable number of members. The state, for example, is a collective of individuals who are grouped together politically, economically and socio-culturally. Constructivism argues that even this type of actor is not natural and no state exists prior to the creation of a subjective perception of the collective group. In other words, states are not really real, there is no such thing as a 'nation' until people 'create' a sense of communal belonging. National anthems, certain versions of historical stories, patron saints and other religious figures, national sports teams, religious beliefs, languages and so on are all socially constructed phenomena, which allow for the creation of a shared identity.

## Illustrating constructivism: US–China relations

The United States and China have a long history of relationships reaching back into the nineteenth century. In the later nineteenth and early twentieth century, the weakening Chinese empire was seen both as a target for trade and US missionary activity and as a power that might resist the rising strength of Japan. After the Allies' defeat of Japan in 1945, the US expected to continue good relations with China; but Americans were shocked by the success of Chinese communism in October 1949. The 'loss' of China (a bizarre expression given the US had never 'owned' the country) led to a long period of conflict and suspicion driven on both sides by ideology as well as power rivalry across the Pacific region. But the initiatives of Nixon and Kissinger aimed to bring China into the world balance of power in the early 1970s, in order to balance the power of the USSR and to gain access to Chinese markets and investments that the US had tried to open before 1918. As the Chinese economy grew rapidly after 1976, the US was first a source of finance and a leading investor. But as the Chinese economy became richer and as the US became increasingly indebted, the US government and US firms and banks borrowed increasingly from Chinese institutions. China enjoyed a huge trade deficit with the US, which enabled it to build large reserves of cash. This trading relationship also led to the growth of Chinese cities and a large middle class. Originally dependent on imported technology, as often Japanese as European or American, Chinese firms started to develop their own capacity for innovation. Chinese research students accounted for around 20 per cent of all PhD students in some science and technology fields in the US. In 1999, the Clinton Administration successfully pushed for the admission of China to the World Trade Organization, arguing that such a growing economic power needed to be incorporated into the fabric of global institutional management and institutional regulation rather then left to be an isolated but powerful outrider of world economic management. Since 2007, China has come to be a leading player in the G20 group of states, has been a continuing player in world trade (despite a lower growth rate in the 2010s), and having an increasingly important role in global money markets. Despite a slowdown in Chinese economic growth and problems of balancing a changed economy as wage costs rose and domestic demand increased, the Chinese economy has become a crucial element of global growth and global stability. Managing 'the rise of China' as a superpower without (so far) a major military or economic conflict has been the result of careful constructive management by both the Chinese and the US, aided by other actors including the major world institutions.

Neo-realism might explain some aspects to the rise of China and the transforming relations between Washington and Beijing since 1911, using concepts of structural change and power position in the world order. But a great deal of this relationship, especially when we look at it in detail and not in very broad generality, has been constructed by both sides. Some neo-realists continue to hold that the rise of China to full superpower status cannot occur without a major world conflict. But it has been changing images and conceptions of national interest, alongside changing domestic politics and changing ideas of what and how world order might be managed, which have shaped this relationship. Today, the Chinese self-image that since they are now a superpower, whatever the United States does China must match it, having equal status in negotiations and in treaty outcomes, is a key condition of agreement (or disagreement) in international management of climate change, trade, intellectual property and security discussions. But much of this history could have been different: constructivists would say only their account provides an adequate explanation of this history.

## Criticisms

For many theorists and scholars of IPE, the constructivist approach has some weaknesses in terms of its explanatory power and coherency. A common criticism of constructivist analysis is simply that it lacks applicability in the realm of IPE and IR. Realists, for example, claim that in order to understand and explain social phenomena and international relations we need to be able to set firm theoretical parameters and outline solid assumptions. Constructivism can be said to be too encompassing in terms of its assumptions of which actors are important and possess significant agency as well as which issues are influential in shaping international interactions. The focus on subjective perceptions and interpretations as well as the emphasis on identity as key determining features of international relations is criticised as being inappropriate. Here, realists argue that there is little value in considering how a person's opinions are formed and how they may perceive others. Ultimately the anarchic world system and the self-interested decision-making of states determine interactions. Individuals have little input and issues such as identity are simply said to be unimportant.

The liberal critique, on the other hand, is based on the assumptions that rules and rational interests govern relations between actors at the international level. The constructivist suggestion that regardless of what rules, institutions and regimes may exist, actors cannot always be considered to be rational maximisers is seen as counter-productive to sound analysis. Liberal critics, and especially liberal economists and those using an economic calculus of interests, reject the constructivist view that identity politics or historical memories may trump what are considered to be rational interests. They also deny the constructivist argument (shared by critical theorists) that 'rationality' itself is a loaded and doubtful concept in most political contexts. Even though individuals do vary in terms of their respective identities, liberal and classic realists hold, they always remain rational and are driven by specific goals. Even though liberals share the constructivist's concern with the human condition, the latter's focus on subjective experiences can be seen by the former as a hindrance to analysis, which considers the roles played by international organisations and regimes. A weakness of assuming that perceptions and values and so on determine behaviour is that as scholars of IPE we cannot necessarily expect to achieve an analysis that considers all the relevant individuals. Put in other words, there are too many individuals to study and if we cannot study all of the individuals and their perceptions then we cannot claim to offer a complete analysis.

A broader critique of constructivism, which is often levelled by advocates of most other approaches, is that constructivism borrows too much from other schools of thought to the extent that it can sometimes be incoherent. For example, many constructivists (Onuf and Sikkink, for example) accept that the non-state actors are often very significant actors; whereas other constructivists such as Wendt express a much more state-centric approach – for Wendt anarchy is 'what states make of it', *not* what states and many other actors make of it. Another example is the position that anarchy does exist in the international arena yet either conflict or cooperation can prevail. Constructivism is, like all of these theoretical labels, a broad church in which quite a lot of diversity occurs. As explained above, constructivists argue that how anarchy is perceived is more important than whether it exists or not. Nevertheless, the view that constructivism sometimes does not offer solid assumptions that remain constant has led to the opinion that it simply avoids inter-paradigm debate.

# Feminism

## Historical development

An area of human relations that has traditionally been ignored in both IR and IPE is the role of women in domestic and international relations as well as in economic and political processes. The existent structures of human societies have often led to the marginalisation, subjugation, exploitation and even exclusion of some elements of society. Women have, throughout history and still largely in the contemporary world, found themselves in this position of being dominated. While there are examples of societies where women's issues, rights and roles in society have been equal with those of men or even primary over men, this is the exception to the norm. However, at various stages in the modern era attention has been paid to the position of women in society and processes of change have been witnessed. The eighteenth and nineteenth centuries, for example, saw much more atten-tion being paid to the political and economic rights of women in Europe and North America, with thinkers such as Mary Wollstonecraft (1996) commenting widely on discrimination. It is important to note that feminism as a school of thought emerged in socio-political realms outside academia but soon was integrated into fields such as sociology, anthropology and politics. Feminism was integrated in earnest into IPE and IR in the second half of the twentieth century.

There are three general historical phases of the emergence and development of feminism as a perspective on human relations. These phases tend to be referred to as 'waves'. The first wave of feminism took place in the nineteenth and twentieth centuries and centred on the women's suffrage movements of Europe and North America. This phase of feminism was encouraged by demands for equal economic and marital rights for men and women but soon expanded to encompass a range of issues pertinent to women's rights, including the right to partake in political processes. The second wave of feminism evolved during the 1960s and is said to have lasted until the late 1980s. Here, 'feminists' built on the earlier efforts and successes of the first wave of feminism and expanded the issue areas of concern as well as the societal scope of feminism. While a range of political and many economic rights had been won for women in Europe and North America as well as (albeit less con-vincingly) in other regions, the 1960s saw feminists focusing on issues of equality in a broader sense.

**AUTHOR BOX**

## Cynthia Enloe

Born in 1938, Cynthia Enloe has been at the forefront of the development of feminist theory. She has placed a particular emphasis on military issues and the impacts these have on women's lives. This relates to both the experience of female military personnel and women who live close to military bases. She has also developed these ideas further in considering how the labour of women is used both to prepare for and to support military operations.

Cynthia Enloe (1989) began to discuss issues such as ending discrimination against women in the workplace or in public office as well as in education and these became central to the feminist remit. Sexual liberation and equality also became key issues. This phase of the development of feminism also saw the spread of the feminist project to many other societies and countries around the world.

The third wave of feminism can be said to have emerged in the early 1990s as a response to the failures of the second wave. This most recent era of feminism has been the most critical as it seeks to incorporate metaphysics into the discussion of equality and emancipation. Earlier forms of feminism are seen by many contemporary feminists as having adopted patriarchal definitions and assumptions of what it is to be female and what is good for women. Third-wave feminists such as Gloria Anzaldua (2010) suggest that how we understand gender needs to be re-evaluated and the goals of feminists need to be re-examined. In short, we need to consider whether equality with men, or masculinity, is what women should be seeking, or should feminists focus more on broader senses of equality and liberty for both men and women to pursue. In this sense feminism as a meta-narrative in IPE offers broader analytical tools that allow us to consider equality and liberty in a more critical manner. Also, we can use feminism to examine not only women's rights but also the rights and experiences of all exploited or marginalised people. It should be noted that throughout the development of feminism men as well as women have been involved in both practical and academic/intellectual ways – you do not have to be a woman to be a feminist.

## Central arguments

■ Women are equal to men and so should be seen as, and treated as, equal to men in all areas of human society and relations.
■ Domestic and international relations are characterised largely by the exploitation of weak, poor and marginalised actors by dominant ones.
■ The individual is an important actor in international relations, and the agency as well as experiences of individuals should be considered as very important in international political economy.
■ Change in contemporary structures and processes is necessary to achieve equality of all people, the emancipation of those who have been exploited as well as a more egalitarian and prosperous world. This requires change in the structure of patriarchy as well as a critique of male-dominated knowledge.

## Specific theories

Feminism is a very broad school of thought with many differing assumptions and specific theories. This is partly a result of the relatively long history of feminist ideology and the adoption of feminist thought in many different academic disciplines as well as the varied range of feminists and the intellectual products they have given rise to. A number of specific theories of feminism (or branches of feminism) deserve attention here with regard to their use in IPE. Socialist feminism, often called Marxist or Marxian feminism, is founded on the core assumption of exploitation in human relations. Here, the exploitation of women is connected to Marxist explanations of injustice as resulting from capitalist economic structures. In order to achieve equality and emancipation for women the capitalist system, which maintains patriarchy through economic competition, must first be overthrown. This can be done through social and military revolution and requires all societies in the world to be engaged in revolutionary action. Socialist/Marxist feminism is therefore a global theory and not restricted to a small number of states or societies.

Liberal feminism advocates the pursuit of equality between men and women through legal and institutional means. The inherent good nature of humans is a key assumption here, as is the ability of humans for rational calculation and peaceful cooperation, issues that Betty Friedan (1982) commented on at the start of the second wave of feminism. Inequality and exploitation of women is seen as a result of historical processes that were shaped by a more anarchic and competitive global system. In the contemporary era of globalisation, where institutions and regimes are increasingly leading to integration and cooperation between states and peoples, the environment is being created for egalitarian relations between men and women. Unlike socialist feminism, liberal feminism sees dialogue and the collaborative creation of institutions, norms and rules as the way to ensure equality between men and women. In a similar manner to socialist feminism, liberal feminism can also be global in scope. Radical feminists (who may also take a radical environmental position known as 'ecofeminism'; see Chapter 9 on the environment) put more emphasis on issues of gender and sexuality, and ask questions about a different agenda of rights and equalities in terms of women's control over their own bodies. They are also interested in the body (male, female and other) in the political economy, and in the political economy of body art and the possibility (or impossibility) of representation of emancipation in gender and sexual relations. Radical feminists are as concerned with rights as liberal feminists, and as concerned with patterns of work and economic justice as Marxist feminists, but they put more emphasis on these other factors, arguing that 'the personal is political' and that inequalities and injustices that arise at a global and local level often do so most significantly in the global South or in the margins of developed societies, including the questions and issues confronting trans people in all societies.

## Human trafficking

The issue of human trafficking is a global problem. The US State Department estimates that between 600,000 and 800,000 people are trafficked across international borders every year, although the nature of this illegal operation makes it difficult to obtain accurate figures. The majority of those trafficked are women and children, many of whom are likely to become part of the international sex trade.

Several feminist writers have focused their work on aspects of prostitution. The political economy of the sex trade deals with issues such as health, wealth, power, control and emancipation. It not only looks at gendered power relations but also deals with the interface between the personal experiences of the sex trade, for prostitute, pimp and punter. Beyond that it considers the factors that may lead to an increase in trafficking, which may be as a result of a 'push' factor to escape conflict zones and other disadvantaged areas. There can also be 'pull' factors, such as the increased demand for prostitution services during major international sporting events such as the World Cup or the Olympics.

The recent historical experience of imperialism and colonialism is seen by some feminists as the cause of inequality and exploitation in developing states. This includes exploitation by one class over another and the subsequent inequality. However, post-colonial feminists also claim that relations between men and women have also been affected by this historical experience in many places. While women from developing regions are not seen to be inherently and timelessly obedient, marginalised and passive, they are seen to be exploited and marginalised in more recent times. Post-colonial feminists claim this is because the societal, political and economic structures put in place in former colonies during the era of imperial domination mirrored patriarchal structures from the former imperial powers. In effect patriarchy was exported to the colonies following subjugation as part of the process of imperial domination. In order to achieve equality and full rights for women, therefore, neo-imperial relationships such as economic dependency must be removed and full national independence achieved.

Christian and Islamic feminism share a number of key assumptions with other forms of feminism but differ in others. The historical experience of both Christianity and Islam often suggests that these religious belief systems have inherent structures that encourage patriarchy. Nobel Peace Prize winner Shirin Ebadi (2003) has often argued that Islam, for example, does not prohibit women's rights. Instead Islam can be used to guarantee such rights and it is varying (patriarchal) interpretations of Islam that have led to discrimination in some Islamic societies. However, both Christian feminism and Islamic feminism highlight the religious grounds of equality before God of all men and women and the role of women in both religions' histories to argue for divinely ordained rights for women. For the former, the role of women in establishing and maintaining the early Christian communities is highlighted to demonstrate how men and women had equal roles and rights. For Islamic feminists a similar focus on women as key parts of the early Islamic community and passages of the Quran that are dedicated to outlining the importance of women's rights are highlighted. In the contemporary era, religious feminists call for a return to earlier forms of their respective religions as a way to liberate women from patriarchal systems on a global scale.

## Criticisms

Feminists have been the target of many criticisms levelled by practically all schools of thought in IPE as well as by anti- or post-feminists in sociology, anthropology and politics. In terms of the traditional theoretical approaches discussed in Chapter 2 there are two main strands of critique. The first is centred on questions of agency and actor behaviour. The second strand is concerned with theories of processes at the international and global levels. Realism, for example, does not share the feminist belief in the agency of the individual in international relations. Even neo-realist theories do not offer any significant consideration of the individual. In fact realist theories reject outright the relevance of individuals as important actors. Instead, the primary units of importance are the state and, in neo-realism, also MNCs, IGOs and perhaps civil society groups (although most realists would also disregard these latter actors). Individuals are seen as simply lacking in agency or the ability to significantly act in international relations on their own and so are not seen as worthy of consideration. Furthermore, the equality of women with men is not seen as a significant issue as it is claimed to have little influence on relationships of power between states in the global arena.

While liberals place more emphasis on the agency of individuals, they too suggest that focusing too much on individuals as opposed to states or international institutions is counter-productive. Some of the key assumptions of liberalism do deal with the human condition, or in other words the experience and well-being of human individuals (indeed, some of the core premises of classical liberalism revolve around the emancipation of humans as they pursue liberty and happiness). However, this concern is secondary to the neo-liberal focus on enhancing international cooperation, stability and prosperity. Even though individuals are seen as important in terms of their inherent worth, they are not seen as possessing enough agency on their own to influence international relations in a significant manner. The feminist concern with and focus on individuals is therefore not suitable for the study of the world in IPE.

Marxists and structuralists share many of the concerns of equality and freedom from exploitation that feminists hold as primary. In Marxism the main goal of Marxian thought is change of the global system and structure of modern human society to allow for the equality of all and the eradication of marginalisation and exploitation of poorer and weaker segments of society. This mirrors some of the concerns of feminism. On the other hand, however, Marxist and structuralist analysis focuses on the impact of economic materialism and the capitalist system as the causes of inequality and exploitation. This is in contrast to the argument in most strands of feminism that patriarchy and historical socio-cultural processes lead to inequality and exploitation. Furthermore, Marxists and structuralists do not focus on any perceived distinction between men and women as opposed to the bourgeoisie and proletariat. In other words, these schools of thought claim exploitation and inequality are perpetrated by one socio-economic class against another as opposed to the feminist claim that the divide is between genders.

# Postmodernism/poststructuralism

## Historical development

The history of postmodernism can be linked to the earliest (classical Greek *and* Hindu) examples of philosophical thinking and attempts to justify knowledge or truth claims. More accurately postmodernism should be seen in relation to, and in a critical position with regard to, all such claims. The essence of postmodernism is to highlight that there is no wholly objective 'truth' and that all knowledge claims must be seen as originating from a particular perspective; we must, it is proposed, recognise that such perspectives are formulated and framed within a set of power relationships and structures. The nature of postmodernism makes it difficult to determine when it emerged or even how it has evolved. An initial assumption may be that it emerged after the 'modern' era, given its name. There is some 'truth' in this; but this is more obviously associated with emerging movements in the fields of art, poetry, literature, architecture and music from the early decades of the twentieth century. The word was first actually used by architectural critics in the mid-1960s. For IR and IPE there was a greater emphasis on social change and the questioning of established norms and values in the 1960s. This, in turn, led to a more clearly defined branch of IR and IPE postmodern thought being developed, albeit with numerous facets, in the 1980s.

Postmodernism is a widely used but unsatisfactory term because it is so difficult to pin down beyond a certain scepticism. Some postmodernists owe a significant debt to Marxism (e.g. Lyotard); but others largely ignore this heritage. Many scholars would prefer the term 'post- structuralism', which implies that postmodernism has moved specifically beyond and away from the structuralism of Marxism, which was indeed its origin in France and German in the 1970s. This label is helpful because if we ask how far or near writers described as postmodern are from Marx it may help understand their work better. To more fully understand postmodern arguments, we need to draw on the language of philosophy which they use, ontology and epistemology.

**CONCEPT BOX**

## Ontology

Inquiry into, or theory of, being. In twentieth-century IPE usage, ontology is the general theory of what there is. For instance, questions about the mode of existence of abstract entities such as numbers, imagined entities (which underpin different perspectives) and impossible entities such as square circles and so on. In IPE this question matters where we talk about structures that cannot be immediately seen but that can be detected through their effects, including some of the most important structures of power. It also includes ideas of discourse, class and patriarchy (the latter central to many feminist writers). The mainstream arguments discussed in Chapter 1 tend to have conservative (small 'c'!) ideas of ontology and restrict what they think counts as a cause or a reality. Postmodern writers may not agree on what they count as existing, but they agree widely on the importance of asking critical questions about ontology, and suggest that scholars who fail to ask these questions carry a concealed bias or agenda in their unquestioned assumptions. The only thing postmodern scholars will agree on is the principle: 'question everything!'

## Epistemology

Epistemology is the theory of knowledge: the branch of philosophy that enquires into the nature and possibility of knowledge. In other words, 'how we know what we know'. In IPE, epistemological questions derive from the methodologies used by the leading perspectives because each orthodox approach has a different epistemological framework, for example, (and in general terms) feminists are normative – they have a set of explicit values or norms that they bring to their work; realists are positivists; some liberals agree they are normative, although other claim to be 'objective' even though liberalism has explicit moral and theoretic assumptions about values. For another example, one might look at feminist authors, who often claim there is something distinctive about the knowledge women have derived from distinctive experience both in developed societies and in indigenous communities (see below). You should also be aware of the term 'epistemic communities', which is sometimes used to designate a certain perspective and its approach to epistemology where knowledge is said to define the boundaries of a group or network (again, see discussion of networking below).

Postmodernist writing can include reference to ancient philosophers such as Socrates and Plato. Martin Heidegger (1991) placed particular emphasis on the nature of 'being' and, crucially, how 'being' is understood. This immediately places individuals, institutions and events in the realm of the social and the subjective. Each become subject to interpretation with each interpretation, by definition, being formulated from a socially constructed position and open to critique. With this in mind it is unsurprising that various strands of postmodernism have emerged at particular times in relation to dominant values and social structures. Revolutionary ideologies clearly pre-dated the 'counter-culture' movement of the 1960s. However, this was a period of particularly creative output from leading postmodern thinkers, especially in France. Notably, they were not 'traditional' social or political revolutionaries who wished to overthrow one system and replace it with another. Rather, they questioned the concepts of all systems. They highlighted aspects of power to be found in the use of language and the framing of discourses. In his 1597 essay *Meditationes Sacrae*, Francis Bacon said 'Knowledge is power'. Postmodernists expose the basis for such knowledge claims and challenge the power relations that follow from them.

## Central arguments

- All 'truth' claims are subjective and based on prejudiced interpretations of events; to understand human experience is above all to understand it in its context(s).
- Claims that are made are self-serving with regard to certain socio-economic and political agendas.
- No alternative claims are being made to replace the 'truth' claims being challenged. IPE can deploy methods (some borrowed from other fields of social understanding and some of its own) that enable it to understand human experience more fully than projects to imitate the natural sciences only once it has abandoned the attempt to be scientific or positivist.

## Specific theories

As indicated above, there is a vast array of thought and criticism that can come under the broad heading of postmodernism. In its most inclusive meaning it can refer to anything that challenges widely accepted principles of style and order that emerged in the so-called 'modern' era of the early twentieth century. The years immediately following the First World War saw a burgeoning of literary and artistic movements that attempted to challenge and reshape the existing establishment forms and endeavours in these areas. Narrative styles changed, as did the use and representation of space and even time. This was in line with changes in the modern world that were even more far-reaching than those of the Industrial Revolution. The inter-war years were times of upheaval in terms of rebuilding war-torn societies and also facing the economic downturn of the Depression era. Political and cultural theorists reflected this change by turning their attention to far-reaching questions about the underlying premises and assumptions that were used to either justify change or retain the status quo.

James Der Derian and Michael Shapiro (1989) have written about how power politics are driven by the interplay of different texts, referring to not only the written and verbal meaning given to certain terms and phrases but also the implications of these meanings and their usage in social settings that necessarily involve power relationships. For example, the attacks on the World Trade Center on 11 September 2001 have been subject to a bewildering array of interpretations. Postmodernists question the meaning of these attacks and how what 'happened' on that day is interpreted. How should these events be understood? This is far more complex than determining who the perpetrators of these attacks were and what their motivations were. What factors need to be taken into account to explain, understand and react to this event? It is inevitable that differing explanations and interpretations will lead to differing understandings and reactions; for postmodernists this demonstrates that nothing can ever be established as undeniable truth. The whole project of the 'war against terror' is fraught with misunderstanding and open to deliberate misrepresentations of issues and events.

---

**AUTHOR BOX**

## Jean Baudrillard

Jean Baudrillard's collection of three essays entitled *The Gulf War Did Not Take Place*, written in 1991 (and later collected into a short book in 2004), is a deliberately controversial analysis of the Gulf War, intended to highlight the use of language and the different meanings that can arise from various interpretations. The underlying point being made was that the engagement between US and Iraqi forces was so unequally in favour of the United States, and that the technology and methods available to the far superior military might of the United States meant that this conflict could not be considered and understood in the same way that previous wars have been. Moreover, the visual representation and overall reporting of the war in the Western media could be seen as something more akin to the imagery associated with computer games rather than the 'reality' of bloody warfare. As with the attack on the twin towers, Baudrillard does not deny that a conflict occurred. What he does argue is that the way in which this conflict was generally reported was so far removed from the 'reality' of events that its meaning had been lost on the majority of those listening to or watching media reports. This is a characteristic postmodern approach where the actual event is seen as almost less important than the interpretation, or very often misinterpretation, of the event.

Although not particularly regarded as postmodern authors (they are radical liberals), it is appropriate to refer to the work of Edward Herman and Noam Chomsky here. Their text *Manufacturing Consent* (1988) looks at the way in which the media, often in conjunction with government press offices, can frame certain issues to suit political agendas. Notably this may be by excluding the reporting of some issues altogether. Alternatively the use of language can be employed to create a particular tone or attitude towards the 'facts' that are subsequently presented. This is straying into the field of discourse analysis but this is a fundamental aspect of postmodern approaches. Any approach that is reliant on interpretation must acknowledge the ways in which language is used to project a particular meaning, and that this meaning has an aspect of power associated with it. In the post-9/11 world anything that has the word 'terror' associated with it has gained a deeper meaning. One only has to look at national legislation brought in by a large number of states to enhance police power in the name of counter-terrorist policies. The definition of who might be regarded as a 'terrorist' or what might constitute activities that could bring these new powers into play has been expanded significantly. Again this highlights the power relationships that are in play surrounding these issues.

Aspects of power are also dealt with in the works of IPE writer Susan Strange. Again, this is someone who would not normally be 'pigeonholed' as a particularly postmodern writer but certain aspects of her work lend themselves well to this discussion. In her seminal text *States and Markets* (1994) she describes four key structures. These are security, finance, production and knowledge. The knowledge structure includes the advantage of being more advanced in research and development in all aspects of science for military, economic or any other competitive endeavour. Importantly it can also refer to what is considered to be 'known' or true. This clearly relates to the postmodern aspect of understanding or meaning. Strange develops this point with particular reference to how power relationships are developed, enforced and maintained. In the context of IR and IPE this can be in terms of the way in which terms such as 'progress' or 'development' are understood and promoted. These may appear to be self-evident in their meaning but on closer inspection they are profoundly subjective and open to manipulation. Policies described as 'progressive' may have highly negative impacts on various individuals and communities.

Chomsky and Strange both deal with issues that are also of interest to postmodern writers but their approach is qualitatively different. Both highlight inequalities but they also suggest ways in which these inequalities might be addressed and rectified. This is in complete contrast to postmodern writers who will criticise the knowledge claims presented in various positions taken, but who do not offer alternative claims. Far from it, as their whole point is to show that *all* positions and arguments should be open to be challenged and discredited. They explicitly do not offer alternative standpoints as this would, by definition, undermine their own approach of universal scepticism. This, however, has led some critics to doubt the usefulness of postmodernism as an approach.

## Criticisms

Although there is much to be said in favour of adopting an openly sceptical approach when assessing various arguments, positions and schools of thought, there may be a problem in taking this to extremes. Critics of postmodern thought argue that if everything is open to questioning and disbelief then what hope can there be for even beginning a field of inquiry? James Rosenau (2007) has identified several aspects of postmodern thought that he argues are contradictory. First, he argues that even an anti-theoretical stance is, in essence, a theory in itself. Second, postmodernists stress the irrational, yet employ rationality and reason to further their own arguments. Third, although they stress the importance of intertextuality they often consider certain texts in isolation. Fourth, postmodernists decry inconsistencies in other approaches, yet fail to remain consistent themselves.

Finally, by rejecting the truth claims of other approaches postmodernists are making judgements, thereby undermining their claims to avoid the subjective and judgemental. What one might conclude from this is that there are 'strong' or radical postmodernist scholars who are inclined to develop the idea of critique from critical theory to the point where they are forced by their own logic to reject any certain conclusions other than a critique of others' arguments and claims to truth; and there are 'weak' or more pragmatic postmodernists who develop an axiom taken from the French philosopher Jacques Derrida that one should be sceptical about everything. But being sceptical is a relative idea – one can and should be sceptical about an idea or argument until it has been tested, and one can test ideas and arguments without always testing them to destruction. In IR theory, radical postmodernism is a minority, but quite influential movement; in IPE, with its dominating concerns about practical issues such as the failure of development in the global South, the problems of economic and energy security, the difficulties of managing a global banking and financial system, and the power of lobbies and institutions representing the powerful against the relatively powerless groups ('the 99 per cent'), radical postmodern epistemology is very much the view of a tiny minority of scholars, and weaker forms of postmodernism (which may still be radical in their values and ontology) are often combined with other positions (anarchism, feminism, green politics).

Postmodern thought plays an important role in highlighting the underlying agendas that may lie behind certain arguments and positions. This is particularly the case when looking at the terms that are used and the way in which arguments are framed and presented in such a way that what may be seen as 'common sense' prevails. For postmodernists, though, there is no 'common' sense. All knowledge is interested, that is it reflects particular interests and the particular context in which it was formed; it will always be potentially open to manipulation and even abuse. In the latter case this can be a direct contributing factor to how power relations are created and reinforced. The most important insights of the philosopher and psychologist Michel Foucault (1926–1984) develop the idea that if knowledge is power, then changes in forms and patterns of knowledge and the ways in which they are expressed, changes in 'discourse' underpin the ways in which power in society and economy work. This idea has made discourse analysis, the 'deconstruction' of practices of language and power, one of the most widely used research tools in IPE used to explain power relations, and one now used well beyond the group of postmodern researchers who originated it. This can be applied at all levels of interaction, be it between states, civil society organisations, state-managed institutions or individuals. Even this analysis can be criticised for being anthropocentric and failing to take into account other species and the wider ecosystem. In essence, postmodern thought is generally negative in tone in that its emphasis is on being critical of all claims to knowledge and truth. This does not mean that it does not have a useful role to play in the overall panoply of IR/IPE approaches. In some respects it is a healthy position to take to require falsification of statements and to require arguments to be adequately justified. Unfortunately for many postmodern writers there can be no justification as they are unwilling to accept claims that they see as inherently loaded and, therefore, suspect.

## Gramscian approaches to IPE

### Historical development

Antonio Gramsci (1891–1937) was an Italian Marxist activist and theorist, most of whose work was written in miserable conditions in prison under Mussolini. Originally a fairly orthodox Leninist, his work became increasingly imaginative and wide-ranging. This partly reflected specific conditions in Italy, which was not a highly developed capitalist economy, but that had a highly developed political culture. Gramsci recognised that divisions between north and south, the diversity of oppositional groups – anarchism was at least as strong as communism, especially in central Italy, and the strong ties that both conservative and opposition groups had outside Italy meant that orthodox Marxism had to be critiqued before it could be applied. Not translated into English, French or German until the 1950s, Gramsci's work played a key part in the development of a distinctive 'Western marxism' in the 1960s (i.e. a non-Russian, non-communist Marxist understanding of society, culture, economy and international relations). It was largely influential in the emergence of an academic field that came to be called 'cultural studies' in universities in European and North America. His ideas, not necessarily in a form he would have accepted, and also channelled through the work of Frankfurt School exile Herbert Marcuse, were influential in the formation of the 'counter culture' in the US in the 1960s and 1970s. Gramscian approaches to IPE have been an important research area in the last twenty years and continue to be a fruitful way of approaching the explanation of the field since the 2007–2010 global financial crisis. It has also been extensively used to critique globalisation and its effects, to analyse the continuing growth in the power and impact of the largest multinational companies, and to explain the growth and distinctive characteristics of the global new media and Internet.

## Central arguments and concepts

■ Power is organised around hegemonic blocs that include coalitions of dominant interests both at a national and international level; these coalitions are not always stable because of the differences that arise between the interests and understanding of different powerful actors within these blocs.

■ While these hegemonic blocs are grounded in class and economic activity and the ownership of the key lever of power, economics alone does not determine the nature of social power: culture, language and social behaviour are much more important than the orthodox Leninist view suggested and they evolve partly independent of the economy.

■ Resistance to the power of dominant groups (counter hegemony) also involves the formation of blocs that change shape and effectiveness, but that encounter many opportunities for effective resistance if well led.

■ Because of the vulnerability of the divisions within capitalist power and because of the potential of counter hegemonic groups to form together, it is easier to imagine alternatives to established power structures than the rather pessimistic long-term vision that many more traditional Marxists suggest.

■ At some points in time, the global system will appear to be relatively stable and unmoving, while at others the opportunities for change and intervention by counter-hegemonic forces are greater – drawing on popular press language of the First World War, Gramsci labels the first a period a 'war of position' and the second a 'war of movement'.

■ Intellectuals and people who cross class, gender and other social barriers can play key roles in the critique of the established power system so as to identify and then take advantage of its weaknesses.

■ People who Marx would call 'working class' acquiesce in their domination by powerful interests and organisations; in Gramsci's phrase, they 'knit their own chains'. They do not do this merely because they are saps manipulated by 'false consciousness'. The management of cultural power is more sophisticated and more deep-rooted than that suggests. As a result, dominant powers do not need to rely solely on violence. Resistance to this domination begins with the analysis of how ideas such as nationalism and patriotism are managed to effect social control. But a whole gamut of media and social forces combine to do this, including the underpinnings of advertising, soap operas and other institutions of popular culture, including much of the education system. These vary from country to country, and often within countries, and cannot be easily explained by a single overarching theory. Scholars such as Stuart Hall and Raymond Williams as well as Noam Chomsky have carried these ideas into the study of literature and the arts.

## Specific theories

Robert Cox was largely responsible for a particular form of Gramscian argument in IPE. Through his teaching and writing, he has been enormously influential on American and European scholarship as well as in his native Canada. Cox suggested in *Production, Power and World Order* (1987) that world order reflected a dominant hegemony that encompassed both state governments and economic actors such as firms and banks. But the underlying structures of hegemony were not necessarily evident to empirical observation directly. Like other social and economic structures, they could be observed and assessed indirectly, through their effects and through the power they wielded. If this idea seems obscure, the concept of 'class' is widely used in social science; although we cannot see or touch or smell class, we can identify its effects and find evidence of how and where and when it is significant. This notion of the importance of structures that we can only observe and study indirectly is widely shared across both Marxist and non-Marxist social science. The key concept in Cox's view is that of world order, which he takes both from Gramsci and from other sources. The world order is capitalist; but to say that is not to give an adequate account. For Cox, and for other Gramscians, the question is how capitalism works, how it shapes lives, how it is challenged, and above all how it changes over time. Gramscian scholars such as Cox, along with Stephen Gill and Mark Rupert recognise that capitalism is immensely powerful, as Marxists agree, but as some more orthodox Marxists do not agree, it is capable of changing its forms and methods of operation. These ideas also influenced the Regulation School (discussed below).

Cox focussed in his original study on the relationship between forms of production, the power of the state, the role of major multinational corporations and their impact in constructing and reproducing global hegemony. Hegemony is domination that does not need to use violence all the time, although it may always have the possibility of resorting to violence. But it is deeply embedded in everyday practice, and in everyday ideas, so that it is harder to question or challenge. Hegemony is not simply about one or two dominant states. It needs the state to manage legal relations and impose contracts, as well as to deploy military force. But hegemony is a dominating structure of interests, institutions, social groups (what Gramsci called hegemonic blocs) and academic, media and other organisations and ideas. Thus the US and European Union are crucial to the actual day-to-day management of global order, but global order is not reducible to one or the other or both of these state powers. Cox planned to go on to write a parallel volume to his *Production, Power and World Order*, and to explore both the historical sociology of global dominance and its key institutions. He particularly wanted to write more about the character of work and labour in contemporary hegemony. But he was unable to do so. These tasks have been taken up by others, including Stephen Gill and Bob Jessop, but also Owen Worth (on austerity and hegemony), Phoebe Moore (on labour and trades unions), and Mark Rupert (on the ways consumer societies acquire values and social practices from the systems of employee training and management of the major corporations). James Mittelman is one of a significant group of scholars from the US who have drawn on Gramscian ideas in a critique of globalisation and its impacts especially on the global South, but also across the international system. What all Gramscians writing in IPE have in common is first of all a strong critique of liberal arguments as description but also as explanation of the field, but also a critique of established orthodox Marxist writing. Gramscians appear to have rather more in common with realist writing, including their concern with power structures and the ways in which power is used, which overlaps with neo-realist theory. But this is a misleading appearance, since Gramscian authors also make compelling criticisms of many aspects of realism (including its neglect of political economy and its misunderstanding of power relations).

## A. Claire Cutler

Claire Cutler is a Canadian scholar who has worked at the University of British Columbia and then at the University of Victoria. Her specialisms are the interactions of international law and international political economy and she has written extensively (among many other things) on the emergence of new forms of private authority in IPE. In the past, while power may have been held by many actors, authority – legal as well as political – was vested in individual states. Naturally, they could grant authority to institutions by agreement, as they have done to many UN institutions such as the IMF and UN Development Programme. But apart from these public international organisations, many private institutions have acquired not just power, but authority, and this authority is in many cases recognised by states. Cutler and colleagues in the field have asked how this came about, what theoretical and practical challenges it presents, and how law and politics interact to create new challenges in the world system. Their answers suggest that while it suits the interests of major state actors to allow trade associations, industry groups, large companies and other actors to take on authoritative roles, making rules and managing key aspects of the global system, they (the major state actors) may not always be in control of how the structures evolve. In accounting regulation, the management of global mergers and acquisitions, credit rating agencies (all discussed in Chapter 7 on finance) private regulation has grown to be of great importance. In development aid, private bodies including some of the leading non-governmental organisations (NGOs) not only manage aid distribution, but also have accounting and auditing devolved to them by both the European Union and major international development agencies. Private authority may often work within the framework of state approval, as it does in managing global standards of safety of many traded goods (electrical and electronic items, for example). But the global Internet and World Wide Web are not managed by any one power, and do not belong to any one actor. They are owned and managed by a network of firms, inventors (who hold patents and copyright), state actors and state regulators; but the most powerful actors are those with knowledge and large market share (including Apple, Google and Facebook) rather than states. It is into this field of IPE that Cutler has led the exploration and explanation, using concepts and ideas drawn from a range of sources, but primarily from Gramscian IPE.

## The global political economy of austerity

Gramscian scholars such as Owen Worth and Bob Jessop have made important critiques of the ways in which policies of austerity have shaped social as well as economic (and education) policies during and after the 2007–2010 financial crises in the developed economies. They also note that the impact of the crisis has been a changing balance of who holds hegemony and how it is wielded, something best evidenced by the eclipse of the G7/G8 organisation (founded by France in 1974 and including only the largest developed economies, the US, Japan, Germany, France, Italy, Britain and Canada plus Russia), and its replacement by a broader framework, the G20. This larger group of twenty states includes China, Indonesia, India, Brazil, Mexico, Saudi Arabia and others alongside the original developed G8 members. All these major countries have found themselves responding to the outcomes of the financial crisis by imposing policies of austerity, cutting public spending, apparently reducing the role of the state in the economy, preaching doctrines of privatisation and the reduction of welfare. These policies have been imposed most rigorously in those economies most damaged by the crisis, including in Europe Ireland, Portugal, Spain and Greece. The Eurozone crisis since 2010 (when the Greek currency collapsed) was dominated by a hegemony within the European Union led by Germany. Its principles were shaped primarily by German banks and German government ideas (which themselves were shaped much more by German history in the 1920s and 1930s than by ideas of integration or cooperation in Europe). Any account of austerity must first of all take account of its international and regional contexts – austerity may be a national government policy, but in none of the countries affected by the crisis has it been a purely national issue. Second, there have been powerful anti-austerity movements, leading to new political parties in many countries, and to anti-establishment movements in pretty much all of them including the US. But these have failed to coalesce for both local and broader political and social reasons. The culture of austerity is now deeply embedded in established institutions including government bureaucracies, but also in companies, pressure groups and international institutions. Its assumptions have been very hard to shift. The core concepts of Gramscian political economy provide ways of understanding these developments, and the lack of really effective opposition to austerity despite the '99 per cent' and anti-banker demonstrations, the attacks of 'Wall Street' and the rise of many local anti-capitalist movements in countries across the developed and emerging capitalist world.

## Criticisms

Gramscian approaches to IPE have been subject to three quite distinct kinds of critique. First, more orthodox Marxists have proposed that the approach has simply abandoned key tenets of Marxism to the point that it has lost coherence and usefulness. Second, there are important debates within Gramscian writing, and especially between those who claim to carry a banner for Gramsci himself, such as Stephen Gill and Bob Jessop and those who, often under the banner of 'neo-Gramscianism' have adapted Gramsci's work in IPE, often drawing on a broader critical theory position, and sometimes also on some aspects of poststructuralism. Both Jessop, Bieler and Morton have been particularly critical of what they see as lapses into the unorthodoxy of post-modern concepts where a more rigid adherence to the coherence of Gramsci's own ideas might be stronger. This is a debate that will persist and that raises questions about methods as well as about which 'face' of Gramsci is the correct interpretation. Third, critics from a wide range of positions and political viewpoints have questioned whether the core values of Gramscian IPE, as well as its key concepts such as hegemony, global order, the nature of power and the significance of discourses of power, have a value in the study of IPE. These are issues the reader must address for themselves.

# Green thought

## Historical development

Human awareness of interaction with our physical surroundings is as old as recorded history. It has played a part in our survival as a species from the successes of the earliest hunter-gatherer communities, through settled cultivation of land and animal husbandry to more recent developments with regard to our understanding of the physical consequences of resource exploitation. That said, it is only in the last few decades that environmental concerns have been formulated into a range of theoretical approaches that put these concerns at the centre of an understanding and analysis of IR/IPE.

Rachel Carson's seminal text *Silent Spring* (1962) is widely regarded as one of the first pieces of writing to highlight the serious consequences of human impact on the natural environment. In this book she explained how the introduction of the pesticide DDT resulted in unintended consequences as this poisonous substance entered the food chain. The 'silence' in the title refers to the lack of birdsong following the spraying of this product on farmland. The initial impact had been positive, as the pesticide had indeed killed the insects that were damaging the crops. However, these insects were then easy prey for birds that ingested the harmful chemicals as they ate the insects. Subsequently this led to a softening of the shells of the eggs laid by these birds, to the point that they broke before they were fully hatched. This had a devastating impact on the following generation of birds. By making these connections Carson opened a whole field of inquiry regarding human impact on the environment.

The 1970s saw a burgeoning of interest in, and writing on, environmental issues. Governments were beginning to recognise that growing interdependence was not simply restricted to economic ties. All domestic and international interactions take place within the confines of our finite planet. The notable exception of course is extra-terrestrial activities, such as space flights. The first manned flight to leave the Earth's orbit was the Apollo 8 mission in 1968. It was from this spacecraft that the classic image of a small, blue planet was photographed. This is argued to have had a profound impact on popular and political consciousness in terms of how the world is perceived. There are no political boundaries or ideologies visible from space. Land and water masses and weather systems dominate. More recent satellite images have highlighted issues such as deforestation and advancing areas of desert. Such technological capabilities have been fundamental in demonstrating the scale of the problems faced due to environmental degradation. Green thought has evolved with different writers emphasising various aspects of the relationship between humans and the physical environment. Some 'deep' green theorists argue that it is unhelpful to think of this as a 'relationship' and that it is preferable to take a more eco-centric view, which, rather than separating humans from their environment, sees humans as being an inextricably linked part of a single environmental whole.

## Central arguments

■ Both 'light' and 'deep' green theorists agree that humans have the capacity to have a disproportionate impact on other species and their habitats.

■ The planet is viewed as a finite resource and the majority of human activities are seen as depleting the 'capital' of the Earth's resources in a non-sustainable manner.

■ Human activities cannot be separated out from the consequences they have on the natural environment; we need therefore to understand how societies and economies can adapt to become more sustainable and resilient to environmental shocks, but however we respond to environmental challenges the complacency of existing global powers has to be challenged.

## Specific theories

Green thought can be roughly divided into two main camps, those taking an environmental or anthropocentric approach and those that are eco-centric. The former sees humans as somehow separated from the natural environment, often at odds with it and trying to overcome difficulties. This approach, therefore, has some similarities with power politics, as it appears to think in terms of conflict and zero-sum games. On the other hand, eco-centric approaches are much more holistic, placing humans alongside other species as part of a complex web of interconnected habitats and biodiversity. The latter is most famously associated with James Lovelock's Gaia thesis (2000).

---

**AUTHOR BOX**

### James Lovelock

The Gaia thesis was named after a Greek goddess associated with fertility and creation. Lovelock's emphasis was on a series of connected 'feedback' systems that keep the Earth's biosphere in balance. For example, the atmospheric cycle of the conversion of carbon dioxide into oxygen via plant photosynthesis. Human activities that generate excessive amounts of carbon dioxide risk unsettling this balance. With deforestation reducing the area of what are known as carbon 'sinks' this adds to the imbalance in this particular feedback system. There are many such systems in the natural world and Lovelock highlights how they interconnect and that it is impossible, even actively dangerous, to assume that actions in one area of the biosphere will not have consequences elsewhere within what is a closed system. Unfortunately the political system of sovereign states can also be seen as a 'closed' system, albeit a socially constructed one. Regardless of the legitimacy of Lovelock's analysis, human organisation is dominated by the nation state system and the concept of sovereignty. As such it remains problematic to manage the feedback systems, which have no regard for political boundaries.

---

The concept of managing ecosystems is more closely related with anthropocentric approaches, although one may assume that Lovelock would also argue in favour of first recognising and then managing, or at least working in balance with, these feedback systems. Environmental approaches tend to focus more on finding a balance between humans being able to exploit natural resources and minimising the impact this has, both in terms of the rate at which resources are depleted and also the potential negative impacts of pollution and other factors associated with resource extraction, transport and manufacturing processes. This can either be at the level of national government or, increasingly, via international bodies such as the Intergovernmental Panel on Climate Change (IPCC). Here green thought intersects with other theories, such as neo-liberal institutionalism, which deals with the conflicts and cooperative actions of governments in institutional settings. As environmental issues have come to the fore in both domestic and international political agendas this has been reflected in how what might be thought of as 'non-green' theories have dealt with these issues.

## Resource scarcity and competition

Thomas Homer-Dixon (1994) has written about environmental issues, but in a manner that classical realists could easily comprehend and relate to. His emphasis is on the reduction in resources and, therefore, increased competition for access to dwindling supplies. Although this is a form of green thought, as it places natural resources at the centre of the analysis, the way in which this is done highlights traditional power politics concerns of competition and potential conflict. Access to oil and gas reserves has long been a contributing factor to a number of the world's protracted conflicts. A similar analysis can be made of access to water supplies, although there is also an argument that, because the parties involved all need access to water, then this could be seen as the issue that might bring them together in a more cooperative conflict resolution-based scenario. For example, riparianism in the Jordan River system has led to intense competition between rival states (in particular Israel and Syria). During the 1967 Six Day War a strategic objective of the Israelis was the capture of the head waters of the Jordan River in the Golan Heights and complete control of Lake Tiberias. Almost by definition, environmental issues are so all-encompassing that they lend themselves to all manner of interpretations by the various stakeholders involved, including a growing number of politically active non-state actors.

The range of actors involved in environmental issues is in line with liberal pluralist approaches, which highlight the diversity of international actors. Green thought is divided over the extent to which multi-stakeholder negotiations are beneficial. Some environmental pressure groups are in favour of sharing platforms with governments and multinational corporations in order to find common ground and possible solutions to environmental degradation. Others take a much harder line and prefer to stay at some distance from the actors they are critical of, fearing engagement may lead to co-option and the hijacking of the debate in favour of corporate interests. The whole issue of corporate social responsibility in particular has been labelled as 'greenwash' by certain groups, who highlight that while some MNCs may promote what green credentials they have, these usually represent only a small fraction of their overall business, which continues to cause enormous environmental damage.

## Criticisms

As demonstrated above, green thought is a very diverse array of approaches and, therefore, the criticisms of the various schools of thought differ accordingly. One of the most high-profile debates on environmental issues is the credibility of the science behind the claims and counter-claims involved in the prediction of trends. This has been a particularly bitter dispute with regard to climate change and alleged global warming. For example, if you were to view Davis Guggenheim's Oscar-winning documentary film *An Inconvenient Truth* (2006), featuring Al Gore, followed by the television programme *The Great Global Warming Swindle* (2007) you would hear two wildly differing arguments on this issue. Both sides accuse the other of presenting dubious scientific analyses in misleading ways. There is even an accusation that predictions of climate change have been exaggerated to support the vested interests of a 'climate change industry' made up of scientists, journalists and academics who have self-serving agendas associated with presenting climate change as more of a problem than it actually is.

The producer and director of *The Great Global Warming Swindle*, Martin Durkin, has also made documentaries arguing in favour of genetically modified crops and a particularly notorious programme entitled *Against Nature* (1997), which suggested that some environmental activists were actually holding back development strategies. One of the examples used was the opposition to a large hydroelectric dam project being built in India. Durkin suggests that without this dam thousands of poor Indian villages will be denied access to electricity. This, in turn, means they will be reliant on the burning of cow dung for their heating and cooking, which causes ill health and shortened lifespan due to inhalation of toxic fumes. While there is some truth in his claims about respiratory illnesses, the manner in which the overall criticism of the environmental groups referred to, including Friends of the Earth, was questionable. Numerous complaints about this programme were made to the Independent Television Commission, some of which were upheld. Environmental issues are clearly emotive and there is a lively debate among green theorists and activists themselves, as well as criticisms of the environmental movement as a whole.

*Against Nature* also featured an academic who questioned the validity of the argument for maintaining the Earth's current range of biodiversity. One might imagine that the 'default' position would be that the extinction of a species should be avoided, hence the protection afforded to endangered species. However, the position taken here is that species come and go and that the world is no worse off for no longer having either the dodo or any number of dinosaurs still roaming the Earth. This appears to fly in the face of the logic of the Convention on Biological Diversity adopted at the Rio Earth Summit. That said, it is an interesting position to take and one that goes to the heart of humanity's position as part of, or in relation to, the natural world. The academic who took this position, Professor Becker, appears to be saying that individual species do not necessarily have a value in and of themselves. Rather, they should be seen in terms of how they add to, or perhaps detract from, human experience and well-being. They are simply to be seen as a resource to be exploited or as something that plays a part in ensuring we have a healthy bio-environment.

## The new institutional economics: networks of power, networks of exchange

Classical political economy was always as concerned with institutional behaviour as it was with quantifiable market interactions. Adam Ferguson (1723–1816) emphasised how important social networks and the civility and mutual trust of a civil society were for economic growth (and for civilisation generally). Alfred Marshall (1842–1924) put a particular emphasis on the institutional nature of market behaviour alongside many other insights into economic behaviour. But in the mid-twentieth century, many of the insights of this kind of work were lost in a farrago of mathematical economics, which came to dominate much of the discipline, and especially microeconomics. For this reason, the rediscovery of the field is often called the 'new institutional economics' although it is actually as old as political economy itself. Scholars have explored how institutional behaviours including collaboration between supposedly competing firms have shaped outcomes. This approach has burgeoned rapidly in the last two decades.

Oliver Williamson focused on explaining how firms managed their transaction costs. Transaction costs are the costs of doing business, including managing supply chains, managing communications, and of management decision-making. Williamson argued that while the management of transaction costs is rational and may be measurable, it is generally neglected in conventional microeconomics. Firms decide whether to manage a particular function – personnel management, distribution, out-sourcing of component manufacture – internally or whether to contract them to outside businesses depending on calculations of how transaction costs can be minimised. Williamson observed that as firm structures and market behaviour became increasingly complex, these decisions assumed ever-greater importance: the firm that managed transaction costs better had a clear competitive edge. These ideas also matter when governments are making decisions of whether to do or outsource particular functions, which in turn has important implications for the privatisation of roles that the state has taken on. It also has implications in international trade: as tariff barriers to trade have fallen under successive agreements, transaction costs have assumed an increasing importance in shaping patterns of world trade as an important element in non-tariff barriers, which free trade agreements have sought to reduce. Williamson's theory has also been used to explain patterns of intra-firm trade (meaning trade within a multinational firm but across national borders), which accounts for roughly a fifth of all world trade in goods and services.

Williamson's fellow Nobel prize winner (still the only woman to have won the Nobel Economics Prize) Elinor Ostrom worked in a comparable field, but looked more specifically at economic governance. She argued that economic relationships were more social than a basic microeconomic model suggested. They involved a certain level of trust, without which economic exchange became difficult if not impossible. They also engaged reciprocal relationships between individuals and social groups. These two ideas of trust and reciprocity made economic management more reliable and so significantly reduced transaction costs. Ostrom is largely responsible for the much greater emphasis on trust, which characterises discussion of finance as well as technological and research collaboration between firms and countries. It also has powerful policy implications. Much of her work focussed on the value of effective governance in developing societies as well as in less developed regions of developed countries such as the US. She was also passionately committed to amplify the implications of her work for environmental policy, where neo-classical economics tended to distort the real costs of environmental damage on both communities and on future economic activities. Williamson and Ostrom worked in different but complementary fields of microeconomics; their influence remains one of the most powerful critical presences in economics and political economy including IPE.

As international economic organisation has become more complex, as trade organisations and lobby groups have become more powerful, and as the distinction between what governments do and what private actors do diminishes, network theory has sought to explain how power lies often in networks rather than in the hands of their individual participants. Mark Granovetter is one of a large group of scholars who have examined how networks manage the exchange of information as well as values and ideas of how to compete more effectively. Joint research networks have become important agents in high technology industry—especially networks between universities, but also between firms and research institutes. Granovetter has described the impact of networks that at first sight are apparently not so powerful in the phrase 'the strength of weak ties' (otherwise 'the strength of weak linkages') in a paper published in 1973 that, although initially rejected for publication, has since become among the most widely cited articles in all social sciences. Granovetter, a sociologist by training, has become one of the most widely used sources of network theory in economics and hugely influential in business studies and strategic management. These ideas have been developed by many other researchers, especially in relation to public sector management in the UK and in Scandinavia, and in the study of global supply chains, as well as in the management of family businesses. As noted above, key to this approach are the ways in which information is handled and transformed within networks, and the ways in which information acquires specific meanings for network players. This goes beyond pricing information in markets, which neo-classical economics also holds to be important.

Network theory suggests that networks themselves hold power and are capable of causing change. This is a kind of systemic or structural argument. It implies that networks are not only important because of the activity or ideas of individual actors within them. Networks themselves have the capacity to act, a view that makes sense to many observers, but that causes some to raise philosophical objections turning on the view that only human beings rather than abstract structures can truly be said to have agency in IPE.

## Criticisms

The idea of institutional structures and relations as significant in political economy is neither new nor very contentious. But critics do ask how one can operationalise the idea of institutions as agents of change, and question whether the core approach of the 'new institutional economics' is rigorous enough to compare with other forms of knowledge in political economy. There are two replies to this criticism. One was adopted by Williamson and Ostrom to show with great care how their methodology could lead to testable and reproducible results. For this reason, a major part of both their work is concerned with questions of methods and cumulative knowledge creation. The other response to the criticism is to show how different forms of knowledge add to the body of work in IPE, especially if the scientific credentials of mainstream social science are held to be bogus: IPE cannot copy the natural sciences and has something different to offer. The idea that institutional structures or networks could operate independent of state power has been challenged both from the right and from the left. They do not operate wholly independent of state power, it might be agreed; but they do exercise a relative autonomy from other structures, which justifies a focus on both institutions and networks. Transaction cost analysis is valuable because it adds something to IPE that one could not access in any other way. What network theories also claim to do effectively is to link micro-studies of social and political relations within economies to larger scale macro processes and outcomes, and very few critics have denied this.

Network theory is perhaps more heavily criticised for what critics see as the vagueness of the concept of 'network'. They also ask whether a network can in itself be an actor separate from those who make it up. This is ultimately a philosophical question rather than a matter of empirical fact; there are strong defences of this position and equally strong ways to attack it. But the ontological argument that networks do not really exist as separate actors from their elements, which was proposed by some (empiricist) critics of network theory when it first emerged in the 1970s has largely disappeared: it is more common for a wide variety of scholars from many different positions to speak of the rise of network society and of the importance of networks, on the new media, online and in more long-established social contexts. The essential element here is the bringing of the social and the political into the arena of microeconomics, which is widely but not universally welcomed.

## Regulation theory and IPE

### Core arguments

While there are a number of different descriptions of economic regulation, many of which are important, and most of which are either liberal or neo-liberal, regulation theory as an explanation of IPE represents a specific school represented by (among others) Bob Jessop in the UK, Michel Aglietta and Robert Boyer in France, as well as the environmental activist and political theorist Alain Lepietz. The theory also has supporters in North America and elsewhere in Europe. Regulation theory (sometimes called the 'regulation school') argues that at a local, national and global level, economic activity forms distinctive systems or 'regimes of accumulation'. These structures are shaped by patterns of ownership and control, by social relationships and distinctive cultural patterns in each country (or region) but also operate at a global level. The key question for regulation theory is, how is an economic system regulated, by whom and with what powers, and how does this regulation form patterns that shape labour relations, investment, management, the incentives to entrepreneurs, as well as the core activities of production, trade and exchange? These ideas derive in part from Marshall's work on industrial districts as well as on Schumpeter's understanding of the relationship between technology, democracy and the working of market economies, especially as refined by Karl Polyani (in *The Great Transformation*, 1958). It owes something to a reading of the Marxian and critical theory tradition; it owes a lot to the experience of political and environmental activists who have helped to shape its theorisation. Regulation theorists agree that markets are social institutions as much as economic ones, but they also identify key features of the economy that shape society, in which sense it is a body of ideas that is at once political and economic.

**CONCEPT BOX**

## Key concepts of regulation theory

Regulation theory introduces or develops four key concepts, which lead it beyond critical theory in IPE to form a distinctive approach. Much of the development of these ideas has been by French and German scholars, although it has distinguished adherents in many countries. These four key concepts are:

*Regime of accumulation*: Different systems have enabled capitalism to survive and evolve despite very great changes in its forms of control, technologies and political contexts. In the early twentieth century, the most influential regime of accumulation was introduced in the car industry with the growth of partly automated, integrated production lines (integrated in the sense that raw materials and components went into the factory and completed vehicles were driven out). Following its originators, this regime was called Fordism. It was progressively carried into most industries, including steel, textiles and clothing, pharmaceuticals and the making of electronic goods. In the 1970s and onwards, deindustrialisation saw the decline of Fordist patterns of production and the growth of the international division of labour. It also saw the rise of new production systems, very often originating in Japanese factories. These introduced new levels of automation and computer controlled systems. It was also characterised by new patterns of work including team working, the end of long rigid production lines, and new technologies of the control of labour and work, including especially IT-managed systems. Although these originated in manufacturing (especially textiles and clothing), they quickly spread to other manufacturing sectors, but also to services of all kinds. These post-Fordist (sometimes 'postFordist') patterns of management reach into social organisation, business practice and international labour and trade, not least through the enlarged development of the international or global division of labour in manufacturing and in global labour markets. Although some writers have chosen to say that by the 2010s the world economy was increasingly 'post post-Fordist', this term does not add much to our understanding: although post-Fordist production has not stood still, the key transformation is still understood to be that from Fordism to something else.

*System of regulation*: the 'mode of regulation' (Boyer) or system of regulation is the body of laws, rules, conventions and unspoken assumptions, which together regulate the regime of accumulation. The system of regulation changes over time, and may evolve quite rapidly in response to changes in power patterns or technology. Regulation theory carries a sense that existing forms of capitalist society and economy are not especially stable, and capitalism needs to keep re-inventing itself in order to continue to survive, which it is able to do through these adjustments. The system of regulation may include a higher or lower level of state regulation as opposed to private or non-state regulation, and the shift to post-Fordism has typically been characterised by growing privatisation of state functions in the economy and in economic law.

*Flexible specialisation*: flexible specialisation (the concept originally comes from Adam Smith) reflects changes in working practice away from large-scale factory systems with production line manufacture. These are replaced by smaller team-working groups with multiple skills, which are quicker to adapt to changes in market conditions. Smaller team-working based firms and institutions are often said by their advocates to demonstrate the qualities of competitive furry mammals in the face of large but slower and more unmanageable dinosaur organisations. Flexible workgroups (a) absorb and manage information more rapidly; (b) have lower transaction costs (term explained in the section above on networking); (c) organise skills and know-how more effectively; and (d) are capable of shifting production styles and designs much more quickly as markets and fashions change. In an old industrial economy such as car or clothing manufacture, these newer techniques and qualities still matter; but they matter very much more critically in an advanced economy where knowledge-based industries, new media marketing and rapidly changing research and development create much more dynamic competition. Examples include advertising and mobile phone construction, but also university management, which has changed radically along these lines since the 1970s. The best examples may be the working of rolling news services for business such as Bloomberg and CNBC.

*Globalisation*: regulation theory assumes that a global economy is already here, that it presents uniquely complex environment for firms and for governments, and that regulation takes place at a series of levels including the global and regional, which set the terms for regimes of accumulation and in effect set the rules for who has authority, how profits are to be measured and audited, and how rules in investment (which means here also how rules on cross-border takeovers and acquisitions are regulated) are managed. Many regulation theorists have also paid particular attention to the impact of global economic activity on the environment, and on ways in which a critique of the systems of regulation, trade and accumulation opens up the possibilities of alternative forms of environmental activism and environmental policy. This has been especially important in France and Germany, where politicians in Green Parties with a good deal of influence have shaped policy on energy and agriculture as well as conservation. Similar movements have been less powerful at a federal level in the US, but even so they have had a significant influence in debates at a local level in some states (Oregon, California) and in many of the major city governments.

## Criticisms

Regulation theory can be criticised – especially by Anglo-Saxons – for its relatively nonchalant origins in French and German economic debates. Does it have real substance that can be tested in detail? But its proponents are likely to reply that, as noted earlier, it has its origins as much in practice and activism as in economic theories of any kind. It has also produced a significant volume of detailed research. It can also be criticised for its apparent liberal idealism, for its core values are much more derived from liberal optimism than from anything in Marx (orthodox Marxists reject it out of hand for this and other reasons). More sympathetic critics might note that although interesting, it is not clear how much it adds to other existing accounts, including Gramscian and network theories of economic behaviour. Discipline-based critics observe that while it purports to be an overall economic and social theory, it has very little to say about key questions regarding the behaviour of either firms or individuals; it is, they suggest, much more a macroeconomic account of its subject than a usable microeconomic theory.

## Summary

In considering the above alternative approaches they cover a range of concepts and interpretations of IR and IPE. They each emerged as a response to either an existing set of theories or particular issues and events. Constructivism, postmodernism and Critical Theory are all concerned with the presentation and perception of socially constructed phenomena. As such they emphasise the inherently subjective nature of knowledge and so-called truth claims. Feminism is also concerned with socially created institutions and structurally determined relationships. However, feminism has more of a normative dimension in that this approach not only highlights deficiencies and inequalities in existing structures, it also provides an alternative scenario and prescriptions for change. Finally, green thought is perhaps the most varied of the approaches considered here, particularly with regard to the position of individuals. The lighter green environmentalists share the anthropocentric view adopted by the other approaches discussed above. Deep green eco-centric approaches reject subjectivity as they are more concerned with physical/natural processes. This chapter concludes the section of this book, which considers the wide range of theories applied to the study of IR/IPE. We now move on to look at a series of issues that are central to processes of globalisation.

## Reflective questions

### Critical Theory

1   In what ways is knowledge a social and political phenomenon?
2   What are the Marxist roots of Critical Theory and how have they informed arguments for change in social relations?
3   What structures are inherent in the capitalist world system that seem to perpetuate inequalities between people?
4   What forms of action do Critical Theorists advocate in order to achieve change in the world system?

### Constructivism

1   To what extent does constructivism remain engaged in the inter-paradigm debate within IPE?
2   What is the role of subjective perceptions and interpretations on actor behaviour?
3   Is anarchy what states make of it?
4   What are some of the risks associated with considering the subjectivity of individuals in IPE analysis?

**Table 2.1** Chapter summary

| Approach | Key process in IPE | Idea of the state | Institutions | Key notion of power | Structure vs agency? |
|---|---|---|---|---|---|
| Critical theory | Critical reflection on knowledge production by actors and by the researcher; culture and language matter as well as material economic and military factors | States are reflections of dominant interests, but not directly determined by economic structures alone. States are powerful chameleons having the potential to change and evolve to maintain power | Like states; but institutions are also arenas of conflict and contention | Hegemonic discourse; power practices in social relations. But power is also physical, military and economic and often coercive | Tend (with exceptions) to structural explanations, but structures include culture and language and social practice as well as class, economy, finance, etc. |
| Constructivism | Actors mutually construct social and political relations; this is a power-based process but also reflects perceptions of interests and contexts | For Wendt and supporters, states are the key actors; for others (e.g. Onuf, Ruggie) social process is more diverse and a much wider range of actors matter along with states | Institutions are complex arenas within which construction of global politics takes place, but they also have a role of their own; most constructivists see institutions as very important | Power is complex, elusive and central to constructivism (Guzzini); power varies depending on the agendas at hand and is not a constant | Constructivists claim to have managed the structure-agency problem more effectively than anyone else, establishing how the two interact, rather than explanations that favour one or the other |
| Feminism | Social relations that are always also political; 'the personal is political'; knowledge creation and norms that exclude or diminish women and marginalised people | State is an expression of patriarchy, but so are other social institutions and economic actors | Institutions are complex and diverse; they are capable of change, which critique aims to create. Women have a marginalised position in institutions, which needs to be critiqued and re-valued | Power articulated in many forms, but underlying them is a patriarchy, a ubiquitous structure of domination | Different feminisms recognise the question but treat it differently |

| | | | | | |
|---|---|---|---|---|---|
| Postmodernism | Interlocking power structures and discourses of dominant actors and powers. Some postmodernists are pessimistic about the possibility of change and focus only on critique; some are more optimistic about change or resistance | The state forms a complex structure that can/should be deconstructed in its operation and underlying discourses and effects | Institutions like the state need to be deconstructed and revalued. Institutions make claims that are not to be trusted; but some institutions, e.g. civil society bodies may be sites of resistance | Power is diffused through discourse and knowledge as well as material forms of power. Imbalances of power are reflected in inequalities in social and economic outcomes | Postmodernists vary on how far they are more structure oriented or more agency and subjectivity oriented. Key structures include discourse not just balance of power or financial/economic structures |
| Gramscian theory | Hegemony; domination; discourses of power; resistance | Broadly Marxist idea of state but more sophisticated in its working and its ideological and social power | Institutions the site of important conflicts and interactions and may be the site of effective resistance, but liberal idea of institutions seen as being overly idealistic | Power is economic and cultural and (for some) discursive | Although originally structuralist (Marxist), Gramscians have understood the S/A question in more nuanced terms similar to constructivism |
| New institutional economics networking | Markets and states manage key economic and business relations; these are best understood through analysis of networks and social exchanges by various means. The world economy includes intense networks of relationships we need to analyse to understand IPE | Provides framework for networking and exchange | Networks and exchange or supply chains provide key institutions alongside other recognised institutional frameworks | Power is both diffused and centralised in the political economy; forming and better managing networks enables the effective use of power | Does not engage directly with the S/A question. Implies important role for institutions as embedded structures |
| Regulation theory | Accumulation; domination; exclusion of those outside key power structures; resistance | The state is an important but not unique actor in the system of regulation, accumulation and domination | Similar to view of the state: diverse institutions function within a system – analysis focuses on critique of that system and it impacts on institutions and firms | Power articulated through frameworks of accumulation and their regulatory structures, which reach from macro level into detailed micro level | Regulation theory sees an interaction between structure and agency in everyday practice but tends towards a more structural account in the long run |

**Table 2.1** Continued

| Approach | Key process in IPE | Idea of the state | Institutions | Key notion of power | Structure vs agency? |
|---|---|---|---|---|---|
| Green thought | Human interaction with the natural environment, although important to note that 'deeper' Green theorists do not make such a clear distinction between humans and environment. The rate at which resources are used is also a key process | States and their governments are social constructs, which usually pursue short-term national interests at the expense of longer-term sustainability of resources. That said, most Green thinkers also recognise the importance of states to manage sustainability through international fora such as the Earth Summit process | Public and private institutions are seen as significant actors in relation to environmental issues. The United Nations' Environment Programme is one example of this. The private sector is often represented in negative terms with many MNCs being accused of promoting non-sustainable practices and generally promoting a culture of mass consumerism | From a Green perspective the most powerful forces are related to the natural environment, such as extreme weather events – increasingly caused as a result of human activity. More positively some Greens, including various Green Parties and environmental NGOs, refer to 'people power' and the importance of people recognising and reducing the environmental impact of their lifestyle options and choices | From Green perspectives several types of structures are relevant. The global ecosystem is the ultimate structure from a Gaian viewpoint. Politically the role of states and their generally inward-looking self-interest is seen as an impediment to sustaining the 'global commons' of the natural environment. Similarly the neo-liberal economic system that rarely puts sustainability over short-term profit is also criticised. In terms of agency in the age of the Anthropocene, where the natural environment is being shaped and usually degraded as a result of human activity then it is individuals that are seen as having the greatest level of agency – either negatively or (potentially) positively |

## Feminism

1   What do feminists claim have been the primary negative characteristics of the relationship between men and women in most societies throughout history?
2   Feminism has become a widely advocated and used approach to study in IPE. In what ways is it a useful approach to understanding international political economy?
3   In a feminist critique, what are the major causes of forms of inequality and exploitation in the contemporary world?
4   Is there a problem with focusing on the agency and experiences of individuals at the expense of other types of actors such as the state or MNCs?

## Postmodernism

1   What 'agendas' can you identify in relation to various approaches' truth claims?
2   How useful is postmodern thought if it refuses to allow a foundational basis from which to explore ideas and concepts?
3   What types of language might be used to frame an argument in such a way that postmodernist writers would critique such terms?

## Green thought

1   To what extent do you agree that non-human species and environmental habitats should be seen wholly in terms of their direct benefit to humans?
2   Does Lovelock's Gaia hypothesis make 'sense' in a world of sovereign states?
3   What do you consider to be the major contemporary environmental concerns and how might they be addressed?
4   What role do states, MNCs and civil society actors play in the environmental issues you have identified?

# | Suggestions for further reading

## Critical Theory

Adorno, T. and Horkheimer, M. (1997) [1944] *Dialectic of Enlightenment*, London: Verso Books.
Cox, R. (1987) *Production, Power and World Order: Forces in the Making of History*, New York: Columbia University Press.
Falk, R. (1995) *On Humane Governance: Toward a New Global Politics*, Cambridge: Polity Press.
Frank, A. (1967) *Capitalism and Underdevelopment in Latin America: Historical Studies of Chile and Brazil*, New York: Monthly Review Press.
Galtung, J. (1984) *There Are Alternatives! Four Roads to Peace and Security*, Nottingham: Spokesman Books.
Gramsci, A. (1998) *Selections from Prison Notebooks*, London: Lawrence & Wishart.
Habermas, J. (1972) *Knowledge and Human Interest*, London: Heinemann.
Horkheimer, M. (1982) *Critical Theory: Selected Essays*, New York: Continuum.
Linklater, A. (1990) *Beyond Realism and Marxism: Critical Theory and International Relations*, London: Macmillan.
Murphy, C. and Tooze, R. (eds) (1991) *The New International Political Economy*, Boulder, CO: Lynne Rienner.
Roach, S.C. (ed.) (2007) *Critical Theory and International Relations: A Reader*, London: Routledge.

## Constructivism

Ashley, R.K. (1988) 'Untying the sovereign state: a double reading of the anarchy problematique', *Millennium: Journal of International Studies*, 17(2) (Summer): 227–262.

Fierke, K.M. and Jorgensen, K.E. (2001) *Constructivism in International Relations: The Next Generation*, London: Routledge.

Onuf, N. (1997) 'A constructivist manifesto', in Burch, K. and Denemark, R. (eds) *Constituting Political Economy*, New York: Lynne Rienner, pp. 7–20.

Ruggie, J. (1998) *Constructing the World Polity: Essays on International Institutionalisation*, London: Routledge.

Wendt, A. (1999) *Social Theory of International Politics*, Cambridge: Cambridge University Press.

Zehfuss, M. (2002) *Constructivism in International Relations: The Politics of Reality*, Cambridge: Cambridge University Press.

## Feminism

Anzaldua, G. (2010) *The Gloria Anzaldua Reader* (ed. A. Keating), Raleigh, NC: Duke University Press.

Ebadi, S. (2003) *Democracy, Human Rights and Islam in Modern Iran: Psychological, Social and Cultural Perspectives*, Bergen: Fagbokforlaget.

Enloe, C. (1989) *Beaches, Bananas and Bases: Making Feminist Sense of International Politics*, London: Pandora.

Friedan, B. (1982) *The Feminine Mystique*, new edn, London: Penguin Books.

Pettman, J.J. (1996) *Worlding Women: A Feminist International Politics*, London: Routledge.

Staeheli, L., Kofman, E. and Peake, L. (eds) (2004) *Mapping Women, Making Politics: Feminist Perspectives on Political Geography*, London: Routledge.

Steans, J. (2013), *Gender and International Relations*, 3rd edn, Cambridge: Polity Press.

Whitworth, S. (1996) *Feminism in International Relations: Towards a Political Economy of Gender in Interstate and Non-governmental Institutions*, London: Palgrave.

Wollstonecraft, M. (1996) *A Vindication of the Rights of Women*, new edn, New York: Dover.

Zalewski, M. (2009) *Feminism and the Transformation of International Relations*, London: Routledge.

## Postmodernism

Ashley, R. (1996) 'The achievements of post-structuralism', in Smith, S., Booth, K., and Zalewski, M. (eds) *International Theory: Positivism and Beyond*, Cambridge: Cambridge University Press, pp. 227–262.

Bacon, F. (2015) [1597] *The Meditationes Sacrae*, London: The Perfect Library.

Baudrillard, J. (2004) *The Gulf War Didn't Take Place*, Sydney: Power Institute of Fine Arts.

De Goede, M. (2006) *International Political Economy and Poststructural Politics*, London: AIAA Publishing.

Der Derian, J. and Shapiro, M. (eds) (1989) *International/Intertextual Relations: Postmodern Readings of World Politics*, Lanham, MD: Lexington Books.

Derrida, J. (1997) *Politics of Friendship* (trans. G. Collins), London & New York: Verso.

Edkins, J. (ed.) (1999) *Poststructuralism in International Relations: Bringing the Political Back In*, Boulder, CO: Lynne Rienner.

Edkins, J. and Kear, A. (eds) (2013) *International Politics and Performance: Critical Aesthetics and Creative Practice*, London: Routledge.

Foucault, M. (2002) *Archaeology of Knowledge* (trans. A.M. Sheridan Smith), London: Routledge.

Heidegger, M. (1991) *The Principle of Reason* (trans. R. Lilly), Bloomington, IN: Indiana University Press.

Herman, E. and Chomsky, N. (1988) *Manufacturing Consent: The Political Economy of the Mass Media*, New York: Pantheon Books.

Kiersey, N. and Stokes, D. (eds) (2011) *Foucault and International Relations: New Critical Engagements*, London: Routledge.

Rosenau, J. (2007) *Distant Proximities: Dynamics Beyond Globalization*, Princeton, NJ: Princeton University Press.
Strange, S. (1994) *States and Markets*, 2nd edn, London: Bloomsbury Academic.
Walker, R. (1993) *Inside Outside: International Relations as Political Theory*, Cambridge: Cambridge University Press.

## Gramscian approaches to IPE

Ayers, A.J. (ed.) (2008) *Gramsci, Political Economy and International Relations Theory*, Basingstoke: Palgrave Macmillan.
Bieler, A. and Morton, A.D. (eds) (2006) *Images of Gramsci; Connections and Contentions in Political Theory and International Relations*, London: Routledge.
Cox, R. (1987) *Production, Power and World Order*, New York: Columbia University Press.
Cutler, A. C. (2003) *Private Power and Global Authority: Transnational Merchant Law in the Global Political Economy*, Cambridge: Cambridge University Press.
Gill, S. (2008) *Power and Resistance in the New World Order*, 2nd edn, Basingstoke: Palgrave Macmillan.
Gill, S. and Cutler, A.C. (eds) (2014) *New Constitutionalism and World Order*, Cambridge: Cambridge University Press.
Gramsci, A. (1998) *Selections from the Prison Notebooks*, London: Lawrence & Wishart.
Worth, O. (2013) *Resistance and the Age of Austerity*, London: Zed Books.
Worth, O. (2015) *Rethinking Hegemony*, Basingstoke: Palgrave Macmillan.

## New institutional economics and networking theories

Granovetter, M. and Swedberg, R. (eds) (2011) *The Sociology of Economic Life*, 3rd edn, Boulder, CO: Westview.
Menard, C. and Shirley, M.M. (eds) (2008) *Handbook of New Institutional Economics*, Berlin/London: Springer.
Ostrom, E. (2005), *Understanding Institutional Diversity*, Princeton, NJ: Princeton University Press.
Wienges, S. (2009) *Governance in Global Policy Networks*, Frankfurt: Peter Lang.
Williamson, O.E. (1983) *Markets and Hierarchies: Analysis and Anti-Trust Implications*, revised 2nd edn, New York: Macmillan.
Williamson, O.E. (1985) *The Economic Institutions of Capitalism*, New York: The Free Press.

## Regulation theory

Adkins, L. and Dever, M. (eds) *The Post-Fordist Sexual Contract: Living and Working in Contingency*, London: AIAA.
Aglietta, M. (2015) *A Theory of Capitalist Regulation*, revised edn, London: Verso.
Amin, A. (ed.) (2011) *Post-Fordism: A Reader*, Kindle edn, Oxford: Wiley/Blackwell.
Boyer, R. (ed.) (2001) *Regulation Theory: The State of the Art*, London: Routledge.
Labrousse, A. and Weisz, J-D. (eds) (2000) *Institutional Economics in France and Germany: German Ordoliberalism versus the French Regulation School*, Berlin/London: Springer.
Ostrom, E. (2012), *The Future of the Commons: Beyond Market Failure and Government Regulation*, London: London Publishing Partnership.
Polanyi, K. (2002) [1985] *The Great Transformation: The Political and Economic Origins of Our Time*, Boston, MA: Beacon.
Stiglitz, J. (2015) *Globalization and Its Discontents*, Harmondsworth: Penguin.
Sum, N-L., and Jessop, B. (2015) *Towards a Cultural Political Economy: Putting Culture in its Place in Political Economy*, London: Edward Elgar.

# Green thought

Bookchin, M. (1997) *The Politics of Social Ecology: Libertarian Municipalism*, Montreal: Black Rose Books.

Carson, R. (1962) *Silent Spring*, London: Penguin Books.

Conca, K. and Dabelko, G.D. (1998) *Green Planet Blues: Environmental Politics from Stockholm to Kyoto*, Oxford: Westview.

Dodds, F. and Pippard, T. (2005) *Human Security and Environmental Change: An Agenda for Change*, London: Earthscan.

Durkin, M. (2007) *The Great Global Warming Swindle*, Orpington, UK: Pinnacle Vision.

Eckersley, R. (1992) *Environmentalism and Political Theory: Towards an Eco-centric Approach*, London: UCL Press.

Guggenheim, D. (2006) *An Inconvenient Truth*, Los Angeles, CA: Paramount Classics and Participant Productions.

Homer-Dixon, T. (1994) 'Environmental scarcities and violent conflict: evidence from cases', *International Security*, 19(1) (Summer): 5–40.

Lovelock, J. (2000) *Gaia: A New Look at Life on Earth*, 3rd edn, Oxford: Oxford University Press.

Paterson, M. (2006) *Consumption and Everyday Life*, London: Routledge.

Vogler, J. and Imber, M.F. (eds) (1996) *The Environment and International Relations*, London: Routledge.

# 3 Business and marketing theories and global business behaviours

## Chapter learning outcomes

After reading and thinking about this chapter, the reader should be able to:

- Identify the main ways in which theories of international business and international economics shape the activities of large and smaller global corporations.
- Understand the key vocabulary of international business relevant to IPE, including (for example) firm strategy, product life cycle, monopoly competition, barriers to entry in a market and rent-seeking and lobbying behaviours.
- Identify and understand some of the main theories of contemporary business behaviour.
- Explain how the complexity of multinational enterprise behaviour and strategies contributes to the complexity of the IPE.
- Give specific examples of important kinds of that behaviour.
- Have a basic understanding of business case study methods, in order to begin to identify key factors in other cases.
- Recognise and explain how management decisions react to and in turn shape the cultures, working practices, diffusion of innovation and global management practices that constitute key elements of the IPE.

## Introduction

In this chapter, we ask how the global political economy evolves through the ideas, strategies and behaviours of major firms. The conventional 'international relations' literature tends often to ignore the fact that it is not governments, institutions or regulators who make the wheels of global political economy turn, but company and investor activity. The critical literature considered in the last chapter may more carefully consider what companies do. But these critical scholars, however important their work may be, do not always have a very clear idea why and how large corporations actually work. In this chapter, we examine the major theories of business strategy, many derived from economics or sociology, which shape international business behaviour. We then turn to the role those theories have in decision-making in companies, including the pervasive and often rather selective influence of business school teachings. We ask how power is created and used in business activity, power that shapes the global political economy in every aspect. We then turn to specific examples. The reader will quickly realise that there are enormous varieties of business strategy and business theory. We aim to look at some of the most important. The analysis in this chapter grows out of, and contrasts with, the previous two. Specific issues that arise from it are developed in the later chapters in this text, but especially in Chapters 6 and 10 on trade and on technology, as well as the discussions of globalisation and its significance.

'Business studies' is an eclectic field that only exists through drawing on other disciplines. A student working for a major business qualification (such as an MBA) will almost certainly study the key elements through the subjects that business studies draws on. So they study some economics, some organisational theory, which derives in turn from politics and sociology, as well as accounting, finance and business law. They will also explore the business environment, including the global contexts in which business decisions are made and that leads them into questions of culture and how to shape a negotiation or plan for effective operations in different countries and regions with their own traditions. Only after all that will the student integrate these different fields of study into an attempt to understand the 'whole picture'. The main vehicle for this will be the study of business strategy – for the purpose of IPE students, that means multinational business strategy – often through the use of case studies. Academic writers have emphasised the importance of business strategy as a set of choices made by managers and investors – the emphasis is on managing what the Boston Consulting Group christened 'strengths, weaknesses, opportunities and threats' in a fluid and changing setting rather than the fixed structural constraints that surround them. Strategy may sometimes in this way over-emphasise the degree of choice decision makers have in the global business environment. But good strategy also recognises those structures, constraints and limitations, including the limitations of knowledge and of capacity (skills, technology, access to quality components among others) that frame any decision-making.

# Four key basic ideas

International business practice is dominated by four elements, which form the starting point for any discussion. Different theories, from the different disciplines that contribute to both IPE and business studies, shape how these practices can be understood. These four elements define how both actual business behaviour and theories of global business run through the international political economy. Their analysis is primarily drawn from economics. These are basic things that need to be understood before we can begin a more sophisticated discussion:

> *competitive structures* – of markets and corporate structures;
> *competition for market shares and profitability*;
> *rent-seeking and barriers to entry* – including high costs of movement;
> *technology change* – and the changes they promote.

*Competitive structures* are first of all the patterns of major actors in a market or business – is it dominated by one, two, a few or many influential actors? This is not just a question of how many firms there are in absolute terms, but of how many influential or innovative firms there are. In most economic sectors, there are many small actors, but they have no or little influence on the pattern of competition. The most important idea here is that the idealised form of market (the touchstone of 'open competition' in a simple model of economic behaviour) where there are many buyers, many sellers, and where there is open knowledge of both prices and specific qualities of goods and services offered, does not exist *anywhere* in the 'real world' of international business. The 'free market', in other words, does not exist in the global economy. All internationally traded goods and services are bought and sold within a set of political, technological and economic restrictions, structures that usually mean there are only a small number of effective actors. True monopoly or monopsony markets (where there are respectively only one seller or only one buyer, who is therefore able to control prices, quality and the number of sales) also almost never exist. Nearly all international trading, including insurance and banking as well as investment finance and manufactured goods, and also primary products (minerals, raw foodstuffs, oil, gas and nuclear fuels and so on), is managed through *oligopolies* where there is only a small group of dominant firms. You have only to look at how many makers of mobile phones, laptop computers, operating system software, civil airliners or oil refiners there are to see that generally very small groups of very large, very profitable multinational enterprises dominate international business. And yet at the same time, many small businesses – or even 'microfirms' employing a handful of people – can be global in reach and global in their purchasing patterns; but they cannot define the terms of competition unless they have a unique innovative product or technology.

The vast majority of businesses worldwide are small firms, including family businesses. But the largest firms have the most influence in politics and in spreading ideas and business practice as well as in economic terms.

Table 3.1 demonstrates the dominant roles of a small number of key firms in several important sectors. It also demonstrates the differences in market structure: where there are more firms, there may be more competition, but there may (as in insurance) also be more barriers between markets set up by regulators or by national traditions. In looking at this kind of data, we should also remember that around 24 per cent of all international trade is intra-firm, meaning it is trade within the same multinational but between different national divisions of Toyota or PWC or Hewlett Packard or whichever firm we study. If you read ahead to Table 3.2, you will also note that different sectors tend to have very different levels of profitability (divide the assets by the profits figure to check this), and different sectors have different average levels of profitability partly as a result of their structure. The global political economy is not composed only of 'states and markets'; it is also constructed sector by sector by different firms and varying technologies, and the study of sectors has always been an important approach to IPE.

What economists call economies of scale – being able to operate or sell or purchase more efficiently because one is operating on a global scale – are key to an understanding of oligopoly market structures. Being bigger than anyone else means that firms have the resources to take risks and withstand the consequences of mistaken earlier decisions. It also erects what have been called 'natural barriers to entry', giving existing players the scope to operate in markets using technology and knowledge that others can only copy at such enormous cost that they are in effect excluded from markets. There are also potential diseconomies of scale. Quite often, large firms have merged with each other in the last twenty or thirty years only to find that the merger did not work, which has led to a break-up, a demerger. De-mergers have sometimes been expensive choices by leading executives, but they have most often occurred where powerful shareholders insisted that they would get better value for their investment if part of a large firm was sold off and the successor managements of both of the resulting companies concentrated on their more focussed tasks more sharply. Economies of scale and barriers to entry may be subject to government regulation including controls on mergers and on abuses of dominant positions, as both US and EU legislators have intended, but laws against oligopoly practices are a relatively small part of the constraints that shape firms' conduct and sector structures and outcomes. For the most part these are shaped by three major economic forces and two major political powers. The major economic forces are: (i) the working of the market – just because competition is limited in some ways does not mean that major firms do not compete, often savagely; (ii) the availability of money – in other words the working of the global financial system (see Chapter 7 on this); and (iii) the availability of skills and knowledge including specific technologies and the relative ability (or disability) of managers in using them. The two political factors are: (i) the effectiveness of the state in managing its responsibilities for producing a stable currency and enforcing contracts through agreed procedures; and (ii) the effectiveness of whatever systems of business regulation are in place (whether they are controlled by state, private or international organisations).

One powerful tool to explain this kind of market is the concept of monopoly competition developed thirty years ago by Henryk Kiezlowski and John Sutton. Large firms do not generally

**Table 3.1** Leading firms and oligopolies: competitive structures in selected sectors (listed by size within each sector)

| Sector | Key firms | Location | Commentary |
|---|---|---|---|
| Civil aerospace | Airbus | EU | Only two global competitors; China |
| | Boeing | US | and Brazil both aim to break this oligopoly but have not done so far |
| Pharmaceutics | Pfizer | US | A group of 12–15 firms dominate |
| | Novartis | Switzerland | the sector in research, with these |
| | Sanofi-Aventis | France | 7 leading in sales volume. One of |
| | Merck | US | the few sectors where EU firms |
| | Glaxo-Smith-Kline | UK | clearly lead rather than US or Asian |
| | Roche | Switzerland | firms |
| | Astra-Zeneca | UK/Sweden | |
| Aircraft engines (Civil use) | Pratt and Whitney | US | These dominate engine market for |
| | General Electric | US | civil planes. SNECMA smaller than |
| | Rolls Royce | US | the others but important in EU and |
| | SNECMA | France | Africa |
| Accounting/ consultancy | Deloitte | | All four have a global reach with |
| | PWC | | subsidiaries pretty much everywhere |
| | Ernst and Young | | and key roles as auditors as well as |
| | KPMG | | accounting and business consulting services to governments and international organisations as well as large and smaller firms |
| Shipbuilding | Mitsubishi Heavy Industry | Japan | Reflects the dominance of E Asian firms after the shift in production |
| | Hyundi Heavy Industry | South Korea | from the US, Sweden, UK, |
| | STX Group | South Korea | Germany in the 1970s. These |
| | DSME | South Korea | firms also play a leading role in |
| | China Shipbuilding | China | oil exploration platforms, marine engines and marine servicing |
| Insurance (all types) | Generali Group | Italy | The global insurance market is more |
| | China Life Insurance | China | fragmented than others listed here |
| | Much Re | Germany | because of regulation and history, |
| | Metlife | US | but has been consolidating very |
| | Zurich Financial Services | Switzerland | quickly and can be expected to keep |
| | AXA Group | France | doing so. All nine firms listed here |
| | Travelers | US | are busy acquiring |
| | Ping An Insurance Group | China | |
| | Tokyo Marine | Japan | |
| Computer chip makers (semiconductors) | Intel | US | These six firms dominate the market |
| | Samsung | South Korea | with a total of over 300 billion |
| | TI (Texas Instruments) | US | dollars in sales between them and |
| | Toshiba | Japan | Intel having nearly half of that total. |
| | RenesasQualcom | Japan | But there are many smaller very |
| | | US | successful specialist chip makers for the many varied uses chips now have, which often dominate specific specialised applications |

*Source*: Forbes 500 List (2014); also various issues of: *Wired*; *The Economist*; *Financial Times*.

simply gang up on consumers or governments, as some Marxist and others predicted; but they do not compete as the free market theorists of eighteenth-century liberalism (Adam Smith in particular) and their later neoliberal successors often suggest. This idea, together with the important contribution of theorists of regulation and regulatory behaviour developed in the 1990s, shape this chapter in important ways. These ideas are still at the heart of much business theory and much business practice, albeit filtered through business school teaching by authors such as Michael Porter, Gary Hamel and Yves Doz (all discussed below).

*Competition for market shares and profitability*: what do multinational businesses *aim* to do? They must first satisfy their shareholders that they are doing their best to increase the value of assets that belong to those shareholders. But they do not necessarily aim for gross profits in the short term. They may aim for technology leadership (requiring very high levels of investment on innovation); they may seek greater brand prominence (through marketing); they may also pursue increasing market shares in key sectors. All these goals reduce profits — because they can be very expensive and demand a great deal of capital. In the longer run, they are only worthwhile if they lead to greater shareholder value. But that is, of course, what they are designed to achieve. In the short run, to take two examples, a civil aircraft manufacturer or a drug producer would almost certainly get more profits by just putting their cash into a hedge fund rather than investing in a ten- or fifteen-year project. But if they want to maintain their position in their competitive and difficult markets, leaders in both sectors have to think long term. They have to plan their capital investments so as to maximise their chances of strengthening their competitiveness in the longer run. It is always the case that firms aim to achieve high profitability. If they don't satisfy activist shareholders — usually powerful financial institutions such as banks and hedge funds — they can expect trouble. But they also aim to do so through building market share. This can weaken the competition; in other words it weakens the ability of other firms to compete with them. It also builds the ability to take economies of scale — since production volumes presumably rise as market share rises. And greater market share may make it easier for multinational businesses to compete in one of the most acutely competitive arenas they face, the market to raise additional capital. A generation ago, there were three major civil airliner makers, Boeing and Macdonald Douglas, both American, and Airbus, a European joint venture based primarily on French companies once heavily subsidised by the government in Paris, but with participation from a number of other companies in other EU member states, and relying on British, American or French aero engines. Macdonald Douglas' civil aviation production suffered by being squeezed between two larger and more politically influential competitors, but they also produced a series of plane models that had technical problems and a series of damaging crashes harmed their public image. As a large company it lost a PR battle, but it also lost a battle with economies of scale and innovation where the two larger competitors in effect wiped it out. They lost market share, losing technically skilled staff, getting into increasing difficulties with both customers and shareholders. The end result was that MD was split, with Boeing swallowing the surviving civil aircraft business separated from the military aviation divisions.

Most large companies have not got bigger just by increasing sales and their customer base (there are important exceptions, including Google and Facebook, which work to other business models). They grow rapidly by mergers and acquisitions: they take over the competition and so enlarge their market share and technical capacity. Firms also often aim to satisfy their workforce — especially in high-technology sectors they must keep their most skilled staff at almost all costs. And they form strategic alliances, usually either to get access to difficult markets in emerging economies or to share technology and research and development risks, or to strengthen their power vis-à-vis regulatory authorities. The mixed motives of firms are inevitable and in addition managers themselves form an important constituency to satisfy; but confusion over aims is a recipe for failure and the most important single reasons why corporations have defined strategies (which may or may not be reflected in the public documentation of 'mission statements' and PR).

*Rent-seeking and lobbying activities*: large multinationals also engage in a wide range of political activities. They lobby, engage in public relations, meet politicians, form trade associations and try to influence regulatory authorities. Much of this work is a natural element of a free society in which 'civil society' works independently of the state. But at the same time, this kind of activity is likely to subvert democratic decision-making. It shifts the priorities of key legislators and decision makers and changes the fundamental role of the state in the economy. Politicians may claim that they are not really influenced by lobbying by large companies; the companies may pretend that this is so. But large companies would not be so foolish as to spend billions of dollars on PR, lobbying and supporting trade associations if they were not fully confident that they delivered what they aimed to do in terms of political influence.

Rent-seeking behaviour – one important strategy for all firms – is to try to influence government policy. That includes shaping the ways in which regulators work, as well as the regulatory environment for product approval, including safety, working conditions, and taxation. What is a 'rent' here? A rent in economic terms is a profit greater than normally predictable if the market is efficient. It is not the same as a rent from letting property (real estate). It is assumed by economists, who accept the doctrine of a free market to be abnormal – there are no rents in efficient markets. But however important market forces are, multinational business is never characterised by the simplicities of perfect competition as taught in 'Economics 101' courses. Rent-seeking is at its most important, and sometimes its most covert, where large firms and government decision makers and regulators have very close private relationships. This happens in all countries, and in international regulatory institutions as well as in national economies. It easily phases into open corruption, as the doyen of classical economics, Adam Smith, sarcastically observed in his *Wealth of Nations* (1776). The most obvious example of a rent is the additional gain made by monopoly businesses through their ability to dominate sales and set prices higher than they would be in a more competitive market. But here 'rent-seeking' is where companies set about achieving additional profits and/or a more favourable position in a market through public relations campaigns, lobbying, close interaction with government and by influencing state institutions (Boddewyn and Brewer, 1994). Large and small firms club together in trade associations, which also have important effects on government and regulators, employing PR firms and specialist consultancies, often spin-off businesses from the major global accounting firms, to represent their interests in trade talks and in the framing of regulations and legislation. Justin Greenwood (2011) has explored a series of cases where large firms or groups of firms have dominated decision-making within the European Union. One remarkable thing about this process – which of course is replicated in all countries – is that EU law not only allows, but requires consultation with business operating within EU boundaries. This means that lobbying and pressure group activities are accepted as routine provided that non-EU firms from the United States, China or Japan have (at least formally) equal access to the decision process as EU organisations.

Barriers to entry exist where it is difficult or impossible for new entrants to start up in a particular sector. Economic theory holds that, other things being equal (they never are in practice), firms that have the prospect of operating efficiently should be able to get into a particular market and muscle aside less efficient or less innovative rivals. The possibility of new entrants keeps existing firms on their toes and protects public policy interests in having efficient markets. But barriers to entry are obvious in specific examples. Although there are a good number of medium-size corporations in the oil industry, they specialise (for example, in exploration or equipment supplies). To set up a rival to Exxon, BP, CNOC or Shell would demand huge investment and huge risks. They already have the technologies and the contracts, and they have the financial resources (including large cash stocks as well as borrowing power) to see off potential rivals easily. Governments create barriers to entry when they insist that only trusted companies produce their telecommunications equipment, do military research or exchange computing contracts with government departments. Regulators create barriers to entry when they insist on higher safety standards, which require longer periods of expensive testing that smaller manufacturers cannot meet – as they do for justifiable reasons (public safety) in pharmaceuticals and food processing. But barriers to entry also arise from the natural conditions of the market, as Kierzlowski and Sutton argued, most obviously in high-technology products. Here, simply being able to produce or process advanced goods and services may be a unique advantage, because of patenting, but also because a workforce may have a unique ability to produce the products or processes effectively. Natural monopolies arise in rapidly moving high-tech markets, and by the time the patent has been exhausted or the tricks of skilled production understood by rivals, the effective market leader will have moved on to new products and new services. One of the main reasons why Apple and Samsung have gone through rapid evolutions in the smart phones and tablet markets is to keep technically ahead of their rivals and to project a brand image of perpetual innovation that consumers might want to be associated with when they buy the products.

Barriers to entry are very different where customers have different levels of knowledge. Selling to other players in the same markets is dangerous because they know as much as the manufacturing firm about the product specifications and the changing technologies. Markets for industrial machinery or assembly robots, to take two examples, are among the most competitive in the world, although there are only a small numbers of producers, because the buyers are also large firms with a great deal of knowledge and expertise. Selling to 'ordinary' people makes different demands – they need to have information about the product and they want to be attracted by design and ease of use. Corporate customers buying manufacturing systems or negotiating large, long-term energy contracts (steel manufacturers, for example) know a great deal about the products available, the quality of service agreements and the likely future changes in their market. Selling within a sector to other large companies is a difficult but important art. Much multinational activity is directed towards this intense activity in which small numbers of firms try to meet the very demanding requirements of customers. For example, computer chip manufacturers such as Intel need to persuade the user of their products – mobile phone, tablet and computer makers, as well as many others – that their specific products will be the best available for a foreseeable future so that their customers do not have to take on the high costs of adapting to new chip specifications more often than they want. Aircraft engine manufacturers such as Rolls Royce control the product standards not just of the sub-contracting firms that supply their main components, but also insist that the sub-contractors include Rolls Royce quality supervision standards in their contracts with their own suppliers along the supply chain.

*Technology change and market transformation* have always been factors in the evolution of the modern economy. Even in a longer perspective, technology change shaped the evolution of the economy and the distribution of power, although change tended to happen more slowly than it has since the start of the industrial revolution. One of the founding theorists of IPE, Susan Strange, argued that two of the most influential but often overlooked authors in the field were Joseph Schumpeter, whose writings on capitalism and democracy took account of the tendencies to monopoly, and Karl Polanyi. Schumpeter was one of the few writers whose work affected international relations theories more generally who took technology and the problem of understanding technology change seriously. Karl Polanyi's thesis in his account of the modernisation of the global economy, *The Great Transformation*, put a careful emphasis on the interplay of technology, markets and social and political forces in order to critique both orthodox Marxian and orthodox liberal accounts of major shifts in industrial capitalism. This chapter cannot wholly ignore technology factors, but technology change within the IPE is discussed in more detail in a separate chapter later.

## The global business environment and the different legal environments of business

Much of the recent business strategy literature has focussed on the difficulties and opportunities inherent in working in a global market where the environment is rapidly changing. Theories of globalisation mostly originated in business school literature and spread to other social science and humanities. The concept of globalisation has been perhaps the most powerful single idea in social science in the last generation. It originated with business school theorists such as Kenichi Ohmae, whose book *The Borderless World* (1999) remains one of the leading optimistic analyses of the advantages of liberal globalisation. These ideas have also been much criticised (see the previous chapter) from a wide range of different positions. But apart from globalisation, the study of business environment also tries to take account of the varied cultural and social contexts that firms face in working across frontiers. It aims to recognise the importance of cultural diversity among both customers and employees, and tries to think through how different social contexts frame different ways in which firms need to work. This filters through to issues such as brand identities (the colour red is seen as lucky and encouraging in China and East Asia but may be threatening to Western eyes, while white may suggest purity in some cultures but death in others). HSBC has for some years been running a global advertising campaign that stresses the bank's sensitivity to local identities and business practices, which appears to have been widely successful. But other attempts to create a 'global' corporate identity have been more difficult to achieve, and some, such as the once famous and then infamous advertisements for the Italian clothing firm Benetton, have had powerfully negative effects.

Understanding the global business environment also necessarily involves making sense of the political and economic environment in national or regional markets and changes in technology and working practices. All this argues for the importance of studying IPE in business schools alongside the other parent disciplines of business studies. In this sense, much of the rest of this book concerns the business environment.

Businesses operate within different legal and taxation contexts. This shapes their behaviour and their capabilities. US corporations that can do so locate in Delaware because that state has laws that give substantial incentives to business, especially to finance and insurance. For the same reasons, UK companies that can do so locate in the Channel Islands or further offshore, while Russian financial interests have moved to London or Cyprus. Although the European Union has been able to create a relatively efficient 'level playing field' through the common market in goods trade across national borders, it has been rather less successful in regulating company size and corporate cooperation. Both the EU and its member governments have been very unsuccessful in regulating business taxation arrangements to prevent large global corporations such as Apple and Starbucks from paying very little tax in the countries where they earned income. They have done this through entirely legal, but largely unintended and unwanted effects of a long series of international agreements on corporate establishment and taxation dating back to 1923.

Global corporate structures have become immensely complex, but not just for taxation reasons. Companies generally believe it is valuable to have local subsidiaries in all the countries they operate in; in many cases they are required to do so by local regulations. But dividing a firm into division or profit centres within an overall holding company of some kind enables the senior management to see more easily which elements are more profitable or more innovative and which are in need of more careful attention (or closing down). Hewlett Packard, the global computing and computing component manufacturer, has subsidiaries in over a hundred countries. Although all the staff in these firms have a common corporate identity pressed upon them (and all, in Japanese corporate style, learn about the common corporate culture, a corporate song, and the 'HP way'), the separate units based in different countries compete directly with each other for research resources and to demonstrate the most effective financial control. If a sub-division creates an important new component or manufacturing technique, this is not shared freely around the larger company; it is sold by that division to its colleagues, with bonuses going to the team in the subsidiary that produced it. In this way, HP executives hope to keep the separate divisions on their toes, to maximise competitiveness and to redouble their capacity to keep each division under the closest scrutiny.

Japanese and Korean companies are often said to have the most convoluted structures, with cross-ownership between subsidiaries and shared research and development, as well as in-house sources of technology or finance. So the Mitsubishi group includes heavy industry units that employ the products of the robotics division and the Mitsubishi Bank invests in the separate divisions as a shareholder as well as a provider of loans. This structure of inter-ownership of separate divisions is very common in some Asian countries. It helps to prevent outside intervention or takeovers; but it also weakens external supervision. It is a practice that has been weakened under pressure from other countries (notably the US) through World Trade Organization (WTO) discussions. It would be illegal in the form it is often practised in both the US and the EU. But it can also be claimed to have served the emerging Asian economies very well as they became efficient rapidly-growing capitalist economies between the 1950s and the 1990s. There is not a common form of company structure in the global economy, just as there is not a common form of management of debt to equity balance in corporate financial structures – Anglo-Saxon practice uses equity much more than some other economies in both continental Europe and the global South. So-called 'hostile takeovers' are only possible in those economies such as the Anglo-Saxon ones (in the UK, Canada, Australia and the US in particular), which allow corporate financial and organisational structures which make them possible.

## Theories of multinational business behaviour and impacts

In this section, we simplify the range of theories by identifying three main contrasting theories. Each of these explains business behaviour and market outcomes in very different ways. Each has an analogy in mainstream theories in anthropology, sociology and criminology, as well as in IR. They are, broadly speaking, structural models; decision-making models that emphasise the quality of decision-making including leadership; and models of firm uniqueness, which deny that there can be generalised or scientific theories. The latter are often called 'postmodern' theories and resemble postmodern approaches to anthropology and sociology (on which they draw) although they are rather more distant from most postmodern approaches to IR.

*Structure–conduct–performance (SCP)* models of business behaviour derive directly from theories of market competition in economics. But unlike many economic theories, they do not idealise how markets work. They also draw on theories of imperfect competition and recognise that firms are driven by complex motives and are complex organisations. But there are two very different kinds of SCP model. The first takes the structure of competition in a given segment or technology as the key starting point. Firms will behave differently depending on whether the market is oligopolistic, largely a monopoly, and on whether there are a group of competing companies all of roughly equal skill and profitability. The structure of competition will also vary depending on whether there are many actors of different sizes or a small number of more or less equal competitors. And it will vary depending on product life cycles (are the goods or services sold well established mature products or new and still innovating and dynamic). This theory was articulated most fully by Scherer (1970), although it can be found in a wide variety of scholarship in the 1960s and 1970s, and is still significant today.

The implications of the SCP approach are important for global economic behaviour. They imply that managers will want to integrate around economies of scale. Financial economies of scale were often seen as being the most important, which partly explains why in the most developed economies in the 1960s and 1970s, very large firms were created that did not have a single focus, but had divisions that (for example) engaged in mechanical and electrical engineering, shipbuilding, defence and food processing. It also implied that large firms became very bureaucratic and hard to manage efficiently, which was the most difficult problem facing firms like British Leyland (car and truck makers) in the UK and IBM (computing and business services) in the US. Large conglomerate firms became close to government, which often encouraged still more mergers, sharing the belief that bigger is better regardless of quality or focus. In such a market, each firm will form a strategy with an eye on its competitors, learning from them; but all tend to learn the same lessons, and firm strategies are not very clearly differentiated. Since the theory predicts that leading firms will dominate by getting increasingly large, all firms aim to grow using takeovers and mergers, barriers to entry and internationalisation.

To take a specific example, at the end of the 1980s, there were only two global firms in the industrial gases market (British Oxygen, now BOC) and Air Liquide (French). They competed primarily by vying for the chance to take over as many smaller firms in different industrial gas and medical markets as possible. Since 1990, both have faced serious difficulties, both have restructured, selling off many of their earlier acquisitions, and both have become more efficient. Each has also become more specialised and both have moved into increasingly high-value market niches leaving some of the high-volume, low-value niches to new entrants. Asian and US and Canadian firms have all entered these markets, where the segments for industrial gases and for medical gases have in effect become separated. (To follow up on this or any other examples used in this chapter, a valuable source will always be company annual reports, on which this discussion is based here).

*A second very different kind of SCP model* explains business behaviour through looking at the structure of corporate organisations. How are businesses organised and how do they manage the complex inter-relationships embedded in their structure? Much contemporary writing on business strategy has focussed on change management, meaning the leadership of change through organisational restructuring. That has included the growth of 'team working', which is meant to be more cooperative rather than hierarchical, and where members of a team contribute ideas and share skills rather than each working in only one highly specialised function. This enables the firm to be more flexible and to respond more quickly to changes in the market or the business environment. It also implies that firms may have a 'flatter' structure, with fewer levels of middle management between the firm leadership and the front line employees. That flatter structure is enabled in part by information processing and sharing through computer networks. The most obvious and successful examples of this structure are the relatively new social media and online businesses such as Apple, Google and Facebook, although many advertising and media companies also have this form of organisation. It is, however, also true that large firms have sometimes adopted the language of team working and quick response, while keeping teams in a layered hierarchy, which enables the centre to keep a high level of control but may often combine the worst of both forms of organisation.

*Strategy/marketing-based theories*: by contrast, there are arguments that evolved critiques of the SCP theories. These start from the view that SCP theories undermine the choices and opportunities for innovation that managers can seize. Again, there are many versions of these ideas, but far and away the most influential author has been Michael Porter. For perhaps two decades in the 1980s and 1990s, Porter's work dominated the syllabuses of most business schools, and they promoted a wide variety of imitations. Porter argued that firms do not achieve competitiveness by tending to do the same things. Instead, they need to design much more specific strategies that identify their own strengths and their own potential to compete and that aim to understand the market where they sell better than their competitors. Putting it a little crudely, while the SCP model tended to identify a market structure inhabited by large corporate actors who easily became bureaucratic dinosaurs, Porter's conception of marketing based strategy saw firms – or the divisions or business groups within firms – as sharp-toothed mammals, smaller, quicker, much more intelligent and much more responsive to changes in their environment. Through moving faster and knowing better, firms gained competitive advantage over others.

Table 3.2 shows that the largest companies in the world are mainly financial institutions or energy giants, although if one goes down the list there are also the multinational car makers and industrial equipment makers, which thirty years ago stood at the head of such a list. Table 3.3 explores the leading manufacturing companies in the world economy. Attentive readers will see that the figures in Table 3.2 are in billions of $US, while those in Table 3.3 are in millions of $US. This domination of finance is discussed in more detail in Chapter 7 on finance and financial markets. The two tables together also illustrate the core strengths of major companies, identifying in particular the shift from Western to Asian (mainly Chinese) company leadership. Reading Table 3.1 above alongside Tables 3.2 and 3.3 gives us a fairly rough but valuable picture of the dominant corporate players in the world economy, also suggesting something about the strategies they have pursued. All the companies listed have of course achieved large size; but they also have achieved strong reputations for their capabilities in specific markets. None of them is the kind of generalised conglomerate that characterised much business activity in the 1970s.

**Table 3.2** Leading twenty world companies all sectors listed by end December 2014 stock market valuation (figures in $US billion)

| Company | Sector/industry | Sales | Profits | Assets | HQ location |
|---|---|---|---|---|---|
| ICBC | Banking/finance | 149 | 42.7 | 3,125 | China |
| China Construction | Engineering/construction | 121 | 34.2 | 2,449 | China |
| Agricultural Bank of China | Finance | 136 | 27 | 2,405 | China |
| JP Morgan Chase | Finance | 106 | 17.3 | 2,435 | US |
| Berkshire/Hathaway | Finance/fund management | 179 | 19.5 | 493 | US |
| Exxon Mobile | Energy | 394 | 32.6 | 347 | US |
| General Electric | Engineering/defence | 143 | 14.8 | 656 | US |
| Wells Fargo | Finance/logistics | 89 | 21.9 | 1,543 | US |
| Bank of China | Finance | 105 | 25.5 | 2,291 | China |
| Petrochina | Energy | 329 | 21.1 | 387 | China |
| Royal Dutch Shell | Energy | 451 | 16.4 | 358 | Netherlands |
| Toyota | Automotives | 227 | 18.8 | 386 | Japan |
| Bank of America | Finance | 102 | 11.4 | 2,114 | US |
| HSBC | Finance | 80 | 16.3 | 2,671 | UK |
| Apple | Electronics/computing | 173 | 37 | 225 | US |
| Citigroup | Finance | 94 | 13 | 1,883 | US |
| BP | Energy | 379 | 24 | 305 | UK |
| Chevron | Energy | 212 | 21 | 254 | US |
| Volkswagen | Automotives | 262 | 12 | 447 | Germany |
| Walmart | Retail/logistics | 477 | 16 | 205 | US |

*Source*: Forbes 500 List (2014).

**Table 3.3** Leading fifteen world manufacturing companies by revenue rank order

| Company | Industry | Annual revenue (in $US million) | HQ location |
|---|---|---|---|
| Toyota | Automotive/engineering | 235,364 | Japan |
| Volkswagen | Automotive | 221,551 | Germany |
| Samsung | Electronics | 148,944 | South Korea |
| Daimler | Automotive | 148,139 | Germany |
| General Electric | Engineering/defence | 147,616 | US |
| Ford | Automotive | 136,264 | US |
| Hewlett-Packard | Computing/electronics | 127,245 | US |
| Bombardier | Aerospace/transport | 122,734 | Canada |
| Hitachi | Engineering/electronics | 122,419 | Japan |
| Nissan | Automotive | 119,166 | Japan |
| Hon Hai Precision Industry | Electronics | 117,514 | Taiwan |
| Exor | Automotive | 117,297 | Italy |
| Siemens | Engineering | 113,349 | Germany |
| Apple | Computing | 108,249 | US |
| IBM | Electronics/business services | 106,916 | US |

*Source*: Forbes 500 List (2014).

According to Porter (and his many followers), how then do large firms compete? Like all businesses, they direct investment towards activities that they expect will bring them profitability, which will build their brands, which will identify unique selling points to exploit, and create competences and strengths in markets they already occupy or that they want to move into. The distinctive point about larger firms is that they do have a global reach and a global conception of strategy, and that they very often have a significantly longer time perspective than smaller companies. In this account, it is most important that managers analyse their firm's situation and competitors accurately before acting on that analysis. Firms compete in Porter's account by adopting one of three strategies. In Porter's earlier publications, these strategies are exclusive – they cannot be efficiently combined; in his later work he came to partially revise that view.

The three generic corporate strategies are:

1 *Cost leadership* – the ability to dominate competitors in a specific sector through using resources more effectively and through continuous monitoring of ways of cutting costs. This strategy is especially important in large volume businesses with mature technologies and a mature stage of the product life cycle. If the strategy works, it tends to produce reliable but not outstanding profits; if it fails, the firm will quickly lose market share and fail (low-cost supermarket chains that buy as cheaply as possible and sell in large volumes are an example).

2 *Specialisation*, including advantages in the use of technology such as robotic production lines and meeting the specific needs of customers more effectively than competitors – this is a customer oriented strategy that relies on an understanding of customer responses; cost control still matters, but firms achieve a higher level of profitability through seeking to differentiate themselves and then in effect charging a higher premium than they otherwise could for delivering greater customer satisfaction (high-end, high-street fashion chains and high-quality transmission manufacturing for car production are good examples).

3 *Focus* – often called *niche* strategy, in which firms achieve a *unique* (not merely distinctive or differentiated) combination of customer satisfaction and sector leadership, the most obvious

ways to do this including patenting of innovations that give the firm a unique product, but may also include a unique quality of customer service, unique branding or design (Ferrari cars offer a good example).

In Porter's work, the second and third have sometimes merged, but it remains conceptually helpful to distinguish them. Each strategy implies different forms of competition. At a global level, each strategy implies different relationships with customers and with government and regulators. The first requires very large-scale activity and today global scale production and/or selling are often necessary to achieve profits; in general, profit percentages may be low, but very high-level activity is capable of generating very large profits. The second is more profitable so long as a firm can maintain its differentiation from rivals effectively. The third may be the most profitable in terms of the percentage return on investment, but by definition tends to be smaller scale even with a global product. Firms that grow large on the basis of unique niche advantages may also be seen as 'too big' by regulators and come under threat of state or legal intervention to protect consumers.

In this global competitive environment, how do small firms survive? One cannot begin to answer questions about small firm survival without acknowledging that many of them do *not* survive. Although everyone can cite the examples of Facebook or Starbucks, as well as many other software and services business, which started in a front room or a garage and grew to global dominance, the vast majority of small firms fail. A significant number of those that succeed do not grow into global players: when they are seen to be profitable and to have a unique technology or brand, are bought by existing major firms looking for new patents or new skills or just for rejuvenating new blood. Small firms also have strategies, and they are primarily strategies of survival. Having a unique skill set may be important. Small high-technology firms may have been spin-offs from university research where the owners have developed a specific innovation and are aiming to market the product or process protected by intellectual property rights. Small firms also evolve where managers or technologists from large multinationals set up an enterprise selling back to their original parent company services which can be managed more efficiently outsourced rather than produced in-house in the large firm. In summary, small firms in global markets draw on the lore of the infantrymen in Norman Mailer's famous book about the American experience of the Second World War: they are either quick or dead.

*Against Generic Strategies?* Peters and Waterman established a contrasting approach to management strategy in which they argued in essence that *there is no such thing as 'generic' corporate strategy.* They insisted instead that each firm – each well-managed firm – is unique and presents its own combination of skills, factors, marketing and human resource management. Rather than try to learn from business models derived from the practices of other companies, managers should seek to understand and build on what is unique and powerful about their own enterprise. They offer a series of eight varied themes rather than anything as rigorous as a specific business model. These models provide advice to the manager, which needs to be adapted to be applied in a specific context – some of these ideas have come to be commonplace ('stick to the knitting' – stick to what you know), but are still useful and relevant. They offered a series of case study examples not so that readers could follow those examples, but so that they could learn how to learn from examples and then practice those skills on their own company. The success of their work created a wave of what has sometimes been called 'postmodern' management practices. But these case study led approaches were not critical in the way that most social science 'postmodern' theories have tended to be; they also made it harder to think how a cumulative understanding of business strategies might be possible. The detailed case study approach on which Peters and Waterman built has been widely adopted across all kinds of business theory, without necessarily accepting some of the assumptions they made about the impossibility of building an effective more general image of how and why businesses succeed or fail. Minus the 'postmodern' word, their approach remains a useful one, not least because it also points to the importance of understanding the history of firms and sectors.

*Synthesising the core models*: most contemporary teaching texts try to integrate the different theories outlined here, but it is hard not to lean more towards one or the others. Johnson and Scholes' influential textbook has gone through a series of editions, which reflect some of these changes in debates (and in fashions in business thinking). Gary Hamel's work over a number of years is another important example (Hamel, 2012).

Contemporary research in international business reveals a great deal of work on leadership in large and small organisations, on succession planning (the replacement of a generation of leaders by another) in family businesses as well as large corporations, on niche marketing and specialisation and on the capacity of firms to respond to changes in global labour markets. Some of this work has been dominated by more recent writing by Tom Peters, but there are many scholars in the field. Globalisation in itself is no longer contentious in this literature (although it certainly is in IPE). Innovation strategies remain as important as ever, and studies of innovation (usually sectoral studies) remain important elements in the table of contents of major journals even beyond those (such as *Research Policy* and *Innovation and Technology*), which specialise in that area. As always, many books aim at a market of quick-fix management with practical guides to specific problems, but there is too a large literature aimed at a more thoughtful or academic readership. It has also always been the case that many managers sneer at the academic fashions that shape that literature, although fashions in academic literature pass (often via popularising short books) fairly quickly into business practice, as a survey of large company annual reports will quickly show.

The example box below sums up some of the key contributions of scholarly and consulting work that this chapter discusses. It gives a (very selective) overview of key thinkers and theorists who have worked across the IPE/business studies frontier, whose work has reflected and shaped the theories that this section examines.

---

**EXAMPLE BOX**

## Leading thinkers in at the business/IPE frontier

**Claire Cutler** – Canadian theorist who has explored the growth and significance of private authority in the global business political economy and the transfer of regulatory power from state to non-state actors, using a critical theoretical approach.

**Boston Consulting Group** – probably the most influential innovative consulting group as the creators of new research designs and research tools for business analysis, which are widely used in market analysis and company performance evaluation.

**Yves Doz** – French scholar and influential teacher at the INSEAD business school who has analysed the growing power of multinational business including the flexibility and technical awareness that successful firms use to create dominance over others.

**John Dunning** – leading British business educator of the last thirty years, whose work emphasises the complexity of the multinational business environment and the difficulty of applying conventional microeconomics to business behaviour. Dunning has often crossed the IPE/business frontier, collaborating with others such as Susan Strange. Also influential as the author of higher-level textbook and through his doctoral-level teaching.

**Gary Hamel** – London Business School-based US academic and consultant who applies a diverse range of approaches to analyse marketing and business strategies; Hamel is perhaps the doyen of the contemporary approach that integrates insights from both the marketing strategy and structure–conduct–performance (SCP) approaches with a focus on the urgent need for the management of change in organisations and technological capabilities to meet future challenges.

**Kenichi Ohmae** – early theorist of globalisation. Working in consultancy, Ohmae had a distinct practitioner view of change in the global IPE. His work has been criticised for its over-optimistic thinking about the positive aspects of globalisation, but remains hugely influential.

**Eleanore Olstrom** and **Oliver Williamson** – joint Nobel Economics Prize winners for their work (done separately) on how networks shape business behaviour and restructure institutional arrangements that more traditional economic and business theories fail to explain. Influential even before their work was used to explain key dimensions of the growth and success of online business, online consumer awareness and online network development.

**Tom Peters** and **Richard Waterman** – co-authors of an influential approach to business analysis based on individual case studies. Drawing on ethnographic concepts of 'thick description', they argue that all generalised models of business behaviour are suspect and that a better approach is the case study that aims to understand how and why individual firms have unique combinations of qualities that enable them to succeed. Peters went on to become one of the leading scholars of business leadership as a source of competitive advantage in the current literature.

**Michael Porter** – still very influential after thirty years, the Harvard Business School Professor, sometimes described as the most highly paid academic in the world, explored how firms gain competitive advantage by creating and exploiting unique strengths through strategic analysis of their position within specific ('segmented') markets. Porter's argument implies that there are not generic strategies that all firms of a given size within a market should pursue, but that each should strive to differentiate themselves from their competitors in order to succeed. This often – but not always – points to the advantage that first entrants gain into a market. It also emphasises the importance of strategic analysis as a factor in decision-making and less controversially stresses the value of moving quickly to outwit more sluggish bureaucratic rivals.

**Joan Robinson** – important Cambridge economist in the 1930s and 1940s, who formulated a theory of 'imperfect competition' that has shaped a great deal of theorising about business behaviour even among scholars who rejected some of her assumptions. Her stress on large firms' willingness to trade profits for market share and on their willingness to seek rents through close links to government even when they preach 'open markets' retains its importance in the work of many more recent thinkers.

**Frederick M. Scherer** – one the principal (and the most rigorous) of the creators of the 'structure–conduct–performance' (SCP) model of business behaviour and firm strategy in the 1960s and 1970s, which dominated business research and teaching before Porter. His work, building on insights by Edward Mason, remains very important although partly overtaken by the dynamic strategy approaches that became fashionable after Porter. But many management approaches seek to merge some form of SCP approach with the marketing strategic approach (for example, Gary Hamel above), and the consultancy McKinsey recently asserted that the work of this group of scholars, which dates from the 1960s, has retained its importance in the contemporary business environment.

**Richard Sennett** – Professor of Sociology at the London School of Economics, who has simultaneously held chairs in US universities. Sennett has written widely on the changing nature of contemporary capitalism including the experience of work and labour processes. His *The Culture of the New Capitalism* (2006) integrates critical thinking about economic processes and globalisation and has been recognised as one of the most important recent contributions to understanding the context of contemporary business.

**John Stopford** and **Susan Strange** – both had distinguished careers in business, journalism and academia and their impacts on contemporary IPE are evident at many points through this book. Each pioneered sectoral studies of different aspects of the world economy. Their collaboration *Rival States, Rival Firms* (1991) initiated a crossover between business studies, IPE and IR, which much later work followed.

## Regulation and multinational business strategies

Multinational businesses face a complex welter of regulation. They are supposed to conform to the national government regulations of each country in which they operate. They may also be subject to all kinds of international regulation process. The most obvious examples are those – however effective or ineffective – shaping financial regulation. Trade policy and negotiations through the World Trade Organization also include important regulatory processes. But in the absence of free competition, it is a sound economic as well as political principle that regulations should manage aspects of corporate behaviour to prevent excessive profits, breaches of law, the formation of cartels and the cheating of both consumers and tax authorities. Repeated anti-corruption campaigns in China have marked the limits of what the state would tolerate, which all the same has allowed some extensive abuses. In the past, campaigns against the monopoly power of large conglomerates such as that in the US in finance and production against the 'robber barons' of the 1880s and 1890s led eventually to important anti-trust legislation. In unregulated markets including, for example, the market for cocaine and heroin, it is easier to see how lack of regulation produces imbalances of power between consumers and comprador traders, and also between those same traders and the actual producers, usually small farmers in Colombia or Afghanistan, who have little leverage against the gangsters they are forced to sell their crop to. Both the argument for the strict control of the global drug trade and those who argue for the relaxation of illegality to allow a more open market are arguing that better regulation (of different forms) would make the global drug markets less dangerous, less unbalanced in terms of who has the real power and less unsafe for individuals involved. Multinational businesses compete in trying to influence governments as rent-seekers, discussed above. They act individually as well as forming trade associations where they collaborate to influence legislators and regulators (this has already been discussed above).

## Private authority and IPE

One important consequence of the growth of increasingly complex regulatory systems is the transfer of authority from the state – or from state-based international institutions such as the World Bank – to authorities that are private rather than public in legal basis and in responsibility. 'Authority' here may mean legal authority; legal powers to manage a market or sector are passed to private actors, which may in some sense be responsible to state power, but that also have a high degree of autonomy. That autonomy may be defined in law within an individual state, but it may also be gathered through a recognised competence or awarded by a political process. This whole process may arise because the state agrees not to do something; it also arises sometimes when the state is unable to manage these responsibilities. Scholars such as Virginia Haufler and Claire Cutler have mapped the increasing growth of private corporations, lobby groups or more or less 'independent' para-statal regulatory bodies in the world economy, and have criticised the use of very specific forms of power they use. That power is often informal and sometimes undemocratic. It also encourages even closer relations between regulators, politicians and major firms since many regulators are recruited from the leading firms, politicians move onto corporate boards when they retire, and specialist knowledge of a field is essential for competence as either a manager or a regulator, narrowing the pool of those qualified to work in either role. It does not deny that conspiracies between regulators, politicians and business are possible (and it is easy to find examples) to say that close contacts between them are inevitable.

## Knowledge as a global commodity

Knowledge and value in global business: many firms are not engaged in the production of specific goods, and cannot really be said to perform a 'service' in an early twentieth-century sense. Instead, they produce or process knowledge. They are engaged in symbolic processing. This affects the kinds of work undertaken by their employees and their experience of work. It also forms one of the most basic elements of the reconstruction of the global economy, as Richard Sennett has observed. Academics, accountants, consultants of different kinds, but also middle managers in almost any business work to manipulate figures, produce data or records, manage the image of the firm, or produce narratives that can be shared by employees and customers wanting to understand the core identity of their products and services. Apple is one of the best examples; Zara, the Spanish owned middle-range clothing store is another. Both establish a core identity, which includes style, design, quality. Both have a certain reputation on which they try to build. Both have an identifiable price niche. Innovation is absolutely key to their image as well as to the detailed specification of the products they sell. In these senses, although both Apple and Zara sell 'things', they also sell an image of themselves and of their customers. To sell this image, they have to be able to create and reproduce it – to process the symbols that express it as well as the reputational factors that bring them strength and keep customers coming back. Even where tangible things change hands, what is being sold is a narrative and an identity as much as a product. If one compared the detailed advertising of Apple with (for example) Samsung, or Zara's advertising and store window displays with a comparable rival such as H & M, it would not be difficult to identify the ways in which products are bought and sold within a set of narratives that express the strategy and self-image of the company. Equally, when a firm loses its identity or fails in its reputation, as the accounting firm Arthur Andersen did in the wake of the Enron scandal in the United States, the result can be disastrous: Andersen acted as auditors for Enron and approved corporate accounts and reports that were in large measure fraudulent; although Andersen had no knowledge of the fraud, the sense that they ought to have done ruined their reputation and forced them out of business, even though they had previously been one of a handful of the largest accounting and consultancy firms in the world.

One specific sector that has global reach and global significance is the supply of business information. With the development of rolling news a decade or so ago, business information services and broadcasting came to merge. Firms such as Pearson (owners of the *Financial Times*), Reuters, Al Jazeera, CNBC and the London based Economist Intelligence Unit (EIU) found that they faced much more acute competition in the provision of instant, reliable market news. Business information is all the more valuable when it is gained before others, but information may include not just specific news about key players in a market. It may also include a generalised sentiment – is the market going up or down? Are employment prospects improving? How does this or that political decision influence the future business environment? If equities are going down, are bond sales rising (as they often do when money is transferred from the less promising area of investment)? Or if both bond and equity markets are falling, where is money going – to gold, to property, to emerging markets? Or are holders of cash preferring to hold on to it rather than spend it anywhere? The most valuable business information may usually be anything that reduces the risk in decision-making. Insider trading is obviously a way to reduce – or remove – risk because the sharers of that information know in advance for sure what is going to happen. Insider trading is illegal because it eliminates risk in decision-making in ways that distort market dynamics because it gives some players a radically unfair advantage over others.

The growth of the Internet has had a range of varied impacts on every kind of business. That includes online stock and bond trading as well as buying information (see above) or buying books, music downloads, clothes and even large ticket domestic items. It has also always included the buying and selling of pornography and of sex, as well as illegal sales of drugs and (often faked) pharmaceuticals. The impact of online business and e-commerce has been to introduce new elements of competition – could one grocery store manage its e-business better than another? This has often turned on the quality (and failures) of software systems. There is, as even the most casual observer would notice, an enormous emphasis on online business in popular magazines and books, and elsewhere. Online businesses can be small and yet have a worldwide reach. They may also be important sources of innovations in a sector. They are most important because generally speaking they demand relatively low capital at the start, which makes it much easier for entrepreneurs without a track record to manage a business start-up.

This body of business practice has a number of impacts on the global political economy that are central to any account of the global political economy (GPE). These include the patterns of competition that tend over time to strengthen the position of major corporations and institutions. This strengthens existing patterns of hegemony. It may also operate against broader public interests – for example, with respect to the global environment or the interests of consumers. It may also mean that suppliers of large firms have a weaker position in an unequal relationship, as supermarket suppliers have often complained in all major economies. The patterns of power and authority which have emerged through the processes of globalisation are significant in thinking about any aspect of power in the world, including the relationship between dominant firms and leading governments in the management of 'hegemony' (discussed in Chapter 2), or the structure of a global balance of power between dominant interests and dependent interests across the global stage. The shift to private authority has included the growth of private security firms, which have taken increasingly diverse roles in developed countries and in the global South. It also includes the ever-greater capacity for data collection of the largest Internet firms and social media, where one might ask what they do with the data they collect, how it is secured, and how it is kept out of the hands of others.

# International business history and case study analysis

International relations does not make very much sense without a knowledge of international history; nor, despite the mathematic abstraction to which some scholars are addicted, can one understand economics without a solid understanding of economic history. By the same token, international political economy that is studied without some knowledge of history is likely to be weak and inadequate, and also likely to suffer from the kinds of broad generalisation that do not help understand anything or formulate any specific policy responses. The history of individual processes, individual sectors and individual firms is important. For different theoretical positions, history may matter for different reasons: Marxian or critical theory places economic and social history at the centre of any study of the changing nature of the IPE (as Marx and leading critical scholars such as Cox have always argued); liberal theorists generally – with exceptions – reject Henry Ford's position that 'history is bunk' and argue that the historical trajectory of ideas and institutions offers one of the main keys to understanding; feminist and postcolonial writers want to understand the history of different forms of exploitation or patriarchy; postmodern theory tends to frame explanation and understanding in terms of context and changing linguistic practices.

Much of the development of business studies and its related economic, psychological and organisational studies has been built around case study analysis. The in-depth use of business cases was originated by the Boston Consulting Group, a private consulting group created in the 1960s. Since then, the 'Harvard style' of case study has become popular. This involves a form of simulation involving cases drawn from 'real world' experience in which advanced students are asked to form teams to master and respond to hundreds of pages of detail on a particular company situation. The quality of these kinds of case studies depends on having up-to-date reliable information and on the commitment of students, but above all on the quality of feedback from tutors as they observe the decisions and conflicts that the teams have. Not all business cases need to be so large scale or so intense, although it will always be true that the more current and 'real' the information they use the better they will be. You can build a repertoire of case studies for yourself either in class or as an individual as a way to better understand how business behaviour and theories of global business both influence IPE. It will become clear if you do this how relevant some of the key ideas in this chapter are to an understanding of how business behaviour plays such a large role in constituting the global political economy. The obvious way to do this would be to choose a sector or a large corporation and do some research to follow up its significance.

Individually or in small groups, students can identify a key sector in the world economy and use online sources, including company annual reports and consultancy reports on the sector, as well as sources such as the *Wall Street Journal*, the *Financial Times*, and the weekly business magazines, in order to build an understanding of a sector. From this core data, they can then start to ask questions about the political and social impact of the sector and the different kinds of power that key actors may play. They can also enquire into the regulatory environment that firms deal with and ask whether regulators are over-intrusive or inadequate. Sector case study analysis is one important way in which IPE and business studies overlap – as you will quickly see if you explore articles through a search of journals such as the *Cambridge Review of Economics*, the *Harvard Business Review*, and many others.

## Summary

The main aims of this chapter have been to demonstrate the importance of global corporations and their activities in shaping the global political economy. Activities that are especially important include mergers and acquisitions, the management of global supply chains, the relationships between parent corporations and subsidiaries, the flow of foreign direct investment and the patterns of innovation (whether in production technologies, products or management styles and policies). There is a global balance of power among major companies as there is among major states; as in the world of states, changes in that balance shape the behaviour of all actors and the outcomes in the principal arenas. To achieve these objectives, the chapter has left some important gaps, which will be addressed in later chapters.

Major firms are largely responsible for a great deal of the important dynamics of the global economy. Their competitive behaviours are one of the most important factors that create the dynamism of contemporary IPE. They shape change, manage risks and cause crises. They also have the potential to create innovations that meet human needs, ending food shortages, providing economic security and remedying environmental problems. It is imperative that any students of IPE has at least some outline sense of the importance of both the behaviour of major firms and the dynamics of government–industry relations, and the study of business cases provides a way of doing this. At the same time, the main theories of multinational business form an important body of work, which has importance because it shapes the opinions and actions of managers. Equally important, it provides an ideological basis for the role that business plays in the IPE. That is to say it provides the ideas and theories that justify how firms behave as well as trying to explain and predict them in a more 'scientific' way. Business schools form one of the most creative and rapidly changing sources of ideas, some of which may be mere temporary fashions, but at least some of which – like Porter and Dunning's work discussed here – comes to have a powerful influence because, at least to a major extent, it seems to help managers make better decisions.

This chapter has also outlined some of the most influential theories of international business behaviour. It has demonstrated how both those theories and the actual management and strategy of firms, especially large powerful multinationals, matter in any consideration of IPE. This is not just a question of 'adding some bits' to existing IPE theory. Arguments about business strategy suggest how the underlying structures of the global economy work, and how, when and why they change. Although there is an important weakness in this discussion if it is taken in isolation, which is a tendency to take the politics out of analysis, other chapters and arguments keep the politics at the front of one's mind, as the other chapters in this book show. But at the same time, if we take the business, the role of major firms, the role of major shifts in the centres of gravity of firm activity out of IPE, it quite often just does not make sense. The leading scholars in IPE have always recognised the importance of business history and the evolution of business strategies. The chapter has explored three separate groups of theoretical approach. First, it examined theories of structure–conduct–performance (SCP), which have been used from the 1950s to explain how firms behave, how they succeed or fail, and how sectoral structures rise, change and decline. The internal organisation and leadership of firms also shape behaviour and outcomes and constitute a variation on the SCP model. In different forms, these theories remain significant today. Second, we looked at the contrasting arguments that Michael Porter and others developed. These ideas have transformed both business practice and business teaching since the 1980s and 1990s. They emphasise the value of good strategic decision-making, using generic strategies of cost–cutting, differentiation/specialisation or unique niche exploitation, making a firm distinct in a market, or, where possible, of achieving and exploiting wholly unique qualities (of products, services or production methods). They also put a strong emphasis on the role of firm leadership and speed of response to changes in the business environment. Third, we examined theories rooted in individual case study analysis and the varied dimensions of success that could be crudely summarised as 'whatever you are doing, be excellent at it!'. This third approach has something in common with other theoretical approaches in other social sciences, which try to build rigorous ideas of understanding without building more general theories. They are sometimes called 'postmodern', but they might equally be labelled a 'business history' approach to analysis. In Tables 3.1, 3.2 and 3.3, the chapter outlined the strength and size of some of the key players in global business. They also note the shift from older manufacturing companies towards energy, finance and fund management, and the steady rise of major Asian companies in world markets. The example box 'Leading thinkers in at the business/IPE frontier' then summed up the impact of the work of a selective group of key theorists, scholars whose work is drawn on in this chapter, and that readers might want to explore more fully for themselves.

# Reflective questions

1   Why are international business sectors generally oligopolistic? Why are some more oligopolistic than others?
2   How do the larger global corporations compare in size with major states (compare turnover and/or assets with state GDP)?
3   Explain the main strategies adopted by multinational businesses in order to compete successfully. Which of these do you find gives a more convincing explanation of the emerging power structures in the world economy?
4   How do governments and large firms interact? Do state actors effectively control large businesses? Whether your answer is positive or negative, give your reasons.

# Suggestions for further reading

The most useful reading a student can do to follow up this chapter is to follow a specific business sector or company in the media, and/or go online to trace through the recent history of the strategy successes and failure of particular cases. You might do this by taking Table 3.1 and adding to it or exploring the specific patterns of competition that have evolved in the different sectors. If this is done in class in smaller groups for different sectors, it will quickly emerge how differently firms may behave even in similar environments. If you look at global sectors, you will also discover in more detail how problematic it can be to work across very different local environments. Another activity would be to take one or both of Table 3.2 and Table 3.3, and then add a longer list of companies. Which sectors are the most profitable (divide assets by profits)? Which are large but less profitable by this measure?

Look in the *Economist, Financial Times, Wall Street Journal, Le Monde Economique* or similar sources, depending on the languages you can use, and the main business journals. More advanced students may then want to go back to the IPE journals and see what gaps they have and where they are influenced by the business literature – you should find that there are very important crossovers, but also some odd gaps.

Bartlett, Christopher, Doz, Yves and Hedlund, Gunnar (2013) *Managing the Global Firm*, London: Routledge.

Boddewyn, J.J. and Brewer, T.L. (1994) 'International-business political behaviour: new theoretical directions', *The Academy Management Review*, 19(1): 119–143.

Dunning, John and Lundam, S.N. (2008) *Multinational Enterprises and the Global Economy*, 2nd edn, Cheltenham: Edward Elgar.

Germain, Randall (2012) 'Governing global finance and banking', *Review of International Political Economy*, 19(4): 530–535.

Greenwood, Justin (2011) *Interest Representation in the European Union*, Basingstoke: Palgrave Macmillan.

Hamel, Gary (2012) *What Matters Now: How to Win in a World of Relentless Change, Ferocious Competition, and Unstoppable Innovation*, Chicago, IL: Jossey Bass.

Johnson, G., Scholes, K., Whittington, R., Angwin, D. and Regner, P. (2013) *Exploring Strategy Text and Cases*, 10th edn, New York: Pearson.

Kierzkowski, Henryk (1989) *Monopolistic Competition and International Trade*, Oxford: Oxford University Press.

Neilsen, Jeffrey, Pritchard, Bill and Yeung Wai-Chung, Henry (2015) *Global Value Chains and Global Production Networks*, London: Routledge.

Ohmae, K. (1999) *The Borderless World*, London: HarperCollins.

Peters, Tom and Waterman, Robert (2004) [1982] *In Search of Excellence: Lessons from America's Best Companies*, 2nd edn, New York: Profile Business Classic.

Porter, M.E. (1980) *Competitive Strategy*, New York: Free Press.

Porter, M.E. (1987) 'From competitive advantage to corporate strategy', *Harvard Business Review*, May/June, 65(1/2): 43–59.

Porter, M.E. and Kramer, M.R. (2011) 'Creating shared value', *Harvard Business Review*, January/February, 89(1/2): 62–77.

Scherer, F.M. (1970) *Industrial Market Structure and Business Performance*, Chicago, IL: Rand McNally.

Sennett, Richard (2006) *The Culture of the New Capitalism*, New Haven, CT: Yale University Press.

Smith, A. (2003) [1776] *The Wealth of Nations*, New York: Bantam Books.

Stopford, John and Strange, Susan (1991) *Rival States, Rival Firms: Competition for World Market Shares*, Cambridge: Cambridge University Press.

Strange, Susan (1994) *States and Markets*, London: Pinter.

Sutton, John (2001) *Technology and Market Structure: Theory and History*, Boston, MA: MIT Press.

Talalay, Michael, Farrands, Chris and Tooze, Roger (1997) *Technology Culture and Competitiveness*, London: Routledge.

Unoki, Ko (2014) *Mergers, Acquisitions and Global Empires*, London: Routledge.

# 4 Globalisation and IPE

## Chapter learning outcomes

After reading this chapter students should be able to:

- Engage in the main theoretical debates about the nature of globalisation.
- Understand the concept of globalisation as a set of processes of integration and understand the debates between hyperglobalists, transformationalists and sceptics as to whether or not globalisation is actually taking place and to what extent.
- Explain the expansion of the European system since the 1500s and how this relates to the emergence of globalisation.
- Understand the roots of the global financial system.
- Comprehend contemporary processes of globalisation in a number of issue areas including: trade and finance, media, environmental challenges, the rise of MNCs and elements of an emerging globalised culture.

## Introduction

Globalisation has become one of the key terms in describing and analysing life in the contemporary world. Different authors have focused on different parts of the structures and processes that contribute to global trends and phenomena. There is some disagreement in terms of what should be the primary focus of such studies. Moreover, there remain disputes over the significance and implications of so-called global trends. Hirst *et al.* (2009) question many of the underpinnings of basic assumptions about globalisation. In particular, they have queried the extent to which current trends are essentially 'new'. Rather, they ask whether such trends should be seen as an extension of a nascent global economy with historical roots stretching back several centuries. This chapter will consider the manner in which current aspects of globalisation have developed, and continue to evolve, over time. It will also give you a sense of how the theoretical perspectives, outlined in the first section of this book, have addressed the actions and issues associated with globalisation. As such this chapter is the bridge between the earlier theoretical chapters and the following issue-based chapters.

First of all there remain fundamental disagreements and debates surrounding what it is that constitutes globalisation. Differing schools of thought focus on various aspects of international relations. What is focussed on can clearly colour one's analysis and, therefore, conclusions. This applies to all aspects of IR and IPE. The study of globalisation is no exception. Here we highlight how each of the, broadly defined, three main paradigms of realists and neo-realists, liberal pluralists and structuralists/Marxists consider globalisation in terms of how it impacts on national interests. We also go on to outline the response from feminism, green theories and postmodernism.

## Realism/neo-realism

For realists the basic idea of interdependence between states is contradictory to their core beliefs. States are seen as unitary actors in a zero-sum game scenario of absolute gains and losses. That said, processes of globalisation could be acknowledged within this paradigm in terms of the domination and subordination roles of various states relative to each other. Globalisation might have altered the means by which states attempt to maximise their power. For example, there is generally less emphasis on invasion and occupation by military means. More likely in contemporary relationships, power and influence are increased by way of biased trading relationships and, perhaps, socio-cultural factors. This point on the increased role of the economic sector in promoting state power, or weakness, is more closely associated with the neo-realist variant. The neo-realist approach can be seen as highlighting the economic dimension of globalisation, whereas classical realism continues to adhere to the political dimension.

## Liberal pluralism

Liberals, in contrast to realists and neo-realists, do not view the state as the only/predominant unit of analysis. As such this range of views is more in tune with the complex interactions characterised by globalisation. They consider the role of various institutions, IGOs, INGOs and a wealth of civil society groupings. Importantly many liberals highlight the individual as a significant unit of analysis. This is undoubtedly a more complex milieu of actors and processes than the 'simple' state-centric approach. It is important to note that part of this complexity is the dual processes of greater connectedness at some levels (transport, communications and so forth) yet also wildly differing experiences and opportunities at the individual level. Liberal pluralism highlights both political and economic dimensions of globalisation. Political liberalism focuses on issues such as human rights and forms of governance. Economic liberalism is more concerned with economic growth. The 'greater good for the greater number' idea might mean that particular individuals suffer or are marginalised from the benefits of such growth. Currently economic liberalism is at the forefront of the dominant states' 'programme' for the twenty-first century. The political liberalism of the pro-democracy agenda can be seen as part of this programme, but running well behind that of the economic drivers.

## Structuralism/Marxism

This range of approaches is concerned with the historical evolution of structures and processes that determine and reinforce patterns of power, domination and resistance. Unlike the above approaches this paradigm is explicit in highlighting levels of exploitation within various structures. Here globalisation is predominantly seen in negative terms, with an emphasis on working conditions and resource depletion. Yet simultaneously this paradigm also acknowledges that aspects of globalisation, such as improved communication networks, actively aid resistance to the negative effects. In terms of distinguishing between the political and the economic, structuralists/Marxists concentrate on the economic sector as the means by which political power is maintained. Importantly this can be seen at both the domestic and international levels. Political power is discussed at distinct levels with, on the one hand, recognition of the ongoing power of governments. On the other hand, political power is often described in terms of individual and collective action for equality of opportunity, with globalisation seen as an inequitable process.

## Feminism

As with liberal approaches the emphasis within feminism is based at the level of the individual. It could also be argued that there are connections with structuralism in that many feminist writers highlight the position of women in patriarchal structures and societies. Issues of cultural relativism can also be seen as relevant here. Just as the political and economic spheres can be viewed differently by various approaches, equally cultural issues can be highlighted as significant factors when comparing experiences of globalisation. Also the emancipatory dimension of structuralism is evidenced within feminism. In terms of globalisation feminism is relevant with regard to the concept that 'the personal is political'. Feminism, arguably, goes further than liberal approaches in pointing out the role and responsibility of individuals to recognise their own position in relation to others, and to work towards greater equality and opportunities for all. The UN Conference on Women, held in Beijing in 1995, represented an acknowledgement by the international community that women have particular issues to be addressed. The specialised agency UNIFEM promotes women's health and education issues. Processes of globalisation, such as the general shift towards cash-based economies, have been critiqued as disadvantaging certain groups. Women, in particular, may be seen as disadvantaged if they are employed in a low-earning capacity while also maintaining a relationship that is gender stereotyped. This could include taking on paid employment while simultaneously also maintaining household and child-rearing responsibilities.

## Green theory

Green theories are particularly associated with transboundary issues and the need to view the world as a totality rather than artificially fragmented units. There is a huge range of what has been described as 'light' and 'dark' green thought. 'Light' green environmentalists refer to lobbying national governments to reform policies on resource usage and pollution. In contrast, 'dark' green activists call for far more radical measures involving a revolutionary approach to overthrowing capitalism. More extreme elements take exception to the anthropocentric nature of most international relations. They prefer to think in terms of eco-centrism, which does not assume that humans are the centre of the universe. Given that the dominant process of globalisation is the pursuit of a model of development that extols mass consumerism, it is unsurprising the green analysts and activists are concerned about how sustainable such a model is. Pollution and resource degradation, including loss of biodiversity, are side effects of globalisation. There are arguments that it doesn't have to be this way and the promotion of issues such as technology transfer from the developed to the less-developed parts of the world are potential responses to these problems. The Earth Summits of 1992, 2002 and 2012 (see Chapter 9) are evidence that the international community, at the level of national governments, can come together to discuss environmental issues. Yet, to date, there has been scant progress in reversing the more negative trends associated with processes of globalisation. The 2009 Copenhagen climate change summit largely failed because the drive for short-term economic growth continues to be the dominant factor in relations between states. The deep green theorists also place emphasis on individuals to reflect upon and amend their patterns of behaviour in response to environmental problems. This can be seen as a further example of the personal being political.

## Postmodernism

A central concern of postmodernism is the use of language. With regard to globalisation it should already be apparent that there are numerous definitions and explanations as to what is happening at the global level and what the ramifications might be. As with the above approaches it is important to note what aspects of politics, economics or socio-cultural factors are being considered. For post-modernists the state is but one of many possible foci for understanding the contemporary global political economy. Similarly issues of personal identification can be seen as relevant and powerful forces. The actual processes of globalisation, such as the apparent reduction of time and space in trade and other patterns of interaction, are important. While not discounting the ongoing relevance of the nation state system, postmodernists stress the need to challenge dominant worldviews, such as state-centrism. Unlike other approaches discussed here they do not offer an alternative vision. On the contrary they suggest that all views are open to question and, controversially, have equal validity. As argued above, individuals have differing experiences of globalisation. Therefore, it is understandable that there will exist myriad interpretations and views on the relative merits and disadvantages of various aspects of globalisation. In this respect postmodernism can be seen as useful in helping to recognise the variety of experiences, although perhaps less useful as a tool for rigorous analysis.

# The globalisation debate

The above outline of differing approaches to interpretations of processes of globalisation is a useful starting point in understanding how globalisation is differently viewed and interpreted. In many ways this is simply an extension of an ongoing inter-paradigm debate. To take this a stage further we will now consider more specific disagreements over the extent to which globalisation is an essentially new phenomenon and how far-reaching the consequences of it might be. In particular this will address the debate over the existence of an emerging global economy and the promotion of human rights.

'Hyperglobalists' are those that believe we are experiencing an era of unprecedented global connectivity and political, economic and social change on a scale never previously experienced. They are made up of a diverse range of analysts who are either positive or negative in their assessments of this scenario. For the positive camp globalisation represents the promotion of neo-liberal economics and democratic forms of governance. This camp would include authors such as Kenichi Ohmae (1999) and Martin Albrow (1996). They can be associated with the so-called 'trickle-down' effect whereby, in the longer term, all people will benefit from an emphasis on economic growth. They often downplay the role of governments in this process and advocate development via market forces. Negative hyperglobalists, such as Hans-Peter Martin and Harold Schumann (1997), agree that there is unprecedented connectivity, but they highlight the non-sustainable level of resource exploitation, poor working conditions and lack of individual freedoms as economies compete in what these critics see as a 'race to the bottom'.

In contrast to the hyperglobalists there are also a number of globalisation 'sceptics'. These authors, such as Hirst *et al.* (2009), argue that many of the processes associated with globalisation have a long-standing history. They point to the expansion of the imperial and colonial systems and the way in which resources and labour were exploited across the globe. However, they make a distinction between these international connections and a system that is truly global in terms of coordination and governance. It is also noted that the greatest level of integration and cooperation is at the regional level, and usually in the more developed parts of the world, for example the European Union. In terms of trade and the movement of goods and services, the greater percentage of such trade is found within the EU, rather than between the EU and the rest of the world. Similarly, roughly two-thirds of the international transfer of capital and goods happens between the subsidiaries of MNCs rather than by way of engagement with other companies or states. Also, in opposition to the idea that the world is becoming increasingly uniform due to the spread of dominant ideas and values, the sceptics point to areas of resistance and what Samuel

Huntington (2002) has described as a 'clash of civilisations'. Sceptics would argue that despite the rise in rhetoric regarding human rights, the reality is that state power and the demands of market forces continue to have priority over the establishment of a meaningful human rights regime at the global level.

There is also a middle position located between the two outlined above – the transformationalists. They believe that we are in the midst of a period of significant change, experiencing phenomena of a new and unique order. However, they do not take their claims as far as the hyperglobalists. As with the sceptics, the transformationalists do not see these changes as having yet evolved to the point of a global world order. It should be noted that the transformationalists do not suggest any particular form that the process of globalisation is leading towards. Rather, they place their emphasis on the dynamic of change. There clearly are changes taking place in the fields of, for example, information and communication technologies and the types of issues on the international agenda. Transformationalists accept that new relationships and divisions are emerging, both within and between states. This in turn is impacting on the agendas of governments and a range of non-state actors. Manuel Castells' (2013) work on the 'network society' is an example of highlighting these new forms of relationships and the issues that arise from them. Transformationalists tend not to express views as dogmatically as either the hyperglobalists or the sceptics. They adopt more of an observational position, simply stating how institutions and related actors are evolving. For example, with regard to coordinating economic issues, the General Agreement on Tariffs and Trade (GATT) has evolved into the World Trade Organization (WTO). Similarly, concern about

**Table 4.1** Conceptualising globalisation: three tendencies

| | Hyperglobalists | Sceptics | Transformationalists |
|---|---|---|---|
| What's new? | A global age | Trading blocs, weaker geogovernance than earlier periods | Historically unprecedented levels of global interconnectedness |
| Dominant features | Global capitalism, global governance, global civil society | World less interdependent than in 1890s | 'Thick' (intensive and extensive) globalisation |
| Power of national governments | Declining or eroding | Reinforced or enhanced | Reconstituted, restructured |
| Driving forces of globalisation | Capitalism and technology | States and markets | Combined forces of modernity |
| Pattern of stratification | Erosion of old hiearchies | Increased marginalisation of South | New architecture of world order |
| Dominant motif | McDonalds, Madonna, etc. | National interest | Transformation of political community |
| Conceptualisation of globalisation | As a reordering of the framework of human action | As internationalisation and regionalisation | As the reordering of interregional relations and action at a distance |
| Historical trajectory | Global civilisation | Regional blocs/clash of civilisations | Indeterminate: global integration and fragmentation |
| Summary argument | The end of the nation state | Internationalisation depends on state acquiescence and support | Globalisation transforming state power and world politics |

*Source*: adapted from Held and McGrew (2003).

environmental issues has resulted in the Earth Summit process and related conventions. In terms of human rights, transformationalists would note that international human rights campaigning has certainly raised its profile in recent years. Yet at the same time the post-9/11 era can also be viewed as one where individual rights and freedoms have been undermined in the fight against terrorism. In each of these examples change has clearly taken place; what is debatable is whether these changes are positive or negative.

## Origins of globalisation

Jan Art Scholte states that 'globalisation has no origin' (Scholte, 2005). At best we can pinpoint certain events that herald the start of a significant era. For example, the invention of the printing press, the first manned flight or the first photograph of planet Earth taken from space. In their own ways each of these can be seen as symbolic, even iconic, examples whereby the world is somehow 'transformed' for its inhabitants. Not all of these had immediate widespread impacts. The initial print runs of the Gothenburg press were very limited, not only in terms of the numbers of copies produced but also the distance they could be distributed and the number of people able to read them. Similarly the Wright brothers, at the start of the 1900s, represented the infancy of manned flight. From these early pioneers of this technology there quickly developed an industry that had major implications for warfare, trade and more widespread movement of people and ideas. Finally, and perhaps the most literal example of the concept of globalisation, the images of Earth relayed back from Apollo 8 in 1968 gave many people a sense of substance to trends that had been occurring for centuries. These trends could previously have been thought of as occurring in bilateral or multilateral arrangements or in regional terms. The image of the 'blue planet' suspended in space highlighted that this was a finite area with finite resources. Until space programmes are developed to take us to the next stage of exploration, and possibly off-planet settlement, humans are going to have to interact within certain limitations. Patterns of interaction at individual through to state level are still evolving. Processes of globalisation are increasingly a part of humans', and non-human species', interaction. Before looking more closely at specific examples of such interactions in the fields of communication, trade, environmental issues, culture and military issues, it is useful to briefly review the historical roots of each of these areas. Each of these will then be discussed in more depth in the following chapters.

## Expansion of the European system

The development of technological advances in travel, communications, trans-shipment of goods and multi-centred production processes has evolved over several centuries. Non-European civilisations, such as the Chinese, have a history of exploration well beyond their borders, with evidence of Chinese traders venturing as far as Africa by the 1400s. However, it is the experience of European exploration and settlement that can be argued to have had the most profound and long-lasting impacts. Beginning with the explorations of the Portuguese and Spanish and their appropriation of resources (gold and silver from Latin America) followed by the more reciprocal trading relationships of the Dutch and then the imperial competition among other European powers, notably France and Britain, there evolved a pattern of domination and subordination/resistance between Europe and the rest of the world. This has been characterised by patterns of colonial rule, preferential patterns of trade, social and cultural impacts and the establishment of a global economy that has underlying socio–economic and political structures.

World-system theory (WST), as outlined in Chapter 2, places great emphasis on the historical evolution of relations between imperial powers and their colonies. Crucially this approach highlights the ongoing dynamics of these relations that have their roots in the colonial era. Even when formal independence was achieved, for many states in the 1960s and 1970s, a fundamental determinant of their future development has been the manner in which their economies continue to be linked to their former rulers. Dependency theory also looks at relations between the global North and the global South. It should be noted, though, that 'dependency' can be viewed as a two-way process. By this we mean that although the dominant model of dependency would be one whereby the South would be dependent on the North, for development assistance or other forms of support, equally it can be argued that the North is reliant on both raw materials and markets in the South. As such, a complex pattern of relationships can be seen to be involved within the global economic system of trade and related socio–political and cultural influences. That said, there remain identifiable advantages and disadvantages for the various actors and institutions involved. Again WST is relevant here as these are structural determinants. A notable feature of the processes of globalisation being considered here is that structural features, such as the dominance of key political and financial institutions, have led to the embedding of certain powers to the point whereby they dominate the international system. Such a situation has arisen on several occasions over previous centuries as particular powers have gained predominance.

Hegemonic stability theory (HST) is relevant here in terms of explaining the various periods when certain powers, for various reasons, have come to the fore. In relation to European expansion and imperialism it is important to be clear what constitutes a hegemonic power. Although Spain and Portugal were important powers with regard to the amount of wealth they extracted from Latin America and the relative advancement they therefore enjoyed in comparison to other European powers at that time, this is not an example of structural power; it is relational. In contrast the Dutch developed a trading system that involved the acquiescence of trading partners, despite the Dutch gaining relatively more in the course of each transaction. In a sense this might be seen as a quasi-structural relationship. Although their trading partners will have experienced some advantage, it was the Dutch who were the dominant partners controlling shipping routes and, to some extent, market prices. The first truly global hegemonic power did not emerge until the 1700s with the rise of Britain as the predominant naval and trading power. Earlier examples might be cited, such as the Roman or Mongol Empires; however, these were mainly based on continuous territorial expansion of their respective 'known' worlds. Britain went beyond this in that, by control of sea-lanes of trade and communication, they established an extensive network between the major trading ports around the globe. This influence and control was expanded further after the Industrial Revolution with the development of railways into the interiors of various countries. This practical control was reinforced by the active governance of large swathes of territory to the point when, at its height, 'the sun never set on the British Empire'.

After the Second World War there was a significant decline in the power and international influence of the European powers. In some respects this redistribution of power was in line with previous rises and falls of empires. The United States emerged as the dominant power in the post-Second World War era, to some extent balanced by the Soviet Union but having the distinct advantage of sustaining no infrastructural damage on its continental landmass and leading the formulation of the major post-war political and financial institutions. HST is again relevant in explaining the significance of the US role in directing the emerging post-war order. Just as Britain had come to dominate the maritime world, the US not only filled the power vacuum left by Britain's decline, but it also took advantage of emerging trends in global trade and development. These include a greater openness in trading and political relations, as they were no longer as closely tied to former colonial relationships. Some of the newly independent states of the 1960s and 1970s were drawn towards the Soviet-influenced command economic approach with clearly directed government intervention in the market. Many more though were capitalist-driven economies. This was a direction that was actively supported and encouraged by the US. The operations of the leading multinationals of this time, which were predominantly owned and operated by US citizens, reinforced the rise of the US to the position of a global hegemonic state. Simultaneously this was further characterised by developments in the fields of technology, notably the emergence of nuclear weaponry and advances in lines and methods of communications.

The development of nuclear weapons was significant for two main reasons. First, once parity in nuclear capability had been achieved by the Soviet Union, a nuclear stand-off emerged, which meant that direct confrontation was largely avoided for fear of escalation to the nuclear level. Yet ideological competition continued between the two superpowers. Part of this competition involved the active promotion by the US of liberal democratic systems of governance, at least in terms of stated political intent. Second, was the promotion of free market economic policies. This approach dominated not only the direction of the US economy but also that of Western Europe and the majority of the newly independent states. Despite actively disavowing territorial gains from its involvement in the Second World War, the US undoubtedly gained from the way in which the post-war world order evolved. The 'empire' of the US is based on much more than territorial expansion. It is characterised more by extending influence in the fields of economics and, increasingly, culture.

The movement of goods and services in increasingly large amounts, at cheaper costs and greater speed, enhanced the position of the leading powers, enabling them to dominate this sector of the emerging global economy. For example, larger cargo ships with the capacity to 'globalise' the production cycle of many goods and the technology to disperse the production process. The emergence of a global economy is most notably characterised by the shift away from local patterns of production to one increasingly reliant on imported goods and services. An extreme example of this would be to consider the spectrum of economic activities ranging from subsistence, drawing solely on local resources, to those that are completely divorced from the local environment and rely on cash income to buy in all goods and commodities, including foodstuffs. Each individual and community is placed somewhere along this spectrum. A key point to note though is that the dominant trend in current economic practices, and even the dominant discourse of what consti-tutes 'development', appears to be moving towards the cash-based economic model. Later chapters will discuss in more detail the implications of how sustainable such a model of development might be. At this point we wish to focus on the primary architecture and actors that are facilitating and encouraging such a trend. We will also cover additional aspects of globalisation and at the end of each section we will consider how each of these issues is reflected upon by hyperglobalists, sceptics and transformationalists.

## Globalisation of trade and finance

Following the end of the Second World War a major conference was held in San Francisco in 1945 to manage the transition from the League of Nations system to that of the United Nations. A key dimension of the emerging order was the role and influence of the main financial systems designed to monitor and control post-war economic developments. This was the first time that multilateral agreements had emerged that took into account the increased connectivity of trading relations on a global scale. Below are brief descriptions of each of the leading financial institutions.

---

**INFORMATION BOX**

## The International Monetary Fund (IMF)

**Headquarters:** Washington, United States

Aims: The IMF was established to create a multilateral system of payments between nation states based on fixed exchange rates and the full convertibility from one currency to another in order to maintain currency stability and world trade. All members had to peg their exchange rates to the US dollar or gold, while the US pegged the dollar to $35 per ounce of gold. Furthermore, each member would have to pay a subscription charge that would be used to support those states that ran into temporary balance of payments problems. Following the 1971 'floating' of the US dollar and the subsequent collapse of the regime, the IMF was left without its central purpose. It is now one of the main advocates of the 'Washington Consensus', which is a narrow view of the world economic system based on market efficiency and the free flow of capital, goods and services. This is also known as the neo–liberal economic model. IMF assistance to states in crisis is now dependent on reforms aimed at advancing this system.

*Source*: www.imf.org/

---

**INFORMATION BOX**

## The World Bank (WB)

**Headquarters:** Washington, United States

Aims: Following the Second World War, the International Bank for Reconstruction and Development (IBRD), now known as the World Bank, was established to revive the war-torn European economies. This mandate was later extended to all developing states. The Bank raises its funds through borrowing from international markets and by dues from member states. The loans made by the Bank to developing states are given at a lower interest rate than commercial banks and are aimed at supporting the construction of infrastructure projects (roads, power plants, hydroelectricity dams and so on). Similar to the IMF, the WB has also been a staunch supporter of the 'Washington Consensus'.

*Source*: www.worldbank.org/

---

**INFORMATION BOX**

## The World Trade Organization (WTO)

**Headquarters:** Geneva, Switzerland

Aims: The WTO replaced the General Agreement on Tariffs and Trade in 1995. GATT was one of the original Bretton Woods initiatives created to establish rules for the governance and liberalisation of international trade. The main goals were to lower tariff and non-tariff barriers (NTBs) to trade that had crippled the global economy prior to the Second World War. Seven rounds of negotiations, often lasting several years, were carried out to reduce tariffs and NTBs, finishing with the Uruguay Round (1986–1994), which resulted in the creation of the WTO. The WTO includes the core agreements of GATT but solidifies them and expands the capabilities for the enforcement of the agreements through trade sanctions and provides greater avenues for future agreements. While GATT focused on trade in goods, the WTO also includes negotiations for the liberalisation of trade in services through the General Agreement on Trade in Services (GATS). GATS covers areas such as telecommunications, banking and transport. There are also agreements that cover trade-related intellectual property rights (TRIPS) and trade-related investment measures (TRIMS).

*Source:* www.wto.org/

Both the actuality of the process of globalisation of world politics and the study of this process require the occurrence and study of the parallel process of the globalisation of economies. As most scholars in the field of IPE will advocate, politics and economics are inseparable and need to be understood and explained in conjunction with each other. The distribution of power and its application to world affairs (politics) is integral to the distribution, exchange and use of resources (economics) and vice versa. As countless discussions have shown, contemporary international politics have become increasingly global in their nature. At the same time advancements in technology, communications and transport as well as the often sporadic process of industrialisation have resulted in a globalisation of the production process and, by extension, trade. It is now possible to produce a product almost anywhere in the world, using resources originating from anywhere and for sale in any market, which at each stage of the process requires trade. The globalisation of trade has largely been a 'natural' phenomenon due to advancements in the human condition dating back to the nineteenth century. However, since the end of the Second World War and increasingly since the 1970s this process has been consciously facilitated by a number of states and international and global institutions, which have as their agenda the globalisation of both trade and finance.

Advocates of globalisation describe contemporary globalisation of trade and finance as a stage in the long-term development of a global society. In this view the globalisation of trade and finance are not merely a more intensified version of the processes of internationalisation and regionalisation but rather the breaking of official (state) controls on the movements of goods, people and services. This 'liberalisation' of the international political economy allows for the replacement of 'international' trade, finance and production with 'global' trade, finance and production. This emergent globalised economy characterised by global trade and financial processes will (as advocates argue) lead to a more prosperous, developed, democratic and peaceful world for all. In this view (often termed neo-liberalism) the occurrence of economic depression, authoritarian regimes and intra- and inter-state conflict in the twentieth century is attributed to the disruption of the process of the globalisation of trade and finance by tightening border controls in the first half of the last century.

During the latter half of the twentieth century trade liberalisation and globalisation increased markedly. Through the General Agreement on Tariffs and Trade (GATT) a number of inter-state accords were reached that led to major reductions in customs duties, quotas and other non-tariff barriers that had previously restricted cross-border trade. In the more prosperous states, for example, the average tariffs on manufactured products fell from over 30 per cent in the 1930s to less than 4 per cent at the turn of the century. This was largely facilitated by GATT. From 1986 to 1994 the Uruguay Round of international trade negotiations were held with the aim of progressively advancing globalisation of trade. The result of these negotiations was the establishment of the World Trade Organization (WTO) as a replacement for GATT. The WTO was established to be a more homogeneous institution with greater ability to enforce existing agreements and to pursue at greater pace further trade liberalisation.

From the 1950s onwards, national borders have also opened considerably to money flows. This was facilitated by the adoption of a 'gold–dollar standard' exchange mechanism that emerged and was enforced by the International Monetary Fund (IMF) in 1959. Under this international exchange regime the major currencies such as the United States dollar could circulate the globe freely and be converted into local currencies at an established and fixed exchange rate. Following the unilateral decision by the United States government in 1971, a 'floating' exchange rate regime emerged in 1973 and was formally inaugurated by the IMF in 1976. Furthermore, increasing regional integration throughout the world led to the bilateral and multilateral reductions in the import and export of national currencies. Combined, these developments led to unprecedented levels of foreign exchange, which by 2000 had reached over $1 trillion.

*Hyperglobalists* point to the creation of the above institutions, especially the WTO, as evidence of a concerted attempt to coordinate, integrate and govern global processes at the economic level.

*Sceptics* acknowledge that there is increased interaction between economies, but deny that this represents an undermining of the basic autonomy of national governments. Some states may indeed be advantaged or disadvantaged under this system. Yet the system itself remains one of individual states interacting, rather than a form of global governance.

*Transformationalists* focus more on the dynamic of change and the opportunities this creates for some, although others may be actively disadvantaged by such changes.

## Corporate globalisation

Globalisation is about more than moving towards a generally common mode of production. The ownership and control of economic activity has increasingly moved away from government control and has also become more centralised in the hands of a relatively small group of parent companies coordinating various multinational corporations. The implications of this are that global trends are becoming ever more uniform. It is important to note, however, that this does not necessarily lead to uniformity of experience for various individuals and communities around the world. Far from it, as the emphasis on cash-based economies has led to a wide diversity of income generation and amount of disposable income available to individuals. The rise of multinationals is indeed characterised by a spread of branded products, albeit with some regional variations in how they are marketed. Yet this global profile does not mean that all of these products are equally available to all consumers.

Corporate globalisation is the spread of big business across the world. As big business grows, it gets more powerful, often meaning that other actors in the international arena, such as national governments and people, witness varying degrees of loss in sovereignty and autonomy. There are five main identifiable trends in corporate globalisation, each of a controversial nature:

1   The first is that the private market place is becoming dominated by large multinational corporations (MNCs).
2   A second trend is the accumulation of wealth within a small number of economic actors, both public and private.
3   Third, the divide between the rich and poor, which can refer to individuals, states or companies, is growing both within and between states.

4    Fourth, the divisions of labour and multi-centred production are also contributing to growing differences of experiences and opportunities.
5    Finally, the political, social and cultural influences of the corporate sector are increasing in line with their economic influences.

The rise of the MNC is not a recent phenomenon. The spread of imperial rule referred to above coincided with the growth in private investment in international trade. Famous examples of this include the Dutch East India Trading Company and the Hudson Bay Trading Company. The operations of such companies had the dual effect of disrupting existing local economies and reinforcing the emerging dominant position of the 'core' states. MNCs outperform smaller companies and locally owned and operated family businesses. For example, high-street coffee stores around the globe are continually replaced by chain stores such as Starbucks. This is a result of the greater efficiency and profitability of the larger firms. Patterns of wealth accumulation also include take-overs and mergers between MNCs. A result of this has been the ever-greater concentration of wealth under the control of a decreasing number of larger and larger firms (see Table 4.2). This accumulation of wealth and prestige can also be identified at the level of the state. Neo-realists argue that MNCs can be viewed as 'agents of the state', thereby acting as conduits for enhancing the power bases of MNCs' home states. However, it is important to recognise that, with the exception of arch realists, most analysts acknowledge that the state is not a unitary actor. Therefore, although the overall power and prestige of some states may be enhanced by processes of globalisation, there can also be many divisions emerging both within and between states.

These divisions are significantly driven by the spread of capitalism. Indications of this are clearly evident; of the more than 6 billion people in the world, approximately 2.8 billion live on less than $1.20 a day. Over 60 states had lower per capita income in 2004 than they did in 1990. Furthermore, the 475 richest individuals have a combined wealth that is greater than the poorest half of people in the world. As will be discussed in more depth in subsequent chapters, there are contentious arguments with regard to the ideology of capitalism. Whereas some, such as World Bank economists, consider free market economic policies to be the solution to poverty, others hold diametrically opposed views. For anti-capitalists the problem lies in the lack of accounting of social and environmental costs in 'free' market economics. They point to environmental pollution, non-sustainable resource usage and poor working conditions as evidence that capitalism is fundamentally exploitative and, therefore, flawed. While acknowledging that processes of globalisation, including the spread of free market economics, have created more connectedness between economies and societies, this does not necessarily mean that all are sharing in a common experience of these processes. Far from it, as processes such as multi-centred production practices are increasingly creating distance between the production and consumption of goods and services. Compare, for example, a locally-orientated subsistence-based economy with that based on the export of manufactured or assembled goods. In a mass consumer society labour costs are driven down by the contracting out of certain aspects of the production process to labour markets with low unit costs. This has a knock-on effect in terms of relative purchasing power. In the field of computers and related technology the consumer is benefiting from both better products and cheaper prices over time. In contrast, the workers producing such goods, although arguably benefiting from the expansion of this sector, are often not in a position to be able to afford the goods they produce.

*Hyperglobalists* see the operations of MNCs as further proof of the extension of a global economy. Their emphasis is on the global networks that have arisen with multi-centred production processes.

*Sceptics* recognise the operations of MNCs but view them more in terms of state power and the reinforcement of a system based on national economies.

*Transformationalists* focus more on the relationship between MNCs and the state. This can include both the positive aspects of MNCs as agents of a particular state, and also where states

**Table 4.2** Top twenty-five MNCs by rank based on composite scores for sales, profits, assets and market value

| Rank | Company | Country | Industry | Sales ($bn) | Profits ($bn) | Assets ($bn) | Market value ($bn) |
|---|---|---|---|---|---|---|---|
| 1 | Industrial and Commercial Bank of China | China | Banking | 148.7 | 42.7 | 3,124.9 | 215.6 |
| 2 | China Construction Bank | China | Banking | 121.3 | 34.2 | 2,449.5 | 174.4 |
| 3 | Agricultural Bank of China | China | Banking | 136.4 | 27 | 2,405.4 | 141.1 |
| 4 | JPMorgan Chase | United States | Banking | 105.7 | 17.3 | 2,435.3 | 229.7 |
| 5 | Berkshire Hathaway | United States | Financial services | 178.8 | 19.5 | 493.4 | 309.1 |
| 6 | Exxon Mobil | United States | Oil and gas | 394 | 32.6 | 346.8 | 422.3 |
| 7 | General Electric | United States | Conglomerates | 143.3 | 14.8 | 656.6 | 259.6 |
| 8 | Wells Fargo | United States | Banking | 88.7 | 21.9 | 1,543 | 261.4 |
| 9 | Bank of China | China | Banking | 105.1 | 25.5 | 2,291.8 | 124.2 |
| 10 | PetroChina | China | Oil and gas | 328.5 | 21.1 | 386.9 | 202 |
| 11 | Royal Dutch Shell | Netherlands | Oil and gas | 451.4 | 16.4 | 357.5 | 234.1 |
| 12 | Toyota Motor | Japan | Automobiles | 255.6 | 18.8 | 385.5 | 193.5 |
| 13 | Bank of America | United States | Banking | 101.5 | 11.4 | 2,113.8 | 183.3 |
| 14 | HSBC Holdings | United Kingdom | Banking | 79.6 | 16.3 | 2,671.3 | 192.6 |
| 15 | Apple | United States | Consumer durables | 173.8 | 37 | 225.2 | 483.1 |
| 16 | Citigroup | United States | Banking | 94.1 | 13.4 | 1,883.4 | 145.1 |
| 17 | British Petroleum | United Kingdom | Oil and gas | 379.2 | 23.6 | 305.7 | 148.8 |
| 18 | Chevron | United States | Oil and gas | 211.8 | 21.4 | 253.8 | 227.2 |
| 19 | Volkswagen Group | Germany | Automobiles | 261.5 | 12 | 446.9 | 119 |
| 20 | Wal-Mart Stores | United States | Retailing | 476.5 | 16 | 204.8 | 247.9 |
| 21 | Gazprom | Russia | Oil and gas | 164.6 | 39 | 397.2 | 88.8 |
| 22 | Samsung Electronics | South Korea | Consumer durables | 208.9 | 27.2 | 202.8 | 186.5 |
| 23 | AT&T | United States | Telecommunications services | 128.8 | 18.2 | 277.8 | 182.7 |
| 24 | BNP Paribas | France | Banking | 123.2 | 6.4 | 2,480.5 | 98.6 |
| 25 | Total | France | Oil and gas | 227.9 | 11.2 | 239.1 | 149.8 |

*Source*: De Carlo, S. (ed.) (2013) 'The World's Biggest Companies: The Global 2000', *Forbes*, 17 April 2013.

(mainly but not exclusively in the developing world) are in an inferior power relationship with the MNCs they interact with.

## Global culture?

For the greater part of human history separate cultures have existed in a state of relative isolation from the influence and impact of others, with the exception of intermittent trading. The processes of political, economic and social globalisation have brought cultures into closer contact. Technological and communicative advancements and expanding interaction between cultures have highlighted the problems and possibilities different cultures face with regard to maintaining traditional patterns of culture and social order. Furthermore, cultural interaction and homogenisation no longer requires the direct physical contact of different people. Through channels such as television and the Internet, cultures can interact and blend. As relations between separate cultures have developed further through activities such as trade, migration and even conflict, the level of isolation and individuality of cultures has slowly decreased. In this sense there are relatively few contemporary cultures that are wholly unique. Despite some distinctive features most cultures now share a degree of commonality. By this we mean cultures are open to increasingly common phenomena, such as the free flow of capital and information via the Internet. However, such phenomena may be experienced differently and 'filtered' through local norms and values.

The intense interaction between the different cultures around the globe has not evolved evenly in scope and range of effects. The dominance of what is labelled 'Western' or occasionally simply 'American' culture has been the source of much controversy since the 1970s. The key practices, features and ideologies of Western/American culture can be found in practically all regions of the globe and most if not all cultures. 'Fast-food' chains such as McDonald's and Kentucky Fried Chicken and the related Coca-Cola franchise are good examples of the American and, in general, Western impact on the rest of the world. In addition to influencing dietary habits, and patterns of health, American influences have also been noted in more fundamental aspects of culture. An example would be the promotion of individualism as the focus of a society, where previously the broader community would be the focus. Although this shift to the individual might promote greater equality at the political level it can also promote greater rates of mass consumption and inequality at the economic level.

However, it is questionable whether we can talk of a world of over 6 billion people becoming a monoculture. It is true that the process of globalisation is resulting in increasingly close contact between cultures and rising, albeit asymmetrical, influence of some cultures on others. Nevertheless, as mentioned above, cultures are rarely insulated from outside influence and globalisation does not necessarily result in the loss of traditions and values. New forms of media such as the Internet have in fact proven a powerful means of strengthening the customs, norms and values of traditional culture. For example, many diasporic groups have actively reinforced their sense of cultural heritage by way of developing interactive websites. In the 'liberal' conception of global cultural homogenisation the constant quest of capitalism to produce and sell necessitates a level of multiculturalism. In this way, cultural integration and homogenisation does not necessarily imply the loss of many traditional values, practices and ideas, rather a synthesis of these at one level of culture while preserving others at another level.

Alternative interpretations regarding the impacts of globalisation on culture do exist. As well as the homogenising impacts of globalisation on all cultures also comes the development of reactionary forces. The largely 'Western'-dominated macro-culture that is seen as being spread by the asymmetrical dominance of American and European cultural influence has resulted in large levels of resistance in less-dominant cultures. The West has widely been discredited for its irresponsible individualism, lack of moral responsibility and capitalist ideology that has been perceived as exploitative and unequal as opposed to emancipatory. Harvard Professor Samuel Huntington, in his article and later his book with the same title, *The Clash of Civilizations* (2002), presented a more negative outlook of the results of cultural interaction in the globalising era than the 'liberal' idea. Huntington argues that the interaction at the highest level of culture, that is the civilisation, will determine world affairs in the post-Cold War world. This interaction is likely to be characterised by resistance and confrontation rather than homogenisation and cooperation.

**AUTHOR BOX**

## Samuel P. Huntington

*The Clash of Civilizations* is Huntington's seminal work on the future prospects for world affairs. In this article that was later developed into a book Huntington offers a new paradigm that focuses on patterns of international conflict and cooperation. He argues that civilisations (the highest point of cultures) will shape these patterns in the decades to come rather than nation states or private actors. Huntington suggests that there are eight identifiable civilisations that will determine world politics. These are Western, Confucian, Japanese, Islamic, Hindu, Slavic-Orthodox, Latin American and African.

While for Huntington the history of the international system has fundamentally been about the conflict and cooperation between monarchs, nations, states and ideologies within Western civilisation, the end of the Cold War has altered this. In the post-Cold War era non-Western actors are now important 'agents' within the international system. Furthermore, there are four main processes at work in the international system that is facilitating this clash of civilisations. These are: first, the decline of the West in relation to other regions; second, the rise of the Asian economy, with China potentially going to become the greatest power in global affairs; third, the resurgence of Islam due to increasing Muslim populations and the end of imperial domination; fourth, the impact of globalisation on flows of commerce, information and people and subsequent impacts on cultural identity.

The emergence of 'resistance' to global cultural integration or 'dominance' in an ever-smaller world plays a major role in ushering in this era of a clash of civilisations.

Regardless of one's position in relation to the clash of civilisations debate it is undeniable that culture is an important factor within all societies. Processes of globalisation can be seen to have aspects of both challenging and, on occasion, reinforcing cultural identity.

*Hyperglobalists* generally concur with the view that there is an emerging global culture.

*Sceptics*, such as Huntington with his clash of civilisations thesis, argue that no such global culture is emerging.

*Transformationalists* focus on the dynamic of change. They acknowledge the forces driving a nascent global culture, but also highlight the forces of resistance.

## Media

One of the main conduits for both the presentation and, possibly, promotion of globalisation is the wide array of media channels. Marshall McLuhan (2013) famously said that the 'medium is the message'. McLuhan is also credited with coining the phrase 'global village' and his work focused on both how the world appeared to be 'shrinking' and the methods employed that gave this impression. For McLuhan the term media was expansive, including not only print and broadcast journalism, but also wider cultural phenomena such as films and television programmes. The rise to prominence of the Internet takes McLuhan's ideas to another level. Part of the medium of the Internet is whether you are even connected. This has become known as the 'digital divide'. It is not simply what information is being presented but also how it is being received, if at all. We can identify a historical progression of media that can be traced back to significant developments, such as Caxton's printing press from the fifteenth century through radio transmissions, long-distance undersea cabling and on to satellite-based communication. As each type of media has developed, so too have the issues that surround them. Issues of editorial control, accessibility, interpretation, ability to act as a result of information received are all relevant to a discussion of the media. In terms of globalisation, the relationship between the local and the global is becoming more complex. This also applies to the manner in which this relationship is reported.

The numbers of people that can be reached by different forms of media has grown exponentially over time. The early printing presses were not the first examples of the promotion of texts. The library of Alexandria, for example, or the illustrated religious scripts of the early Christian era clearly pre-date the invention of the printing press. But the advent of print technology began the process of moving towards greater circulation of texts. Of course, the level of literacy had also to rise before mass consumption of printed texts could take place. Here there is a link to cultural issues, especially with regard to the expansion of empires. Both the British and the French have placed great emphasis on the promotion of their own languages in their former and current overseas territories. As such there is a clear link between the level of technology being used and the political agenda that underscores its usage. In the context of power relations the example of imperial control and resistance is pertinent here and relevant to many contemporary situations. The manner in which different types of media are utilised is illustrative of this point. Imperial powers would communicate to their subjects via mainstream media, such as newspapers and later broadcasting. Resistance movements might use similar techniques, but on a smaller and usually more localised scale. By definition, imperial powers had a form of global reach and global interests. In contrast, pro-independence movements have a more localised focus, and more restricted resources to draw upon. A typical example would be the circulation of *The Times* or *Le Monde* compared with pamphlets produced by local political activists. Here it is not so much the numbers of people being reached as much as the content that is being provided.

Increasingly there is a division among various types of media where some might be described as 'corporate' and others as more 'independent'. By corporate we are thinking of businesses such as Fox News and other arms of Rupert Murdoch's media 'empire'. An example of a more independent form of media would be Indymedia (www.indymedia.org), which presents itself as an 'alternative' news source, often highlighting anti-globalisation actions. In terms of relative power the corporate examples have greater access to financial resources, often raised by way of advertising. They are also in a privileged position in terms of access to politicians and the corporate business community. Furthermore, they are seen by many in the mainstream audience to be a trustworthy source of information. In contrast, the smaller more independent providers of 'news' tend to have far more limited financial resources to call upon. Although the growing Internet usage provides Indymedia and similar sites with a potentially vast audience, they have to be proactively accessed by their audience. The same might be said of needing to buy a mainstream newspaper or to tune into a mainstream radio or television broadcast. However, the latter is far more part of the cultural background that surrounds people. Increasingly the mainstream media are extending their reach by means of embracing new technologies; they now exist in print, broadcast and electronic formats. The implications of this are that the underlying political agendas of the corporate media are being promoted, perhaps implicitly rather than explicitly. As with the spread of cultural norms and values cited above, corporate media plays a significant role in delivering such images and views. Simultaneously the spread of independent websites, down to the level of the individual site developer, can be seen to be presenting a wide range of alternative views. Despite such developments there remains a structural bias that favours and reinforces the role of the mainstream providers of news and commentaries.

In addition to the news media it is important to also consider the role and impact of the entertainment industry. As above, there is a sense of division between what can broadly be described as the mainstream corporate industry, especially in relation to the Hollywood studio 'system', and that of more independently minded (and financed) film-makers. In addition to the world of cinema, the same can be said of the music industry with major and independent record labels. Although there will be cultural differences in various parts of the world, it is possible to identify an underlying power dynamic involving a corporate core of mainstream entertainment media and a generally sub-servient periphery of more marginal independent producers and consumers. Just as the news media is important in presenting a particular view of the world, albeit challenged by some counter-views, the entertainment industry can have an impact in terms of influencing audience beliefs and atti-tudes. This is clearly related to issues of culture but focused upon here due to the manner in which these cultural products are presented, distributed and accessed. As with the Indymedia example above, the role of technology in allowing greater accessibility to these products is telling. The phe-nomenon of file-sharing on the Internet has allowed an ever greater platform for the presentation of such products. This includes raising the profile and accessibility of film-makers and musicians who remain outside their respective corporate mainstream. There is also an issue of the illegal file-sharing of products that bypasses the traditional routes of access, and therefore also bypasses the generation of some of the revenue for the larger players. There is an ongoing debate surrounding the morality and business implications of such practices, inside as well as outside these industries. With regard to globalisation, file-sharing is a truly global phenomenon, it bypasses national and regional distribu-tion agreements. It also changes the previously existing dynamic between the core mainstream of these industries and their peripheral or marginalised components. As such, in line with McLuhan's argument, both the media and the mediums of communication are evolving, and important.

The position and role of various media are closely interrelated to processes of globalisation. This is in terms of both actively promoting aspects of globalisation, highlighting some of the crit-icisms of these processes, and more generally informing, or perhaps misinforming, debates about globalisation.

*Hyperglobalists* see forms of media as the conduit for dispersing the norms and values of the dominant powers, thereby continually reinforcing their position of dominance.

*Sceptics* present a counter-argument whereby the processes of globalisation actually stimulate an oppositional dynamic that can provide a greater sense of local identity.

*Transformationalists* recognise the role of media sources in presenting images and views of the wider world, but that this is more likely to result in evolving forms of cultural hybridity.

## Global environmental degradation

The aim of this section is to highlight the core environmental issues that have emerged and wors-ened since the 1970s and that are of a 'global' nature (as in affecting multiple states and regions) and the 'global' responses to such issues. The main issues included here are as follows: greenhouse gases due to increased industrialisation and fossil fuel consumption and associated global warming; rising sea levels due to global warming; resource degradation including forests, water and fish-stocks. Fossil fuel consumption is a twin problem with both depletion of stocks and also increased pollution due to their usage.

A key factor regarding environmental issues is that the liberalisation of international trade and investment risks worsening the impacts of human activity on the environment. Critics point to many channels through which globalisation may adversely affect the environment. First, with the increasing levels of, and greater opportunities for global trade there is the potential for further exploitation and use of oil and other non-renewable resources. The result of these is a rise in levels of land, air and sea pollution, deforestation, soil erosion, floods and other ecological imbalances. Second, more trade often means goods and people travel a longer distance and in greater numbers, resulting in even more consumption of fuel resources and subsequent emissions of pollutant gases. While on the one hand global networks of trade and consumption increase choice in the marketplace, for those that can afford to buy these goods, it also creates a false impression of the true cost of many of these goods. With the exception of the niche market of Fairtrade products, the dynamic of the free market rarely passes on social and environmental costs to the consumer. One of the dominant trends of globalisation continues to be the spread of mass consumerism around the world. Unless this is checked, or technological improvements allow for more environmentally friendly patterns of growth, this is a scenario that is likely to be increasingly divisive and create increased conflict between individuals and states.

Attention towards environmental issues began to emerge in the 1970s and by the turn of the millennium environmental problems had become a focus of international concern. Understanding the causes, impacts and possible responses to global environmental problems has become increasingly urgent. Since the early 1970s an awareness of the number and severity of environmental problems has emerged. Some scientists dispute the more pessimistic predictions for resource depletion. Yet the majority agree that not only is this depletion occurring but also that the more negative impacts on the environment are as a direct result of human activity. As such it should, therefore, be possible for humans to correct their behaviour and activities to improve this situation. The difficulties in achieving this are twofold. First, we continue to operate in an international system driven by individual national governments. Although some progress has been made in terms of binding conventions and treaties, these are currently insufficient to address the serious nature of most of these problems. Second, a lot of environmental problems are a result of lifestyle options and choices at the level of the individual. It is difficult to legislate against such behaviour, especially when the two main strands of the dominant development process are market growth and personal freedoms. For example, indicators for development tend towards levels of economic growth and a population's ability to consume.

Advocates of globalisation highlight other tendencies fostered by the processes of globalisation. They would argue that increased trade liberalisation allows for the spread of more environmentally friendly technologies and practices. Integration with the global economy should lead to increased wealth and industrial development, allowing for the more efficient use of resources and the means to regulate and combat negative impacts on the environment. This position is correct, in theory, but in practice the mass consumer society tends towards greater divisions of wealth, opportunity and environmental conservation. There are some examples of altruistic redistribution of wealth; however, the general tendency is for 'developing' societies to become more focused on self-interested individualism and materialism. This can still include technological advances to enable greater efficiency of use of resources, but these are usually relative savings in the context of a net increase in resource use. For example, fuel efficiency of the internal combustion engine has advanced over time, yet these savings have been more than overtaken by the rapid increase in the number of cars. Therefore, the key determinant here is not so much the level of technology but rather the way in which this is applied. Similarly, awareness of environmental issues needs to be distinguished from practical action to address relevant policies and individual behaviour.

The nature of many approaches looking at environmental issues often describe them in global terms. Concepts such as global warming and the description of certain resources such as forests or oceans as 'global commons' build up a holistic picture of the issues to be addressed. While there is some validity in this perception it is also the case that these issues are generally moderated through the ongoing system of national governments. As such there is a fundamental conflict between short-term national interests and longer-term global interests. This problem is also exacerbated by the previously mentioned drive towards individualism and mass consumerism. Under such circumstances there continues to be a significant divide between the growing awareness of environmental issues and the desire to actively confront these, at both the level of the individual and the state. See Chapter 9 for a more detailed discussion of environmental issues and the impact of integration at the global level.

*Hyperglobalists* can envisage environmental issues in both a positive and negative light. Negatively they consider resource degradation on a global scale, highlighting issues such as global warming, climate change, over-fishing and excessive deforestation. More positively they also draw attention to the Earth Summit process and the ability of nation states to come together in a global forum to agree, or at least debate, global environmental concerns. The dominant model of development is relevant here with multi-centred processes of production and manufacture feeding into the ever-expanding spread of mass consumerism.

*Sceptics* cast doubt on the very existence of some environmental issues, such as global warming. They also doubt the ability of essentially selfish states embracing a global environmental agenda at the expense of their individual national interests. In terms of concerns about mass consumerism the sceptics are less concerned about this as they would allow for the 'technical fix' argument to offset the worst aspects of resource depletion.

*Transformationalists* acknowledge that environmental issues are now part of the international diplomatic agenda. However, they see this as only the beginning of a process that has much further to develop before national interests are subsumed by a truly global agenda. Moreover, the transformationalists are less committed to a determined outcome. One outcome could be that societies and economies continue to 'develop' in a non-sustainable manner with resulting resource exhaustion and conflict over dwindling supplies. On the other hand, growing awareness, national legislation and international cooperation could lead to a more sustainable future.

## Multi-globalisation

In looking at processes of globalisation it is apparent that there are a variety of approaches and explanations as to the extent and likely consequences of these processes. Moreover, it is possible to discuss globalisation at many different levels, to the point that apparently competing viewpoints are more accurately seen as describing differing phenomena. For example, the above sections have placed emphasis on political, economic, socio-cultural and environmental issues and agendas. Each of these has also been impacted upon by technological developments.

At the political level many national governments are experiencing difficulties in maintaining autonomy, or sovereignty, over their policies. Rather, although they maintain the right to adopt whatever policies they choose to within their own territories, many are increasingly restricted in their policy options due to external factors. Hyperglobalists would point to this as an example of how all states are becoming interconnected. However, as sceptics would point out, this is not the same as saying a truly global community of states is emerging, as some states are more profoundly impacted upon by these interconnections than others. Also at the political level is the role and influence of civil society. Just as national government experiences should be differentiated from each other, this is even more the case at the level of the individual. With a global population now in excess of 6 billion there are myriad personal experiences of the processes of globalisation. For the individual the political sphere encompasses issues such as national citizenship. Yet it is also much more. Beyond identifying with a particular state, individuals think of themselves in terms of family affiliations, sexual orientation, ethnicity, religion or simply personal tastes and interests. Processes of globalisation can have a bearing and impact on each of these categories of identification. This then leads to a further complexity in the shaping of individual and collective responses to these processes.

One of the key components of globalisation is the relationship between the political and economic spheres. Even those who are sceptical of the degree of global interconnectedness would accept that this is a key relationship in international relations. Although explicit political agendas can be identified, such as the promotion of human rights, these tend to be subsumed within the dominant ethos of the promotion of economic growth. Furthermore, the drive towards economic growth also has both domestic and international political consequences in terms of the securing and exploitation of resources, some of which may be located in territories under another political jurisdiction. This can lead to either policies of cooperation or of conflict. Again hyperglobalists would highlight the level of symmetry in bringing together economic systems and institutions to facilitate international trade and consumption. A more sceptical view may well acknowledge that such structures are in place, but that they continue to be dominated by certain powerful states and related interest groups. Similarly, some MNCs now have annual turnovers well in excess of the gross domestic product of some national governments. Despite this indisputable fact there remains a debate around the extent to which this represents a true separation of the political and economic spheres. Neo-realists, for example, would dispute the extent to which MNCs are autonomous actors, preferring to describe them as 'agents of the state'. It would be more accurate to view MNCs as being part of a public/private spectrum along which some states and MNCs are in a more privileged position than other states and MNCs. At any given time, each of these international/global actors will be either more or less advantaged or disadvantaged along this spectrum. Put another way, some are closer to the core of the international trading system while others are more peripheral or marginalised from the potential benefits of this system. This analysis can also be applied at the level of the individual. Disparities of opportunities and achievements exist at all levels of community, be it sub-national, national or international/global. Globalisation is, understandably, normally perceived and articulated on a grand scale. However, at both the political and economic levels the opportunities and restrictions of this are experienced at the individual level.

As discussed above, there is a sense that globalisation is leading to a more common political, economic and cultural environment. This view is controversial with active resistance to this process taking place. There is even an argument that it is the very processes of globalisation that are reawakening aspects of cultural identity at a more localised level. This has led to some hybridisation of local cultures and external influences. In part this is a result of the mixing of cultural influences due to the increasing exchange of both goods and services. Processes such as urban drift are also playing a part in the mixing of various influences. The spread of communication technologies and related media sources have also enabled a greater mix of ideas, interests and activities. Therefore, although the concept of cultural imperialism or cultural homogeneity can be challenged, there are identifiable influences that ensure cultures are dynamically evolving. It is, of course, a value judgement to say whether they are developing for better or worse. Even allowing for an element of impartial objectivity there is a strong position to be taken with regard to the equity and sustainability of any given system.

## Summary

This chapter has outlined the three main theoretical positions with regard to the existence and extent of processes of globalisation. It has also highlighted the manner in which different theoretical approaches emphasise particular actors and issues, thereby arriving at differing conclusions about the impact of globalisation. Attention was drawn to certain issues that illustrate both the positive and negative aspects of globalisation. These issues will now be explored in further detail in the following chapters of this book. It is recommended that as you read these chapters you consider how the various schools of thought outlined in the first section of this book would interpret and analyse these issue areas.

**Table 4.3**  Chapter summary

| | Key actors | Key processes | Emphasis on political economy | What causes change? | Global institutions? | View of conflict in global relations? |
|---|---|---|---|---|---|---|
| Hyper-globalisation | MNCs | Capitalist production, exchange and consumption; cultural homogenisation; technological revolutions (especially in travel and communication); the spread of media (especially social media) | Central driving force is the expansion and embedding of capitalism | Capitalism | A largely political response to the global processes of market integration; but also an element of the continued rapid pace of globalisation | Perhaps can be seen as a result of the intense and rapid integration taking place; ultimately will not prevent globalisation from continuing apace |
| Globalisation as a slow transformation | MNCs | Capitalist production, exchange and consumption; increased travel, migration, and trade | Long historical process of interaction and integration largely driven by economic activity (especially trade) and political interactions (especially war and diplomacy) | Capitalism (but in different ways to the understanding of hyper-globalists) | A largely political response to the global processes of market integration; certainly facilitates closer cooperation and interaction between different states, peoples, markets and so on, but limited by national interests and sovereignty | Long a feature of international relations at a more local or regional level, made possible at the global level due to developments in technology and warfare; not necessarily caused by globalisation, and does not imply anything significant for its future |

# Reflective questions

1 What arguments are used to support or deny the existence and/or extent of processes of globalisation by hyperglobalists, transformationalists and sceptics?
2 What factors led to the spread of the European/US system and its influence around the world from the 1700s?
3 How are various divisions within the global political economy exemplified in terms of who gets what, when, where and how?
4 Explain the origins and evolution of the contemporary global financial system.
5 What roles do MNCs play in facilitating and promoting processes of globalisation?
6 In what ways are issues of environmental sustainability being addressed at the global level?
7 What evidence suggests that a single global monoculture is emerging? And how does resistance to cultural homogenisation manifest itself?

# Suggestions for further reading

Albrow, M. (1996) *The Global Age: State and Society Beyond Modernity*, Cambridge: Polity Press.
Castells, M. (2013) *Communication Power*, Oxford: Oxford University Press.
Coleman, L.M. and Tucker, K. (eds) (2015) *Situating Global Resistance: Between Discipline and Dissent*, London: Routledge.
De Carlo, S. (ed.) (2013) 'The world's biggest companies: The Global 2000', *Forbes*, 17 April.
Hassoun, N. (2014) *Globalization and Global Justice: Shrinking Distance, Expanding Obligations*, Cambridge: Cambridge University Press.
Held, D. and McGrew, A. (eds) (2003) *The Global Transformations Reader: An Introduction to the Globalization Debate*, 2nd edn, Cambridge: Polity Press.
Hirst, P., Thompson, G. and Bromley, S. (2009) *Globalization in Question: The International Economy and the Possibilities of Governance*, 3rd edn, Cambridge: Polity Press.
Huntington, S.P. (2002) *The Clash of Civilizations: And the Remaking of World Order*, Reading: Cox & Wyman.
Kacowizcz, A.M. (2013) *Globalization and the Distribution of Wealth: The Latin American Experience, 1982–2008*, Cambridge: Cambridge University Press.
Lechner, F.J. and Boli, J. (eds) (2015) *The Globalization Reader*, 5th edn, Chichester: John Wiley & Sons.
McLuhan, M. (2013) *Understanding Media*, 2nd edn, Berkeley, CA: Ginko Press.
Martin, H.P. and Schumann, H. (1997) *The Global Trap: Globalization and the Assault on Democracy and Prosperity*, London: Zed Books.
Ohmae, K. (1999) *The Borderless World: Power and Strategy in the Interlinked Economy*, 2nd edn, New York: Harper Paperbacks.
Roberts, J.T., Hite, A.B. and Chorev, N. (eds) (2015) *The Globalization and Development Reader: Perspectives on Development and Global Change*, 2nd edn, Chichester: John Wiley & Sons.
Scholte, J.A. (2005) *Globalization: A Critical Introduction*, 2nd edn, Basingstoke: Palgrave.
Steger, M. and James, P. (eds) (2015) *Globalization: The Career of a Concept*, London: Routledge.
Stiglitz, J. (2007) *Making Globalization Work: The Next Steps to Global Justice*, London: Penguin Books.
Thrift, N., Tickell, A., Woolgar, S. and Rupp, W.H. (eds) (2014) *Globalization in Practice*, Oxford: Oxford University Press.

# 5 National, international, regional and global governance

## Chapter learning outcomes

After reading this chapter students should be able to:

- Understand the concept of governance and be able to differentiate it from coordination and management.
- Explain how governance differs/remains consistent at the national, international, regional and global levels.
- Engage with theoretical debates that discuss the nature of globalisation and its impact on international, regional and global governance and how both state and non-state actors are involved.
- Understand and explain how processes of international cooperation have intensified over the past century and how this intensification is leading to forms of governance.
- Understand a range of contemporary issues in international relations and the global political economy which require some form of governance, including: security, health, travel and transportation, trade, communications and finances.

## Introduction

This chapter considers how far the governance of processes of globalisation is being managed at a national, international or global level. Hirst and Thompson (2009 – also discussed in Chapter 4) contend that despite an increasing number of issues having a global dimension, they continue to be responded to at the governmental level, and by ad hoc collectives of states rather than by an overarching global governing authority. While the popular belief of some conspiracy theorists might be that the UN fulfils the role of a global government, the number of UN resolutions that are ignored or actively broken contradicts this view. Important UN agencies contribute to global governance, but do not 'do' global government. Certain aspects of the work of the UN, notably its specialised agencies, have a very important role. However, this is not a *supranational* organisation. It does not have coercive power. Rather, it is a voluntary collective of states that all retain their sovereign autonomy. It works by consensus (although, as we shall see later in the chapter, consensus can also be powerful). This raises questions about the fundamental definition and workings of international and/or global governance. Is 'governance' simply the coordination of national policies, or does there have to be a greater sense of the rule of law and, crucially, of its enforcement? Does this create a different kind of authority in international relations? Or does it reinforce and develop existing patterns of domination – global hegemony?

# The nature of governance

The answer to these important questions might well be 'neither'. Governance is first of all the coordination of national policies. But in order to make this policy coordination work, quite a lot of authority may need to be transferred to a global level. Some aspects of that authority may be changed in the process, some not. This is especially the case where technical decisions require technical knowledge. And other actors, non-state actors, might well have important roles even if the lead role is formally held by states and state-run international bodies. It is also the case that governments very often do much less than appears at first because their actions at national level are shaped by consultation with a range of trade associations, firms, NGOs and advisory bodies, which, while they do not carry formal authority, have both knowledge and the capacity to act effectively without which government cannot function. Rather crudely, we might use the word 'government' for those areas of international economic activity where there is a united structure of authority and where decisions have a relatively direct impact on implementation. We might then use the word 'governance' for those kinds of coordinated inter-institutional management of policy where there is no single authoritative body able at the same time to make and to implement policy (see Table 5.1). To think that power and authority in complex international situations is only held by states may often be confusing. Even if states hold the formal role, they are not able to manage the responsibilities that the role brings without working with both other states and other actors. This is especially the case in three situations: in markets, in highly technical areas of policy management and in areas where complex networks have evolved to coordinate policy responses. To repeat, even if (and this is not always the case) states have the formal legal authority, and so retain formal sovereignty, they may well have conceded both authority and effective action to others. Governance is thus about complex multi-

**Table 5.1**  Global governance vs global government

| Government | Governance |
|---|---|
| Direct control | Indirect control |
| Direct authority to act (usually rooted in constitutional arrangements) | Authority achieved through consensus and often risks evaporation at crucial moments |
| Although some governments may be coalitions, most governments do not require the remaking of the coalition to initiate policy | Rooted in a coalition of different types of actors (which may include governments, private agencies, firms, international organisations, NGOs and regulatory bodies) |
| Not all governments are centralised – e.g. federal systems – but governments generally have a measure of central control over policy implementation as well as policy making | Decentralised and dependent on cooperation of a range of actors for implementation as well as decision-making – and sometimes on different coalitions for implementation and for policy making |
| Ideally described in a hierarchical structure | Although it may have elements of hierarchy – some actors are more senior or powerful than others – the essence of governance is a relatively 'flat' structure of power and authority |
| Power in this structure rests on constitutional position | Power in governance rests on technical expertise and ability to deliver at least as much on formal position |

*Note*: This table represents both as 'ideal types' for purpose of explanation – there are plenty of variations on the main themes.

lateral policy management; it is not primarily about law or formal sovereignty, although of course it may have a bearing on both. Confusingly, some commentators and some politicians may use the word interchangeably with 'government'; but it is much more clearly understood as distinct from government, and that is generally the way it is used in academic discourse including across the IPE literature.

Governance at the domestic level can be reduced to the fundamentals of law making and enforcement along with domestic and foreign policy making and implementation. In political economy, much of this activity will be some form of regulation. Yet within these fundamentals there can be myriad differing examples between states, especially when one considers the relationship between the individual citizen and the ruling regime. Some regimes are far more authoritarian than others. To transpose this to the global level, such differentiation is, by definition, not possible as we are referring to something that is supposed to be universal in character and action. Therefore, governance at the global level would need to include aspects of law making and enforcement plus policy making and implementation. The 'domestic' level would become redundant, and 'foreign' would presumably refer to any off-planet relations that might occur at some point in the future. That said, there remain difficulties in extrapolating concepts such as citizenship, rights and duties to the global level. These are not universally agreed ideas and practices across various states. As such they will not easily transfer to a system of global governance. This issue is, therefore, perhaps best understood in terms of a range of possibilities with regard to levels of governance, some of which are more straightforward to implement than others. As a tool of analysis and explanation, the framework adopted in Chapter 4 that refers to hyperglobalists, transformationalists and sceptics can also be utilised here. These positions will be considered in relation to political, economic and socio-cultural aspects of governance.

One important debate here is concerned with the extent to which issues in international political economy are actually subject to some form of governance, and whether this governance is international, regional or global in scope. We can identify a great many issues such as trade, conflict, environmental change, democratisation and integration in various forms. Most of the issues that we can identify can also be seen to be managed to some extent at the international level. Around the globe many conferences, for example, take place with state and non-state actors being represented, organisations and regimes are established with a particular agenda and so on. However, it is more difficult to identify when issues are governed at the international level. For example, climate change issues such as rising sea levels and the impacts on coastlines are often addressed by the international community but are these activities about reacting to, managing or governing these issues? Furthermore, who is involved in these processes and who is not? To take another example, global financial governance failed in the financial crisis of 2007–2009; the story of which organisations have been involved and how and why they have failed is an important and complex one that illustrates much of this debate – but it will not be discussed further here since it is discussed at some length in Chapter 7.

Hyperglobalists would argue that the processes driving globalisation are resulting in radical changes in the nature of how issues are dealt with at the international level. There is, in this perception, a change over time in international relations, which means that as modernity progresses, the way issues such as trade are dealt with evolves. Initially states would seek bilateral and then multilateral mechanisms to manage and govern the relations between them. But as the complexities of a global system emerge, so too does the need for greater cooperation. The result is a change from bilateral to multilateral to international and then global management. Further integration and cooperation leads to governance at the international or global levels.

The counter-argument, however, is that very little has changed since the end of the Second World War and that in fact states and non-state actors respond to international issues by managing them at the regional level at most. Advocates of this view claim that any attempts at global management are ultimately unsuccessful. Furthermore, there is little credence given to the concept that international governance takes place.

Yet others argue that not only is management taking place at the international level but a level of governance also takes place between states at the regional level as well. The EU, as mentioned above, is the prime example of this level of governance but not the only one. This camp does not, however, perceive there to be any real measure of governance at the global level.

A separate important theoretical debate is between those who broadly see the growth of global governance as an extension of liberal activism and plural management of the international system and those who see it as the extension of some form of hegemonic or imperial power. This question has dominated much of the discussion of global governance in IPE since the early 1990s. The debate includes, in the first camp, those who are inclined to welcome globalisation but who do not see it as an unqualified benefit (such as Thomas Freidman, 2007). It also includes liberal theorists who have welcomed the extension of global governance so long as it meets conditions of transparency and accessibility (such as Barnett and Finnemore, 2005). The second critical group of writers includes Gramscian scholars such as Mark Rupert (2000) and James Mittelman (2005) (this question was discussed in more detail earlier in Chapter 3).

How does international governance (regional, global or whatever) arise? One answer would be to look at the theory of the state itself. Over the past 200 years, the modern state has evolved in response to a series of pressures on it for territorial and military security, but also for economic security. In the mid–nineteenth century, an increasing number of states started to provide technical education and basic standards of education mainly to respond to economic needs, but also to try to promote social stability in the face of rapid and socially fragmenting growth during the Industrial Revolution. An enlargement of state education was followed by the beginnings of welfare systems such as pensions and basic healthcare. After 1918 this was extended in many countries to housing and to state support for other welfare systems, including state aid for higher education. By the 1950s, most states had extensive welfare agendas, and although the US federal government was only spending around 18 per cent of GNP, most European states and many elsewhere were spending in the region of 40–50 per cent of GNP. Some of this was on defence, but much of it was to meet welfare demands of different kinds, including full employment and high levels of education, training and healthcare. This produced a crisis of the state in the 1970s, a crisis of expectations where governments were facing much greater demands than they could match and looked for ways to respond. One part of the response was a neo–liberalism that proclaimed the need to reduce the role and power of the state in the economy and in social life. But although this argument produced a great deal of noise and conflict, the percentage of state involvement in GDP hardly fell, and in some cases (notably Mrs Thatcher's Britain) it actually rose. In practice, one key strategy adopted by many states was to internationalise the problems and demands they faced. Developed countries created a series of institutions (such as the G7) or adapted others (such as the European Community) to address complex demands from society and economic actors. It was the state that demanded an expansion of international governance. As Alan Milward (2000) has suggested in the case of the EU, we might even see international organisations as being the saviours of nation state institutions. What Anthony King (1997) called the 'crisis of overload' on the state in the 1970s was managed partly by depressing expectations, and partly by political manoeuvres in domestic politics, but it was also managed by the creation of international institutions that offered governance-based solutions to failures of government. In some cases these organisations actually took on the role of the state more and more, and in other cases they provided smokescreens or scapegoats for the state authorities to pass blame to. It is fair to say that the most important such body, the European Union, has in turn taken all three roles.

# International cooperation

One of the earliest examples of international cooperation and a form of governance was the creation of the International Telecommunications Union (ITU) in 1885. In the previous few years European states had been developing their telegraphic capabilities and were entering into numerous bilateral arrangements with neighbouring states. As the telecommunications sector expanded, the number of such agreements was becoming unmanageable and, in a 'form follows function' response, an international body was created to oversee this sector. Twenty European states agreed a framework convention to facilitate and govern the process of trans-border communication. Common rules were agreed to standardise equipment, adopt uniform operating instructions and create international tariffs and accounting rules. This feature of commonality is something that will be returned to in several parts of this chapter. It is important to make a distinction between commonality with regard to overarching principles and processes and the actual 'content' or practices adopted by the actors who are party to such agreements. For example, the ITU would embed its position as a governing body as more states join or more television or radio stations are granted broadcasting licences. However, although this reinforces the role and position of the ITU this does not necessarily lead to greater homogeneity of content. The reverse is more likely as the increased mass of programming creates a growing diversity of broadcasts. Conventional thinking might equate growing coordination with a subsequent reduction in diversity. As referred to in the previous chapter, hyperglobalists equate coordination at the global level with concepts such as cultural imperialism and less heterogeneity. Globalisation sceptics, of course, would highlight ongoing, or even exacerbated, differences.

Similarly, at the political level the history of emerging structures of governance has been both incremental and contentious. A certain trajectory can be traced from the creation of the League of Nations (LoN) (1919) to the United Nations (UN) (1945) and to the first truly supranational body, the European Union (EU) (1957: Treaty of Rome). The LoN had a particular historical context being formed in the immediate aftermath of the First World War. Its explicit aim was to foster greater understanding and cooperation between member states as a form of conflict avoidance. It had more of a managerial remit rather than explicit governance of member states. The UN took this approach to another level after the Second World War. This organisation had a much broader membership, which further expanded following the political independence of former colonies. It also expanded its remit, as characterised by its specialised agencies such as the World Health Organization (WHO), UN Educational, Scientific and Cultural Organization (UNESCO) and the Bretton Woods institutions. Despite this expanded role and capacity the UN's style is also more managerial rather than governing. In political terms the only international body with a truly governing role and capacity is the EU. All member states of the EU are subject to the rules and regulations that they agree to upon accession to this body. Although this remains a voluntary system a key principle of membership is that the sovereign rule of national governments is superseded by the rule of the *governing* bodies of the EU.

The structure of the EU comprises the European Commission, the Council of the European Union, the European Council, the European Court of Justice, the European Central Bank and the European Parliament. The decision-making process of the EU is a combination of achieving consensus between member states and supranationalism where decisions may be imposed on dissenting members. The latter point is also very significant in relation to the concept of sovereignty. Although membership of the EU is voluntary, no state that has joined has ever left and in fact the EU has continued to expand its membership. As such we can conclude that while occasionally individual states may not always achieve all of their objectives, they do, on balance, gain more from membership than they lose.

The above example of the EU is the exception rather than the rule in terms of international governance. While the UN is widely recognised as the forum for dealing with global issues it remains a collective of individual nation states. State-centric interests, even rivalries, continue to inform the debates and processes of managing global issues. States can be seen as agents of change. In addition, the relative power capabilities of the various member states continue to be of relevance. The ability of states to react to and influence the global agenda differs greatly. Non-state actors in the private and voluntary sectors are increasingly involved and influential in discussions on and actions related to issues arising from processes of globalisation.

# Actors

Some approaches to the study of IR and IPE continue to be predominantly state-centric (as discussed in Chapter 2). This section will consider the different power capabilities and roles of individual states before moving on to examine non-state actors.

Power can be based on material resources, military capabilities, financial resources, technology, diplomatic expertise and the historical accumulation of these power-related factors. For example, the expansion of the British Empire was based on and driven by certain technological advantages in the realms of maritime superiority and a leading role in the applications of the Industrial Revolution. Similarly, the United States was able to rise to hegemonic status during the twentieth century via a combination of military might, a favourable economic environment and as a result of the relative decline of European powers. Some other states are in a far less powerful position. This may be because they lack the quantity of material resources, military capabilities, financial wealth and are simply too small to compete at the global level. Other states may have some of the above resources in significant quantities but lack the political control to maximise the benefits of these resources. Former colonies in Africa, for example, may be in this last category, being resource-rich but disadvantaged in the current global economic system. Some connections can be made between the relative poverty and disempowerment of some parts of the world and the relative wealth and empowerment of the dominant powers.

Relative power capabilities are relevant to both bilateral relations and also within the context of intergovernmental organisations. Those states that possess greater power capabilities tend to be in a better position to influence outcomes in terms of reactions to and policies towards issues at the global level. On the other hand, states with limited power capabilities tend not to have a great influence.

In order to most effectively promote individual state interests many states will act in concert with others to achieve shared goals. This has the advantage of pooling resources and creating a larger power base from which to negotiate. The motivations behind such actions can vary. For

**Table 5.2**  Actors in the global system

| Actor type | Total number (2015 approximates) |
| --- | --- |
| States | 200 |
| MNCs | 60,000+ |
| Single-state NGOs | 10,000 |
| International NGOs | 25,000 |
| Intergovernmental organisations | 5,000 |

*Sources*: Collated from *Forbes*, OECD, Union of International Associations and UN data.

example, the creation of the EU can be viewed in relation to both the geographic proximity of the member states and also as a reaction to previous conflicts between some of its original members. In contrast, the Alliance of Small Island States (AOSIS) is drawn from several geographic regions but the members, many of which are micro-states, have identified a shared interest in highlighting the problems of, and lobbying for solutions to, issues such as sea levels rising.

---

**EXAMPLE BOX**

## The League of Arab States

Consisting of twenty-two member states, the League of Arab States (often referred to as the Arab League) offers an example of an intergovernmental organisation whose envisioned purpose is much like that of the European Union. Created in 1945 and headquartered in Cairo, Egypt, the League originally consisted of six member states – the independent Arab states at that time: Egypt, Iraq, Jordan, Lebanon, Saudi Arabia and Syria, with Yemen joining later on in that year to become the seventh member. Following independence and accession negotiations a further fourteen states joined through the 1950s, 1960s and 1970s (these are: Algeria, Bahrain, Djibouti, Kuwait, Libya, Mauritania, Morocco, Oman, Palestine, Qatar, Somalia, Sudan, Tunisia and the United Arab Emirates; Comoros was the last state to join in 1993).

The League was established in order to coordinate the international relations of its member states in terms of relations between them and relations between the Arab world and the broader international community. Furthermore, following many years of political and economic domination by external powers the Arab world sought to ensure its sovereignty and independence by encouraging greater integration and cooperation between member states. The League was thus also established in order to offer some form of governance at the regional level while respecting the sovereignty of each member state. There are administrative zones within the League and member states vote on policy, laws and regulations with resolutions often being agreed upon. However, the ability of the League to implement the decisions that are made and enforce the laws and regulations that are agreed upon is limited in practice. For example, in 1997 eighteen of the member states agreed to establish an integrated, single market, which would have no barriers to trade such as taxes on exports/imports, tariffs, quotas or non-tariff barriers. This single market is called the Greater Arab Free Trade Area (GAFTA) and came into effect on 1 January 2005. However, while member states agreed to this project, barriers to trade still remain and some signatories have been slow to meet their requirements in terms of fully liberalising their trade system. The department within the League of Arab States that governs economic issues is the Arab Economic Council. This council has little real power in enforcing the agreement when states such as Egypt do not comply.

In this way, the League can be seen to seek to govern international relations within the Arab world but in practice governance is limited and coordination and management are terms that better describe the functions of the organisation. As noted above, there is also a difference between international and global governance/management. The Arab League, while dissimilar to the EU in terms of its capacities (the EU, as discussed above, being much more of a supranational authority), is similar in that it only operates at the international level and not the global level. It only seeks to govern/manage its twenty-two member states and not a broader global community of states.

A different example of how states promote their interest by working cooperatively is the Organization of Petroleum Exporting Countries (OPEC) where the member states are geographically dispersed but have a common interest in a primary export commodity.

## OPEC

In theory the Organization of Petroleum Exporting Countries (OPEC) acts as an inter-governmental organisation, which governs the oil sector activities of the twelve member states: Algeria, Angola, Ecuador, Iran, Iraq, Kuwait, Libya, Nigeria, Qatar, Saudi Arabia, United Arab Emirates and Venezuela. Here, the member states agree to submit to the governance of OPEC in order to control the levels of oil production, refining and export. The organisation was established in 1961 to regulate the global oil market and influence oil prices. In practice, though, the problems of international governance are evident and OPEC does not successfully govern either the activities of its member states very effectively or the global oil market. In the first instance, member states often exceed the production, refining and export quotas they are set by OPEC in a self-interested pursuit of greater export earnings for themselves in the short term. In the latter case, the global oil market is now relatively saturated with suppliers and OPEC only accounts for approximately a third of global production. Its capacity to govern the global oil market is, therefore, heavily restricted as cutbacks in OPEC production and exports can relatively easily be picked up by other exporters. Recent fluctuations in prices of both crude oil and refined oil on the global market demonstrate this point. Through 2014 prices declined rapidly from an average of between $90 and $120 since 2011 to less than $60 in early 2015. This decline in prices resulted from increased oil production in some states, led by increased production in the USA from oil shale, and lower-than-expected demand in major developed and developing states – in EU members, China and India in particular. OPEC members meeting in late 2014 to decide how to respond (which traditionally came in the form of lowering production to reduce global supply thus raising the cost of oil per barrel) agreed to not act. Some would conclude that OPEC realise that it simply could not influence global prices anymore, while others may argue that OPEC members decided to maintain production levels to maintain their market share and to reduce profits available for investment in future production by rival producers (like the USA post-oil shale revolution). Furthermore, by only having twelve member states OPEC certainly cannot be seen to either govern or even simply coordinate state behaviour at the global level. It is, instead, an international organisation that attempts to govern one aspect of a small number of states' behaviour.

States also work together to promote their economic objectives. Interestingly, while many states compete economically with each other, there is also a high level of monitoring and coordination in the economic sphere. In the post-Second World War order a central pillar of the UN structure was the Bretton Woods Trio of the International Monetary Fund (IMF), the International Bank for Reconstruction and Development – later renamed the World Bank (WB) – and the General Agreement on Tariffs and Trade – later renamed the World Trade Organization (WTO). (See the information boxes on these institutions in Chapter 4.) These institutions act as key elements in the global economic system. The IMF is responsible for ensuring relative stability within global financial markets and domestic economies by providing financial resources via loans and grants to national governments. These payments are conditional in terms of expectations that these national economies will be run along prescribed lines. In order to receive support from the IMF national governments have to adopt policies such as encouraging foreign direct investment (FDI), cutting back on domestic expenditures, privatising national companies and opening up markets. In effect these conditions are aimed at homogenising the global economic system by encouraging universal acceptance of free market liberal economic policies.

In addition to the above global institutions a similar ideological model of liberalism can be identified within various regions around the globe. The EU, the North American Free Trade Area (NAFTA), the Association of South East Asian Nations (ASEAN) and the Asia-Pacific Economic Council (APEC) all adhere to this model. On occasion economic and other disputes occur between member states of each of these organisations. Each organisation has a procedural mechanism in place for dispute resolution. So too does the WTO, which is a significant development in governance compared to the GATT system, which did not include such a mechanism.

All of the above examples are intergovernmental organisations. Civil society actors have the opportunity to discuss economic issues with state representatives when they meet as part of the World Economic Forum (WEF). This forum, established in 1971, brings together politicians and civil society lobbyists to debate important global economic issues and their consequences. This is not a formal mechanism of governance in the same manner as intergovernmental organisations like the WTO, but it is an important forum for generating dialogue and policy recommendations. It must be noted that one of the characteristics of globalisation is the increasing role of non-state actors in engaging and influencing state policy decisions.

Socio-cultural issues are relevant in both the domestic and international arenas. Identity formation, partially in response to aspects of globalisation, is now far more complex than a simple reading of national identity. Multiple identities can exist in an individual simultaneously. These can involve elements of race, class, gender, religion and a whole range of issues and situations that individuals can either identify themselves with or be identified by others. Classical realism does not focus at the level of the individual or collective at the sub-state level. With the emergence of a range of global socio-cultural issues that impact on individuals regardless of their state of origin, the personal experience is rarely if ever shared across a nationality. There are a number of organisations at governmental and non-governmental levels that try to address these issues.

UNESCO is a specialised agency within the UN that deals with issues of socio-cultural relevance. It has an explicit global remit, although its work is often mediated through national governments. The primary mission of this organisation is to promote cooperation and collaboration towards shared understanding of concepts of justice, freedom and human rights. This manifests itself predominantly in the fields of education, science and culture. For example, there is a specific 'Education For All' programme, which aimed to provide basic education for all children and adults by the year 2015. Key stakeholders include national governments, multinational corporations and a range of civil society groups. Public/private projects are increasingly common as national governments and intergovernmental organisations attempt to fund such ambitious endeavours. Similar examples can be found in relation to health.

The World Health Organization (WHO) is a specialised agency of the UN. As such it is an intergovernmental organisation, but in fulfilling its mission it works closely with a range of non-governmental actors. For example, in addressing issues such as HIV/AIDS, heart disease, diabetes, malaria and a range of potential and actual pandemics various stakeholders coordinate their efforts. The Alliance for Health Policy and Systems Research has more than 300 partner institutions from around the world. This brings together medical researchers and practitioners with relevant policy-makers and other interested partners. Although having some country-specific projects, this alliance has an explicit global remit. In relation to tackling malaria a holistic approach is adopted, looking at both preventative and curative measures. This involves local environmental conditions, which may be a factor in the prevalence and control of malarial vectors. The private sector includes key actors such as pharmaceutical companies. The role of private companies can be controversial as they are primarily driven by the pursuit of profit. As such it may be more profitable for such companies to invest in research to create products like effective slimming medication or hair loss treatments. There is a profitable market for such products in the more developed states. Whereas there are concerns with regard to the growing levels of obesity, diabetes and other lifestyle-related disorders, in terms of rates of mortality greater numbers of people die from malaria. Therefore, it is arguable that the private sector should prioritise its research and development activities towards the types of illness and diseases that are responsible for the highest rates of mortality.

The relationship between various public and private stakeholders is interesting and complex. Government agencies increasingly look to public–private partnerships to achieve their objectives. Private companies are beginning to use phrases such as 'corporate social responsibility' but remain accountable to their shareholders who have a reasonable expectation of a profitable return on their investment. Although sometimes presented as having diverging priorities, governments and MNCs can also be seen as having compatible interests. In the field of healthcare, pharmaceutical companies are understandably driven by the profit motive. In comparison, governments are often seen as having an altruistic duty of care responsibility towards their citizens. While this is not a wholly inaccurate view, there is also an argument that governments are equally 'profit-driven,' albeit in a different manner. Citizens are a form of social capital. High rates of illness and mortality are both a drain on national health services, necessarily drawing money away from other potential government expenditure, as well as reducing workforce capacity. Some non-governmental organisations (NGOs) take a much more critical view of the role and impact of the private sector.

One of the leading networks for addressing social/cultural and environmental issues at the non-governmental level is the annual World Social Forum (WSF). Beginning in 2001, this event brings together a wide range of civil society activists who campaign for social and environmental justice. Although explicitly non-governmental in terms of its membership the WSF does receive some funding from national and local governments to support the annual meetings, which take place in different parts of the world (Brazil 2001, 2002, 2003; India, 2004; Brazil, 2005; simultaneously in Mali, Venezuela and Pakistan, 2006; Kenya, 2007; Brazil, 2009 and 2010; Senegal, 2011; Brazil, 2012; Tunisia, 2013; Morocco, 2014; Tunisia, 2015). In 2008 the event was not focused on a particular location but related events were held throughout the world with the common theme of the Global Call for Action. WSF is centrally supported by a permanent head office in Brazil and an International Council that consists of representatives of 129 organisations. This council includes six commissions with responsibilities for the areas of methodology, content and themes, expansion, strategies, resources and communication. While not strictly representing governance in the same manner as that of national governments and intergovernmental organisations, this does represent a high level of coordination and consensus building. The issue of communications is particularly relevant as the emergence of the Internet has vastly increased the ability of diverse civil society groups to offer mutual support and coordinate their campaigns. This theme has become central to the latest WSF events that have taken place with considerations for consolidating democratic movements (in the Middle East, for example), deepen debates about the crisis of the liberal model and new geopolitical issues, and to promote alternatives to ensuring peace, social justice and human rights. These considerations influenced the WSF's decision to hold the 2015 event in Tunisia.

The impact of media and information technologies is not, of course, simply restricted to civil society. National governments are sometimes described as losing elements of sovereignty and autonomous control as a result of such technologies. For example, rapid communication both within and across borders between citizens, possibly reporting on events such as heavy-handed policing of political demonstrations, is very difficult for national governments to monitor and censor. On the other hand, national governments are also able to utilise such technologies to actively enhance and embed political control. This may be via closed circuit television systems, the monitoring of personal communications and financial transactions. Access to digital information can therefore be seen as a blessing and a curse depending on who is using it and how.

In terms of governance, the power of such technologies has been recognised by states, MNCs and NGOs, leading to the World Summit on the Information Society (WSIS), which was held over two phases, first, in Geneva, Switzerland, in 2003 and, second, in Tunis, Tunisia, in 2005. This was a multi-stakeholder forum, which included national governments, MNCs, IGOs, NGOs and specialised agencies. Following the meeting in Tunis participants agreed to create the Internet Governance Forum (IGF). This is an ongoing body that continues to promote the discussion of public policy issues related to the Internet. There is active engagement from the information technology private sector and NGOs concerned with developments in the use and potential misuse of these technologies. One particularly significant aspect of communication technologies is various forms of print, broadcast and digitally available media. These forms of media are major factors, possibly determinants, in the formation of worldviews.

The reporting of various civil and military conflicts, the representation of minority groups, environmental issues and many other phenomena can actively influence individual and societal opinions and actions/reactions. Controversial issues such as the Palestinian–Israeli conflict, the extent or even existence of global warming, the wearing of the *hijab* and civil partnerships are all issues that can arouse strong and conflicting opinions. Given that most people will not have personal experience of many of these issues, the influence attached to their reportage can be a crucial factor in how they are understood. There has been an evolution and proliferation in the forms of media. For example, a century ago a citizen in London would be heavily, if not solely, reliant on information provided by the *London Times*. Subsequently other print-based media emerged, followed by radio and then television. At each stage the speed and immediacy of reporting was taken to another level. The development of the Internet has taken the field of communication to an unprecedented level. In addition to existing media outlets the Internet has disseminated the ability of very small groups or even individuals to compete in the presentation of 'news'.

Until relatively recently the main institutions of news reporting have been concentrated into a relatively small sector. For example, notable press barons such as the late Robert Maxwell and Rupert Murdoch have tended to dominate the sector via their ownership of a vast range of publications and broadcasting companies. The Internet has allowed groups such as Indymedia, or the Independent Media Centre (IMC) to present alternative information. IMC describes itself as 'a network of collectively run media outlets for the creation of radical, accurate, and passionate tellings of the truth.' They gather information directly from local activists, rather than relying on the major press release agencies. This may be seen as an attempt to 'democratise' the news. The immediacy and relative lack of control over these news sources have radically transformed the news landscape and how information is presented. Of course, the greater supply of information may actually create greater confusion rather than clarity. It also raises questions about the political control of information.

Indymedia's web servers are based at numerous locations around the world, each one therefore coming under the political jurisdiction of a particular government. There have been several occasions where national governments have attempted to disrupt Indymedia's operations. In 2004 the US government seized the web servers, followed by a similar incident in the UK in 2005. Around twenty Indymedia websites were disrupted during this period. Subsequently equipment was returned and there were no criminal charges as a result of these actions. This suggests that while national governments are unable to legally prevent these sites from operating they can adopt policies of inconvenience and disruption. This disruption represents a form of governance, albeit a rather negative one. National governments sometimes appear to be trying to interfere with 'alternative' news services. Although it would be too much to claim that mainstream media sources are extensions of government they certainly seem able to operate more freely than groups such as Indymedia.

Having considered a range of actors relevant to aspects of governance we now move on to examine a range of issues that have a governance dimension to them.

# Issues

In classical realist terms security is thought of as pertaining to the protection of national borders and sovereignty. It does not tend to consider the level of the individual other than as a human resource to promote the interests of the state. Processes of globalisation have challenged this concept of sovereignty and individuals' perceptions of their own security are not necessarily indivisible from that of the nation state. Critical security studies have a much broader definition of both security and insecurity. This applies at the levels of individual governments, IGOs, the business sector and a wide range of NGOs.

At the individual state level the more developed states tend to have a high level of domestic political control. Their main security concerns are economic and the protection of access to foreign resources such as oil. There will be a very different set of national security priorities in states where there is less political stability and governments have much shorter-term goals. Collective security arrangements can be identified in previous centuries. However, these tended to have the dual purpose of protecting from external threats and to increase cooperation within the collective. In contemporary international relations military security still remains a very important issue for national governments.

The advent of nuclear weapons and the (practically universally recognised) risk of mutual assured destruction (MAD) have served to solidify military security and its management as key problems. The vast majority of state actors do not seek nuclear weapons capabilities but a number of states do possess such weapons. Due to the destructive nature of nuclear weapons both states that possess them and those that do not have an interest in coordinating policies at the global level to try to ensure they are not used. The Treaty on the Non-Proliferation of Nuclear Weapons (NPT) is a UN-negotiated treaty that manages the development and use of nuclear technology. Membership in the treaty is voluntary but only a small number of states have not signed it. The NPT acts as a policy guide to when and how national governments may employ nuclear technology for peaceful purposes and offers safeguards on this activity. While the NPT is a good example of how national governments have sought to govern nuclear technology on the global scale it has not been entirely successful. Some states, such as India and Pakistan, have not signed the treaty and have developed nuclear weapons capabilities that are not subject to any form of international governance.

The management of the global Internet captures the complexity and technical difficulty of governance. Although the United States has a great deal of power over the Internet, no one part of the US political economy controls it − different actors worldwide play important roles in its regulation and management, and in its growth and innovation (see Table 5.3).

**Table 5.3**  Stakeholders in the governance of the global Internet

| Actors/stakeholders | Process | Power/capability | Scope |
|---|---|---|---|
| The US government, including military and government regulators | Technical legal consultative participation still provides the core hardware on which the Net sits | Monitoring surveillance innovation core rules | Very important but not in control |
| National governments other than the US | Technical legal consultative participation | Variable commitment and capability for censorship | Some significant players – e.g. China – but none in control |
| Internet Service Providers (ISPs) | Businesses that use innovative systems to manage the Net/web | Have crude power to switch off, but difficult to differentiate between different users | In day-to-day control – but do not own the system or the material that goes on it |
| Innovating individuals firms copyright holders | Technical consultative participation legal – copyright, etc. | Copyright protection on political will to prosecute | Primarily dealt with in national jurisdictions |
| UN bodies (WIPO etc.) | Consultative participation. Some limited technical capability | No independent legislative power, but influential in TRIPs discussions | Low-level monitoring – have sought a greater role without success |
| World Trade Organization | Important but strictly limited power – not primary regulator | Formal dispute mechanism | So far limited – some actors would like its power increased over Net. Sub-national |
| Sub-national actors (including regulators, courts and prosecutors) | Regional or local courts have played significant roles in regulation – but often overturned at federal/national level | Limited as they defer to federal/national level | Sub-national |
| E-commerce actors (e.g. Amazon, Bloomingdales, etc.) | Few formal powers | Limited independent power, but these actors represent the actual phenomena of e-commerce | Have acquired great informal power through commercial and copyright/brand control and through advertising spending |
| Financial markets – equities and debt | Funding e-commerce and technical innovation | Finance market instability has power to upset or slow innovation and growth | Global with some key regional and national centres |
| Pornography businesses | Much informal capability – part of e-commerce (see above) but the biggest and most innovative part until recently | Well-funded and embedded in virtually all networked communities | Declining but still important innovators and actors despite their bad reputation |
| 'Netizens' – Net users and lobby groups representing them | Includes Net citizen action groups, illegal downloaders, small innovators, bloggers, etc. – a very large but uncoordinated constituency | Potential to hack into systems for political and non-political reasons | Attempts to democratise the Net/web have largely failed – user groups have some power esp. through 'open source' innovation rather than by direct democracy |

The security agenda of the twenty-first century is qualitatively different in that threats may not come from another state but from non-state sources ranging from global warming to terrorist groups like Al-Qaeda. State-centric governance is increasingly pursued through cooperative action rather than wholly individual national policy making. The concept of security has therefore evolved to require governments to consider a much broader range of issues, as considered below, as part of their security policy-making process.

The issue of health necessarily has an individual dimension. National health services vary tremendously from welfare states' provisions to no provision at all. The so-called health transition, or the shift from predominantly communicable to non-communicable or lifestyle-related illness, has broad implications. Globally there have been some successes in reducing infant mortality rates but this has been accompanied by longer life expectancies and a growing incidence of ill health. The prevalence of non-communicable illnesses in modern societies can be explained by processes such as urban drift and the move away from traditional subsistence agriculture. Dietary habits are moving towards more processed foods, which are high in fat, sugar and salt. Modern societies also lend themselves to more sedentary lifestyles with many office-based jobs and transport systems that require the minimum of exercise. The combination of these trends has implications for both personal health and the overall health of broader national societies.

At the global level modern advancements in transport technologies have resulted in the increasing mobility and ease with which individuals can travel around the world. Advancements in air transport have been very important in allowing more people to be able to travel large distances in a relatively short time. The continuous increases in flight services and the relatively cheap cost of flights have also helped to make international travel easier and prevalent. As people travel around the world more the mobility of communicable illnesses, such as flus of various kinds, also increases. The result is that national governments have had to focus on the international and global levels with regard to health issues. In early July 2009, for example, the Tunisian government placed restrictions on Muslim pilgrims travelling to Mecca in Saudi Arabia out of the fear that H1N1 (swine) flu could be transmitted back to Tunisia. Similarly, in late 2014 the Moroccan government notified the Confederation of African Football (CAF) that it was not willing to host the finals of the January–February 2015 CAF tournament. The reason given by the Moroccan government was concern over the threat of the Ebola Pandemic that began in December 2013 in Guinea and that spread to a number of other states in Africa, Europe and North America throughout 2014 infecting tens of thousands and killing several thousand. Processes of globalisation have thus significantly affected how governments manage some health problems, increasing the need for international coordination.

The advancement in means of transport has become an issue of importance. This is due to the problems associated with organising the mass movements of people and goods across national borders. The private sector has a large role in international transport by offering the goods, services and logistics of transport. Private sector airlines, shipping companies, rail networks and train companies, automotive companies and fuel suppliers are the main actors. As such, the private sector has to a certain extent been influential in the management of international transport. In the air transport industry, for example, a number of airline companies jointly created the 'Oneworld Alliance' in 1999. Membership in this alliance has since increased rapidly. The aim of this alliance is to standardise specifications for engineering, maintenance and servicing operations within the airline industry in order to facilitate air transport. It is worth noting that member airlines of the Oneworld Alliance seek to manage the global air transport sector in a manner that maximises their profits.

National governments have also engaged in international cooperation in order to manage transport policies. In order to facilitate international transport, national governments have had to coordinate policy decisions as well as actual infrastructure and modes of transport. An example of international coordination in a transport sector is the EU-backed project called The European Rail Traffic Management System (ERTMS). This project aims to achieve a homogeneous railway control and command system that will cover the whole EU. As part of this project there are two key elements: the European Train Control System, which standardises on-board train control, and a single system for mobile communications. This project builds on previous mechanisms for railway management in Europe, which include the establishment of a single set of specifications for railway infrastructure.

One of the most visible changes in human relations that have accompanied globalisation has been the rapid expansion of international and global trade. Trade between states, in effect, comprises the majority of *international relations* on a day-to-day basis as individuals as well as public and private corporations exchange goods, services and financial resources over national borders in increasingly large quantities. Advancements in communications, transport and logistics technology have contributed to the ability of economic actors to sell the products, services and capital to others in different states all around the world. At the same time, the socio-economic development of practically all societies to some extent has resulted in increased demand for imports. No state can now supply all its needs domestically. Instead, states must import products, services and even capital to maintain themselves. With the proliferation of trade around the globe since the end of the Second World War has come the need to organise how trade is conducted. The main issues regarding the governance of trade relate to tariff and taxation levels on external trade, protection of intellectual property rights, reciprocity and fairness, and encouraging 'open markets'.

As mentioned above the WTO acts as the main intergovernmental organisation involved in managing international trade. It does this by providing member states with the forum to negotiate bilateral and multilateral agreements and rules, which are enforceable as legally binding once approved. An example is the WTO-negotiated agreement on Trade Related Aspects of Intellectual Property Rights (TRIPs). This agreement came into effect in 1994 and stipulates that all member states must respect the intellectual property rights of public and private entities once those rights have been claimed and approved by a member state's government. This prevents infringements such as the illegal production of pharmaceutical goods, which have not been approved by the company that originally developed them.

Other examples of effective global governance structures in which state authority, firms, international institutional frameworks and NGOs interact include the management of global telecommunications (Fuchs, 2008). In human rights policies, there is a higher degree of politicisation and a greater degree of conflict, especially over the use of torture in the so-called 'war on terror'. But, even if imperfect, the global regulation of human rights has proved to be of value for people in some countries and some situations, and NGOs such as Amnesty International and Human Rights Watch find it valuable to have the key norms they wish to promote, and that democratic governments generally claim to support, institutionalised in frameworks such as the International Criminal Court (ICC) and the various other UN institutions that deal with human rights. Another example of a systemic framework of global governance is found in international police cooperation through Interpol (see example box below), while global finance, which offers an important body of regulation, norm building and communication of values as well as negotiation on detailed policy management, is discussed in Chapter 7.

---

**EXAMPLE BOX**

## Interpol

The International Criminal Police Organisation, commonly known as Interpol, is one of the largest IGOs in the world in terms of membership and operations. First established in 1923 in Austria, Interpol has been headquartered in France since the end of the Second World War. It is the primary agency that coordinates and facilitates international policing operations and at the time of writing has 189 members. As explicitly stated in its constitution, Interpol does not take part in any policing or anti-crime operations that do not cross state borders. Its purpose is exclusively to act as a body that helps national police forces when crimes are transnational or when those perpetrating crimes cross from one state to another.

The need for increased cooperation and coordination between national police forces emerged in the first half of the twentieth century. As processes of globalisation resulted in greater integration between people and increased exchanges such as trade, criminal activities also began to internationalise/globalise. The need for an organisation that would act as a means to combat crime on an international level was clear and in the post-Second World War era has become essential. However, Interpol's activities are limited to a certain extent and its role as an IGO is restricted by its constitution and its budget. The former determines Interpol as a 'coordinating' body rather than a 'governing' body, while its annual budget is only approximately US$60 million – a relatively small amount of money for an organisation with a global remit.

The organisation's ability to operate not only relies on the membership of sovereign states, but also their acquiescence and cooperation – something that is not always forthcoming, and something that Interpol does not have significant influence over. In early 2015, for example, it emerged that a nominee for the post of Minister of Agriculture in Afghanistan, Mohammad Yaqub Haidari, was wanted by Interpol on charges of large-scale tax evasion and fraudulent currency conversion in Estonia. Furthermore, Mr Haidari had been wanted by Interpol since 2003, demonstrating the difficulties that remain in pursuing charges against individuals living in different countries from those in which the charges were placed.

The most striking example of world leaders coming together to address an issue of global governance took place in 1992 with the Rio Earth Summit. Under the auspices of the UN this meeting brought together representatives from 172 nation states, including more than 100 heads of state or heads of government to discuss a perceived crisis of environmental degradation. This was unprecedented in both scale and range of issues under discussion. Civil society was also present but it was noticeable that NGOs had a separate meeting area some miles from the main conference centre. Two major conventions were established, one on climate change and one on biodiversity. Not all states ratified these conventions but their establishment meant that they remained in place beyond the Summit to act as a focal point for ongoing negotiations over environmental issues. Disagreement over the accuracy of the science of climate change has continued and there are complex negotiations regarding the targets to be set for limiting greenhouse gas emissions. That said, the Earth Summit process and work of the Intergovernmental Panel on Climate Change demonstrates a serious attempt to monitor, coordinate and govern a range of issue that impact on all states, communities and individuals.

## Summary

This chapter has explored the types of national, international and global governance that take place in the contemporary world. The core debate in IPE that has been engaged with here is whether or not 'governance' actually takes place and at what levels. There are competing schools of thought here ranging from the position that true governance does not actually take place apart from at the national level to the view that governance does take place both within states and

**Table 5.4** Chapter summary

| | Key actors | Key processes | Emphasis on political economy | What causes change? | Global institutions? | View of conflict in global relations? |
|---|---|---|---|---|---|---|
| National governance | National governments | Domestic law enforcement; provision of national security (against external and internal threats); elections; referendums; nationalism and identity forming practices | Varies depending on dominant national ideology; increasingly about the balance between free market policies and the state's role in welfare | Economic development; urbanisation; industrialisation; demographic growth; revolution; regime change; democratisation | Seen as a potential threat to state sovereignty; provides international framework but limited role in domestic affairs | Often a self-help view of sovereignty, security and survival |
| International governance | National governments | Diplomacy; foreign policy making and implementation; war | Importance of economic development, and economic and political security | War; institutionalisation; embedding of social, political and economic interactions at the state and market levels | Useful in supporting national interests and providing frameworks for international relations; yet can be ignored where possible | Acknowledges international anarchy and the need for the pooling of resources for security and survival |
| Regional governance | National governments; regional inter-governmental organisations; specialised agencies | Diplomacy; foreign policy making and implementation; the 'pooling' of sovereignty; coordination and standardisation; institutionalisation | Central emphasis on the 'politics of economic relations' | War; institutionalisation; embedding of social, political and economic interactions at the state and market levels | Can be compatible with and complementary to regional organisations; emphasis remains on regional level cooperation | Acknowledges international anarchy, but focus on regional coordination to promote regional stability |
| Global governance | National governments; global inter-governmental organisations; specialised agencies | Diplomacy; foreign policy making and implementation; war; international law; hegemony; globalisation; institutionalisation | Pursuit of political and economic goals on a global scale, including: economic development, the advancement of healthcare and human security, environmental protection and combating climate change | War; competition (for example, hegemonic rivalries); globalisation; environmental change | The central achievement of global level institutionalism; essential to the establishment and maintenance of global peace, development and stability; potential to provide law, order and security for all members of the global system | Historically inevitable, but preventable or at least manageable within a globalised system of institutions regulating state behaviour |

between them; a middle-ground approach claims that only 'management' and 'coordination' take place at the international and global levels. Furthermore, governance can no longer be seen as exclusively a function of national governments. Instead, non-state actors from the private sector can also be seen to be involved in management and governance in international relations. In the contemporary world there definitely are issues of a global scope, such as global trade, environmental change and health issues; however, in most cases governance does seem to remain limited to the national or international levels at present.

## Reflective questions

1    What are the distinctions between coordination, management and governance?
2    Can you identify the differentiating characteristics of governance at the national, international, regional and global levels?
3    The primary function of national governments is to 'govern'; however, can you think of examples of non-state actors engaging in forms of governance also?
4    International cooperation in international relations is not new, but have processes of globalisation intensified the nature of interdependence and thus the need for international or global governance as opposed to just cooperation?
5    In addition to traditional security concerns, what new and emerging international and global issues require collaboration between state and non-state actors at the international and global levels? And why?
6    In what ways has the development of global telecommunications and transportation led to global governance structures in which state authority, firms, international institutions and NGOs interact?
7    What roles do civil society groups and private sector actors have in shaping and implementing state and non-state policies related to governance at the global level?

## Suggestions for further reading

Barnett, M. and Finnemore, M. (2005) *Rules for the World: International Organisations in Global Politics*, Ithaca, NY: Cornell University Press.

Bexell, M. (2015) *Global Governance, Legitimacy and Legitimation*, London: Routledge.

Diehl, P. and Frederking, B. (eds) (2015) *The Politics of Global Governance: International Organisation in an Interdependent World*, 5th edn, London: Lynne Rienner.

Fogarty, E. (2014) *States, Non-State Actors, and Global Governance*, London: Routledge.

Friedman, T. (2007) *The World is Flat 3.0: A Brief History of the Twenty-first Century*, New York: Picador.

Fuchs, C. (2008) *Internet and Society: Social Theory in the Internet Age*, London: Routledge.

Gill, S. (ed.) (2015) *Critical Perspectives on the Crisis of Global Governance: Reimagining the Future*, Basingstoke: Palgrave Macmillan.

Hirst, P. and Thompson, G. (2009) *Globalization in Question: The International Economy and the Possibilities of Governance*, 3rd edn, Cambridge: Polity Press.

Karns, M. and Mingst, K. (2004) *International Organisations: The Politics and Processes of Global Governance*, London: Lynne Rienner.

King, A. (1997) *Culture, Globalization and the World-System: Contemporary Conditions for the Representation of Identity*, Minneapolis, MN: University of Minnesota Press.

Mattli, W. and Woods, N. (eds) (2009) *The Politics of Global Regulation*, Princeton, NJ: Princeton University Press.

Milward, A. (2000) *The European Rescue of the Nation State*, 2nd edn, London: Routledge.

Mittelman, J. (2005) *Whither Globalization? The Vortex of Knowledge and Ideology*, London: Routledge.

Nel, P., Nabers, D. and Hanif, M. (eds) (2015) *Regional Powers and Global Redistribution*, London: Routledge.

Pease, K. (2009) *International Organisations: Perspectives on Global Governance*, Harlow: Pearson Education.

Rupert, M. (2000) *Ideologies of Globalisation: Contending Visions of the New World Order*, London: Routledge.

Sinclair, T. (2012) *Global Governance*, Cambridge: Polity Press.

Weiss, T.G. (2013) *Global Governance: Why What Whither*, Cambridge: Cambridge University Press.

Weiss, T.G. and Wilkinson, R. (eds) (2013) *International Organization and Global Governance*, London: Routledge.

Weston, B. and Bollier, D. (2014) *Green Governance: Ecological Survival, Human Rights, and the Law of the Commons*, Cambridge: Cambridge University Press.

# 6 Trade

## Chapter learning outcomes

After reading this chapter students should be able to:

- Understand and engage with the mainstream theoretical debates regarding trade in IPE.
- Understand differing interpretations on the importance of trade and its impacts on international relations.
- Comprehend the characteristics of the contemporary global trade system and its growth in the last few decades.
- Be able to explain free trade agreements, their proliferation over the last decade or so and to offer conclusions on their significance.
- Be familiar with the role played by MNCs in trade and be able to explain patterns of increasing MNC-related trade.
- Understand contemporary criticisms of the global trade system, free trade agreements and the trade-related activities of MNCs.
- Relate discussion of trade to theoretical debates discussed earlier in this book and understand the development of key methodologies used to analyse trade.

## Introduction

This chapter returns to assess some of the different theoretical views on world trade. Only some approaches that have been outlined in previous chapters will be discussed here depending on their relevance to the contemporary trade structure and contemporary discussions of it. The initial sections of this chapter should thus be read while keeping in mind the discussions of theoretical approaches in Chapters 1, 2 and 3. The development of the global trade system after 1945 is surveyed and particular attention is paid to the multilateral management of this system and its successes and failures, as well as key issues of debate. Pertinent issues in world trade are discussed, including the position of developing countries, the role of MNCs and the 'free trade versus fair trade' debate.

## Liberalism

Within IPE liberalism has been said to be more successful as a school of thought than other theoretical approaches (see Chapter 1). This is in part to do with the dominance of trade as an issue of study in IPE and the relationship between liberal economic thought and the development of the global trading system since the end of the Second World War. Liberal economic thought dates back to around the late seventeenth and early eighteenth centuries. Adam Smith (1723–1790) was one of the earliest advocates of notions of free trade which would later be referred to as a single classical liberal approach. Smith's work, including *The Wealth of Nations* (1776), suggested that trade is the predominant form of interaction between people within a state and between states. The exchange of resources, goods, services and even capital from a supplier to a buyer using money as the medium is seen as a natural and peaceful form of international relation. Furthermore, trade between people requires a level of cooperation in order to take place. While liberals share realists' assumptions of anarchy in the international system, they claim that cooperation between people that is centred on trade is possible and desirable.

For liberal economic thought, trade is not a zero-sum game but is in fact a plus-sum game, a form of interaction that actually benefits all who are engaged with it. In this sense the realist/mercantilist assumption that trade benefits one actor at the expense of another is refuted. By exchanging goods and services, for example, for money, one state (or market of people) can gain products that it otherwise would not possess or gain products at a lower cost. At the same time, by supplying another state (or market) it is possible to make greater profits than supplying just your own. At the same time as trade being beneficial for purely economic reasons, liberals also claim that trade has other positive effects on international relations. For example, liberals such as Michael Doyle argue that trade results in greater integration between the trading societies, thus allowing them to become more familiar with each other and strengthen shared interests. The result of this integration is a decrease in the risk of conflict and an increase in cooperation and stability. Early liberal scholars including David Ricardo (1772–1823) developed notions of trade as being a key to economic growth and prosperity. By trading more a state (or market) can further develop economically through developing economies of scale (having large markets to sell many goods and services to), lower costs and increase efficiency (by exploiting comparative advantages in the production of certain goods or services).

As discussed in Chapter 5, there are elements of national governments being involved in the management and governance of global trade through IGOs such as the WTO. However, liberal economic thought calls for the exclusion of national governments from playing a significant role in the economy. Governments, it is claimed, are not capable of organising entire economies efficiently. The free market with its invisible hand of supply and demand is said to be the most effective organiser of economic activity. Liberals say that national borders therefore act as a form of governmental restriction on trade and a restriction on the growth and prosperity it brings. As a result of governmental involvement in the economy, as well as the existence of 'unnatural' borders between markets in the form of state borders, trade is hindered. Thus, liberals suggest a system of limited governmental involvement in trade and the removal of national barriers to trade such as taxes on imports/exports, tariffs and quotas on how much one state may export to another. Many observers, such as David Harvey in his book *A Brief History of Neoliberalism* (2005), point to the embedded nature or hegemony of liberalism in the contemporary free market global economy. There is, quite simply, a liberal dominance in the decision-making processes, which shapes the ways in which trade is facilitated and deregulated to the extent that it often seems there is no other game in town. This discussion is taken further in the section below on the contemporary trade system.

## Realism/mercantilism

Realists tend to place less emphasis on economics in general than liberals do. Nevertheless, trade is seen as an area of significance for realists in IPE and mercantilism has a long tradition of thought as well. The key tenets of realist thought on trade are closely linked to its concern with international anarchy, national security and power. In order to maximise one's own national power capabilities with regard to rivals a state must expand its military power base as well as its diplomatic capabilities. Realists argue that in order to do this it is necessary to develop a strong economic base in order to be able to out-compete rivals by purchasing or developing weapons. One way of doing this is to develop an industrialised economy and encourage an affluent domestic society that can provide economies of scale. However, where domestic populations and markets are insufficient to drive economic growth, new markets to sell goods and services in are needed. Therefore, realists suggest that states seek to engage in international trade in order to gain wealth. However, unlike liberals, realists believe that trade is a zero-sum game and that states can gain trade surpluses at the expense of other weaker states (who subsequently have a trade deficit).

Trade for realists is a means to get richer and more powerful in order to strengthen national capabilities and be able to pursue national goals in the international arena. While liberals argue for free trade and the exclusion or limiting of government involvement in the economy, realists argue for the opposite. Free trade in this sense is about competition between economic actors and if a state is weaker or less rich than its trading partners it will be automatically disadvantaged and unable to compete. The result is a trade deficit and the further weakening of the state. The economy or economic actors in a state should thus be supported by the national government if they are to be able to compete with others in the global market. This policy is termed economic nationalism and is put into action through the protection of domestic markets via barriers to imports such as tariffs, taxes and quotas. Direct financial and technological support from national governments to support domestic industries is also used here.

Realists are adamant in their conception of international anarchy and the lack of ability for cooperation between states and peoples under such conditions. While liberals see cooperation and stability stemming from greater levels of trade, realists see no such connection. Trade makes some rich and some poor and is an extension of the competition for power between self-interested states. Cooperation and stability are therefore not directly linked to levels of trade.

## Structuralism

Structuralist notions of trade can be complex and positive or negative, seeing trade as a very important aspect of the modern world but one that has many different effects. In some cases structuralists see structures of global trade that very much resemble previous economic structures that existed in the era of European imperialism. Here rich states trade with poorer and less economically developed states in a manner that seems to benefit the former. In terms of exports, the less-developed states tend to produce low-value products such as raw materials, low-technology manufactured goods and food. At the same time, more industrialised states tend to export high-value goods and services such as high-technology manufactured goods and financial services. Structuralists, such as Immanuel Wallerstein (1981), see a clear distinction between exports that are worth a lot of money and those that are worth little. The result of trading in this manner is for the advanced economic states to continuously record trade surpluses with their poorer partners. This adds to the *underdevelopment* of the global South and is claimed to be a relationship of exploitation.

Because the global economy is split up into exporters of different types of products, for example, with Japan exporting high-technology computing products and Chad exporting cheap clothing, a relationship of dependency has also emerged. Here, Andre Gunder Frank (1979) claims that poorer states need to trade with richer states to get a range of products, which they cannot supply themselves with. This causes an endless cycle of trade deficits and economic stagnation, meaning these poorer states can never really compete in global trade for more expensive products. At the same time, some structuralists see the benefits of 'fair trade' as a means to transfer some technology and financial resources to poorer states. However, this is a marginal group.

# The contemporary trade system

Of the major theoretical approaches to understanding trade, liberalism has become dominant in international relations. Realist thought on trade had provided most European states with a guide for economic policy during the early modern era. However, by the late eighteenth century and early nineteenth century liberal economic thought had gained in prominence and was influencing policy making in the major European states. The contemporary global economic system is, to a large extent, based upon the dominant themes in liberalism and was consciously formed at the end of the Second World War by the victorious Allied powers. The United States and the United Kingdom led the way in developing institutions that would guide the global economy in the post-war world. The economic structure that was established in the early post-war years largely remains today, with liberalism *embedded* in the global system. So the cornerstones of international and global trade are the liberal notions of free trade, limited government involvement in economics, global institutions such as the WTO and the primacy of the private sector.

It is extremely important to stress that while the global system of trade is governed in a way that is based upon or informed by liberal economic thought, for many states international trade is not entirely characterised as free and without governmental involvement. However, constant efforts have been made over the last half century to move towards a global system where free trade is universally adhered to. It is in many ways very difficult to organise a set of relations such as trade on a global scale and it takes a great deal of time. Nevertheless, the liberal vision of free global trade is, in some ways, getting closer with the proliferation of free trade agreements and the adoption of liberal economic thought by most governments. That said, many impediments to free trade do exist. While trade in manufactured goods is increasingly becoming liberated and total volumes of traded manufactured goods have risen significantly in the last two decades (largely due to free trade agreements), trade in services, raw materials and agricultural goods remain regulated to a large extent. The result is that trade in these sectors is far from free. Indeed the processes of negotiating the full liberalisation of trade in these areas have proven to be unsurpassable since the mid-1990s and have helped block progress in multilateral negotiations in the WTO.

National governments meet via the WTO in order to negotiate agreements that will result in the creation of further rules and norms governing global trade. These 'rounds' of negotiations last for a number of years each and focus on ways in which to reduce barriers to trade between states. There have been nine rounds of negotiations under both the GATT framework and the WTO. Perhaps the most important aspect of WTO-led trade liberalisation is the principle of most favoured nation (MFN) status. Upon joining the WTO states have to automatically agree to certain norms and rules. Here, the concept of MFN status states that any preferential treatment between two WTO member states in terms of the framework governing trade between them must be given to all other members and reciprocated. So, if Japan and China, for example, agree to bilaterally lower barriers to trade in a given economic sector they are seen as giving each other preferential treatment over other states. This runs counter to the aim of the WTO and the liberal values embedded in the global economic system of facilitating free trade on a global scale. Therefore, if Japan and China reduce barriers to trade between them they must also lower their barriers in the same way with all other WTO member states. In theory this would lead to the level playing field of liberal economic thought and would lead to a global free trade regime. However, in practice often MFN status is not recognised or reciprocated. Indeed, bilateral and regional FTAs actually run directly counter to the MFN principle as they are exclusive to the states party to the agreement. At the same time WTO member states have to treat all companies and economic activity as they would treat its domestic companies. This principle of non-discrimination (by not favouring domestic over international actors) is also often difficult to monitor and enforce. However, there are dispute settlement mechanisms within the WTO system that states can appeal to if they feel that the MFN and/or non-discrimination rules have been broken by another member state.

---

**AUTHOR BOX**

## Joseph Stiglitz and Andrew Charlton: *Fair Trade For All: How Trade Can Promote Development*

The dominance of liberal economic thought in contemporary debates and policy with regard to trade (what is called neo-liberalism) is not without its critics. While realists and structuralists present their own critiques of the concept of free trade and the direction in which the contemporary trade system is going, there are those from within the broad umbrella of liberalism who also voice caution. Joseph Stiglitz, a former World Bank head and Nobel Prize winner, and Andrew Charlton raise some concerns about the pursuit of global free trade. At the same time as supporting the claim that trade can lead to greater economic prosperity, international cooperation and stability, Stiglitz and Charlton temper optimism about when this is possible. Here it is argued that free trade among competitive markets and industries will improve productivity and efficiency. However, where underdeveloped markets and industries are concerned, issues of competitiveness and survivability are raised. The lack of ability to actually compete in global markets that have been created through trade liberalisation often leaves poorer states out of the process of trade and therefore the benefits it brings.

In order to fully develop a global economic system that is integrated, characterised by cooperation and peaceful interaction, and is founded on free marketeering Stiglitz and Charlton suggest that *fair trade* should be pursued. This notion is based upon the principle of increasing trade in much the same way as free trade. However, fair trade implies free trade between advanced and competitive states, while allowing for varying levels of openness with regard to developing states. Rather than rapidly opening up economies to competition through free trade, the developed world should allow developing states to gain greater access to their markets by reducing barriers to trade. The latter should be allowed to retain some barriers to trade in certain sectors in order to develop domestic industries, allowing for the full liberalising of trade once these industries are competitive enough to engage with the global economy. The core argument of this concept, according to Stiglitz and Charlton, is that the current global economic system, with its pursuit of free trade, only works for half the planet at best. The other half gets left out and is impeded from developing economically.

---

The latest round of WTO negotiations began in Doha, Qatar, in 2001 but has failed to produce a new overarching agreement on the further reduction of barriers to trade. The key sticking points here have been over trade in agricultural products and services. Developing states, led by India, Brazil and Kenya have pursued liberalisation of trade in agriculture – wanting greater access to the rich markets of the developed states for their agricultural exports. At the same time, the majority of developed states, led by the G7 bloc, have sought greater access to developing states' services markets for their service exports. However, developed states have for the most part refused to eliminate the remaining barriers to agricultural imports or to reduce agricultural subsidies to their domestic industries (the EU has been the most significant actor to refuse this latter point). In return, developing states have refused to lower barriers to services – asking the question of why should they allow developed states' industries access to their services markets (in which developing states' domestic industries are less competitive) while the developed states' agricultural sectors are protected. However, on 7 December 2013 at the WTO's Ninth Ministerial Conference all WTO members approved a new agreement aimed at lowering tariffs and subsidies in the agricultural sector. This agreement is referred to as the Bali Package and stipulates that developed states would no longer be able to introduce quota limits (absolute limits on the amounts of a specified good that can be imported from specific states) on agricultural products from developing states, as has previously been common practice. In their place, developed states will be able to charge increased tariffs on the importing of agricultural goods if they exceed specific limits. Subsidies given to the agricultural sectors of developed states will also be reduced to an extent. While not the total removal of agricultural subsidies and tariffs that developing states had called for, the Bali Package is the first real achievement of the Doha Round and can be seen as increasing the momentum of negotiations in this round.

In part as a response to the lack of progress in multilateral negotiations many states have turned even further to bilateral or smaller-scale multilateral negotiations. The United States, for example, had only three FTAs (with Israel, Canada and Mexico – the latter developing into NAFTA) prior to 2001. By 2014 it had twenty bilateral FTAs in effect and a number of others being negotiated. Regional FTAs have also begun to proliferate or strengthen. In the Middle East and North Africa, the Greater Arab Free Trade Area (GAFTA) agreement, for example, came into effect in 2005 and steady progress has been made in reducing all barriers to trade in manufactured goods between the eighteen member states – natural resources, agricultural products and services are somewhat more restricted still. There are fears that the proliferation of bilateral and small multilateral agreements will detract from the WTO-led global efforts to liberalise trade. Here, states may feel that the WTO process is too difficult and slow and will not serve their national interests. Instead bilateral or regional FTAs may be more likely to result in greater success in facilitating trade. If this is the case then barriers to trade will be removed within regional blocs but will remain between different regions, therefore further limiting inter-regional trade. It may also be the case, however, that the proliferation of bilateral and regional FTAs will simply lead to global free trade by a cumulative process of trade liberalisation.

At the same time as institutions are created and engaged with to pursue free trade on a global scale there are many political impediments that restrict this goal. Political impediments continue to exist even when some form of FTA is in effect or when WTO membership is in place. Normalisation of trade relations between Israel and its Arab neighbours that are members of the WTO and that also share FTAs with the United States along with Israel is far from a reality. Even trade between Egypt and Israel is extremely limited, regardless of the facts that they are both WTO members and privy to the MFN rule, as well as having a peace treaty that calls for economic normalisation between them. Furthermore, being close geographically and having economic characteristics that would complement each other it is surprising that Israel and Egypt engage in so little trade with each other. However, when considering the unofficial boycott of Israel by Egyptian businesses and consumers (due to the Israeli occupation of Palestine and the unresolved conflict between Israel and a number of Arab states) the limited levels of trade and lack of free trade between the two are not so surprising.

## Rising levels of trade

Globalisation has entailed the expansion of trade to the extent that we can now truly talk of a global trading system (see Table 6.1). International trade has expanded so rapidly and so widely that virtually every market on the planet is linked to many others via the exchange of goods and

**Table 6.1**  Trade across regions (2012, value in US$ bn)

| Exports from/to | North America | Europe | Africa | CIS | Middle East | Asia | South and Central America |
|---|---|---|---|---|---|---|---|
| North America | 1151 | 380 | 38 | 18 | 75 | 488 | 217 |
| Europe | 492 | 4383 | 211 | 245 | 208 | 645 | 124 |
| Africa | 74 | 240 | 81 | 2 | 17 | 160 | 30 |
| CIS | 37 | 430 | 14 | 149 | 20 | 127 | 7 |
| Middle East | 118 | 148 | 39 | 7 | 116 | 732 | 11 |
| Asia | 975 | 855 | 177 | 121 | 260 | 3012 | 196 |
| South and Central America | 187 | 128 | 21 | 8 | 17 | 172 | 202 |

*Source*: World Trade Organization (2013) *International Trade Statistics 2013*, Table I.4, p. 21, Geneva: WTO.
*Note*: The total volume of world trade in 2012 was $7.9 tr. The total volume of world GDP in 2008 was $65.4 tr.

services. Historically, over the past three centuries international trade was concentrated into two forms. The first was trade between imperial centres and their colonies. The second was between the imperial centres themselves (largely this meant trade between European states). However, the modern global system is characterised by literally all states engaging in some form of trade with others. This assent of trade as a daily interaction between markets and peoples regardless of whether they are from an economically advanced state or not is a relatively new phenomenon. While the global economy has a GDP of approximately US$65 trillion, international trade totalled approximately US$16 trillion in 2008 (World Bank data). As a total amount and as a percentage of global GDP, trade levels have risen very rapidly since the 1950s. It is worth noting that prior to the First World War international trade levels were also very high in terms of a percentage of global GDP. The level of trade dropped significantly in the inter-war period and during the Great Depression but then began to rebound after the Second World War. Many liberal scholars argue that there was a direct causal link between the low levels of international trade after the First World War and the onset of economic crises, global recession, rise of nationalism and ultimately the Second World War. The embedding of liberal economic values in the revision of the global economic system that followed the Second World War was largely based upon these liberal observations. The architects of the post-war system, including economists and scholars such as John Maynard Keynes, argued that in order to ensure that economic recessions, nationalism and conflict did not return an open and integrated economic system was needed. Therefore, the foundations of the contemporary global economic system were developed in a deliberate attempt to facilitate and encourage global trade.

The patterns of trade have also evolved rapidly so that now trade takes place between all areas of the world and in practically all sectors of production. Rising levels of trade have traditionally been seen between the areas of the 'Triad' of North America, Western Europe, and Japan and Australia. These areas constitute the most economically advanced markets in the world where a majority of economic production has taken place in the last half a century. The Triad represents the most prosperous set of markets in the global economy. Trade between Western Europe and North America, for example, has grown rapidly from around US$50 billion a year in the 1950s to over US$528 billion in 2008. This is compared with much lower levels of trade between other markets in the world over the same period of time. While the Triad markets trade quite heavily, sub-Saharan Africa and the Middle East, for example, have seen much more restricted levels of trade. The

Middle East has the most limited levels of intra-regional trade in terms of a percentage of regional GDP and sub-Saharan Africa comes a close second. Furthermore, these regions have not had as much success trading with other regions such as Europe or North America as others have. Natural resources such as oil and gas do constitute major exports from the Middle East and North Africa in terms of total value and percentage of GDP. However, if we remove these commodities and only consider non-oil or gas exports, this region does not export very high levels of products to the rest of the world. The same can also be said for other developing regions. Table 6.1 illustrates, among other things, not only the regionalisation of global trade, but also the very powerful differences in levels of engagement in world trade between regions.

At the same time as levels of trade between the less economically developed regions and the more developed ones have been limited since the 1950s, trade between less-developed regions has also been quite low. Trade between South Asia and South America, for example, has traditionally been very limited. So, the majority of trade that has taken place between regions since the Second World War has been between more advanced markets. The intensification of processes of globalisation has begun to transform these traditional patterns of trade. Levels of trade have been increasing quite rapidly over the last two decades. Much of this increase in trade has not included the Triad markets but has actually taken place between emerging markets. The emergence of China as a major trading state is the perfect example here. China's levels of trade have increased very rapidly since the 1990s and China now has the world's second largest levels of trade. The development of both low-technology and high-technology manufacturing industries have led to very large increases in Chinese exports of products such as clothes, toys and now even cars. Rising levels of affluence have led to greater purchasing power and subsequently increased imports of consumer products such as high-technology equipment. Industrialisation has also brought a greater need for resources and China is now the second largest importer of oil and gas. But China's trade has not just taken place with the richer markets in Europe, North America, Japan and Australia. Instead, China is trading at high levels with almost every region. Other developing states have also witnessed similar patterns of economic growth and rising levels of international trade. India and Brazil are cases in point, which have managed to develop economically in recent decades and now have many trade links with all regions.

Table 6.2 illustrates world ranking for leading exporters and importers. It demonstrates the growing power of China in world trade, the trade deficits of some countries (the US and UK

**Table 6.2**  Selected ranking of imports and exports in merchandise trade 2012 (value in US$ bn)

| Rank | State | Exports | Rank | State | Imports |
|------|-------|---------|------|-------|---------|
| 1 | Extra-EU | 2167 | 1 | USA | 2336 |
| 2 | China | 2049 | 2 | Extra-EU | 2301 |
| 3 | USA | 1546 | 3 | China | 1818 |
| 4 | Japan | 799 | 4 | Japan | 886 |
| 5 | R. of Korea | 548 | 5 | Hong Kong, C. | 553 |
| 6 | Russia | 529 | 6 | R. of Korea | 520 |
| 7 | Hong Kong, C. | 493 | 7 | India | 490 |
| 8 | Canada | 455 | 8 | Canada | 475 |
| 9 | Singapore | 408 | 9 | Mexico | 380 |
| 10 | Saudi Arabia | 388 | 10 | Singapore | 380 |
| 11 | Mexico | 371 | 11 | Russia | 335 |
| 12 | United Arab Emirates | 350 | 12 | Taiwan | 270 |

*Source*: World Trade Organization (2013) *International Trade Statistics 2013*, Table I.8, p. 25, Geneva: WTO.

in particular), as well as some possibly surprising leading players (Belgium and the Netherlands). It does not show the mix of trade (high/low-technology products) and it excludes services and primary products including raw materials.

**EXAMPLE BOX**

## Shifting patterns of trade

Through the course of the seventeenth to the twenty-first centuries patterns of trade have tended to follow forms of imperial and colonial expansion. In the twenty-first century, while remnants of such forms can still be identified, new patterns are also emerging. Imperial expansion can be seen as politically driven and centred on territorial expansion. The dominant trade dynamic of today emanates from the private sector. Multinationals are not territorially bound. The free flow of capital allows their operations to react to the market demands of production and consumption. They are not driven by political allegiance, even though at times political issues will affect MNC behaviour. Instead they are driven by corporate agendas and the pursuit of profit.

For example, India was referred to as 'the jewel in the crown' of the British Empire. The vast majority of its trade flowed towards Britain and other parts of the empire. Today, India has one of the highest levels of trade within an increasingly diverse portfolio of goods and services. Brazil's experience is quite different in terms of colonial inheritance. In part this is because of the very different nature of Brazilian geography and society. Furthermore, Brazil gained independence from Portugal much earlier than India did from Britain. As a result Brazil did not have access to the technologies associated with the Industrial Revolution, which formed a significant part of India's economic development.

**Figure 6.1**   Regional trade flows

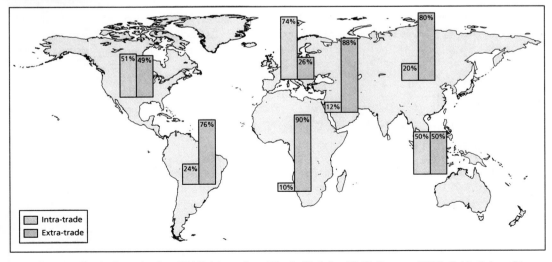

*Source:* World Trade Organization (2013) *International Trade Statistics 2013*, Geneva: WTO, Table 1.4, p. 21.

# Free trade agreements

One of the key features of the contemporary global economic system is the proliferation of FTAs between states. The primary purpose of an FTA is to facilitate trade across state borders by reducing or removing barriers to trade. This is done by two or more national governments negotiating an agreement as to how they can reduce or remove entirely administrative mechanisms such as tariffs, taxes, quotas and non-tariff barriers on imports and exports. These mechanisms often restrict trade by raising the costs of the products and services that are imported or exported. This is because the companies seeking to sell or buy products and services will always try to maximise their profits. If a national government enforces a tax on a given product that is imported or exported then this cost is transferred to the market and not the company, thus raising the cost to the purchaser and making the product less desirable and restricting market demand.

FTAs are based on classical liberal economic thought. In the works by Adam Smith, for example, trade is described as a natural human interaction but governmental management of international trade is not natural. The benefits of trade are restricted by barriers to trade and so a single free market that is unified by the removal of national barriers to trade should be pursued. The benefits of trade will then allow for the maintenance of a peaceful and stable global system that is prosperous. This position is not without its criticism, however, as many scholars, NGOs and civil society groups often highlight. This is discussed in more detail below. The dominant actors that have established and shaped the institutions of the modern economic system have advocated FTAs as a primary mechanism. The WTO is in itself largely a forum for states to meet in bilateral or multilateral settings to negotiate FTAs. The WTO also acts as a forum to ensure that FTAs (once agreed) are respected as international law and are abided by.

There have been two main forms of FTAs in the last few decades. The first type is bilateral FTAs, which are negotiated between two national governments. These agreements can cover trade in all goods and services that are exchanged between the states or only some economic sectors. They also cover trade only between the two parties, although provisions for trade with other states are also accounted for. In the case of the latter point, FTAs have provisions that ensure that a third state does not simply export products to one of the FTA signatories and then re-export them to the other signatory, thus in effect gaining free access to this state without actually reciprocating such access. FTAs are often seen as very desirable for states that are seeking to maximise exports. Gaining free access to a large market such as the United States offers the opportunity for greater exports and greater economic growth. However, reciprocal free access to your own market also raises competition for domestic companies and can therefore be seen as undesirable.

---

**EXAMPLE BOX**

## The political economy of bilateral FTAs

The Jordan–United States FTA

On 24 October 2000 the United States and Jordan signed a bilateral FTA to fully liberalise trade in the vast majority of goods and services. In some ways this FTA was a first in terms of US foreign trade policy and how bilateral FTAs are constructed. The agreement was the first between the United States and an Arab state and only the fourth FTA the United States had signed at the time. It also included provisions for labour rights and environmental protection. Subsequently the United States has signed a large number of FTAs and several of these have been with states in the Middle East. The Jordan–US FTA required the removal of all tariffs, quotas and taxes on all forms of bilateral trade in goods and services by 2010. At the time that it was signed some observers claimed that this agreement was a reward given to the Jordanian government for its support of US policies in the Middle East, in particular with regard to the peace process between Israel and the Arab world. This observation was based on the belief that gaining free access to the US market would result in greater Jordanian exports and economic growth. The United States, on the other hand, was not seen as gaining much from the greater access to the Jordanian market as it is small in size and has not traditionally been a major importer of US goods and services. As such, the agreement was seen as a political rather than an entirely economic endeavour. Nevertheless, others claimed that the FTA was designed as a purely economic project aimed at increasing trade.

The result of the agreement has been quite profound since late 2001 when the agreement came into effect. Bilateral trade between Jordan and the United States has increased from US$390.2 million in 2000 to over US$3 billion in 2014. This near tenfold increase in trade over a relatively short period of time is quite dramatic and can clearly be attributed to the FTA. Importantly the increase in trade value has come about mostly due to the rapid expansion of Jordanian exports to the United States. Jordanian exports rose from US$73.3 million in 2000 to a high of just under US$1.5 billion in 2006 and US$1.2 billion in 2014. The majority of Jordanian exports to the US market have come in the textiles and apparel sector while US exports to Jordan have mainly been higher-value added goods such as machinery and transport equipment.

## The China–ASEAN FTA

The People's Republic of China and the ten members of the Association of South East Asian Nations (ASEAN) (Brunei, Burma, Cambodia, Indonesia, Laos, Malaysia, the Philippines, Singapore, Thailand and Vietnam) launched negotiations for a FTA to cover 90 per cent of all goods traded between them in November 2001. While negotiations were relatively swift the implementation of the agreement was planned and carried out in stages over several years. The agreement called for all tariffs on goods traded between China and the six original ASEAN members (Brunei, Indonesia, Malaysia, the Philippines, Singapore and Thailand) to be fully removed by 2010 and for tariffs to trade in goods with the remaining four ASEAN members to be fully removed by 2015. As with most FTAs each signatory state has been able to maintain tariffs on some sectors in agreement with the other signatories. By July 2005 an early harvest programme for trade in some goods was implemented. This was followed by the finalisation and implementation of a dispute settlement mechanism agreement in the same year. Negotiations to extend the FTA to trade in services were concluded and implemented in mid-2007. Finally, a China–ASEAN investment agreement was signed at the ASEAN summit held in Thailand in December 2008. The result is the integration of over 1.7 billion people into a (largely) zero-tariff market making it the largest free trade area by population and third largest by overall GDP.

Yet as often happens when negotiating multilateral FTAs that involved a relatively large number of states, the negotiations and implementation of the China–ASEAN FTA have not been entirely smooth. Coordination in implementing agreed-upon tariff reductions and the removal of other barriers to trade is complicated and can slow down the process of trade liberalisation. Furthermore, agreements like the China–ASEAN FTA do not always lead to high levels of economic integration, especially in services sectors such as finance and banking, and telecommunications. At the same time as it is implementing the broader multilateral FTA with ASEAN members, China has also been pursuing deeper, more inclusive bilateral agreements with individual ASEAN members to accelerate the process of economic integration and trade-led development. For example, in 2008 China and Singapore signed a bilateral FTA that has more economic scope than the China–ASEAN FTA. ASEAN members in turn have been somewhat cautious about encouraging Chinese domination over ASEAN while at the same time trying to gain from the benefits of increased trade with China. In particular, while ASEAN states seek the economic gains of having duty-free access to the world's most populous state, they are weary of being locked into a regional economic system where they provide raw materials to China and import manufactured goods in return (in effect a core–periphery relationship).

The second form of FTA has been regional multilateral agreements such as the North American Free Trade Area (NAFTA) agreement. Here, the United States and Canada negotiated an agreement with Mexico in 1994, which added free trade between the three states to the bilateral FTA already in existence between the United States and Canada. This multilateral agreement created a single market with free trade in goods and services (but not labour). The EU, in effect, has a multilateral FTA also and states wishing to join the union have to accept this agreement. Because of this FTA the EU represents a single economic market with liberalised movement of goods, services and people across state borders.

Many states now use FTAs as major foreign and economic policy tools. The United States has pursued bilateral FTAs at an increasing rate since 2000 as a means of meeting its political as well as economic objectives. Up until 2001 the United States only had FTAs with Israel, Canada and Mexico. Following an FTA with Jordan that came into effect in 2001 the United States has signed a further fourteen and at the time of writing is negotiating a number of others. The United States has largely focused on signing bilateral FTAs with South American, Middle Eastern and North African states. With regards to the latter two, FTAs form a key element in broader US foreign policy aimed at engaging more with the region.

There are many criticisms of FTAs by individuals and groups that do not share the liberal assumptions about their benefits. Many people see FTAs as damaging to economic development of poorer states. It is argued that by reducing barriers to imports domestic industries, which are often in their infancy or are relatively uncompetitive internationally, will not be able to survive. The increased competition from external actors, which are often more efficient and competitive, will out-compete domestic rivals and thus reduce economic growth in the poorer states. In this argument, barriers to trade are there to protect domestic industries and economic growth and not to impede trade. Some states such as North Korea follow some policies that encourage barriers to imports in order to strengthen or protect domestic industries.

Other criticisms of FTAs are that they encourage the deregulation and removal of governance of the economic sector. Here, MNCs can pursue their activities without the hindrance of national governments regulating their behaviour. In some states, such as the United Kingdom, governmental laws stipulate things like minimum wages, the right of association in unions and working conditions. However, in many developing states such regulations are not in existence and national governments are unwilling to discourage MNCs from operating in their countries. In effect, the modern liberal economic system necessarily entails a race to the bottom as governments seek to offer the most profitable terms for MNCs and foreign capital to invest in their economies. Critics of FTAs claim that these agreements only encourage this process. Exploitation of labour and the environment is seen as a negative result of FTAs. Regardless of whether FTAs are seen as economically and morally desirable or not, FTAs have proliferated rapidly and the liberalisation of global trade has resulted in greatly expanding levels of this type of exchange.

One of the most important contemporary debates with regard to global trade is the importance of regional FTAs and their impact on the WTO-driven pursuit of global free trade. Since the 1980s there has been an emergence of regional trading blocs such as NAFTA, Mercosur (a South American regional trade agreement aimed at creating a fully integrated single market in Latin America) and the EU. These regional trade agreements create preferential treatment for the member states at the expense of states not included. As discussed above, there are concerns that the development of regional trade agreements and the regional blocs they create will actually hinder global trade. This is in direct contradiction of the liberal economic thought that has inspired the contemporary global economic system, which seeks free trade on a global level. It may be the case, however, that regional trade agreements and trade blocs are actually steps on the way to a fully integrated and free trading global system. The EU, for example, negotiates FTAs with other states or groups of states as a single actor. This helps to streamline the process, as is evidenced by the Barcelona Process of integration between the EU and the Middle East and North Africa. States on the southern Mediterranean such as Tunisia only have to negotiate one agreement instead of twenty-seven, making the process of integration more efficient.

## MNCs and trade

Much of the global trade that takes place today is carried out by and on behalf of MNCs. Private sector MNCs account for over US$5 trillion in trade, which is equivalent to nearly 50 per cent of all international trade that takes place; trade within individual companies but across international boundaries – intra-firm international trade – accounts for an estimated 23 per cent of total world trade (all figures from WTO 2009 *Yearbook*; authors' estimates). It is often said that MNCs are the engines that drive global trade. In the liberal point of view, therefore, MNCs are the engines that drive global economic growth via trade. Realists would also argue that MNCs are very important in encouraging international trade and so they are important to the economic development of their 'home' state.

Structuralists, on the other hand, acknowledge the link between MNCs and trade and suggest that this relationship is extremely intense. Ultimately, though, they see MNCs as having an exploitative and damaging effect on people and the environment via international trade. Almost all the international trade that MNCs are engaged with is actually inter-firm trade or intra-firm trade. This means that they trade largely with other MNCs or with different branches of their own corporation that are situated in different states. In the case of the latter it is very interesting to note that while goods or services may be transferred from one branch of a single corporation to another, if these branches operate in different states this transfer counts as international trade. Intra-firm trade actually constitutes a large percentage of trade involving MNCs. It has also become much more prevalent as the operations of MNCs have become increasingly geographically dispersed.

MNC-related trade is driven by global divisions of labour, which allow for the combination of material, labour, infrastructure, technology and financial resources from around the world to be pooled together in one economic endeavour. The utilisation of different markets for different parts of a manufacturing process, for example, helps MNCs to maximise profits. This is done by locating the cheapest labour, resources and infrastructure that are appropriate and employing them in the manufacturing of goods. Of course, divisions of labour that are global in scale are only possible due to advanced and cheap technologies in communications and transport. The nature of the global economy with these divisions of labour mean that MNCs pursuing more profits will move their operations around the world, possibly quite rapidly. This means that states can attract investment from MNCs as they move the operations into new markets. For developing states this is a key source of income and economic activity. Because many states around the world are so keen to attract MNCs to their markets, they are often in competition with each other, putting MNCs in a preferable position where they get to choose where and when to invest. The result can be seen as a 'race to the bottom' where developing states (and in some cases developed states also) will offer incentives to MNCs such as tax breaks, low labour wages and so on. Combined, these processes allow MNCs to be extremely flexible with where they operate and the terms under which they move their activity to other states. Because of this position MNCs are often criticised for evading normal forms of governance – they quite simply can be above the law in many states or move on if national governments cause them trouble.

**EXAMPLE BOX**

## Wal-Mart Stores

One of the world's largest and most expansive MNCs is Wal-Mart Stores. In 2014 Forbes reported that Wal-Mart Stores had total assets of US$204.8 billion, annual profits of US$16 billion, total assets worth US$204.8 billion and a market value of US$247.9 billion. Its annual sales ranked first in 2014 out of all major MNCs and its total market value ranks tenth globally. Founded in 1962 as a discount chain store and headquartered in Bentonville, USA this MNC rapidly expanded in terms of its remit and geographic presence. Wal-Mart Stores now has business operations in twenty-seven different countries on five continents. The primary area of business for Wal-Mart Stores is the operation of large discount depart-ment stores and warehouse stores, and it now operates over fifty different business names, many of which are more familiar to their customers than the umbrella corporation (for example, the Woolco in Canada, the Bompreco supermarket chain in Brazil and Asda in the UK).

It operates in the highly competitive manufacturing and retail industries and in order to remain competitive and maximise profits Wal-Mart Stores, like other MNCs that have to compete in an increasingly globalised economy, has developed a complex division of labour in terms of business development, purchasing, retail and the distribution of its products and outlets. This division means that various operations are conducted in different states and resources and labour are sourced from around the world. Even more importantly, as Wal-Mart Stores is primarily an outward facing retail outlet that has to purchase the majority of the goods it sells, its global trade network for purchasing then transporting and selling products is truly global in scope. While it operates outlets in only twenty-seven states, the products that these outlets sell are either sourced entirely or in part from almost all states around the world. The inter-firm and intra-firm trade that Wal-Mart Stores engages with means that global supply chains are deeply embedded in its overall activities, and it in turn acts as a driver of international trade, particularly in merchandise but also in various ser-vices. Examples of how Wal-Mart Stores' global supply chains operate can be found in the consumer products it sells, ranging from textiles and apparel to food and electrical goods (all of which entail the international exchange of raw materials, transnational manufacturing/processing, and transportation around the world for sale).

For structuralist as well as liberal interpretations, global trade is driven to a large extent by the activity of MNCs. As mentioned above, MNCs do account for a large share of global levels of trade. However, the role of MNCs in enhancing trade is not straightforward. In many ways

MNCs act as the channels or conduits between markets, facilitating the movement of goods, people, capital and services in myriad ways. The ability of MNCs to exploit markets for resources, labour, production and sale around the world is quite extraordinary and with modern forms of communication and technology trade is greatly enhanced by the pursuit of maximising profits. Put in other words, MNCs require trade in order to be profitable and to grow.

## Criticisms of trade

There are a wide range of criticisms of trade and its impacts on the world. These can be categorised into three broad camps or schools. One camp is very much against international trade, claiming that the impacts on the human and natural worlds that come from trade are very damaging. A second camp argues that international trade is structured in a manner that is unfair to many of the world's poorer and less economically developed people. This argument is based on the perception of the global economic system as being based on open competition between economies. In this system those economies that are more advanced and industrialised automatically are in a more advantaged position to compete. The third key school of criticism is made up of those who see international trade as encouraging conflict between states by leading to imbalances in power capabilities as well as relationships of dependency.

For those who see international trade as very damaging there are two key elements of concern. It is argued that international trade and the deregulation of the global economy weakens labour rights and leads to exploitation of workers. Here, the actions of MNCs and how they treat employees are of great concern. Low wages, poor working conditions, long hours, no holiday or illness allowance and even in many cases modern forms of slavery are cited as some of the problems that international trade brings. Furthermore, the movement of goods and people that international trade entails is seen to be adding to environmental problems. As larger amounts of fuels are consumed in order to transport goods and people from one market to another, greater levels of pollution are witnessed. Of importance here, again, are the operations of MNCs. As mentioned above, MNCs often transfer material and people from one branch to another as part of global divisions of labour. By manufacturing products in different states and transporting the different components in the production chain MNCs add to pollution. Some would argue that international trade does in fact add to economic growth. This may be good in terms of raising incomes and national GDP levels. However, this also means that greater levels of consumption and pollution will follow.

We might add that there should be real doubt about whether many governments actually support free trade. Even those that use the rhetoric of free and open trade most effectively jealously guard particular industrial sectors and particular firms. The United States, European Union and Japan each have very elaborate systems of trade control. As powerful agricultural exporters (such as Australia and Argentina) have pointed out, this applies especially to food products. But protection against low-cost products from newly industrialised countries is rife; using health and safety regulation, regulations on common standards, and many other forms of non-tariff barriers is widespread. This is partly because trade protection is so fiercely lodged in domestic politics. But many countries, including those in east Asia, which grew rapidly in the 1960s and 1970s under state management (Taiwan, the Republic of Korea and Malaysia among them) and those in continental Europe, the Middle East and Latin America, which have a long state tradition of government management of economic activity (France, Italy, Argentina and Egypt among them) have not created a political culture in which ideas of free trade stand unchallenged. The ideas of state protection as a basis for growth enshrined in the writings of Friedrich List, the nineteenth-century father of neo-mercantilism, may be disreputable to most economists, but they are still important in political and media views of the economy, especially in response to crises.

One major concern for many in the contemporary global economic system is the problem of fair competition. Advocates of free trade claim that open markets and the removal of barriers to trade will create a 'level playing field' where economic actors all have the same opportunities. Critics would agree that by adopting liberal economic policies of free trade and open markets economic competition is actually encouraged. While liberals see competition as leading to greater efficiency, lower costs and increases in economic activity, others, such as structuralists, see competition as relatively undesirable. They point to the fact that the more advanced economic states achieved their high levels of advancement not through free trade and open markets but by economic nationalism, conquest and the protection of domestic industries. At the same time, critics ask how less advanced economies can expect to successfully compete with the more advanced ones. In this view, therefore, the global economic system of free trade is simply not fair. This position is often referred to as the 'free trade versus fair trade' debate. Advocates of this position suggest that barriers to trade should remain in place for less-developed states so that infant industries can be nurtured and economic development can take place. We could say that this second camp of trade critics is actually pro-trade, but refuses to support 'free trade' in its current form.

---

**EXAMPLE BOX**

## The Fairtrade Foundation

This is an independent non-profit organisation whose objectives are to work with businesses, community groups and individuals around the world in order to support producer organisations in the South in order to improve their trading position and promote the sustainable development of farmers, workers and their communities. The Fairtrade Foundation licenses the use of the FAIRTRADE Mark for products sold in the UK in-line with international fair trade standards. Established in 1992 by CAFOD, Christian Aid, Oxfam, Traidcraft and the World Development Movement and joined by the National Federation of Women's Institutes among others, the foundation's mission is to help facilitate just and equitable development for all. The Fairtrade Foundation sees fair trade as a means to transform existing inequitable and unfair trading structures and practices into ones that favour the poor and disadvantaged. This overall goal is pursued by tackling poverty and injustice through trade; using certification and product labelling using the FAIRTRADE Mark; and helping to develop a citizens' movement for change by bringing together producers and consumers. Its key activities include providing an independent certification of exchange processes; supporting growth in the market for fair trade products; supporting producer organisations; and raising awareness of trade-related injustice and means to combat this.

*Source*: Fairtrade Foundation (www.fairtrade.org.uk).

---

**EXAMPLE BOX**

## The World Fair Trade Organization

The WFTO is a global network of mostly private sector organisations that coordinate to reflect the Fair Trade supply chain. Its network includes producers, marketers, exporters, importers, wholesalers and retailers from over seventy countries that adhere to the principles of fair trade and trade justice. The WFTO offers its members the opportunity to engage in and to promote practices that maintain and enhance equitable trade that ensures fair prices for producers and consumers while promoting sustainable development and environmental protection. Its vision is a world where trade structures and practices work in favour of the poor rather than against them, and in which development and human security are provided for all. As such, the focus of WFTO policies, governance structures and decision-making is on producers, especially farmers and artisans in the developing world. It was founded in 1989 and originally named the International Federation of Alternative Traders (IFAT) and its activities have always focused on promoting awareness of fair trade, offering its members networking opportunities and training, and building global trust in the Fair Trade certification.

In 2013 the WFTO product label was introduced. This label is given to all products that adhere to the principles of sustainable and equitable development, just and fair prices for producers, fair pricing for consumers, and environment-friendly production and provision. Only products that have been traded fairly according to the WFTO's standards and monitoring mechanisms are permitted to carry this label. A key goal of this label is to build trust between producers and consumers, and to enhance the market share of fair trade products.

*Source*: World Fair Trade Organization (www.wfto.com).

A more radical perception of the impacts of international trade is one based on realist assumptions. The belief that trade leads to relative increases and decreases in economic wealth and therefore power capabilities is utilised here. This view suggests that national governments do follow policies of economic nationalism despite the claims to be trading freely and openly. Trade is thus seen as a form of competition between states in itself. Furthermore, rising levels of trade are leading to the transfer of resources, wealth and power from some states to others. For example, economically advanced states tend to have trade surpluses in their trade with less-developed states, resulting in an overall transfer of wealth to the more developed world. This is, in short, a continuation of former imperial economic relationships. The effect can be to further tip the balance of power capabilities in favour of the wealthier states.

## Trade theory and modelling

In addition to the perspectives of the main meta-narratives used in the study of GPE as discussed at the start of this chapter, a number of trade-focussed theoretical models are available for both the study of actual trade relations, and the creation of policy. While Smith (absolute advantage) and Ricardo (comparative advantage) both provided coherent arguments for pursuing liberal trade policies, and offered relatively sophisticated explanations of the nature of trade, by the 1900s their approaches were seen as limited. Ricardo, for example, argued that national advantages in trade were the result of labour productivity alone. Observation of modern patterns of trade suggests that merely focussing on this factor of production is insufficient as advantages in trade also are impacted by other factors such as natural resources, capital and technology (the latter is increasingly important in the twenty-first century). By the 1920s scholars began to search for new ways of interpreting both the nature of trade and the causes of comparative advantages. In the 1920s and 1930s Eli Heckscher and Bertil Ohlin became the most successful scholars attempting to do this.

Heckscher and Ohlin (two Swedish economists) argued that a state's comparative advantage is determined by the availability of specific factor endowments: labour *and* capital, where a state will have an advantage in producing goods that rely on the factor(s) it has in abundance. According to the Heckscher–Ohlin Theorem then, developed states that have an abundance of capital due to their higher levels of wealth and larger GDPs, will have a comparative advantage in producing capital-intensive high value-added goods, while less-developed states that have an abundance of cheap labour will have a comparative advantage in producing labour-intensive (usually low value-added) goods. The Heckscher–Ohlin theorem was widely regarded as the most appropriate method to use to analyse patterns of trade and inform trade policy through much of the mid-1900s. However, it too suffered from some generalisations just as Smith and Ricardo's approaches did. Heckscher–Ohlin assumed, for example, that all states/markets are the same in terms of tastes, consumer practices and levels of technology.

By the 1940s economists (and political economists) started to develop ways to deal with the weaknesses in the Heckscher–Ohlin model. Wolfgang Stolper and Paul Samuelson were two American economists who succeeded in synthesising Heckscher and Ohlin's ideas with a more nuanced interpretation of the ways national economies operate and change over time. They did this by taking into account the role played by domestic interest groups. Their theory has some-times been labelled the Stolper–Samuelson model, the Heckscher–Ohlin–Stolper–Samuelson model, or slightly misleadingly, the Heckscher–Ohlin–Samuelson model. According to this theory there are groups within states that experience the different factors of abundance or scarcity that Heckscher and Ohlin has considered for states as a whole. In this situation trade liberalisation benefits those factors of production that are in abundance while hurting those that are scarce within a state. At the same time some domestic groups (and perhaps different geographical areas within a state) may have an abundance of capital (for example, large metropolitan cities like New York or Chicago) while others have an abundance of cheap labour but not capital (for example, rural/agricultural centres). Therefore, trade liberalisation by one state is beneficial to the owners of capital within that state if capital is in abundance, but detrimental to the workers if labour and natural resources (such as productive agricultural land or oil) are scarce. As a result free trade will be supported by domestic group(s) that would benefit from trade liberalisation (the capitalists in the above scenario) and opposed by those domestic groups that suffer (the workers in the above scenario).

The ideas of Stolper and Samuelson, like Heckscher and Ohlin, have remained relevant in GPE and continue to be referred to. Certainly, the observation that some domestic groups gain from free trade, while other domestic groups suffer from it is useful and a welcome move away from seeing states as merely unitary actors. However, it has become rather common to criticise their approach as being somewhat too simplistic and observations of contemporary patterns of trade cannot be explained using the Stolper–Samuelson model. A major criticism is that this model does little to explain intra-industry trade (trade between different states in the same sector, such as in cars, computers, mobile phones and so on). All of the main approaches from Smith to Stolper and Samuelson approach trade by assuming that goods are homogenous, meaning that they do not consider the possibility of, nor the impact of intra-industry (and intra-firm) trade. Yet a key feature of the contemporary global economic system is intra-industry trade of differentiated products. We do not all have the same style of mobile phone handset, for example, nor do we all drive the same type of car or use the same desktop computer model. This observation is even more important when we consider that most intra-industry trade occurs between states that have similar factor endowments (mostly between developed states in North America, Europe, East Asia and Australasia, which have abundance in the same factors including capital, technology and automated manufacturing facili-ties). Because of this (and other) feature(s) it has been necessary to develop existing trade theories to take into account the complexities of the contemporary global economy.

From the late 1990s in particular a new approach to analysing patterns of trade has become heavily relied on: the *Gravity Model*. This model utilises the factor endowments approach used by Heckscher, Ohlin, Stolper and Samuelson but also acknowledges a range of other variables and is more commonly used by economists rather than GPE specialists. It relies on quantitative analysis and considers factor endowments such as capital, labour, resources, technology and management/organisational capacities. Yet it also considers factors that are not normally associated with production: including variables such as consumer tastes, which can be heavily influenced by religious beliefs, ideologies, values and other socio-cultural factors; geographical proximity, where the argument is that states that are closer to each other are more likely to trade with each other because of lower transportation costs, ease of transport, and less insecurity due to instability in various parts of the world that might disrupt supply (for example, European Union imports of natural gas from Russia that have to pass through third parties like Ukraine); cultural, ideological and other affinities/differences between consumers, where the same ethnicity, religion or sense of nationalism may promote trade, or where opposition due to political, ethnic, ideological, and religious factors among others, might encourage boycotts on trade (for example, most Arab states have a boycott on trade with Israel due to its occupation of Palestine and ongoing disputes with other neighbouring Arab states). Strategic trade policies such as preferential trade agreements can also be considered using the Gravity Model approach. Overall, the Gravity Model approach has emerged as the most effective tool used to understand, explain and predict patterns of trade, and is even used to prescribe trade policy, but like the approaches that preceded it, the Gravity Model is not likely to remain unchallenged.

## Summary

Building on the previous chapters on theory, globalisation and governance this chapter has introduced trade as one of the most important contemporary forms of international relations. The ideological foundations of the structure of global trade have been considered. Here, classical liberal economic thought has been very influential in the establishment of the post-Second World War global economy and the role international trade plays in it. Over the past half a century or so international trade has expanded very rapidly and now we can refer to global trade. At the same time, while international trade traditionally was dominated by the Triad of North America, Western Europe, and Japan and Australia, international trade is now prevalent in all regions. The more economically advanced states still tend to dominate in trade relationships with less-developed states but trade between less-developed states is increasingly important. Also, less-developed states such as China are becoming very large traders.

The proliferation of bilateral and multilateral FTAs since the 1990s has helped to reduce and remove barriers to trade. The facilitation of trade has helped to drive greater levels of international trade. Through these agreements and the global trading regime dominated by the WTO, trade is likely to continue to increase rapidly. At the same time, MNCs play a very important role, accounting for a large part of global trade. Much of this trade is between firms or even between different branches of the same MNC. The expansion of global trade has served to highlight very different opinions on its impact. Liberals claim that trade is good for economic development and international stability should be promoted. The structure of the global trading system is based on these ideas. The realist position is one of economic nationalism and mercantilism, which suggests that trade is good for building power capabilities, but only if a state has a trade surplus. Finally, more critical observers, such as structuralists, argue that the manner in which global trade is carried out is damaging to both people and the environment.

**Table 6.3**  Chapter summary

| | Key actors | Key processes | Emphasis on political economy | What causes change? | Global institutions? | View of conflict in global relations? |
|---|---|---|---|---|---|---|
| Trade as beneficial | MNCs; national governments; IGOs; individuals; NGOs | Capitalist production, exchange and consumption of goods, services, capital, knowledge, and labour leading to: Economic development and advancement | Interaction between markets with each other within a system of states | Globalisation; industrialisation; urbanisation; economic growth; capitalism | Essential to the facilitation of international and global trade; maintenance of laws and structures that promote and encourage trade | Trade as a key form of relationship that can prevent inter-state conflict through increasing interdependence, trust and friendship; conflicts hinder and undermine trade |
| Trade as problematic | MNCs; national governments; IGOs; individuals; NGOs | Capitalist production, exchange and consumption of goods, services, capital, knowledge, and labour leading to: Exploitation; marginalisation; alienation; dependency; underdevelopment | Interaction between markets with each other within a system of states | Globalisation; industrialisation; urbanisation; economic growth; capitalism | Essential to the maintenance of a global order that benefits the rich few while trapping the poor masses in poverty | A key result of the inequalities, greed and competition inherent in the capitalist practice of global trade |

# Reflective questions

1    What is the significance of international/global trade on international stability and economic growth according to liberals, realists and structuralists?
2    How significantly have levels of international/global trade increased since the end of the Second World War?
3    If FTAs seek to encourage trade by reducing or removing barriers to trade, does the proliferation of such agreements necessarily mean that trade will continue to increase? And to what extent?
4    How far can we say that international/global trade is driven by MNCs?
5    How have formal modelling methodologies developed and which would you use to analyse contemporary trade processes?
6    Are there negative impacts of international/global trade?

# Suggestions for further reading

Acharyya, R. and Kar, S. (2014) *International Trade and Economic Development*, Oxford: Oxford University Press.

Baghwati, J. (2003) *Free Trade Today*, Princeton, NJ: Princeton University Press.

Bernasconi-Osterwalder, N., Magraw, M., Oliva, M.J., Tuerk, E. and Orellana, M. (2014) *Environment and Trade: A Guide to WTO Jurisprudence*, London: Routledge.

Bernstein, W. (2009) *A Splendid Exchange: How Trade Shaped the World*, London: Atlantic Books.

Gervais, D. (2014) *Intellectual Property, Trade and Development*, 2nd edn, Oxford: Oxford University Press.

Gunder Frank, A. (1979) *Dependent Accumulation and Underdevelopment*, London: Macmillan Press.

Harvey, D. (2005) *A Brief History of Neoliberalism*, Oxford: Oxford University Press.

Heron, T. (2014) *The Global Political Economy of Trade Protectionism and Liberalization: Trade Reform and Economic Adjustment in Textiles and Clothing*, London: Routledge.

Marrewijik, C. van (2002) *International Trade and the Global Economy*, Oxford: Oxford University Press.

Narlikar, A. (2003) *International Trade and Developing Countries: Bargaining Coalitions in the GATT and WTO*, London: Routledge.

Sampson, G. (ed.) (2009) *The WTO and Global Governance: Future Directions*, New York: United Nations University.

Smith, A. (2003) [1776] *The Wealth of Nations*, New York: Bantam Books.

Stiglitz, J. and Charlton, A. (2007) *Fair Trade For All: How Trade can Promote Development*, Oxford: Oxford University Press.

Van den Berg, H. and Lewer, J.J. (2014) *International Trade and Economic Growth*, London: Routledge.

Wallerstein, I. (1981) *The Modern World System: Capitalist Agriculture and the Origins of the Modern World System*, London: Academic Press.

Wheeler, K. (2012) *Fair Trade and the Citizen-Consumer: Shopping for Justice*, Basingstoke: Palgrave Macmillan.

World Trade Organization (2013) *International Trade Statistics 2013*, Geneva: WTO.

# 7 Global finance

## Chapter learning outcomes

After reading this chapter, students should be able to:

- Understand what makes up the global financial system, and how it operates, including explaining key terms and vocabulary relating to it.
- Have a sound basic understanding of the history of the development of the global financial system, and of why finance is central to all activity in IPE.
- Be able to explain how the institutions and regulation of global finance have changed, and with what effects, before and after 2008.
- Understand the arguments about the main causes of the global financial breakdown in 2007–2010, and be able to debate the relative merits of at least two explanations of the crisis.
- Have a clear sense of why the global financial system is of such importance to all governments and why the major states in the global system have found it impossible to leave the management of the financial system to markets or banks.
- Have an understanding of how and why the global financial system has recovered from the crisis of the 2000s, and the current issues and problems it now faces.

## Introduction

The global financial system is at once (i) a market in which money itself, and financial products, representing credit, debt and risk, are bought and sold; (ii) a structure of exchange, what account-ants would call a pattern of flows of funds, in which first Britain, then the US, then Japan, and most recently China has acted as the dominant provider of funds for the major debtor nations and firms; and (iii) a set of institutional arrangements, including regulators and rules and institutional procedures, most obviously exemplified in recent years by the continuing rise of the G20 bloc of leading developed and developing nations along with global institutions and key market actors who, it could be said, both largely caused the 2007–2009 crisis and enjoyed success (so far) in resolving it. It is also a system of power that distributes gains, losses and the prospects of future gains and losses in a number of different forms.

The chapter takes as a main starting point the global financial crisis of 2007–2008, but of course the world financial system has both a long history, as we shall see shortly, and also more recent issues and problems. The crisis was the greatest in the history of the contemporary world system, and lasted even longer than the crisis of 1929–1932. Reading what follows, bear in mind that (as of 2016; all figures from the *Financial Times* various days) the world GDP, production of goods and services, the 'real economy', is worth roughly $79 trillion. That is 79 with twelve noughts after it. If that seems a very large figure, annual transactions in the global financial system are worth (calculations vary) roughly ten to twelve times that amount, and the total stock of world debt con-siderably more. Global pension funds alone are worth an estimated $128tr, and emerging market economies (including Russia, China, Brazil and others) have added to the stock of global debt by roughly the same amount ($70tr) as total global GDP since 2010. The fact that world debts are rising so much faster than world production is a source of concern this chapter will return to; but it illustrates very well the importance of this topic: finance, credit and debt are prime movers of economic activity, and in crisis are sources of major risks in the IPE. This was not always so, but it has been the case for many years now.

# Two stories of financial globalisation

The financial crisis that began in 2007 demonstrated the vital importance of global finance. It also demonstrates that the financial system that emerged from the 1980s was a good deal less stable than many had imagined when it was leading world economic growth in the early 2000s. Sixty years ago, the total volume of financial transactions in the international system were determined largely by the volume of trade and foreign direct investment (FDI), together with an element for the repayment of debts. But the proportion of international financial transactions grew throughout this time. In the dollar and oil crises of the early 1970s, it already made sense to say that the world economy was dominated by financial structures and processes – in a phrase made famous by the scholar Susan Strange, it had become a 'finance driven global economy'. Globalisation did not start then; but it did continue to accelerate. In the 1980s, led by the US, German and British governments, formal state regulation of financial markets was significantly reduced, markets grew very rapidly, and new kinds of banking were created. World finance became what Strange called a 'global casino' driven by high risk taking for high rewards, and stoked by the circulation of huge amounts of what she called 'mad money'. Many of these funds circulated very quickly around the world system in ways that governments found hard to grasp, never mind control. In this stage of the globalisation of financial activity, financial transactions became significantly but not totally disconnected from the 'real economy' of trade in goods and services, tourism, and international investment and job creation. Rapid flows of 'hot money' – money borrowed for very short terms for speculative investment – came to dominate the financial system. Bankers dealt in risky investments but also provided the finance that fuelled mergers and acquisitions and corporate growth. Governments responded slowly, and in some respects the leading governments responded by trying to do less regulation in finance, partly because they believed they could not actually regulate successfully, and partly because the political leaders in power in the 1980s in the US, Japan, Germany and the UK shared a commitment to neo-liberal values, which suggested that states should intervene as little as possible in economic activity. The globalisation of finance is for the most part a relatively recent transformation, perhaps partly a flight from common sense. We are where we are today because of globalisation, and most of that happened since the 1980s.

That at least is one story. It is the story that, according to many newspapers and blogs, explains the origins of the 2007–2008 crisis. It contains *important elements* of truth; but it is actually *far from being the truth*. We need a more sophisticated and historically informed story. In this view, finance has *always* been international, and the roots of modern capitalism, which lie in the creation of modern banking in the fourteenth and fifteenth centuries, were international from the start. Globalisation is not new, and global finance has been at the heart of most economic activity, including the growth of the modern state, since then. There were important new elements in the post-1980s financial system, of course; but they need to be much more carefully examined than the general story of the previous paragraph.

The story of the origins of banking in the fourteenth century are important here. Rich merchants in wool and metals in Italy and Austria and the Low Countries found themselves with spare money in one place (where they sold their goods) and a need to pay debts (for the wool or spices or precious metals they had bought) or save for future investment in another place far away. This was at a time when much of Europe was in continuous warfare, where mercenary armies dominated much of the continent, and where moving money around in the form of gold and silver was especially risky. The solution was the letter of credit rather than moving cash itself. The letter of credit was guaranteed by the signature on it, and by the reputation of the banking house that issued it; a banker had to be known and trusted to have letters of credit accepted. But at the same time, governments cast jealous eyes on the money that these merchants were gathering. As a banker, you might have two choices. Some monarchs simply took your money on some pretext or other, some of which involved taking your life at the same time. Or you could give cash to the state to fund its wars and bureaucracy, in exchange for the same kinds of letters of credit, hoping they would be worth something later on, that the state would redeem them and pay back the loan they represented. You took big risks: when, to pay for a great war with France in 1346, English King Edward III reneged on all his debts (what we would call bonds) to Italian banks, in a stroke he destroyed all the newly emerging Italian banks he had borrowed from. It took thirty years, and the aftermath of the impact of the Black Death (1348–1351), to recover. Wrecking the established banking houses gave the opportunity for a second generation of newer banks, including most famously the Medici in Florence, to emerge later in the century. The invention of the letter of credit, together with the creation of a new system of accounting, double-entry bookkeeping, and the needs of the emerging modern state for funds created modern banking, and in the process what came to be called capitalism.

Early merchant capitalism was intrinsically linked to early banking, trade and the beginnings of government finance through the creation of a market for letters of credit from merchants and governments. Today letters of credit are still used in international trade. But much of the debt in the international system takes the form of bonds. Bonds are simply corporate or state debt, which can be bought and sold. Any asset that is turned into a document that can be traded and that represents the risks and possible future rewards of something is said to be 'securitised', a term that does not mean security as in the absence of risk. This emerging market financed the activities of trade and state power. It was sold on, giving the buyers freedom to turn their paper back into liquid cash, and redeemed – given back to the issuer in exchange for cash – when their time period runs out. The creation of the letters of credit and what becomes the bond market is the first piece in the jigsaw of modern capitalism, not a relatively recent invention, although of course there have been many changes since the mid-fourteenth century. Governments can benefit from this because it hugely increases the amount they can spend, so long as they are able to continue to pay the interest on debts they can continue to borrow. They do not have to pay back the principal they borrowed. The growth of 'big government' in the sixteenth century depended on it. The growth of even bigger government in the nineteenth and twentieth century followed the same pattern. Small powers that were good at managing debt – like Holland – flourished at the expense of larger but less financially competent rivals. Failure to effectively manage their debt reduced the greatest European Empire of the early seventeenth century, Spain, to ruin. They were replaced as system leader first by Holland, then for a longer term by France. Britain floundered in and out of debt for some time, but found ways of following the Dutch model. To that model, London dealers added the power of a central credit management organisation, the Bank of England, founded in 1694, which managed the state's debts as well as issuing money, something that directly contributed to Britain's emerging trade, military and economic power.

The link between governments and merchant capitalism is fundamental to the whole economic system. All governments have depended on their ability to raise money to fund wars and increased public spending on international markets. But it is not only governments that depend on bankers. The growth in trade and big government in the nineteenth century produced a further evolution in the state. But it also supported the growth of industrial capitalism, capitalism that was founded more on industrial investment and production than on trade in credit notes and bonds. Britain became the world's principal exporter of capital, funding the building of US French and Russian railways and the expansion of several empires as well as her own. But the model was in significant ways the same as before. And the banking system has also always depended on the state and its regulation, its judicial powers, and its capacity to enforce contracts and establish international agreements. The relationship works in reverse. When the global banking system collapsed in 2007–2008, as in 1929–1932, only state action could protect the system. In the 2000s, this action was taken by central banks such as the US Federal Reserve and the European Central Bank, and committed huge reserves to finance and also to insure the system. A few individual banks and bond dealers were allowed to go bust, including most famously the US firm Lehman Brothers, in September 2008. But across the global financial system, the state had an overwhelming interest in protecting the system even at the cost of several trillion dollars of extra public spending. This financial system took 300 years to establish. But what is characteristic about the modern state and the modern financial system is that they are not merely 'interdependent'; they are symbiotic – they have evolved together and each could not exist without the other. All this works only because it works at a global level: it has always been international, but it is even more intensively internationalised today than ever before.

In 1907, 1929, 1987, 1997 and again in 2000/2001, there were significant shocks in the global financial system. The recent 2007–2010 crisis is therefore part of a pattern. A sudden and apparently unpredictable crisis is not new. The most violent of these was undoubtedly the crisis of 1929. The impact of 1929 was very important not just for its tragic consequences in the 1930s, but also for the future of economic diplomacy. International institution building at the end of the Second World War and in the subsequent crises of the 1950s and 1970s was directed primarily to ensuring that the experience of 1929–1932 would not be repeated. Central banks and governments cooperated with the market to achieve this. In the Asian financial crisis of 1997, some banks went bust, mainly in Japan and South East Asia, and there was a knock-on effect on Western financial markets. But the main gainers in the crisis were the US, which re-asserted its power over what had seemed to be rising Japanese and Asian institutions, and China, which mostly stood apart from the bad loans that had helped to cause the crisis. In the 2000/2001 stock market crisis (the 'dot com' collapse), financial markets were not undermined by a powerful shift in investor confidence, partly because of effective government-led responses to stabilise global finance. It looked as if financial crises – famously described over and over by politicians and commentators as 'boom and bust' – were things of the past. They were, of course, mistaken. If anything, the global financial system is more vulnerable to major shocks not just because of its size or its interdependence, but also because of the complexity of the system and the difficulty that follows from that complexity in correctly assessing the risks potential weak points in the system present.

A word on 'stability': the international financial system is not stable, and nor is the international economy as a whole. This is, to put it at its crudest, because global capitalism is not stable, and does not seek stability, and *cannot* remain stable. Global capitalism is dynamic, and only functions effectively if there is instability. Political commentators of all parties invariably say that they want 'stable growth' (does anyone want stable recession?). But stable growth is a contradiction in terms. What they probably mean is that they want manageable or sustainable growth rather than periods of explosively rapid growth followed by dramatic recessionary collapses. But stability has been a feature of international financial markets only if they are measured on a particular timescale. Day to day, they are dynamic, and that dynamism enables markets to trade, and traders to make money out of the changing margins they find. It is a basic principle of capitalism that successful risk takers make money, while unsuccessful ones fail. Over longer time periods, financial markets are also unstable, reflecting not just a 'business cycle' of trade and exchange, but also a cycle of the creation and destruction of credit and asset value in markets for financial products. The task regulators set themselves is not to eliminate instability completely (which would kill the market), but to control its extremes and their consequences. This has never proved easy to do.

## The core ingredients of global finance

Global finance involves the buying and selling of particular assets – money, credit and debt, and financial instruments linked to them. Some of this business is *investment* – money committed for projects, which, in the longer or shorter term, are directed to produce profits, usually called *capital*. Some is the *repayment* of earlier debts. It also includes *deals between governments and government-backed institutions* such as the International Monetary Fund (IMF) and Bank for International Settlements (BIS). But most of this activity is done in the market by banks, firms, insurance companies with money to invest. These markets are regulated where they operate in particular national jurisdictions by a mixture of private and government bodies. But international markets have become increasingly complex, and at the same time have evolved less certain forms of regulation, to which we will return shortly. International trade is still a very significant factor in the demand for money in the world system. But, as already noted, trade has for quite a long time not been the *determinant* of demand for finance. If you buy a foreign car, a Japanese brand electronic item, which was probably made in South East Asia, American software, Indian financial services, Scottish life insurance, or when you book your holiday abroad, you are creating a demand for currency. This is so because people, including workers, suppliers and shareholders in the country your product or service comes from, want to be paid in the currency they use, not in the currency you use. Trade creates a pattern of cash and currency movement, which mirrors the movement of the goods and services themselves. Trade in insurance, including insurance for trade, adds to this pattern. But as already suggested, these 'real economy' flows are only a relatively small proportion of global financial flows, not more than 10 per cent, and arguably now as little as 5 per cent, depending on how the measure is done.

The global financial system is thus not a single market. It consists of a set of separate but interconnected markets. In addition to the markets for money, capital and debt, there are markets for commodities that may substitute for money, most obviously gold, but also for anything in which investors might have confidence, from oil in transit (in other words, oil actually in a tanker at sea may change hands many times before it arrives at a destination port if investors are drawn to short-term investment in the commodity), to land (real estate), and to Chicago pork bellies (an investment vehicle invented at a time when the Chicago commodities exchange was right next to the meat market, and less surprising to Chicagoans than to most other people). Markets for debt exist not just because institutions firms and governments need to borrow money; they also exist because institutions, firms, money and individuals have money to invest and seek out higher rates of return, even though high returns normally signify higher risks. Crudely, if there was no debt market, investors would have to keep their cash under the bed or in the cellar, where it would earn nothing.

All of these markets are not just ways of getting access to funds or ways of investing. They are without exception also channels for speculation. And they are ways of *quantifying risks* – putting a price on the risk of holding *or not holding* a particular asset over a given longer or shorter time period – in ways that allow those risks to be passed on or hedged in a market. All financial markets have this role, which we could describe as an insurance function – they enable dealers to insure against possible changes in price or availability in the future. So financial markets manage several different kinds of risk at the same time. First of all these include the risk of price movements in a given commodity. But they also include the risk of holding a given commodity or bond or debt as against the risk of not holding them, and as against the risks involved in holding any other alternative. Since any risk can be measured (at least in theory), complex mathematical models can measure the trade-off between different kinds of risk.[1] 'Derivatives' are financial products whose value is derived from that of other products using some version or other of these mathematic models, derived from the price or expected change in price of a package of investment products. These emerged in the 1990s as important investment vehicles. By the 2000s, they had taken so many varied forms that is had become impossible to define very accurately what a derivative is or was. Those selling derivatives had to understand both the mathematics and the markets they were dealing with if they were to succeed without simply engaging in a dressed-up gamble. It only became evident after the 2008 crisis from reports to the US Congress, the UK Parliament and other institutions, that most people involved in derivatives markets either did not understand the maths or did not understand the markets. In the reports, it became clear that quite a lot of market players did not really understand either, and that regulators did not understand either the maths or the risk management either, something that they have sought to improve since.

# The growth of a globalised financial system: a little more history

The global financial system evolved fairly rapidly throughout the nineteenth century for four main reasons. First, there was a continuing growth of industrial capitalism that created a growth in trade in industrial goods, and the equally important increases in exchanges of raw materials and food-stuffs to pay for those products, created a growing demand for money and investment. Second, there was rapid growth in financial speculation, especially in government, railway and banking bond issues, particularly in the last thirty years of the nineteenth century. Third, as the 'modern state' emerged, with its greater role in the economy and in social affairs (education, pensions, social provision, local government) as well as the greater cost of advanced technology military equipment led to a transformation of the larger states economies, with a steadily increasing reliance on finance based on the sale of short- and long-term debt. Fourth, imperial competition was an important driver in the growth of global financial interests, and investment patterns (German money in Turkey and the Balkans, France in north Africa, Britain in South America) followed political as well as commercial interests. At the start of the twentieth century, these formed a relatively balanced system under the broad hegemony of British run institutions. Those institutions included the pound sterling, the Bank of England and London money markets. Investment channelled from London funded the growth of the American and Russian rail systems and the beginnings of global oil markets in the 1880s. Rules set largely by British institutions, with some consultation with others, especially French and American banks and investment houses, dominated the global economy. But there was virtually no formal regulation of any international activity other than trade by international inter-governmental institutions. There was little perception that formal regulation could be necessary. This was partly because the system seemed to work, despite the instability of growth and recession over the business cycle. It was also because there was a theory that appeared to explain effectively why the global financial system worked and why it would go on working – free trade liberalism. Free trade liberalism (see Chapter 1 for these basic concepts) was never universally accepted, and most politicians and business people in Germany France and Russia had grave doubts about it. But at the core of the system, including in the main British institutions, the theory was largely accepted by those who managed the 'rules of the game'.

The First World War changed all that. The relative stability of the global system was wrecked from the onset of war. Britain had been the world's leading exporter of capital throughout the nineteenth century, even if German, French and American capital exports started to challenge the

British leadership from about 1870 onwards. Currencies were valued in relation to gold, but a good deal of trade was done in British currency, and the value of sterling underpinned the stability of the world trade system. Quite suddenly, in the spring of 1916, after two years of fighting and the enormous costs of an industrialised war, Britain became a net importer of capital for the first time since at least the mid-seventeenth century, as it sold off foreign assets as well as vast quantities of bonds, in order to pay for the war. It was the US that replaced Britain as the world's main lender. Nationalist-minded political and business leaders in the US may have felt that the switch was only right, but in fact the US was ill-prepared to take on the role of global hegemon, which was implicit in this fundamental underlying shift in the structure of global capitalism. It was not until 1944, and in very different circumstances, that the US assumed a role of effective system manager. The US role in the 1920s was important, especially when US loans underwrote the partial recovery of the global economy and paid for much of the costs of German currency stabilisation after their crisis in 1922–1923. But US administrations were reluctant and inconsistent in taking on the role of global economic manager, and the UK had not completely given up aspirations for that role. The crash of 1929 and its incompetent management by all governments of its economic aftermath, produced a wave of economic nationalism that helped to bring about the Second World War. The instability of the years 1914–1949 was of a different kind to any that had gone before, at least since 1650.

Towards the end of the Second World War, it became clear to most people in business and finance as well as government in the US that they had to take a radically new leading role in global finance. This was out of self-interest, to protect investments and to enable other countries that had no foreign exchange or dollar reserves to access dollars so they could buy the exports the US wanted to produce in a peacetime economy. The stabilisation of global finance, which included the stabilisation of exchange rates, the creation of a new institutional framework, the stabilisation of payments between economies, the greater regulation of government and corporate borrowing by credit rating agencies and banks, and the introduction of more transparent rules for bond markets all helped to create the conditions for growth. This took several years to effect, and the disappearance of Germany from global trade and finance for four or more years made recovery more complicated. However, by 1949 this had changed. International trade and international finance were together the moving forces of global economic growth and global economic integration in the period from 1949–1970. This produced very important benefits. But it is also important to say that it produced an important skew in the distribution of the benefits. The wealthier countries – the OECD group – got much more out of this growth than many developing countries, although it is also true that a small group of developing countries, mostly in East Asia, benefited greatly too.

In the 1950s and 1960s, global financial leaders were also anxious to maintain stable exchange rates. The Bretton Woods system tried to guarantee fixed but flexible' exchange rates by linking the value of all major currencies to that of the dollar. The IMF acted to support governments when they could not keep rates fixed. The US Treasury also in effect acted as an important international player. This was seen as desirable because it provided predictability for investors and stability to boost trade. It worked well for twenty years, but was dependent on the stability of the dollar. In the later 1960s, the dollar lost value due to domestic inflation and the costs of the US international role. The US government lost its willingness to support stable exchange rates if it would cause deflation and unemployment at home. In 1970–1971, the Nixon Administration abandoned the system, a unilateral move that caused enormous disruption for a short time. But the rise of other currencies and economies was bringing the dollar's dominance to an end, and the new system of flexible exchange rates proved more workable than had been thought. Some countries developed currency collaboration, including several different structures in the European Union before the decision to develop a common currency, the Euro, at the end of the 1990s. But the system of flexible exchange rates, which still exists, has proved flexible. One main effect has been that, on the whole, exchange rate policy has become depoliticised, and attention has focussed on other financial problems. But exchange rate instability remains a potential problem, evidenced today by concerns about the continuing relative rise in China's currency and the relative decline in the value of the dollar long term. We cannot rule out a future major currency crisis, marking shifts in global financial power between major players as in the past, but flexibility has tended to create markets where adjustment happens more gradually rather than in sudden shocks.

---

**EXAMPLE BOX**

## Credit creation

In most national economic systems, it is only lawful for banks or the government to create credit. Other financial institutions – funds of different kinds, insurance companies, investment houses' hedge funds and so on – can trade in money and credit and financial instruments that represent them, but cannot *create* money or credit. Governments have the power of credit creation as the issuers of legal money –they can decide how much to issue at any time in order to balance the need to grow the economy and control inflation. But when government-backed currency collapses other forms of money may be introduced – ranging from the currencies of other countries (often dollars, as in Zimbabwe in the late 2000s and much of Central Asia after the collapse of the USSR in the 1990s) to cigarettes and silk stockings (in Germany in the mid-1920s and again in 1945–1949), to almost anything else where people trusted its value more than that of formal money. In desperate food crises, food too, including international aid supplies, have acted as currency. This is obviously harmful since it encourages the hoarding rather than the distribution of the food.

Credit is most often created when a bank lends out more than it has taken in deposits. This is normal banking behaviour, because bankers know that at any one time their customers will only require a proportion of the money they have put in the bank back. If this 'normal' behaviour changes, because customers lose confidence in the bank or the currency, it causes a 'run on the bank', where customers demand all their deposits back at once. Governments normally in effect insure the banks against this by acting as 'lender of last resort' (LLR), being willing to cover a run on the bank, but at interest rates high enough to discourage the banks from abusing their right to create credit. In both British and American law (and in other legal systems too), banks' rights to create credit are very specifically defined, with some banks having greater independence than others, and, as noted above, non-bank financial institutions having no right to create credit. On international markets, however, they may be able to find ways of getting round that restriction. This weakness of regulation was a factor –although not the principal cause – of the 2007–2009 crisis.

Capital ratios are created when governments impose limits on how much money banks can create by requiring them to keep liquid assets (things that they can use in a crisis to pay demands for money – cash, short term debt, gold) in accounts in the national bank, and by requiring them to hold a percentage of the credit they issue as liquid assets themselves. This ties up bank resources so that they are restricted in the credit they can issue. Normally, careful banks would want to do this anyway. But careless or dishonest banking can threaten the banking system and the whole economy.

Measuring the amount of credit and money in an economy is a difficult and controversial art. Measuring the total amount in the world system is even more difficult. The solution has been not to arrive at a 'true' verdict', but to set accounting standards so that equivalent and comparable measures are generally used. Figures from some states, and some banks, are highly unreliable because those standards are not universally maintained.

# What was the 'international debt crisis' and where did it come from?

One aspect of global finance that has been of continuing difficulty has been global debt, usually but not always meaning 'Third World debt'. This emerged as a problem at the end of the 1970s. At various points since Mexico defaulted on huge debts in the early 1980s, a number of countries have created enormous piles of debt, which they have then either defaulted on or threatened to default on if the banks did not radically change the terms and conditions of their loans. Sometimes, as with Argentina's repeated difficulty, the main cause has been persistent government incompetence. But there are usually more complex causes, and the structure of global finance and the working of global markets, has been the principal cause of much of the debt crisis. It is worth adding that in 1976, in the middle of a foreign exchange crisis, the UK borrowed substantial sums from the IMF, as she had for roughly the same reason directly from the US in 1946. In the Eurozone crisis after 2010 (following the global crisis of 2007–2008), Ireland, Greece, Cyprus, Portugal needed urgent loans from international donors to manage their economies, while the much larger economies of Italy and Spain teetered on the brink of a similar fate, and Greece has experienced much graver problems that continue; emerging markets are not by any means the only ones facing borrowing problems.

The origins of the global debt crisis lie in the willingness of investors, some might say investors with more money than sense, to put money into bad business around the world. It is not that simple, but that is a valid starting point. At various points in the history of international finance, good money has gone down a great many bad drains. The purpose, of course, was a search for high profits from high-risk operations. In the 1840s and 1850s, waves of investment poured into railway companies across many countries. Most of the original rail businesses went bankrupt, because they were badly run or overambitious (or both), and some were merely scams to attract investment and steel it. The railway boom only came to fruition when much more carefully run, second generation companies came to expand the market after the initial boom and bust. This pattern was so closely repeated in the biotechnology investment boom of the 1980s and in the 'dot com' boom in Internet business in 1997–2000 that one can only wonder at the ignorance of those who supervised it (banks will pay for most senior executives to do an MBA, but few fund programmes in economic history). In the 1920s, money flowed even faster into the US stock market, whether from large investors, foreign banks or small guys in the diner, only to disappear in the 1929 Crash. In the early 2000s, at a time when stock markets were high and markets for other assets also looked solid, many people, and many institutions, with money to invest committed it to mortgage backed securities in the US in the belief that somehow their risk would disappear in clever mathematics. Mortgages were 'bundled' together in large packages that were said to eliminate the risks from the weaker ones, but the risks, far from disappearing, spread contagion around the market. In the same way, investors in the 1970s had put money into the developing world or global South, especially money gathered from oil producers that grew rich in the early 1970s after the price rise of 1973. Much of this money was invested in high-return, high-risk investments. These investments were generally not in the poorest countries, but in those developing countries with some natural resources or oil or strong agriculture to exploit. At the end of the 1970s, material, energy and agricultural prices collapsed. The prospects of these investments showing a return from cocoa, coffee, oil, copper or iron disappeared. 2008 was not the same as the late 1970s; but it was similar enough that the lesson of the second might well have taught caution to investors and institutions in the second. But the crisis of the early 2000s was predicted, if at all, to very few experts, and they were generally not heard.

These financial crises have been very important for the most developed countries, but they have had even more profound effects for the less-developed countries and economies of the global South.

In the 1970s, developing countries became saddled not just with large debts, but with growing interest payments they could not make. By the end of the 1980s, and ever since, many countries have faced debt repayments much greater than the total value of foreign aid and investment they received. This most acutely affected those countries with some assets (usually raw materials); the poorest and least endowed economies were not able to borrow against the value of assets they didn't possess. Several attempts have been made to eliminate this debt. Some countries have found it easier to default, but the costs are great. Some countries are in effect in default, including some large ones, but it is quietly not recognised. The June 2005 Gleneagles Summit of the G8 attempted to resolve this, partly in the aftermath of huge public campaigning to reduce debt for the 2000 Millennium Development Goals, and partly because developed countries recognised that it was in their own longer-term interest to have healthy growing markets in Africa and Asia. The Summit reached some important agreements, only part of which have been implemented so far. Developing country debt remains an ongoing problem, but one positive side effect of the recent global crisis might be that lenders might become more careful about lending too much to countries that cannot afford it.

# The financial crisis of the 2000s

Suppose you are a relatively ordinary student with not much money. You borrow money from the bank or student loan authority to finance your lifestyle, run a credit card or two which maybe your parents have guaranteed, and so on. If you owe say £6,000 (or $6,000), and the bank for whatever reason suddenly asks for its money back, you have a problem, and possibly a big problem. But suppose you manage to borrow £60 billion (don't think too much about what you might spend it on). At that point, the bank has a problem much more than you do. To lose this amount of money would not simply be a poor image on a balance sheet. It could well threaten the bank's survival, and in turn it might also threaten a national banking system. This is a part of what happened in between August 2007 and September 2008 in the Western banking system, when banks found themselves with huge piles of debt, including bonds they had bought at high prices in boom years that had become worthless. The American banking system in particular nearly collapsed because of debts backed by mortgages on houses and land. The British banking system was also threatened, but less so because there was relatively less bad debt, but there was enough to cause a serious crisis. And British (and European and Japanese) banks had extensive investments in the US economy that had lost a significant part of their value too. The globalised creation of credit rested on trust in the system as a whole and in its fragmented regulators, including central banks, credit rating agencies, underwriters, banking associations and other market managers. This trust proved to be mistaken. The incentives to drive ahead in creating new financial instruments, including the infamous mortgage backed securities (and collaterised debt obligations (CDOs)), outweighed the caution bankers might have felt in dealing with risk in new and very complex ways. Banks had become used to building deals on the back of heavy borrowing from other banks, highly leveraged deals. When, suddenly in August 2008, banks ceased to trust this inter-bank market and stopped lending in it, they equally found it impossible to borrow from it. They could not refinance existing deals, never mind create new ones. For a period of time, much conventional banking activity stopped until government intervention gradually refuelled the system. The crisis grew rapidly because it became a fundamental crisis of trust in the system.

It was indeed government intervention that saved the banking system. Governments in the US, UK, the Eurozone and Asia pumped huge amounts of funding in the form of newly created credit into the global system. The International Monetary Fund (IMF) also played an important role, lending to severely weakened economies. Governments in the US, UK and the Eurozone supported their intervention by creating vast resources of credit based on their sovereign powers (called 'monetary policy easing' at first, and then 'quantitative easing' by central bankers). If they had not done so the entire fabric of western banking and finance would quite probably have collapsed. But doing so runs the risk of leaving an inheritance of high debts into the future. The calculation was always that present stability was necessary despite future risks, which could be managed in due course. Some banks were allowed to collapse, including the long established Lehman Brothers in the US. Others were in effect nationalised. This was not wholly strange in countries with a tradition of nationalisation, including Britain and Germany, but in the US it was a radical step that provoked great political opposition. However, with the hindsight of a further year, it is clear that this action was helpful and saved the core elements of the financial system from meltdown. There are future risks, but a short-term catastrophe was avoided – fairly narrowly.

## Global financial institutions

The global financial system is characterised by some important institutions. Some are very well known; some are powerful but hardly discussed in the media and little known. Some are private, some public, and some in effect cut across the public/private distinction.

### The International Monetary Fund (IMF)

Originally created to manage international exchange rate stability in the post-1944 Bretton Woods System. The IMF has become a major actor both in coordinating aspects of financial policy and in acting as lender of last resort to governments, a role it was originally not intended to have. Power in the IMF depends on the money states put in – the more they contribute the more weighting their votes have. As the mix of leading contributors have changed, the balance of power has changed, but the US and EU continue to dominate the IMF despite the rise of china and Saudi Arabia as contributors, at least so long as they agree together.

### The World Bank (WB)

The World Bank was originally called International Bank for Reconstruction and Development. That title is a better representation of its main roles, which provide funding for development and guidelines and studies on what makes for effective development. The World Bank was powerfully shaped by the so-called 'Washington consensus' in the 1980s and 1990s, cooperating with the IMF and US Treasury in imposing a neo-liberal agenda on the organisation. But by the late 1990s, in response to continuing crises in the developing world as well as changes in the Clinton administration in the US, the WB moved somewhat apart from the IMF and the nature of the Washington consensus shifted and became less dictatorially neo-liberal. The WB's anti-poverty programmes have become a distinctive instrument of funding for development.

Perhaps confusingly, we should note that in most respects, the World Bank acts as a fund, and the IMF acts as a bank. The IMF does not have the independent credit creation powers of most banks – it depends on the direct authorisation of participating governments, and is not a credit creation agency in the way that governments and international banks are; but with the specific authorisation of governments it can create credit through its loans, and it has done so, including in the recent past.

## The Bank for International Settlements (BIS)

One of the least known and least understood of global financial institutions. Important not least because central bankers meet more regularly than anywhere else through the BIS. It therefore acts as an effective coordinator even when it is not trying to act as an enforcement body. Its primary function is to act as a clearing house for international payments between governments and central banks – hence its title. But it has become a main tool of international economic cooperation on finance, and has developed a series of tools on capital ratios (the Basle 2 agreements), which may bring greater stability to international banking if and when they are fully implemented. Formally, its regulatory role is to advise central banks, although it does have some important powers. In practice, its formal role is blurred by the fact that central bankers treat it (among other things) as a principal forum for the joint design of global financial regulation on issues such as the minimum holdings of secure capital, which individual commercial banks should keep to maintain reliable ratios of assets to the money they lend.

## The Organisation for Economic Cooperation and Development (OECD)

The OECD has no executive role over global finance but is an important source of cooperation and policy coordination. It has also been a source of proposals for regulation of global trade in services, which would include banking finance and insurance, and which, if ever implemented, would bring much greater liberalisation to global markets. These proposals are however frozen, widely opposed by developing countries.

## The G7/G8

Founded in 1974 on a French initiative, the G7 was established as a coordinating body to deal with global financial and economic crises after the 1970 dollar and 1973–1974 oil crisis. Its members are the US, Japan, Canada, France, Italy, the UK, and Germany. Russia was later added as the eighth member. The G7 has been widely criticised, and it has sometimes tried to do much more than proved possible in managing financial issues such as responses to the decline in value of the dollar in the 1980s. It has also vastly broadened its agenda to include security, environment, development and so on. This is mainly because the institution has a semi-permanent and very efficient secretariat who have been able to institutionalise the process of agenda setting and issue negotiation.

## The G20

The G20 is a much more recent body. As of September 2009, after the Pittsburgh Summit it has in effect replaced the G7. This gives it a more effective secretariat, wide agenda setting powers and some executive authority. It includes the leading developing countries, Brazil, China, Indonesia, India and Saudi Arabia, as well as all the G8 members. Africa is seriously unrepresented in the G20, as are other smaller states and non-state movements. But it has the ability to represent core world financial actors. It is too early to evaluate whether the G20 will succeed in the missions it set itself at Pittsburgh, but no other body has the authority or power to do what it is attempting. It is a negotiating forum rather than a body with formal supervisory powers, but it has considerable influence, not least because of the scope of its membership and the relative effectiveness of its secretariat.

## Central banks

Each country has its own central bank responsible for regulating banking and financial institutions. While most are long standing bodies, the US Federal Reserve system was only created in 1913 after a series of crises showed the inadequacy of governance by separate state bodies. The European Central Banks was established in 1998 to manage the Euro and the Eurozone, which today has nineteen members, including the main EU member states other than the UK. Central banks cooperate closely in their international functions as well as in coordinating much of their regulatory work. While some central banks are legally independent of government, a model derived from German practice after 1949, all are open to close supervision by government, not least because in a crisis it is the state that underwrites resources central banks may provide to bale out the financial system.

## Credit rating agencies

Tim Sinclair and others have, through research over nearly twenty years, shown how important the credit rating agencies have become in the global financial system, at least up to 2008. Credit rating agencies are independent companies that make judgments about firms and governments by rating their debt. In other words, they make a judgment about the riskiness of the bonds they issue – are they a good risk or not? If they are a very good risk, they carry a 'triple A' rating. This means they have a high status, but also that they will pay less to borrow money. If a firm or bank loses its rating, for example, downgraded from 'triple A' to 'double A', there are several consequences, including a loss of prestige and almost certainly serious damage to the share price, but also an increase in the costs of borrowing money into the future. Exactly the same happens with countries – government debt, 'sovereign debt', is rated by the agencies, and if they are able to maintain a high rating the rates they pay to borrow money are lower and their status as trustworthy is reinforced. All this is done by three major businesses, which are independent of any regulation other than normal company law. Three are based in New York, one of those also in London. Together they act as a global regulator of great importance. Sinclair has argued that they are the only effective regulatory force in the global creation of credit, which has been so important in the last twenty years. They rate bonds and debt instruments –specific financial products – rather than the firm or government as a whole, but inevitably their power is seen as a power to award ratings like stars to leading pupils or films in the popular and media mind.

The credit rating agencies are, however, commercial businesses. They act for the firms and governments that they rate. They charge a fee. If a bank launches a new bond, it invites a rating agency to classify it, and if it doesn't like the outcome, at least in theory it might ask another for a different judgment (although mostly the four agencies follow each other closely). The credit rating agencies thus appear to have a conflict of interest – do they serve the interests of the rated bond issuing firm, the market or customers of the bonds rated? The conflict of interest is, however, illusory. Rating agencies did not choose the role of global regulator, which they have evolved, and their first duty is to their shareholders, their secondary duty is to their customers.

## Hedge funds, shadow banks and 'offshore'

Unregulated banking has always existed on the fringes of the global system. But the emergence of new types of banking activity has caused concern about whether it threatens the stability of the financial system as a whole as well as concern about the risks of unregulated banking and investment. Hedge funds are private investment houses. They are not formally 'banks' in the sense that they do not 'take deposits' or create credit in the technical sense. They invest money from companies and rich individuals, seeking the highest returns while aiming to 'hedge' their bets against risks using complex mathematical modelling. Hedge funds are innately risky vehicles for those with enough money to afford heavy losses, but they also invest heavily in specific businesses to 'turn round' weaker firms, pressing managers to act more effectively and kill off loss-making parts of businesses. Hedge funds have a poor reputation not just because of their risk taking, but because their investments often commit them to manufacturing or service companies that they try to transform. Hedge funds worldwide account for an estimated $4.2 trillion of investment, which is a large figure until one looks at the overall size of global finance and money markets; in fact they are significant but not dominant players even if they agreed (and by their nature they are always first of all competing with each other to attract funds). Shadow banking is banking including credit creation, which is outside official regulation. Shadow banking is of more concern to governments and central banks. It is hard to estimate its size. It grew from a tiny element in 2000 to a major factor before 2007; while some (including the leading economist Paul Krugman) blamed the crisis on the growth of unregulated shadow banks and their complex investment instruments, this is controversial. However, it is not questioned that, after an initial fall in 2008, since the crisis, shadow banking has grown rapidly to account for at least $70 trillion (a 2012 figure). That is the equivalent size of world GNP. Because the crisis led to a significant tightening of regulation and control of 'official' banking, fund managers and their investors have sought more profitable unregulated opportunities. One issue here is that it is almost impossible to judge what risks the shadow banking system holds, and this uncertainty is problematic for central banks and regulators but also for potential investors. Shadow banking includes some activities of hedge funds, but not hedge funds as a whole. It also includes many activities conducted 'offshore' in global financial centres. Offshore includes economies such as the British Virgin Islands, Panama, Guernsey and the Bahamas where taxes are low and financial regulation legally set to be permissive. The continuing growth of shadow banking and offshore have been among the most important (mostly unexpected) effects of the crisis, and present some of the most problematic challenges to central banks and governments, and indeed to the idea of democratic control of financial systems.

## Global accounting firms

Global accounting firms set and implement rules for financial reporting. This is technical and may seem geeky. Do not be mistaken – it is of enormous importance. Accountancy businesses define what counts as profit, loss, capital and debt. They use balance sheets to demonstrate the credit-worthiness of governments as well as firms. Crucially, in a financial system dominated by banks and insurance companies, it is accountancy firms who report on the solvency (or otherwise) of those businesses. To be quoted on pretty much any stock exchange in the world from London to Shanghai, from Tehran to Johannesburg, from New York to Sydney, a firm has to have its books audited and its financial standing confirmed by one of the major accounting firms (which have subsidiaries in every country). There were only four such firms, but one, Andersons, was broken because it had been the accountants for the fraudulent US energy business Enron (once briefly the fourth biggest US firm), and when the Enron scandal emerged, the accounting firm that had reported on its accounts and authenticated them as good was destroyed even though it had probably been deceived itself rather than knowingly participating in the giant fraud. Thus three remaining accounting firms (which each have a couple of hundred subsidiaries operating in every country) dominate world finance and have enormous power. That power is as standard setters, educators and regulators as much as in their auditing and accounting roles.

## The global financial system after the financial crisis

By 2015, the global system had returned to roughly the level of production and the volume of financial flows before the crisis began in 2007. Of course, years of investment, saving and spending had been lost. But after a modest and sometimes hesitant recovery, where does the world financial system stand? Global growth never stopped, thanks to the contribution of emerging markets. But despite the role of debt levels as one cause of the 2008 crisis, levels of debt have continued to rise. That includes public debt, the external debt of countries, but also individual and corporate debt. Today, four main issues stand out as significant in shaping the likely future trajectories of the global financial system. These are: (a) the rise and rise of China as a powerful influence, including the difficulties of managing the Chinese currency and its global consequences; (b) the difficulties and growth patterns of emerging markets and their greater significance for world finance and economic activity; (c) the relatively sluggish performance of many of the most developed economies; and (d) the impact of quantitative easing on world markets as well as on developed economy domestic markets and government and central bank policies. This section will also ask how the main theories explored throughout this book might explain some of the issues and problems that arise when one tries to understand how the global financial system has behaved since 2010.

China's increasing importance in global finance is not simply a matter of size or volume of transactions. In the twenty years or more up to 2015, China was a vitally important net exporter of capital, money acquired through trade in goods, including manufactures and primary products. But the Chinese export boom has weakened significantly, and as Chinese firms and state owned enterprises have sought to create domestic demand to replace a decline in exports, the flow of funds from China has been partially reversed: Chinese banks, firms and private consumers have started to borrow more from both domestic and foreign sources, adding to the stock of total world debt. Chinese officials have wobbled on how they wanted to manage the future value of their currency, and this has added to the instability of the yuan, especially in small but significant crises in August and September 2015. China's reduced demand for primary imports for minerals, coal and oil have had powerful effects on global prices, pushing them down and producing further instability in the world economy. Chinese central bank officials have struggled to balance the different demands of global markets, domestic demand and domestic banking stability as they tried to learn how to manage a (relatively) marketised economy and financial system in more difficult times than the years of steady high growth. This has introduced further uncertainty into the world economy even though China's growth has remained at 6.5 per cent, lower than the previous 9–10 per cent, but still high by comparison with other countries. The unintended effects of adjusting China's internal and international financial position to a changed set of national policies and a changed business environment have resounded round the global system, and can be expected to continue to do so into the future. Whether Chinese institutions will be so willing to fund developed country borrowing as in the past remains to be seen, but the combination of debt management and currency value management alongside the question of how to manage lower demand and declining growth are not only domestic policy questions. They raise issues for the world economy and for the US in particular, which will be resolved in the next decade, or, if not well managed, will be important causes of instability.

But China is not the only emerging market economy that has experienced difficulties since the 2007–2008 crisis. Low oil prices have caused energy producers to face declining and uncertain incomes, which has affected Russia in particular, but also Saudi Arabia, Iran and Iraq (which both have other economic problems) and Nigeria, Mexico and Venezuela. It may seem a paradox that low energy prices that benefit many consumers nonetheless have disproportionate impacts on the producers – why should the benefits not balance out the problems causes by low energy prices?

Since the crisis, debt in the global system has increased for a variety of reasons. A factor has been the growth of emerging country debt as noted earlier. But developed country governments, developed country consumers and developed country corporations have also increased their borrowing. Since established banks have been required by governments and regulators to increase their capital holdings to ensure their safety against another crisis, much of this debt has been based outside the established Western banking system. Banks and financial institutions in the developing world have lent more. Government creation of money and credit through quantitative easing has also contributed to the growth of debt, as has central bank policy on keeping interest rates low or at negative rates. The growth of shadow banking outside the established banking system has given rise to a good deal of concern, and shadow banks and hedge funds have undoubtedly contributed to the growth of debt and credit too. But the most important question here is the growth of debt in the major economies and whether or not that is potentially destabilising for the global financial system as a whole. This is an unresolved debate, but we can illustrate the scope of the problem in Table 7.1.

Perhaps of all these issues, including debt, adjustment to China's changing position, unstable energy prices and low growth and low interest rates, the most opaque is the impact of low growth over the long run, and its tendency towards deflation. One key element here is that as ultra-low or negative interest rates have spread from the deflationary economy in Japan to other slow growth economies, including even the (relatively successful) United States, monetary policy has become harder to use effectively. Crudely, governments have only three tools to manage an economy by direct measures: fiscal policy (raising and lowering taxation, and managing the mix of taxes used; monetary policy (controlling the money supply and controlling or influencing interest rates and the availability of credit in the longer and shorter term; and business management through nationalised companies and intervention in mergers, takeovers and other direct means to control the level of competition in a market (often called strategic trade policy or strategic industrial policy). Since the gradual end of the Depression in the 1930s, governments in all countries with a primarily capitalist economy have relied on what they aimed to create as a balanced mix between the three. In the 1970s and 1980s, as Keynesian economic thinking became less fashionable and less widely used, monetary policy was seen as *the* primary means of government economic policy, especially where political pressures kept taxation low. This has remained so even when governments handed part of the control of monetary policy to so-called 'independent' central banks (some are more independent than others, but sovereign power means that governments can always take back control if they need). But if the changing world economy makes monetary policy instruments less effective, then governments are pushed either to do less, something that, despite some politicians' rhetoric, they cannot easily do after the crisis in 2007–2010, or to use fiscal policy and direct

**Table 7.1**  Public debt as a percentage of GDP 2015 (selected countries)

| | | | |
|---|---|---|---|
| Japan | 232 | Germany | 80 |
| Greece | 188 | Brazil | 66 |
| Lebanon | 147 | India | 60 |
| Italy | 147 | China | 42 |
| US | 107 | Turkey | 33 |
| Eurozone 15 | 106 | Indonesia | 26 |
| UK | 103 | Russia | 17 |

*Source*: IMF Survey of Public Debt (May 2016a), Washington DC, IMF.
*Note*: Public debt is calculated as debt owed by governments and state institutions and so excludes debt of corporations and private debt such as student loans, mortgages and credit card debt.

intervention more, which is possible but not so easy either. In short, governments have found their options for economic policy more constrained than before. This may lead to further crises; it may also lead to a greater level of international policy management to redress the diminishing opportunities for management within a given economy.

## Summary

Let's draw together the key elements of the discussion so far:

1  *International economic activity creates a demand for money* – finance for trade, aid, investment, payment of debts, goods, services, holidays and so on.
2  *Some currencies are seen as more reliable than others, and trade tends to take place valued in those currencies.* All currencies have a value on world markets, but the ones that are most trusted are also used to hold reserves in by firms as well as states. These reserve currencies (including the US dollar, Swiss franc, euro and pound sterling, recently joined by the Chinese RMB) are key elements in the structure of global finance.
3  *All money has two functions: it acts as a store of value and as a medium of exchange.* These two roles are not always compatible, for many reasons, but most simply because as a medium of exchange its value will change depending on the demand and supply for money whereas those who use it as a store of value want it to hold the same value over time and will turn to other forms of value storing such as buying land or gold if they cannot be confident it will at least hold its value.
4  *Capital is not merely 'money'*; it is money invested for a particular purpose, bearing particular kinds of risks and carrying a particular reward – profit (which accountants often call return on investment, or ROI).
5  *In the contemporary economy, money takes many different forms, not just cash in your pocket.* That includes credit card borrowing and other loans. It also includes credit created by both banks and governments. Measuring the total amount of money in an economy is quite a contentious business, and economists do not agree on how to do it; but they do have different measures for different purposes. Measuring the total amount of assets (money + equipment + land + other resources) held by a firm is a matter of accounting conventions as well as of simply adding up. Measuring the amount of money in the world economy is even more difficult since a lot of credit creation occurs across borders, and the conventions globally are not so clear cut. At different times and in different places, 'money' has included gold bars, human beings (slaves), conch shells, cocaine and cigarettes. Now most money in the world system is paper money, which has no intrinsic value (no value in itself of itself) other than the confidence that markets put in the institutions and governments that issue it.
6  *Credit is value created by issuing promises to pay later.* All credit is in some way linked to debt. So markets for credit are also markets for debt – most often in the form of government and corporate bonds, which are bought and sold on specialist markets. The value of credit depends on the confidence markets have in the capacity and willingness of governments to redeem their promises later. Sovereign debt is debt owed by governments, who can default on their promises to pay much more easily (but not without a considerable cost) than individuals or firms.
7  *Complex markets are regulated by a complex system of governance in which no one major agency has control.* This system of governance necessarily involves a range of stakeholders. Although sovereign governments have strong powers in this area, they cannot act unless they both agree among themselves and carry the support of markets and leading market actors. The 2007–2009

**Table 7.2** Chapter summary

| | Origins of the crisis | Process | Key actors | Why/how was it resolved |
|---|---|---|---|---|
| Neo-realism | Decline of US power and authority and rise of challenges to it; US has not 'lost' dominant position but has been sharply challenged | See 'origins'. Resolution includes recognition of role of new players especially China (e.g. in G20) but dominant actors – US, IMF, Eurozone, UK – managed the crisis together | States acting alone and through international institutions that they dominate | Effective state action; but perhaps the 'crisis' was not as potentially harmful as often claimed? |
| Classical liberalism | Crisis caused by market failure and failure of regulation by political institutions, banks and other regulators | Interdependence at work; pluralist actors cooperate even though also some disagreement | Key actors are states but also main international institutions, key firms and also networks of linkages | Crisis resolved by effective (if late) international cooperation; weak regulation a factor but not main cause |
| Economic neo-liberalism | Market mechanisms partly failed because of increasing regulation and poor judgement, but the crisis was caused by governments and banks, not 'market failure' | Crisis accelerated quickly because of preceding conditions; competition between banks helped to resolve outcome after initial government intervention | States in their role as regulators of currency and debt levels; banks and private actors also played a major role; did governments let banks off too easily rather than letting more fail? | Governments fulfilled their proper role but then produced long-term problems through quantitative easing and increased regulation |
| Regulation theory | Weak regulation became necessary for effective accumulation as debts and falling profits pressed investors to take increasing risks | Global institutions neglected social and environmental concerns and allowed hectic accumulation in run up to crisis; some of this was recovered but process also led to greater inequality | States and institutions played important roles but had little autonomy. Crisis and outcomes structured by the systems put in place in thirty years before the crisis | Crisis in many ways remains a factor since effective re-regulation only taken a small step in 2008–2010. |
| Gramscian theory | Crisis has deep historic roots in evolution of world economy including weak regulation and neo-liberal policies in 1980s | Hegemon challenged and then reasserted by leading powers (compare 'neorealist' point above). Inequalities increased in crisis | Non-state actors such as credit rating agencies had gained key powers; but crisis resolved when the large states reasserted their hegemony | Not clear the crisis has been resolved as opposed to managed pro tem |
| Feminism | What was the 'crisis'? Crisis for ordinary men and women not just the abstract 'economy'. Agree crisis increased inequalities sharply, but a gendered difference in gains and losses and threats | Process of crisis one of near collapse followed by reassertion of dominant powers and institutions and dominant ideas and patriarchy | Key actors for dominant theories banks, states, firms, an approach that neglects those who were most damaged by the crisis on the margins of economy and society | As Gramscians: not clear 'resolution' of crisis more than a sticking plaster, but what happened in 2008 was necessary as far as it went |

*Note:* This summary table is intended to be a starting point for discussion – you can add to it, and you should be able to sophisticate it too.

crisis has called this system of governance into question, and it is still in need of revision. But that revision is more likely to be a set of developments and refinements than a major transformative reform.

## Reflective questions

1   What is money? How and why is it traded? Are there contradictions between the different roles money fulfils?
2   What are the main institutions of the global financial system? Looking at any one, try to evaluate its performance since 2000.
3   Summarise how you understand the relationship between finance and the growth of the state.
4   Why was there a financial crisis in 2007–2010? Offer two contrasting explanations using theory learned in this text and compare them.
5   What in your view are the strengths and weaknesses of the rise of China in global finance?
6   What in your view are the strengths and weaknesses of the global financial system since 2010? How vulnerable should we feel to another crisis of some kind?

## Note

1. This is the difference between *risk* and *uncertainty* in the jargon of the market. Risks may be greater or smaller, but can in principle be measured; uncertainty is insecurity of a kind, which can be imagined, but not reliably measured. In general, financial markets like risk because they can speculate in it, and hate uncertainty because it creates loss of confidence and on a large scale can undermine confidence in the markets themselves not just in individual items the markets sell.

## Suggestions for further reading

Bank for International Settlements, *Quarterly Reports*, Basel: BIS, various issues.

Eichengreen, B. (2011) *Exorbitant Privilege: The Rise and Fall of the Dollar*, Oxford: Oxford University Press.

Eichengreen, B. (2015) *Hall of Mirrors: The Great Depression The Great Recession and the Uses and Misuses of History*, Oxford: Oxford University Press.

Hozic, A.A. and True, J. (2016) *Scandalous Economics: Gender and the Politics of the Financial Crisis*, Oxford: Oxford University Press.

Hudson, D. (2014) *Global Finance and Development*, London: Routledge.

International Monetary Fund (2009) *World Economic Outlook: Crisis and Recovery*, April, Washington, DC: IMF.

International Monetary Fund (2016a) *IMF Survey of Public Debt*, Washington, DC: IMF.

International Monetary Fund (2016b) *World Economic Outlook: Crisis and Recovery*, April, Washington, DC: IMF.

King, K. (2016) *The End of Alchemy: Money, Banking and the Future of the Global Economy*, Boston, MA: Little Brown.

Parks, T. (2006) *Medici Money: Banking, Metaphysics and Art in Fifteenth-Century Florence*, London: Profile Business.

Stiglitz, J. (2010) *Freefall: Free Markets and the Sinking of the Global Economy*, Harmondsworth: Penguin Books.

Strange, S. (1998) *Mad Money*, Manchester: Manchester University Press.

Wolf, M. (2014) *The Shifts and the Shocks: What We've Learned and Still have to Learn from the Financial Crisis*, London: Allen Lane.

Woodcock, S. and Bayne, N. (2011) *The New Economic Diplomacy: Decision-Making and Negotiation in International Economic Relations*, London: Routledge.

Zehetner, S. (2014) *Regulation of Credit Rating Agencies: A Comparison of Regulatory Regimes in the US and the US*, Vienna: Akademik Verlag.

# 8 Development

## Chapter learning outcomes

After reading this chapter students should be able to:

- Comprehend contemporary definitions of the concept of development.
- Explain what liberal modernisation is and how it is seen by many as the key to achieving development.
- Understand and be able to analyse the 'development problem'.
- Understand the UN Sustainable Development Goals, how they are being pursued and how progress towards achieving them is going.
- Analyse the agency of the major state and non-state actors involved in pursuing development internationally/globally.
- Discuss examples of major development projects found around the world.
- Relate discussion of development to theoretical debates discussed earlier in this book.

## Introduction

This chapter considers the meaning and role of development in the world economy. The contested nature of the term is highlighted and the historical understandings are outlined in the first section. The shift towards a neo-liberal orthodoxy in development is discussed and the impact of salient issues such as sustainability, foreign aid and the debt crisis is highlighted.

Mainstream economists predominantly think of development in terms of overall GDP and rates of GDP per capita. A more holistic view of development, however, can be found in the UN's Human Development Index, which expands the criteria for the definition of development to include the distribution of wealth throughout societies. Health indicators, such as rates of infant mortality, life expectancy and rates of death, are also considered (see also Chapter 14). Similarly, social indicators, including literacy rates, gender equality and access to secondary and higher education, are seen as key features of development. The development discourse operates at many levels featuring many actors with various, sometimes competing, agendas. These can be broadly summarised as those that favour a 'top-down', economic growth-driven version of development and those more interested in establishing a firm foundation of environmental and social sustainability upon which economic growth can prosper.

Within development discourse there are numerous ideological approaches that encompass views on the political, economic, socio-cultural and environmental dimensions of development. The latter half of the twentieth century was dominated by the confrontation between the United States and the USSR and their respective allies. This can broadly be represented as the division between the capitalist and communist political economic approaches. The early 1970s saw a growing awareness of environmental issues, which fed into the debate on what truly constituted 'development'. In the post-Cold War era there has been growing awareness and discussion of worldviews that are not wholly driven by economic growth as an end in itself. Such views can have an explicitly religious or spiritual dimension, seeing development as the attainment of

spiritual purity. In addition to differing conceptions of development there are also differing methodologies and prescriptions as to how to achieve such development.

Fukuyama's *End of History* thesis (referred to previously) explains the end of the Cold War
as well as the so-called 'triumph' of liberalism. While having some convincing elements to
his argument, it fails to address social and environmental development issues. Below, we first
discuss the dominant model of neo-liberal development theories, followed by critiques of this
approach.

# Liberal modernisation

Central to the liberal perspective is an attempt to theorise and explain issues of economic disparity
between states. The end of the Cold War witnessed the formulation of a new geographical political map as many states broke away from the USSR and gained independent status. Many scholars
turned their attention away from 'high politics' and began to theorise about economic development. The North/South divide is a geographical term that distinguishes the rich developed North
from the poor underdeveloped South. This line of division is not, however, straightforward; split-
ting the world into two hemispheres is too simplistic. Australia and New Zealand are situated in
the southern hemisphere but are essentially rich developed countries. On the other hand, the supposedly rich North includes relatively poor countries such as Turkey and Albania. Similarly there
are also huge disparities of wealth distribution *within* Northern and Southern countries. Despite
these inconsistencies the term North/South divide has become an understandable shorthand. It
is widely used to explain the distribution of wealth, poverty and decision-making capacities of
states in the international arena. It is worth recognising here that there are commonalities in these
regional groupings, for example, states located in the North have all gone through the process of
industrialisation whereas states in the South have all experienced political and economic domination, many acting as colonies to the North. Liberal modernisation is a perspective that seeks to
account for the slow economic progress of 'Third World countries'.

## CONCEPT BOX
## Development terminologies in IPE

The term Third World stems from Cold War terminology and the idea that there were two
mutually hostile power blocs and a third that did not align to either superpower; hence,
'three worlds' were depicted. The First World referred to the capitalist market economy
states, such as in Western Europe, North America and Australia and Japan. The Second
World to the communist/socialist centrally directed economies of Eastern Europe, China,
North Korea and Cuba. The 'Third World' was then a residual term, which referred to the
poorest regions of the world such as parts of Africa and Asia and Latin America. Some have
pointed to the possibility of a 'Fourth World'. This includes indigenous populations of the
world. Many contemporary writers have pointed to the inadequacies of this 'three world'
model, arguing that there exists one world. By using this term it implies that these countries
are not a part of the global economic system. What to call poor states is much contested
and some prefer 'developing countries' or 'least/lesser developed countries' (LDCs). Some
dislike the term developing as it implies that liberal economic development (industrialisation) is the only way forward. Also, the term 'majority world' has been applied in some

academic perspectives. What terminology to employ often stems from personal or political preference; however, arguing over terminology does not alter the fact that the gulf between rich and poor continues to grow.

Walt W. Rostow was a leading academic and American policy adviser, who formulated a controversial thesis on development. His book *The Stages of Economic Growth: A Non-Communist Manifesto* (1960) was in stark contrast to Marxist-inspired approaches. Rostow was explicit in his rejection of state-interventionist command economy ideas. He outlined how and advocated that in order for lesser-developed regions to progress they should industrialise and develop their economies along the same lines as Western liberal economies.

The stages of development theory gained momentum in post-Second World War economics as many formerly colonised states began to gain their independence. This theory was primarily concerned with developing these newly independent nations and development was based on the Western model that industrialisation and market-driven economies are key to a flourishing and successful national economy. As suggested by the title, the theory of stages of growth was an alternative to Marx's theory of social evolution. Rostow argued that underdeveloped economies should follow the path of the industrialised states; in short, they should industrialise. Rostow argued that all the industrialised states had followed the same path and witnessed the same historical stages of development; underdeveloped states were just at an earlier stage on this developmental path. This developmental path is linear and progressive and once states had reached a certain point in this linear path, economies would just 'take off'. An example of how 'take off' can be achieved is given in Rostow's explanation of the different stages of development.

The stages of development fit into five distinct categories. The first of these stages is traditional societies; these are subsistence economies. An example of a subsistence economy would be an agricultural one in which the economic product is consumed by producers or bartered rather than sold in a cash-based economy. In agricultural economies labour is intensive, jobs are carried out by hand or animal as opposed to mechanised forms of production. This meant that a ceiling existed on the level of attainable output (tradable produce) per head. Traditional economies could not reach the levels of tradable produce to participate in emerging global markets, thus having limited quantities of capital and not achieving industrialisation.

The second stage of Rostow's developmental model is labelled the 'pre-conditions for take off'. In this stage traditional societies need to create a surplus for trading and this is achieved by industrialising old methods of working, for example, technology and machinery is incorporated into agriculture. The infrastructure of the society needs to be built up to support the new industrialised industries, for example, roads need to be built in order to secure the easy movement of goods and services. Also, healthcare and schooling sectors need to be built and developed to serve the new workforce. Another important part of this stage is the emergence of entrepreneurs, banks and other institutions that mobilise capital. This stage of development is also referred to as the transitional stage. Rostow argued that traditional societies coexisted with the pre-conditional societies and no time frame was given as to when societies would reach the third stage, which is 'take off'.

In this third stage industrialisation massively increases, with workers switching from land to manufacturing industries, and economic growth is regionalised into a few regions of the country. Cities are established and new political institutions and social institutions evolve to support the industrial economies. 'Take off' is fully achieved when old traditional societies and ways of doing things have been eradicated and modern society becomes the norm. During 'take off' new industries expand, rapid profits are gained, trade relationships are established, and social and political structures are transformed in such a way that steady growth can be maintained.

The fourth stage in this linear process is called the drive to maturity; this means that technological innovation continues to flourish. The entrepreneur class continues to grow, capital is accumulated and 'take off' is sustained with continual steady growth. The last stage is high mass consumption societies; this is where emphasis is on consumption and industry is centred on the consumer society. America and Western Europe have achieved this fifth stage of development, where branded clothes and innovative technology such as smart phones and wireless Internet access have become the 'must haves'. Industry is always driving towards creating new ideas that the consumer will desire.

However, Rostow's view is based on observations and interpretations of previous economic developments. It does not necessarily follow that future developments would evolve in the same context or follow the same patterns. This approach is seen as deterministic and overly rigid in its predictive nature. It must also be acknowledged that states have not been able to follow Rostow's path to development. His theory presupposes that states operate in the international arena as isolated units; for him there are no systemic forces that prevent or hinder the development process. This view does not take into account structural obstacles to development such as the hierarchical nature of the international arena. Also, Rostow's argument is too simplistic in his assumption that all industrialised economies followed the same path. Rostow could be accused of Western-centrism as he devised the five stages of growth based on observations of the West, and from his title (a 'non-communist manifesto') it is clear that his theory is ideologically motivated and developed at the height of the Cold War. If we analysed the most high-performing countries in GDP per head terms since his work was published, which are the East Asia Tiger economies, including South Korea, Taiwan, Malaysia and more recently China, we would find that none were open liberal market economies that combined free markets with open democratic institutions: all of them have been powerfully centralised states with managed industrial growth and very distinctive patterns of human capital by comparison with other developing countries. Their attachment to managed trade and state control of labour markets is hardly a liberal model, but it is perfectly true that they have passed rapidly through the stages of growth. This does not mean that modernising development cannot work; but it is very hard to find contemporary examples that actually fit the narrative Rostow offers.

Nonetheless, Rostow's model can be seen as an orthodox approach to liberal development and still, with adaptation, forms the basis of much liberal development thought. Later development theorists have been critical of Rostow's work, seeing it as too deterministic. The failure of Rostow's model led liberal modernists to re-evaluate their position on processes of modernisation. However, the underlying principles of liberal development and the need for lesser developed states to modernise their economies is still adhered to and modernisation theorists have developed a more refined set of economic principles, which are known as the 'Washington Consensus'. This Consensus was a list of economic policy reforms, which, it was thought, Latin American states should adopt in order to develop. The principles were later applied to Eastern European countries and also to African and South Asian states.

## CONCEPT BOX

# The Washington Consensus

John Williamson is credited with coining the phrase Washington Consensus. Below are the ten policy reforms he identified as representing the preferred policy options promoted by the Washington-based financial institutions of the World Bank and the International Monetary Fund.

- Fiscal discipline.
- A redirection of public expenditure priorities towards fields offering both high economic returns and the potential to improve income distribution, such as primary healthcare, primary education, and infrastructure.
- Tax reform (to lower marginal rates and broaden the tax base).
- Interest rate liberalisation.
- A competitive exchange rate.
- Trade liberalisation.
- Liberalisation of inflows of foreign direct investment.
- Privatisation.
- Deregulation (to abolish barriers to entry and exit).
- Secure property rights for key political groups.

*Source*: Williamson (1990).

The Washington Consensus was an attempt to move away from a tradition of development loans and towards linking loans to specific conditions set by the financial institutions of the developed world. The implementation of the Washington Consensus is most clearly illustrated in the promotion of so-called Structural Adjustment Programmes (SAPs).

Neo-liberal ideas point to the positive nature and aspects of such a system; for example, states and non-state actors and individuals share a common interest and aspire to the same liberal economic goals. This idea has been conceptualised and developed due to the advent of communications technology, which has enabled greater connectivity between individuals and societies. Also, the movement and flow of consumer goods and the spread of ideas, including mass consumerism, have begun to break down cultural divisions and draw the world into what Marshal McLuhan called the 'global village'. However, this conception has been criticised by both realist and Marxist-inspired theorists as not all states and individuals share a common goal; for example, Islamic states and individuals, North Korea and to some extent China do not share 'Western' liberal 'common values'. This idea of the international society has also been criticised due to the fact that only rich industrialised states have access to advanced technologies. This has led Anthony Giddens to reinterpret McLuhan's global village into what he describes as 'global pillage' (for a fuller discussion of these ideas, see Chapter 4).

Neo-liberal agendas are also concerned with the diverse processes that characterise the emerging global economy. These include: flows and patterns of trade and resource use; movement of goods and services; technology transfer; technological 'leap-frogging' and knowledge diffusion; the evolution and implementation of international property rights, patenting laws and bio-piracy. Moreover, the formation and management of international regimes and processes of conflict and cooperation are included.

The value of foreign aid as a tool for development has been widely debated. Liberals have tended to promote aid as a useful means of achieving development goals, at least if targeted and managed well. Neo-liberals and structuralists have both criticised aid, the former because they claim it distorts the working of markets and the latter because they see aid as a form of hegemonic domination or, more succinctly, 'aid as imperialism' (Hayter, 1971). Foreign aid is distinct from aid for emergency relief (which most people agree has great value). There is plenty of evidence that foreign aid cannot be the main cause of growth, and its advocates today would argue that it is an adjunct to effective domestic capital formation and the creation of a skills or knowledge base (through education and training). Aid contributes to growth, they would suggest, rather than being its primary cause. Over the last twenty years, aid programmes have been restructured to meet those objectives by Japan, the

European Union, the US and major international institutions. But this has not removed the criticisms of those who retain their fundamental objections to aid. One powerfully argued version of this is the debate between two widely discussed alternative accounts of development. Moyo (2009) advocates a version of the established Washington Consensus in her rejection of most foreign development aid practice, holding firmly to the view that aid distorts markets and undermines domestic capital formation even if it is not encumbered by corruption. Joseph and Gillies (2008) defend the argument that, if given with focus, attention to the context, attention to human development needs and care to avoid corruption, development aid can be 'smart' and effective. This is an argument that has circulated for at least forty years, but that is worth careful attention. What we might also note is the extent to which development issues have vanished from political agendas – in the 2015 British General Election, all the main parties (with the notable exception of the UK Independence Party) were committed to protect foreign aid and development spending even if other financial cuts were necessary, while in other countries debates about the value of development assistance in whatever form have also been muted in the 2000s.

## The development problem

Despite the lessening of political attention, the 'development problem' in IPE is a complex and heavily debated issue. Within liberal economic thought, development is equated with poverty reduction by way of economic growth. However, where growth has occurred it has rarely been accompanied by the so-called 'trickle-down' effect whereby the benefits of such growth reach all sectors of society. A more likely scenario is the accumulation of wealth among the elite and upper middle classes. Structuralists point to this in terms of clear class-based divisions of wealth, where wealthy and relatively Europeanised elites have the ability to reproduce their social and economic power over or against poorer and often indigenous communities. In addition to this division of wealth, there is a further criticism that can be made of mainstream development approaches. The accumulation of capital can be argued to be based on a false premise. This refers to the lack of acknowledgement of the hidden, or overlooked, social and environmental costs that occur in the pursuit of economic growth. Poor working conditions, environmental pollution and non-sustainable resource use are not generally taken into account when assessing indicators of development. The evolution of multi-centred points of production and consumption also adds to the difficulty of monitoring and taking into account such costs. On the contrary, the dominant model of development is to rely on market forces free from political oversight and legislation. Without social and environmental costs being factored into the market value of particular goods and services, the imagined benefits of economic growth are liable to contain many negative aspects. Structuralists tend towards a more encompassing view than most approaches to the study of IPE. The degree to which relevant factors are acknowledged in determining indicators of development goes to the heart of the development problem.

**EXAMPLE BOX**

## The 'development' of Nauru

Nauru is a small island state in the South Pacific. For many years its economy has been based on the mining and export of phosphate (used in the production of fertilisers). Originally this operation was controlled by Britain and then Australia. Nauru achieved political independence in 1968. Successive Nauruan governments have continued to rely upon this export income, despite the known environmental costs the mining was inflicting on the island. At the height of phosphate export Nauruans had one of the world's highest rates of GDP per capita. However, this situation could not be sustained and as the phosphate deposits have been mined out the Nauruan economy has faced a sharp decline. The majority of the land area has been stripped of its surface soil and the rocky outcrops that remain are unsuitable for crop production, even for basic subsistence. Nauruans are now heavily dependent on importing foodstuffs and other goods, while simultaneously having decreased purchasing power for such imports. 'Development' in economic terms has come at the cost of the local environment and also social costs as many Nauruans are now leaving the island to seek employment and improved lifestyles in other countries.

The above example demonstrates two significant aspects of the development problem. First, it shows how economic growth in itself is only one aspect of development. Second, the Nauruan economy post-independence was tied into a form of production and export-led growth that made it very difficult for the newly 'independent' government to diversify its economy and move away from colonial era reliance on the export of a single commodity, albeit one of a limited and finite nature (IBP USA, 2009). Nauru's experience may be seen as an extreme case but it is illustrative of how this small island state is tied into a wider global economy. The historical evolution of the Nauruan economy has clearly had a lasting impact on the options and choices made by subsequent Nauruan governments.

The above section has outlined the predominant (economics-based) development model and the problems that can arise from this. The following section looks at a response to this at the level of the UN.

# Millennium Development Goals to Sustainable Development Goals

The latter part of the twentieth century saw a proliferation of international meetings and summits focusing on poverty alleviation and other development goals. The UN took the lead in organising conferences on themes including children (New York, US, 1990); environment and development (Rio de Janeiro, Brazil, 1992); human rights (Vienna, Austria 1993); population and development (Cairo, Egypt, 1994); social development (Copenhagen, Denmark, 1995); women (Beijing, China, 1995); human settlements (Istanbul, Turkey, 1996); and food (Rome, Italy, 1996). Several of these meetings established standing bodies to institutionalise ongoing negotiations to tackle the issues that were raised.

The momentum of this succession of conferences led to a meeting held at UN Headquarters in September 2000 at which the General Assembly adopted the UN Millennium Declaration. This comprised eight Millennium Development Goals (MDGs) with a timetable set out to achieve each of them by the year 2015. This represented the most ambitious development agenda ever undertaken and on an unprecedented scale. The eight goals were: (1) end poverty and hunger; (2) universal education; (3) gender equality; (4) child health; (5) maternal health; (6) combat HIV/AIDS; (7) environmental sustainability; and (8) global partnership. Perhaps unsurprisingly, when the mid-point of this period was passed in 2008, despite some notable progress having been made in some fields, none of the MDG agenda were being fulfilled at a rate that suggested the goals would be met in time. In part, this can be explained by a lack of commitment by the major powers to keep to their promises on overseas aid packages for the poorest nations. There were also unexpected downturns in the global economy and crises in relation to food and energy supplies. While some might argue that the MDGs were always unrealistic in their targets and timescale, it should also be recognised that conditions for development were far from ideal. The MDGs are also significant in their process: they represent a globally arrived at consensus to which pretty much all states, many NGOs and most relevant international organisations have given active consent. From a liberal point of view, this is an important step in norm building and institutionalisation, in practical action for development. From a critical theory point of view it is an important step in the consolidation of a global hegemony, which, although apparently beneficial to development, embodies conceptions of development and practices of aid, trade and surveillance that box the poorest peoples and communities into acquiescing in their own domination, in liberal hegemony.

MDG 1 linked two of the perennial objectives of development policies. In many ways these two areas may be seen as indivisible. It is hard to imagine one existing without the other. As outlined elsewhere in this text, there is no simple strategy for reducing poverty. Some approaches that focus on wealth creation may be effective for some sectors of society, but actively impoverish other members. For example, the push towards increased privatisation of services may offer business opportunities, but also push some of these services beyond the financial reach of some of the poorer members of a community. Equally, the increased privatisation of water or other infrastructure needs may help boost needed investment while putting the price out of reach of many of the poorest in society.

The complex relationship between poverty and hunger was graphically highlighted in the mid-1980s during the famine crisis in Ethiopia. Despite food aid being shipped to the country it was discovered that there were actually grain stores within the country that could have been drawn on but there were economic reasons why this food was not being distributed. Food aid also risks disrupting national markets with an unintended negative impact on local producers, as it had in 1984/1985 in Ethiopia. In other cases a country with serious food shortages may be prioritising non-food cash crops such as tobacco, cotton or flowers in order to earn export revenue. Again, this highlights how there are complex economic factors at play at both the domestic and international levels when attempting to meet essential nutrition requirements.

In spring 2010, when clouds of volcanic ash from Iceland cut all flights around Europe for more than a week, flights of vegetables, salad crops and flowers from Kenya to Europe's supermarkets were disrupted. It was announced that this affected up to 12 per cent of jobs in Kenya, around 11 per cent of Kenyan GDP, and around 30 per cent of export earnings (BBC News, 16 April 2010). This trade is no more than ten years old, having evolved largely through the global activities of European supermarket supply chain managers. It contributes to local economic growth and makes a real difference to employment and skills. But it also impoverishes neighbouring non-exporting farms, uses much more than a fair share of available water, and has a grim carbon footprint. The majority of the profits it generates go to Western supermarkets rather than local farmers; the farmers do benefit substantially too, but given the pattern of post-colonial land ownership in Kenya, that too raises problems about who is really benefiting.

MDG 2 focused on the provision of universal education. There are stark divides in terms of how life chances are increased, or not, depending on access to education. Even basic literacy and numeracy skills remain beyond the reach of many children and adult learners. Some advances have been made in countries such as Burundi, Ghana, Kenya, Tanzania and Uganda where the governments have abolished fees for schools in the public sector. This has led to a significant uptake in education opportunities, but with a resulting pressure on these governments to now provide sufficient teachers and school buildings of an adequate standard. Inequalities remain with a lower uptake in rural areas and a marked gender divide with girls being more likely to drop out from education. Governments are faced with the dilemma of investing in future generations while at the same time meeting the demands of current budgetary needs in other sectors of the economy. Education may well be recognised as a priority for longer-term development goals, but may be seriously restricted due to the practicalities of budgetary constraints and shorter-term priorities.

MDG 3 dealt with the issue of promoting gender equality. As the UN Development Programme has repeatedly noted, roughly 70 per cent of the actual work done in developing countries is the product of female workers, although because quite a lot of that work is 'domestic' it may not be counted in GDP statistics. Women not only make the greater contribution to past growth; they also, according to the UNDP, have the greatest potential to contribute to future growth – if you seek future growth, educate and empower women. As noted above, educational opportunities are a key factor in providing for gender equality. Since the launch of the MDGs there has been a marked increase in female school enrolments. That said, there remain marked difficulties in retaining these pupils. In rural areas where water is in short supply it tends to be women and girls who can spend large parts of their day walking to fetch water for the household. Lack of water also impacts on levels of sanitation and female pupils may be reluctant to attend schools with no private toilet facilities. Cultural issues such as this extend well beyond primary school years. Many societies have hugely differing norms and expectations running along gendered lines. Even if a girl is able to access primary education, this is no guarantee that she will be able to progress to secondary or higher education, regardless of intellectual ability. Male students have greater employment opportunities and even when females are able to enter the labour market it is far more likely that this will be in low-paid jobs. One indicator of gender equality is the proportion of women holding parliamentary seats in a national government. There are only twenty countries where women hold more than 30 per cent of parliamentary seats. This gender disparity in direct involvement in political decision-making is even more marked in the senior ranks of government, with even the most developed states still showing a male bias at ministerial level.

MDG 4 sought to reduce child mortality. In reviewing this goal there are noticeable regional variations. Some parts of the world have made progress in this field but sub-Saharan Africa stands out as a problem area with very little progress having been made since 2000. Malnutrition is deemed to be the underlying cause of death for many children under five. Poor access to potable water is another major factor, which has also been linked to the need to promote breastfeeding rather than rely on powdered milk preparations. More than one-third of child deaths occur before the infants reach one month of age. This indicates that early intervention is crucial in order to increase survival rates. With targeted food and medical aid, this figure can be brought down substantially, but getting it down and keeping it down has proved a problem in areas affected by civil conflict or widespread corruption such as West Africa. Beyond this age, immunisation programmes are also important and this is a priority area for national healthcare teams. The likelihood of a child surviving is clearly influenced by the environment into which they are born. Poor sanitation, poor diet, limited water supply and the availability of healthcare support systems all play a part in determining rates of survival. This is a good example of how an integrated approach to development is required to tackle the various MDGs cited here. Although each represent distinct areas of concern it is difficult to have a discrete policy initiative to tackle them in isolation from other considerations, in both the policy domain and other aspects of governance.

The connection between MDGs is perhaps most clearly demonstrated in the relationship between MDGs 4 and 5. MDG 5 related to maternal health. Very often mothers are at risk during the latter stages of pregnancy, during delivery and in the immediate post-delivery period. One of the most shocking examples of the divergence of healthcare provision between the developed and developing world can be found in statistical data relating to health risks during pregnancy. The risk of a woman in Sweden dying from causes that are pregnancy-related is 1 in 17,400. In Niger this figure is 1 in 7. Again there can be numerous factors that lead to this enormous disparity in life chances. These can relate to the overall health of the individuals concerned and their resilience to deal with the physical stress of pregnancy and childbirth. As with rates of infant mortality, a major factor is the level of healthcare and nursing support available during labour and shortly thereafter. Although high-technology healthcare can sometimes be helpful, very often what women actually need in crises at childbirth is simple and reliable care from a qualified midwife within quick reach. Once again the development infrastructure needs to be in place to tackle this particular MDG. The enabling of this has to be set into the context of national governments, and aid agencies, making hard budgetary decisions on the basis of limited funding.

MDG 6 is an interesting case as it dealt with the fight against HIV/AIDS. As such it is something that can be seen as a global issue, although as with some of the above examples there can be extreme variations in incidence between regions. This MDG also refers to tackling the spread of malaria and other diseases. The HIV/AIDS issue is one that has been experienced very differently in various parts of the world. Rates of prevalence are diverse, as is the availability of treatment and even popular beliefs about the causes and consequences of infection and cultural attitudes towards sufferers. Sub-Saharan Africa is, again, one of the most vulnerable regions to infectious diseases. The numbers of people in this region living with HIV/AIDS continues to rise, although antiretroviral drugs are making some progress in treatment. A priority area for the use of these drugs is to prevent mother-to-child transmission. Again this demonstrates the overlap between MDGs as this is clearly an area of work that relates to both child and maternal health. With respect to other diseases, malaria is notable as it appeared to be in decline but has more recently re-emerged as a significant health threat in particular regions, once again Sub-Saharan Africa being a case in point. Malaria has been cited as a disease that should perhaps be given a greater priority in terms of research and development among international pharmaceutical companies that have been accused of focusing their efforts more on products aimed at the developed world. For example, slimming pills may be seen as more profitable products than those to treat malaria and other diseases associated with the poorer parts of the world. In contrast, there have been some examples of pharmaceutical companies working with governments and aid agencies to develop coordinated strategies to tackle particular diseases. The Global Polio Eradication Initiative is a good example of this.

MDG 7 was perhaps the most far-reaching as it seeks to ensure environmental sustainability. This clearly ties in with other UN-led initiatives such as the Earth Summit process. Despite this, it is also one of the more vague of the goals in terms of targets. It is broken down into four subsections. The first refers to reversing the loss of environmental resources, but fails to be explicit about what these are and how to reverse such losses. The second calls for a 'significant reduction' in loss of biodiversity, but neither sets targets or proposes a plan of action for this goal. The third calls for improved access to sanitation and potable water. The final sub-goal calls for a 'significant improvement' in the lives of 100 million slum dwellers. To some extent this is the MDG that reads like more of a 'wish list' than something where a coherent strategy is being promoted via inter-state or multi-stakeholder cooperation.

The final MDG 8 dealt with the concept of a global partnership for development. Although the UN is, by definition, state-centric it also promotes cooperative action with a range of stakeholders from civil society and the private sector. In terms of North/South cooperation there has been a long-standing target of 0.7 per cent of developed states' gross national income (GNI) being set aside for overseas development assistance to the less-developed states. This has only been achieved by a small number of Scandinavian countries, with the vast majority of developed states falling well short of this target. The international conferences referred to above routinely include pledges of additional financial packages to aid development projects, but these are often unfulfilled. More recently governments appear to be placing greater emphasis on public/private partnerships whereby MNCs are encouraged to invest in development projects. In part this can be seen in the context of the broader project of neo–liberalism and greater emphasis on the private sector driving all aspects of society. Civil society groups are also engaged with in relation to identifying development needs and facilitating the delivery of aid. This can lead to some eclectic alliances of stakeholders and tensions can occur with MNCs being essentially profit motivated, NGOs tending towards the more altruistic and governments seeking to balance pledges of aid with myriad other budgetary pressures. Table 8.1 charts the progress of each of the eight Millennium Development Goals by 2015.

By the start of 2015 some significant progress had been made towards achieving aspects of the MDGs. That said, there remained a stark North/South divide and where progress had been made it tended to be sporadic, localised and sometimes reinforcing of existing inequalities. It was clear that reaching the endpoint of the MDG period was far from the end of the development process. In order to address the ongoing international development agenda the UN formed an Open Working Group (OWG) made up of thirty member states drawn from five geographic regions in order to provide a reasonably representative group of states. Civil society was also engaged with

**Table 8.1** Millennium Development Goals 2015 progress chart

Photo credit: © UNICEF/Newar

## Millennium Development Goals: 2015 Progress Chart

United Nations Member States gathered together at the start of the new millennium to shape a broad vision to fight poverty and combat numerous issues hampering development progress. The vision was translated into eight Millennium Development Goals and has remained the world's overarching development framework for the past 15 years. This framework, set to expire in 2015, includes time-bound goals, targets and indicators to monitor progress on extreme poverty and hunger, education, gender equality, child survival, health, environmental sustainability and global partnerships.

This chart presents the final assessment of progress towards selected key targets relating to each goal. The assessment provides two types of information: progress trends and levels of development, which are based on information available as of June 2015. The colour shows progress made towards the target and the text in the box shows the present level of development. For most indicators, 2015 projections are used to assess progress; for a few indicators that do not have 2015 data or projections, the latest available data of 2013 or 2014 are used.

2015
TIME FOR
GLOBAL ACTION
FOR PEOPLE AND PLANET

**Table 8.1** Continued

| Goals and Targets | Africa | | Asia | | | | Oceania | Latin America and the Caribbean |
|---|---|---|---|---|---|---|---|---|
| | Northern | Sub-Saharan | Eastern | South-Eastern | Southern | Western | | |

**GOAL 1 | Eradicate extreme poverty and hunger**

| | | | | | | | | |
|---|---|---|---|---|---|---|---|---|
| Reduce extreme poverty by half | low poverty | very high poverty | low poverty | moderate poverty | high poverty | low poverty | — | low poverty |
| Productive and decent employment | large deficit | very large deficit | moderate deficit | large deficit | large deficit | large deficit | very large deficit | moderate deficit |
| Reduce hunger by half | low hunger | high hunger | moderate hunger | moderate hunger | high hunger | moderate hunger | moderate hunger | moderate hunger |

**GOAL 2 | Achieve universal primary education**

| | | | | | | | | |
|---|---|---|---|---|---|---|---|---|
| Universal primary schooling | high enrolment | moderate enrolment | high enrolment | high enrolment | high enrolment | high enrolment | high enrolment | high enrolment |

**GOAL 3 | Promote gender equality and empower women**

| | | | | | | | | |
|---|---|---|---|---|---|---|---|---|
| Equal girls' enrolment in primary school | close to parity | close to parity | parity | parity | parity | close to parity | close to parity | parity |
| Women's share of paid employment | low share | medium share | high share | medium share | low share | low share | medium share | high share |
| Women's equal representation in national parliaments | moderate representation | moderate representation | moderate representation | low representation | low representation | low representation | very low representation | moderate representation |

**GOAL 4 | Reduce child mortality**

| | | | | | | | | |
|---|---|---|---|---|---|---|---|---|
| Reduce mortality of under-five-year-olds by two thirds | low mortality | high mortality | low mortality | low mortality | moderate mortality | low mortality | moderate mortality | low mortality |

**GOAL 5 | Improve maternal health**

| | | | | | | | | |
|---|---|---|---|---|---|---|---|---|
| Reduce maternal mortality by three quarters | low mortality | high mortality | low mortality | moderate mortality | moderate mortality | low mortality | moderate mortality | low mortality |
| Access to reproductive health | moderate access | low access | high access | moderate access | moderate access | moderate access | low access | high access |

**GOAL 6 | Combat HIV/AIDS, malaria and other diseases**

| | | | | | | | | |
|---|---|---|---|---|---|---|---|---|
| Halt and begin to reverse the spread of HIV/AIDS | low incidence | high incidence | low incidence | low incidence | low incidence | low incidence | low incidence | low incidence |
| Halt and reverse the spread of tuberculosis | low mortality | high mortality | low mortality | moderate mortality | moderate mortality | low mortality | moderate mortality | low mortality |

**GOAL 7 | Ensure environmental sustainability**

| | | | | | | | | |
|---|---|---|---|---|---|---|---|---|
| Halve proportion of population without improved drinking water | high coverage | low coverage | high coverage | high coverage | high coverage | high coverage | low coverage | high coverage |
| Halve proportion of population without sanitation | moderate coverage | very low coverage | moderate coverage | low coverage | very low coverage | high coverage | very low coverage | moderate coverage |
| Improve the lives of slum-dwellers | low proportion of slum-dwellers | very high proportion of slum-dwellers | moderate proportion of slum-dwellers | moderate proportion of slum-dwellers | moderate proportion of slum-dwellers | moderate proportion of slum-dwellers | moderate proportion of slum-dwellers | moderate proportion of slum-dwellers |

**GOAL 8 | Develop a global partnership for development**

| | | | | | | | | |
|---|---|---|---|---|---|---|---|---|
| Internet users | moderate usage | low usage | high usage | moderate usage | low usage | high usage | low usage | high usage |

---

The progress chart operates on two levels. The text in each box indicates the present level of development. The colours show progress made towards the target according to the legend below:

■ Target met or excellent progress.
■ Good progress.
▫ Fair progress.

■ Poor progress or deterioration.
▫ Missing or insufficient data.

For the regional groupings and country data, see *mdgs.un.org* Country experiences in each region may differ significantly from the regional average. Due to new data and revised methodologies, this Progress Chart is not comparable with previous versions.

**Sources:** United Nations, based on data and estimates provided by: Food and Agriculture Organization of the United Nations; Inter-Parliamentary Union; International Labour Organization; International Telecommunication Union; UNAIDS; UNESCO; UN-Habitat; UNICEF; UN Population Division; World Bank; World Health Organization - based on statistics available as of June 2015.

Compiled by the Statistics Division, Department of Economic and Social Affairs, United Nations.

*Source*: adapted from the UN's Commission on Sustainable Development's Millennium Development Goals: 2015 Progress Chart, www.un.org/millenniumgoals/2015_MDG_Report/pdf/MDG%202015%20PC%20final.pdf

more than had been the case when the MDGs were formulated, which had largely been driven by a relatively small group of officials and consultants within the UN system. In the post–2015 development phase the MDGs were extended to become seventeen Sustainable Development Goals, as follows:

1 End poverty in all its forms everywhere.
2 End hunger, achieve food security and improved nutrition and promote sustainable agriculture.
3 Ensure healthy lives and promote well-being for all at all ages.
4 Ensure inclusive and equitable quality education and promote life-long learning opportunities for all.
5 Achieve gender equality and empower all women and girls.
6 Ensure availability and sustainable management of water and sanitation for all.
7 Ensure access to affordable, reliable, sustainable, and modern energy for all.
8 Promote sustained, inclusive and sustainable economic growth, full and productive employment and decent work for all.
9 Build resilient infrastructure, promote inclusive and sustainable industrialisation and foster innovation.
10 Reduce inequality within and among countries.
11 Make cities and human settlements inclusive, safe, resilient and sustainable.
12 Ensure sustainable consumption and production patterns.
13 Take urgent action to combat climate change and its impacts.
14 Conserve and sustainably use the oceans, seas and marine resources for sustainable development.
15 Protect, restore and promote sustainable use of terrestrial ecosystems, sustainably manage forests, combat desertification, and halt and reverse land degradation and halt biodiversity loss.
16 Promote peaceful and inclusive societies for sustainable development, provide access to justice for all and build effective, accountable and inclusive institutions at all levels.
17 Strengthen the means of implementation and revitalise the global partnership for sustainable development.

While much of the intent and ethos of the MDGs can be identified with the extended SDGs there are some significant amendments, in part reflecting some of the issues and interests that had emerged since the inception of the MDGs. For example, SDG 11 is noteworthy at a time when more people are now living in urban rather than rural areas. Similarly energy security has become sufficiently concerning to warrant its own goal. The manner in which these goals have evolved may, in part, be explained by a combination of changing international circumstances but also the much higher level of engagement with civil society that fed through to the process of drafting the SDGs. While it remained the UN member states of the OWG that formally presented the proposed SDGs to the UN for adoption, this was a much more transparent process with a broad range of civil society groups paying close attention to what was included in an attempt to ensure their particular development concerns were addressed.

## Major groups

The multi-stakeholder concept has its origins in the UN Commission on Sustainable Development's Agenda 21 and the designation of 'major groups' with identifiable interests and roles in the promotion of sustainable development: (i) business and industry; (ii) children and youth; (iii) farmers; (iv) indigenous people; (v) local authorities; (vi) NGOs; (vii) scientific and technological community; (viii) women; and (ix) workers and trade unions. Each of these groups represents a particular constituency of actors and agendas. The following section looks at each of these groups in turn and locates them within the broader development process.

Business and industry has been seen in both a negative light as one of the main reasons for environmental degradation, and more positively as a source of potential solutions. Either way this is a sector that clearly plays a key role in the development debate. The text of the Agenda 21 document calls on businesses to look towards more efficient forms of production, to minimise pollutant discharges and to recycle and reuse component parts of the manufacturing cycle as much as possible. For its part, the private sector has responded in a rather ad hoc manner with some businesses engaging much more fully with this process than others. Some of the larger MNCs have formed the World Business Council for Sustainable Development (WBCSD). Some of this group's members are drawn from the oil, gas and mining industries. These are precisely the companies that environmental groups have targeted their campaigns towards, citing them as being some of the worst polluters and responsible for environmental degradation on a massive scale. The more cynical or, at least, sceptical in the environmental movement are suspicious of the WBCSD and the whole concept of 'corporate social responsibility' (CSR). It is difficult to judge the extent to which corporations are truly trying to make their operations more environmentally benign, or if this is simply a public relations exercise to counter the campaigners' arguments – and to attract the 'green pound' of environmentally conscious consumers.

Children and youth are the group that are arguably the most relevant to sustainability, given they are likely to be inheriting either the ongoing problems or the more positive solutions of the current environmental crisis. The UN has a long-standing commitment to the promotion of children's rights via agencies such as UNICEF, the above MDG on child healthcare, special reports on child soldiers, access to primary schooling and so on. Many of the UN's publications are aimed at a younger audience, highlighting the organisation's peace and development work and the need for intercultural understanding and cooperation. This attitude is also mirrored in many local and national governments' documentation that is distributed via school networks. Similarly, many NGO groups have a youth membership category with their campaigning messages pitched at younger age groups. Children and youth comprise roughly one-third of the world's population. In many parts of the developing world there remain relatively high birth rates, which means that in these states the younger age group is beginning to outnumber the older population. Demographic patterns vary between states but there is a growing correlation between the areas where environmental vulnerability is at its most extreme and a high level of children and youth as a proportion of the population. In that regard, getting the message of sustainability across to the younger age groups is even more important.

Farmers are highlighted as a significant group in the context of sustainable development. This makes sense given the relationship between the agricultural sector and the natural world. The use of pesticides and the evolution of genetically modified crops may be cited as examples of some farmers moving away from a reliance on the 'natural' balance of ecosystems. That said, this only applies to certain sectors of the farming community and the underlying principle for the vast majority of farmers is that one needs to care for the land if they want to have successful crops year on year. About one-third of the world's land surface is given over to agricultural production and this is the foundation of most rural communities. As such it is crucial to sustain this sector. This is doubly important when one considers that it is this production that also sustains urban dwellers. A distinction needs to be made between the small-scale subsistence farmer who may produce little more than what is required to feed an extended family, and the huge conglomerates that represent farming on a massive industrialised scale. This is not to say that small-scale farming never includes harmful, non-sustainable practices. However, it is farming at the industrialised level where most criticisms of environmentally damaging methods can be cited. For example, extensive use of chemical fertilisers and pesticides can create toxic run-off, which pollutes local water supplies.

High levels of nitrogen in water has been noted as having damaging impacts on numerous fish and amphibian species. Such pollution can also be harmful once it enters the food chain, up to the human level.

Indigenous peoples are cited as a major group for several reasons. They are recognised as having a special connection to their lands. This point can be contentious in some areas where land ownership is seriously contested and also where indigenous peoples are no longer the majority group in their home state. The latter point can raise questions of identity and the perceived legitimacy of the national government. Although all states can lay claim to having some element of an indigenous population this is more easily identifiable in some parts of the world than others. For example, in areas where there was expansion of European influence and colonisation the indigenous population is more easily identifiable, such as in Australia or New Zealand. The same applies in the US where, although no longer formally part of a European-led imperial strategy, the post-independence US drove westwards into the territories of many indigenous tribes. Over the years mixed-race relations have blurred the indigenous/non-indigenous divide. That said, there remains a strong sense of indigenousness in many parts of the world and traditional concepts of stewardship of the land, as opposed to over-exploitation of resources, is being turned to as a more sensible and sustainable model. There are also powerful models of development that draw on indigenous knowledge and indigenous practice in agriculture, aquaculture and medicine. It is clearly a mistake to see a dramatic opposition between the demands of indigenous peoples and the prospects of development when the know-how that specific groups in Amazonia, the Pacific Islands or elsewhere can offer provides a basis for bottom-up patterns of sustainable growth, as organisations such as Survival International have been arguing for some time.

Local authorities have been at the forefront of promoting the Agenda 21 message. Local Agenda 21 projects have been particularly successful in the UK and other parts of Europe, notably Germany. One of the mantras of the environmental movement is to 'think globally – act locally'. Local authorities, such as city and district councils, are particularly well-placed to communicate 'green' initiatives and policies to local communities. They are also often significant employers in terms of both numbers of staff employed and also the environmental impact the provision of their services can have. To some extent they represent the interface between national governments and citizens. They can act as promoters of recycling in relation to waste management schemes, they are providers of public transport systems to reduce car pollutants, and they can support environmental education initiatives in schools and colleges. Many local authorities in the developed world are involved in twinning projects with counterparts in the developing world, thereby fostering education opportunities and potential exchange visits. Such projects can be somewhat unbalanced as one partner will tend to have considerably greater access to resources than the other. However, recognising this is part of the education process.

Having NGOs as a major group is appropriate, even necessary, but this represents one of the most diverse of the groups. The breadth of this group covers representatives from several of the other groups such as farmers, women and, of course, women farmers. The groups are not mutually exclusive and the diversity of the NGOs represented here illustrates the tremendous range of interest groups related to the field of development. Some issue areas are covered by several different NGOs. If one were to take tropical deforestation as an example, then there are interest groups in both the NGO sector and within the other major groups. Survival International has campaigns that deal with protection of tribal peoples threatened by logging operations (see: www.survival-international.org). Similarly, the Rainforest Alliance is attempting to protect rainforests, but may have a greater emphasis on the overall ecosystem rather than the more anthropocentric approach of Survival. The World Wide Fund for Nature may focus efforts on the protection of a particular endangered species living in a rainforest habitat. The interests and agendas of these groups lead them towards cooperative actions, although priorities and action plans may sometimes differ.

Through the mechanisms of the Cotonou Convention (2000), the European Union has adopted a programme of active involvement of civil society groups in development programmes, which is also an important source for the legitimisation of specific programmes and for genuine involvement of local communities (see: ec.europa.eu/development/geographical/cotonouintro_en.cfm). This is, however, not always welcome to national governments, which quite often – but not always – try to control or undermine civil society NGOs, which they see as a source of opposition, and the African, Caribbean and Pacific (ACP) governments in the Convention have a veto over EU development programmes. In giving formal recognition, some power, and sometimes not a little authority to NGOs through the Cotonou programme and through Echo (its emergency relief organisation), the EU is following behind what is widely seen as the 'good practice' of other regional and UN-led institutional frameworks.

The scientific and technological community plays a very important role in development policy making. If one looks at the debate on climate change there have been serious disagreements on the causes, rapidity and consequences of changes in climatic conditions. Without a firm basis for predictions on what will happen in the future it is difficult to plan accordingly. While strongly reliant on scientific input, the climate change debate has become heavily politicised. Various interest groups have lobbied to present scientific findings as either overdramatising the likely impact of climate change, or even disputing the methodology and interpretations of these conclusions. The Global Climate Coalition (GCC) was formed in 1989 with an apparent remit to counter the claims being made by scientific advisers to the IPCC. For the better part of a decade it included prominent members from the oil, gas and automobile manufacturing industries. These were the sectors deemed most responsible for producing high levels of greenhouse gas emissions and most at risk from tighter regulation of harmful emissions. As the science of climate change became better understood and more difficult to dispute, many of these members left the GCC and began to investigate how to reduce their carbon footprints. The nature of scientific inquiry is such that it is virtually impossible to achieve 100 per cent certainty on outcomes and scientists prefer to present findings in terms of probability percentages. That said, there is now a widespread acceptance that not only is climate change occurring, it is also significantly impacted upon by human activity. Therefore, human activity needs to be modified in order to reduce the more extreme negative impacts of climate change. This has a direct bearing on development policy in that the transfer of knowledge and skills in renewable energy and low-carbon technologies is an important goal of development policy actors including the EU and Japan. It also provides an area of development action that offers commercial advantages to the stakeholders, who are able to research, develop and promote green technologies more efficiently: economic development is not invariably an obstacle to environmental improvement – or vice versa.

Technology is therefore double-edged and, depending on its application, may lead to greater environmental degradation or greater protection. It plays a key role in the promotion of development goals. Science and technology are fundamental elements in meeting the majority of the UN's MDGs, be it in healthcare, agricultural production or sustainable energy supplies. Technical fixes are sometimes cited as the solution for many development problems. There is an argument to be made here, and *some* technologies may have a demonstrable development and environment benefit; but it does risk avoiding the underlying issue of what is creating a problem in the first place. For example, there is a very lively debate on what types of energy supply should be utilised from a range of fossil fuels, renewable sources or the nuclear option. There is less discussion on reducing energy consumption and, perhaps, even slowing economic growth. There is also a risk of assuming that technology will continue to advance and we will find future answers to problems that we are currently aware of. For example, in the 1950s it was suggested that nuclear power would be 'too cheap to meter' and that there would shortly be a solution found to the problem of the safe storage or disposal of harmful radioactive waste. Nuclear waste remains a problematic issue and the cost of nuclear power generation, when waste disposal and decommissioning costs are factored in, is actually far more expensive than originally predicted.

Women are undeniably a major group and play a very important role in the context of the MDGs. This is partly because they are often at the centre of many of the development issues to be addressed. This is especially the case in rural communities where it is women who are often at the forefront of providing food and water for households. They are both the bearers of and main care providers for children. The UN has recognised the importance of promoting gender equality and highlighting the role women play in development issues, especially since the 1995 UN Women's Conference in Beijing (which was actually the fourth UN Women's Conference). Embedded within the UN framework are bodies such as the Division for the Advancement of Women, the Development Fund for Women (UNIFEM) and the International Research and Training Institute for the Advancement of Women (INSTRAW). There are also a great many NGOs that focus on the issue of women's rights or development issues where women are the central focus.

The final major group involves workers and trade unions. Again this is a very large sector to cover and it includes a broad range of workers drawn from all aspects of rural and urban economies. While there may be less formal employment in rural areas there are often mining or agricultural workers, some of whom may be unionised but many who are not. Workers' cooperatives are increasingly seen as a way in which land use can be retained in the control of local communities. This is not to say that MNCs do not continue to engage in interaction with such groups; but they may play more of an intermediary role by sourcing their supplies from cooperative farms and then selling these on to the international market.

This has the advantage of allowing the cooperatives to have access to markets they might not otherwise have, but also maintains a greater sense of stewardship for the land than might otherwise be felt by MNCs with no personal connection to the land. Involving workers and trade unions in a more engaged manner also provides some sense of shared planning and 'buy in' to development planning. The whole thrust of the major groups initiative is to recognise that there are shared interests and to try to avoid some potential tensions and conflicts, such as between workers and employers.

Having considered how development has been defined, explored potential problems with this, and reviewed the main development goals and the major development actors, it is useful now to look at some specific examples of development projects to assess how they are implemented and how successful, or not, they have been.

## Development projects

In the 1960s and 1970s, there was a wave of decolonisation, with many states achieving political independence from their former colonial rulers. It is important to note here, however, that political independence as represented by a head of state, government officials, national flag and national anthem does not necessarily equate to full economic independence. Many of these states were, and to some extent remain, tied into neo-colonial patterns of dependence. They often sought development aid in the early years of independence with a view to increasing their infrastructure capacity and investing in major schemes such as large hydroelectric power generation schemes. The large dam schemes, such as the Aswan High Dam in Egypt, are classic examples of such large-scale investment projects. While they have undoubted benefits in terms of both power generation and flood control, there are also some serious negative consequences of such projects. The initial building of such dams almost always involves the forced relocation of communities. The silt that would normally flow with the river that has been dammed is held back in the reservoir that has been created by the dam. This has two significant impacts. First it prevents the nutrients in the silt enriching the land downstream, with a result that farmers there are then forced to use artificial fertilisers, which may have a harmful environmental effect. Second, the amount of silt is often underestimated and as it builds up it shortens the projected productive lifespan of the project. More recently the World Bank has recognised that the negative impacts of such major dam projects outweigh the benefits. The World Commission on Dams has led a review of such projects and they now have considerably less support with international funding reduced or withdrawn altogether from several projects. India's Namada, Turkey's Ilisu and, perhaps most controversially of all given the scale of the project, China's Three Gorges Dam have all faced significant international criticism.

At the opposite end of the development planning scale there are also examples of much smaller-scale projects. Many development consultants and campaigners prefer the grassroots or community-based approach. A UK-based development NGO called Practical Action highlights the role of intermediate technologies to provide low-cost community projects such as the digging of wells and other irrigation projects and micro power generation (see: www.practicalaction.org. uk/home-uk). Solar cookers and wind-up radios are also examples of very small-scale initiatives that don't grab the headlines in the same way that the major projects do, but have a far-reaching impact in terms of the lives improved by these small initiatives. This reflects two very different approaches to development. As highlighted elsewhere in the chapter, it is possible to take either a top-down or a bottom-up approach to development. The MDGs and the major groups discussed above can be seen to combine elements of both approaches. Almost by definition something emanating from the UN may be seen as top-down as it attempts to coordinate action on a global scale. That said, when one looks at the majority of practical plans within the majority of the MDGs they tend to be focused at the individual and local community levels. Some of the major groups are more community-focused than others. Yet even with some of the more economic-growth-first-and-then-'trickle-down'-later members, such as the main MNCs, there appears to be a growing awareness that development has to be inclusive and is not something that can be simply directed from above. Development is a combination of global processes and local impacts, and responses.

# Critical frameworks for rethinking development

A variety of studies offer more critical ways of looking at development issues, drawing on the kind of literature we have already discussed in Chapter 4 above. These include more radical approaches, sometimes looking at resistance to globalisation and its development dimensions from a neo-Gramscian perspective (e.g. O'Brien *et al.*, 2000) or a feminist approach (e.g. Peterson, 2009; Parpart and Marchand, 1995). Much of this critical work begins by questioning the very conception of development, going back to the arguments rehearsed earlier in this chapter and asking how we can better understand what development actually means, how specific discourses and social practices associated with development have been produced, and how their meaning is controlled. Probably the most influential work in this field is Escobar's *Encountering Development* (1995 – although there are several competitors for this title). Escobar invites us to question the project of development as envisaged in both the liberal/radical and neo-liberal/neo-realist camps, drawing particularly on Foucault's work on understanding the construction of discourse and the forms of power it involves. This also turns attention in development studies to the varieties of forms of power that are involved within the academic discipline of development studies itself, as Pieterse (2000) shows. The extensive literature on development theory and sustainability and the varieties of liberal arguments about development can also be explored through a reading of his account.

Critical theory and postmodern theory raise at least one question in application to development, which is at the same time an ethical and a policy concern. This body of broadly critical analysis of development processes has great value in formulating sharp questions and suggesting research strategies to find answers to them. But at the same time, their approach is one of critique, which, as Robert Cox argued (see discussion in Chapter 4), makes a sharp division between practical knowledge and critical thought. But development, although it might justify a critical approach, surely also justifies a practical approach, one that engages with practical realities and needs that people face every day – surely it cannot afford the luxury of merely thinking critically without some form of effective response. But while this raises some important theoretical questions, the shorter answer to the dilemma is that it is a false distinction, and that most development debate is at once critical (from whatever standpoint, including that of Gramscians and postmodern Foucauldians and neo-liberal writers such as Moyo (2009)) and practical, at least in its aspirations. The more important question may be to ask, who controls development processes, in whose interests, and with what assumptions?

# Summary

This chapter has aimed to introduce a range of ideas and arguments about development. These touch on questions of political economy, of course, but they also confront political economy with questions of justice and ethics, with questions of how political economy itself studies its subject, or, less abstractly, it challenges the choices we each make when we choose to study aspects of it. And it raises questions about the wide range of groups and organisations that have become increasingly involved in the 'delivery' of development policies.

**Table 8.2**  Chapter summary

| | Key actors | Key processes | Emphasis on political economy | What causes change? | Global institutions? | View of conflict in global relations? |
|---|---|---|---|---|---|---|
| Top-down development | States, firms, markets | Economic growth and 'trickle-down' | Dominance of neo-liberal model seen as a positive force for development | Free-market neo-liberal economics | The UN, World Bank, IMF, WTO | Conflict is seen as working against the realising of many development goals |
| Bottom-up development | Individuals, communities and civil society actors | Community cohesion and environmental sustainability | Greater recognition that structures of power are actively holding some back from developing | Civic activism | World Social Forum and range of INGOs that operate at the global level | As above but grassroots view expands on this to look at aspects of structural violence and dispossession |

## Reflective questions

1  Why is the concept of 'development' considered to be problematic?
2  Who are the key actors in the development process? And what role do they play?
3  What factors impeded progress towards the achieving the MDGs and remain relevant in relation to the SDGs?
4  Is there simply a technical fix for development problems, or are there more deep-rooted problems that need to be addressed?
5  What is the core discourse of development? How far does it pit liberal and neo-liberal ideas in opposition to each other and how far does it absorb them into a single structure of ideas and social practices?

## Suggestions for further reading

Adams, W.M. (2008) *Green Development: Environment and Sustainability in a Developing World*, London: Routledge.

BBC News (2010) 'Kenya flower industry hit by flight cancellations', *BBC News Online*, 16 April 2010.

Brinkerhoff, J.M. (2002) *Partnerships for International Development: Rhetoric or Results?* London: Lynne Rienner.

Chari, S. and Corbridge, S. (eds) (2007) *The Development Reader*, London: Routledge.

Escobar, A. (1995) *Encountering Development: The Making and Unmaking of the Third World*, Princeton, NJ: Princeton University Press.

Fukuyama, F. (1992) *The End of History and the Last Man*, London: Penguin.

Hayter, T. (1971) *Aid as Imperialism*, London: Penguin Books.

Hopkins, M. (2008) *Corporate Social Responsibility and International Development: Is Business the Solution?* London: Earthscan.

IBP USA (2009) *Nauru Recent Economic and Political Developments Yearbook*, Washington, DC: International Business Publications.

Joseph, R. and Gillies, A. (2008) *Smart Aid for African Development*, Boulder, CO: Lynne Rienner.

Moyo, D. (2009) *Dead Aid: Why Aid Is Not Working and How There Is a Better Way for Africa*, London: Allen Lane.

O'Brien, R., Goetz, A-M., Scholte, J-A. and Williams, M. (2000) *Contesting Global Governance: Multilateral Global Institutions and Global Social Movements*, Cambridge: Cambridge University Press.

Parpart, M. and Marchand, J. (1995) *Feminism/Postmodernism/Development*, London: Routledge.

Peterson, V.S. (2009) *Global Gender Issues in the New Millennium*, 3rd edn, Boulder, CO: Westview Press.

Pieterse, J.N. (2000) *Development Theory: Deconstructions/Reconstructions*, London: Sage.

Roberts, J. Timmons and Hite, A.B. (eds) (2006) *The Globalisation and Development Reader: Perspectives on Development and Global Change*, Oxford: Wiley Blackwell.

Rostow, W. (1960) *The Stages of Economic Growth: A Non-Communist Manifesto*, Cambridge: Cambridge University Press.

United Nations (2014) *Human Development Report 2014: Sustaining Human Progress: Reducing Vulnerabilities and Building Resilience*, New York: UN.

Williamson, J. (1990) 'What Washington means by policy reform', in *Latin American Adjustment: How Much Has Happened?* Chapter 2. Washington, DC: Peterson Institute for International Economics. Available at https://piie.com/commentary/speeches-papers/what-washington-means-policy-reform.

# 9 Environment

## Chapter learning outcomes

After reading this chapter students should be able to:

- Recognise and describe why environmental issues are now an important element of the international political agenda.
- Explain the role of a range of actors in creating/responding to environmental issues, including governments, MNCs, international non-governmental organisations and individuals.
- Understand and explain a range of contemporary environmental issues, including resource depletion, declining biodiversity, food security, water security, energy security and the meaning and significance of the Anthropocene era.
- Analyse global processes of dialogue and cooperation that focus on responding to, or resolving environmental issues.
- Discuss the role of the media in formulating popular perceptions and opinions in relation to environmental issues.
- Discuss the role of individual lifestyles in relation to global environmental issues.
- Relate discussion of environmental issues to the theoretical debates discussed earlier in this book.

## Introduction

Environmental issues are inextricably linked to human existence, from the earliest hunter-gatherer groups through to the settlement and cultivation of territories, and subsequent competition for land and associated resources. Yet it is only relatively recently that environmental issues have become a significant part of the international political agenda. During the late 1960s and early 1970s environmental consciousness was raised and the environment became, and remains, a highly politicised issue. This chapter will look at the actors, issues and processes relevant to the political economy of the environment.

The interaction between actors, issues and processes can be viewed in a variety of ways. None of these categories are homogeneous. There are enormous differences between the material situations of various states and individuals in terms of their physical resources and the impact that environmental change can have as a result of exploiting these resources. Similarly, MNCs and NGOs are also broad categories that mask a variety of agendas and capabilities. The issues that will be referred to below have varying degrees of impact and importance to the diverse range of actors under consideration here. It therefore follows that the processes involved in the interaction between this complex array of actors and issues will also be variable. While there is a case to be argued that there may be a single 'process' of global environmental degradation taking place over time, it is important to highlight that this process will be experienced, understood and acted upon differently by different actors depending on their individual interests and level of agency.

In the early 1980s researcher Eugene Stoermer was the first to coin the term 'Anthropocene', referring to human impacts on the planet and likening these to previous geological era. Atmospheric chemist Paul Crutzen, specifically in relation to ozone depletion, developed this idea further. Professor Will Steffen, former Executive Director of the Australian National University's Climate Change Institute and others have developed these ideas further still, especially in relation to what they consider to be human-induced climate change. Despite a small, but very vocal, minority of climate change deniers the overwhelming body of scientific knowledge is now clearly demonstrating that human activity is having an increasingly detrimental impact on humans, other species, habitats and inter-connected ecosystems around the world. The World Wide Fund for Nature's *Living Planet Report 2014* indicates that more than half of the world's wildlife has been destroyed since 1970. This figure is based on surveys of over 10,000 representative populations of birds,

**Table 9.1**  Survey of attitudes towards environmental issues in the EU 2014

**QA1 How important is protecting the environment to you personally?**

| | Total 'Important' | Diff. EB81.3–EB75.2 | Total 'Not important' | Diff. EB81.3–EB75.2 | Don't know | Diff. EB81.3–EB75.2 |
|---|---|---|---|---|---|---|
| Europe 28 | 95% | +1 | 5% | = | 0% | −1 |
| Sweden | 100% | +2 | 0% | −2 | 0% | = |
| Malta | 99% | −1 | 1% | +1 | 0% | = |
| Slovenia | 99% | +1 | 1% | −1 | 0% | = |
| Cyprus | 93% | −2 | 2% | +2 | 0% | = |
| El Salvador | 97% | −1 | 3% | +1 | 0% | = |
| Luxembourg | 97% | +1 | 3% | = | 0% | −1 |
| Netherlands | 97% | +4 | 3% | −4 | 0% | = |
| Portugal | 97% | +2 | 3% | −2 | 0% | = |
| Denmark | 96% | | 4% | | 0% | = |
| Estonia | 96% | +2 | 4% | −1 | 0% | −1 |
| Spain | 96% | +2 | 4% | −1 | 0% | −1 |
| Belgium | 95% | | 5% | = | 0% | = |
| France | 95% | −2 | 5% | +2 | 0% | = |
| Italy | 95% | +1 | 4% | −2 | 1% | +1 |
| Hungary | 95% | −1 | 5% | +1 | 0% | = |
| Bulgaria | 94% | −4 | 5% | +4 | 1% | = |
| Germany | 94% | −1 | 6% | +1 | 0% | = |
| Ireland | 94% | = | 6% | = | 0% | = |
| Slovakia | 94% | −1 | 6% | +2 | 0% | −1 |
| Finland | 94% | +1 | 6% | −1 | 0% | = |
| United Kingdom | 94% | = | 5% | −1 | 1% | +1 |
| Czech Republic | 93% | −2 | 7% | +2 | 0% | = |
| Croatia | 93% | – | 7% | – | 0% | – |
| Latvia | 93% | −2 | 7% | +2 | 0% | = |
| Lithuania | 93% | −1 | 7% | + 2 | 0% | −1 |
| Austria | 91% | +1 | 9% | −1 | 0% | = |
| Poland | 91% | −1 | 8% | +2 | 1% | −1 |
| Romania | 91% | −1 | 8% | +2 | 1% | −1 |

*Source*: European Commission (2014) *Attitudes of European citizens towards the environment*, Special Eurobarometer, 416, p. 10. http://ec.europa.eu/public_opinion/archives/ebs/ebs_416_en.pdf.

reptiles, mammals, amphibians and fish. The leading causes for this catastrophic decline are unsustainable levels of hunting and fishing, degradation or loss of habitats and other actors associated with climate change. How the relationship between humans, other species and the ecosystems necessary to support life on Earth are understood and responded to are, arguably, the most significant challenges facing individuals and their governments through the twenty-first century.

The huge variation in interests and agendas of the diverse actors concerned with environmental change means that it will always be problematic attempting to reach a consensus on what action needs to be taken, if any. The conferences of the parties to the UN Framework Convention on Climate Change (UNFCCC) illustrate the difficulties in reaching agreement between nearly 200 states. These Conference of the Parties (CoP) events are also subject to intense lobbying from both MNCs and other civil society NGOs.

Table 9.1 illustrates public perceptions and attitudes towards environmental protection within EU member states. There are clearly variations across this region, as there will be in other regions of the world. There are also some apparently illogical inconsistencies, such as 48 per cent of UK respondents expressing concern about growing amounts of waste, yet only 16 per cent of the same group highlighting problems with their patterns of consumption. In part this reflects the manner in which environmental issues are ranked relative to other social concerns, and the connections made, or in this case probably not made, between these issues. How these concerns are formed, understood and addressed will be determined by a range of actors and issues, as outlined in the following pages.

## Actors: governments

National governments are not a homogeneous group and some have more impact on the environment than others. However, they are central to environmental issues in terms of their capacity to enable environmentally mindful legislation and to attempt to formulate, monitor and, where appropriate and possible, police international agreements seeking to secure environmentally sustainable goals. Looking at how the global economy has developed over the last few centuries it is reasonable to argue that the economic growth that has driven the accumulation of power among the core states has largely not taken environmental degradation into account. Far from it, as natural resources have been plundered in many parts of the world in order to fuel this growth. Even when colonial rule has been supplanted by political independence for former colonies the underlying economic dynamism has tended to rely on the extraction of primary products to generate export income. Multinational corporations facilitate much of this, thereby highlighting the combination of actors that feed into environmental politics. In addition, numerous civil society groups, such as Friends of the Earth and Greenpeace International, have been extremely active in highlighting environmental problems and lobbying both governments and MNCs to move towards more sustainable economic development practices. This initial section will consider how governments, MNCs and civil society actors have responded to the emerging environmental agenda from the early 1970s onwards.

The UN Conference on Environment and Development, held in Stockholm in 1972, marked a significant breakthrough in international diplomacy whereby the major powers acknowledged that there was a clear connection between economic development and environmental conservation. It was recognised that it was not possible to continue to emphasise economic growth without an understanding of associated environmental costs that accompany this growth. The Brundtland Commission's report 'North/South: a programme for survival' highlighted the vested interests that the governments of the global North had in avoiding the social disruption that would be caused by excessive environmental degradation taking place in the developing world. This was in terms of ensuring access to a steady supply of primary resources, and also to secure markets for their manufactured goods. There was also a desire to maintain stability in the developing world to avoid pressure to intervene, by military or other means, should political control in the global South break down to the point that Northern strategic interests were threatened. While a myriad of issues may lead to conflict around the world, aspects of resource depletion, erratic weather patterns leading to both floods and droughts (which are often also associated with crop failure) are seeing greater numbers of people migrating or coming into conflict with neighbours as competition for increasingly scarce resources intensifies. Such factors are most obviously and extremely experienced at the local level, but do also have significant international contexts and consequences. However, despite a growing awareness of the interconnections at a global level the majority of international relations have continued to be based on relatively short-term national interests.

All governments face difficult choices when trying to address environmental issues. The more developed ones have more diverse economies and the capital to provide for some environmental conservation, both domestically and as part of their overseas aid programmes. Even these, though, have been criticised by environmental groups for failing to restrict pollution, and to manage vulnerable species and habitats appropriately, and generally continuing to prioritise economic growth over sustainability. The less developed states are often at the forefront of major environmental crises in the forms of spreading desertification, deforestation and loss of biodiversity. These are also the governments that tend to have fewer budgetary resources to draw on for conservation projects. Their position in the global economy is such that they draw heavily on their natural resources for government revenue. This may be in the form of mining operations, which often have severe polluting characteristics, or the clear felling of swathes of tropical rainforest. The latter raises some export income but the environmental consequences can be far-reaching. These include loss of habitat, reduced biodiversity, increased soil erosion and even damage to mangrove and reef systems as a result of higher levels of silt in river systems. Governments may be fully aware of the environmental consequences of some of their policies but feel unable to take more direct conservation measures due to the short-term economic costs involved.

The latter part of the twentieth century saw some headway being made with national governments at least opening discussions on how to address perceived environmental problems. Initially this was focused on the fear that fossil fuels were being depleted at such a rate there would be significant energy shortages and potential conflicts over access to dwindling fuel supplies. Some of the more extreme 'doomsday' predictions of the early 1970s suggested that coal, oil and gas supplies would be close to exhaustion by the turn of the century. This has clearly not come to pass but it should be acknowledged that this is largely because of the willingness of consumers to pay significantly more for these fuels. Because of this, reserves that had not previously been considered economically viable to exploit were added to the overall reserves available. Although these secondary fuel supplies continue to be depleted far in excess of the natural processes that would replace them there is now less concern regarding the amount of fossil fuels available for use. Rather, the concern has shifted to the pollution associated with such usage, not exclusively but predominantly in relation to greenhouse gas emissions. This issue has formed the basis of the main international negotiations at the governmental level, as illustrated by the Earth Summit process and the formation of the Intergovernmental Panel on Climate Change (IPCC). Despite growing awareness and acknowledgement of the pollution caused by mainly relying on fossil fuel-based energy supplies the general trend for most of the larger, more powerful states is to continue in this manner rather than shift to renewable energy sources. For example, since the first edition of this text was published in 2011 the UK government has actively reduced its investment in renewable energy sources while at the same time exploring the exploitation of fossil fuel shale oil and shale gas reserves.

The Rio Earth Summit of 1992 will be looked at in more detail below but it is worth noting here the significance of this event. This Summit meeting built on the environmental platform established in Stockholm in 1972, but took this debate to a more profound level. This was in terms of both the number of governments that were represented at Rio and also the fact that this included a great many heads of state and heads of government, including those from the most powerful developed nations. There were also legally binding agreements presented for ratification in the form of Conventions on both climate change and biodiversity. Not all of the states present were wholly enthusiastic in ratifying these agreements. George Bush, the US president at the time, had appeared reluctant to even attend the meeting and in a speech shortly before his arrival he had stated that he would not sign any agreement that would cost US jobs. His agenda was still focused very much at the level of national interest and not acknowledging that global environmental concerns necessarily included the national interests of all states. This attitude goes to the heart of the dilemma of dealing with global issues at the national level. Pursuit of national interests has been a central part of international relations since the creation of the Westphalian nation state system. Although this socially constructed political system simply overlies the reality of the natural world and environmental processes it has gained a predominant role in how humans interact with this wider environment. There may be a mismatch between what is actually happening and how we deal with it but national governments retain a key role in how these events are mediated and dealt with, or not in many cases.

Although the above point highlights the ongoing significance of national governments it is worth reiterating that some are in more powerful positions than others to deal with environmental crises. For example, the low-lying island states of the Pacific region contribute virtually nothing in terms of greenhouse gas emissions, yet this issue is a threat to their very survival with some of these islands already being inundated as a result of sea-level rise. Adapting to a rising sea level via building coastal defences is not a viable option for most of these states. Mass migration is also problematic both in terms of where to relocate to and issues of identity. Ideally the problem should be dealt with at its source, which are the emissions generated by the industrialised states. The only way these small island states can influence this scenario is by arguing their case at international forums such as the IPCC. This reinforces the state-centric nature of international relations, but also highlights the power politics dimension of this whereby the interests of a few thousand Pacific islanders are unlikely to alter the course of the major powers of the United States, China, Russia and other significant greenhouse gas emitters. Although the major powers are discussing reductions in such emissions they are generally rather modest targets in comparison to what would be required to halt, or even significantly slow down, the encroachment of the ocean being experienced in low-lying regions of the world. One of the problems with the 'front lines' of environmental crises is they happen in particular places and unless this is within the boundaries of a major power they are unlikely to be acted upon in a significant manner. Despite the recognition that problems such as sea-level rise or tropical deforestation have global consequences they largely continue to be seen as something to be managed at the national level.

While national governments are geographically fixed in terms of their sovereign territory the same cannot be said for their interests. The above example graphically demonstrates the Pacific islands' interests being intertwined with events taking place well beyond their political boundaries. Similarly, the most developed states have overseas interests in terms of access to resources and markets. When looking at the emerging environmental agenda from an international political economy perspective it is difficult to maintain a wholly state-centric view as so many relevant issues cross national boundaries. The growth of transnational and interdependent relationships is a key feature of processes of globalisation. Within that context it is important to look at the role that MNCs play with regard to environmental issues.

# Actors: multinational corporations

Chapter 4 outlined the significance of MNCs as major international actors. Regardless of seeing them as wholly independent actors or as 'agents of the state', their impact is undeniable. Many of the environmental crises currently taking place around the world are a direct result of MNC activities. Resource depletion and resultant pollution from all manner of manufacturing processes are overwhelmingly conducted with MNC involvement. With the minor but worthy exception of the very small percentage of international trade that can accurately be described as 'fair trade', the vast majority of international trade does not factor in environmental, or social, costs when fixing the price of tradable goods. This is not to say that no MNCs have any sense of environmental awareness or the need to promote sustainability. Some of them do have long-term strategies and recognise that in order to protect their business interests this requires at least some degree of environmental sensitivity. But these tend to be the exceptions to the rule and the latter part of the twentieth century saw the emergence of the phrase the 'race to the bottom' as both governments and MNCs tried to pursue economic growth by any means necessary. The consequences of this have slowly emerged with a growing recognition that such practices are short-sighted and need to be fundamentally reassessed. That said, just as national governments are a wildly varying collective, so too are MNCs with some much further advanced in their environmental awareness and strategies than others.

The World Business Council for Sustainable Development (WBCSD) is a coalition of some of the world's largest MNCs. These include major fossil fuel companies and representatives of the mining, shipping, airline and automobile industries. As such it features many of the companies responsible for the most dramatic environmental issues on the planet. In recent years the phrase 'corporate social responsibility' (CSR) has been coined to acknowledge the central role that MNCs play in impacting on the environment. As with many such phrases it is open to a wide range of meanings and interpretations. The companies themselves, understandably, say this highlights their environmental and social concerns. Others, notably some of the civil society environmental campaign groups, have criticised this approach as 'greenwash' and a shameless public relations exercise to both divert attention from ongoing environmental damage caused by these companies, and also to attract the 'green pound' of environmentally aware and concerned consumers. Short of an admission of guilt from the MNCs this is a debate that cannot be satisfactorily resolved one way or the other. No doubt there are some who work in the private sector that do have sentiments that extend beyond the basic profit motive. The Body Shop and Ben and Jerry's are both examples of MNCs that have gone out of their way to source, manufacture and promote their respective products in a sustainable manner. They do also highlight this in their advertising but this does not diminish the value of these practices.

Energy companies are at the forefront of the climate change debate. They are also among the most high profile when it comes to flagging up their CSR credentials. British Petroleum is a good example of this with a redesigned logo that resembles a green flower and a marketing slogan that reads 'Beyond Petroleum'. This is a reference to their research and development work on renewable energy sources and products. This certainly exists but it represents a very small proportion of the company's overall business, which remains firmly based on highly polluting and non-sustainable use of fossil fuels. Their attempts to rebrand with enhanced green credentials came under close scrutiny following the Deepwater Horizon oil spill in the Gulf of Mexico in 2010. Their logo was repeatedly lampooned by campaigning organisations such as PR Watch (see below). The major automobile manufacturers are also developing hybrid products that highlight fuel efficiency and reduced carbon emissions. Again, this is to be welcomed but the underlying problems of resource depletion and pollution associated with an emphasis on multiple car households as opposed to investment in public transport infrastructure remains in place. In the broader context of development policies based on consumerism MNCs are the principal actors in facilitating this. Governments can play a role in terms of taxation and other forms of market intervention, such as health and safety legislation. Individual consumers are also clearly crucial as the 'end users' of manufactured products. Yet it is MNCs that provide the drive and momentum for this by way of both producing products and actively promoting them, often creating a market that would otherwise not exist. Markets can also be artificially created by built-in obsolescence. Added to this the constant redesigning of products to create a sense of them coming in and going out of fashion demonstrates this is a system that is built on ever-expanding levels of consumerism, and related environmental degradation. Very few markets are ever truly saturated and with many millions of new consumers entering these markets in India and China alone this is a process that has potentially very serious environmental consequences.

Governments and MNCs have both been the target of a broad range of environmental lobbying groups covering an equally diverse array of campaign issues. The early 1970s was again a significant period for this group of actors as it saw the formation of some of the leading organisations, such as Friends of the Earth and Greenpeace International. Their agendas and methods have evolved over time but they remain fundamentally concerned with environmental conservation and sustainability. Initial campaigns were based on the detrimental impacts of human activity on the environment. The Greenpeace organisation was born out of protests against US nuclear testing in the north Pacific. Success in this campaign led to protests against the French nuclear testing programme and the remit of the organisation quickly evolved to cover many other campaigns. Notable among these was their opposition, along with other conservation groups, to the annual seal cull conducted in Canada and Newfoundland. Both the cull and the protests remain ongoing. Greenpeace was one of the first campaign groups to highlight both the role of direct action and the importance of recording and publicising these actions. MNCs are not alone in their public relations exercises. The protest groups operate at various levels. They highlight the environmental damage caused as a result of MNC activities. They attempt to influence governments to adopt more environmentally aware and responsive policies and legislation. They also encourage members of the public to join their organisations and to lobby both MNCs and governments on their behalf. Advances in telecommunication technologies have radically enhanced the latter point.

## Actors: non-governmental organisations

NGOs previously relied on writing to newspapers or conducting high-profile actions that would ensure their arguments would receive press coverage. As these actions became more commonplace their newsworthiness subsequently declined. However, the Internet has provided a valuable platform for highlighting issues via these organisations' own websites and it is also becoming a conduit for the practical coordination of campaigns and related actions. This also enables connections to be made highlighting how the consumption of products, for example in the UK, may have far-reaching consequences for people, other species and habitats far across the globe. The organisation of consumer boycotts, or at least raising awareness of more sustainable-sourced alternatives, has played a significant part in these groups' actions. The role of the individual has become increasingly important as patterns of consumption have evolved to such a degree that lifestyle options and choices have impacts well beyond a person's immediate locality. NGOs have capitalised on this by highlighting these connections and illustrating the level of empowerment this bestows upon individuals. It is no longer the case that citizens are restricted to exercising a level of political power once every few years by casting a vote in an election, assuming they have the right to vote. Now many people are making actively 'political' choices in relation to thinking about the implications of their consumption of all types of goods and services. This can be in relation to where they take their holidays, how they travel, whether they are using energy-saving light bulbs or avoiding leaving electrical items on stand-by. These are day-to-day activities that are increasingly recognised as having environmental consequences.

---

**EXAMPLE BOX**

## Think global

This section has looked at how different types of actors interact in the pursuit of their various interests in relation to environmental issues. Often they intersect as issues relate to government policies, private sector practices and civil society concerns and activism. An example of an NGO that seeks to engage with UK government policy, European Union initiatives as appropriate and relevant private sector activities is Think Global. This is a development education organisation with a particular focus on the promotion of the concept of global citizenship, especially in the fields of environmental awareness and sustainable development. Its motto is 'Promoting education for a just and sustainable world'. It has an emphasis on how environmental and broader developmental issues are taught in schools, although its remit also extends to a lesser extent to higher education and general public outreach initiatives. As such its main focus is raising awareness among individuals to make lifestyle choices, to the best of their abilities, which are environmentally aware and sensitive. What options people have to make such choices are often bound by government policies and the context of their socio-economic circumstances. Again this illustrates the complex dynamics between the public and private spheres and individuals' relationship with the environment.

---

Having looked at the range of actors that are influential on and impacted by environmental change we now turn to look at specific issues and how each of these actors relate to them. None of the following are completely 'stand alone' as, in line with Lovelock's Gaia theory, they are each interconnected as part of a global ecosystem. Some have very locally specific dimensions, but all are best understood in terms of their place in relation to broader environmental impacts.

## Issues: resource depletion

Resource depletion has been a concern since the earliest days of the environmental movement. As mentioned above, there have been varying predictions and disagreements over the rate at which supplies are becoming exhausted. However, there is virtually unanimous agreement that the vast majority of resources are being consumed in excess of natural replenishment. Fossil fuels appear to have a degree of market elasticity, which means that supplies can 'expand' in relation to their market value. The same cannot be said for other resources such as forests or fish stocks. Both of these have been excessively exploited, to the point of systemic collapse in some areas. These are interesting examples in terms of issues of ownership and sovereignty. Forests are obviously located within a specific sovereign territory, yet they have also been described as the 'lungs of the world' and should therefore be seen as a form of global commons. This is obviously a contentious point with states that wish to exploit their forest resources arguing that they have political autonomy and every right to use these resources in any way they see fit. A fair point in the current nation state system, but one that is at odds with the more holistic perspective that recognises the importance of these forest areas as carbon sinks, which play a crucial role in the global climate system. Some developing states, notably Malaysia, have been very forthright in condemning the more developed states for what they see as the denial of development and the opportunity for these states to better themselves. The UN has devised a set of 'Forest Principles' that attempt to monitor, if not police, the use of forest resources in a sustainable manner. This is directed towards governments but has implications for the MNCs involved in the timber industry and also NGOs such as the Rainforest Alliance, which promotes forest conservation.

## Issues: deforestation

The debate surrounding forest resource use and conservation is highly politicised with potential disagreement over land use at the domestic and intergovernmental levels. Added to this is the economic dimension with big business involvement, plus numerous NGOs that campaign for forest conservation. The latter include those that may be campaigning for the protection of a particular species, such as the orangutan. They argue that the best way to protect a species is to protect its natural habitats, in this case tropical rainforest. There are other groups that campaign on behalf of indigenous peoples, for example the Yanomani in Amazonia, who are threatened by loggers and mining prospectors. Tropical rainforest is home to the most concentrated and diverse range of biodiversity on the planet and this also raises its profile as both a resource, notably for medicinal plants, and as an ecosystem to be valued in its own right beyond the market value of any extractable timber. The political economy of tropical rainforest is as complex as the flora and fauna that inhabit this ecosystem. There are a wide range of actors with competing interests and agendas involved over the fate of this habitat.

## Issues: biodiversity

One aspect of protecting biodiversity is to reduce the number of extinctions of species that occur. The International Union for Conservation of Nature (IUCN) produces a 'red list of threatened species'. This currently lists over 16,000 species at various levels of risk up to highly endangered. As the natural world has evolved, unless you are of a creationist persuasion, many distinct species have emerged and subsequently disappeared. This raises some interesting points on the 'value' of species. Does it matter that we no longer share the planet with the dodo? The answer to this question is likely to revolve around the extent to which species and habitats are perceived as having inherent value, or if this only occurs in terms of a 'use' value for humans. This is an illustration of the distinction to be made between those who separate out humans from our natural environment and the deeper green approach, which sees humans as simply another species, albeit one with a disproportionate ability to impact on all other species. Here we are touching on the realms of moral philosophy but the answer to the above question is of great significance to some of today's most pressing environmental debates. To return to the rainforest example, protecting biodiversity can be on the grounds that it is the most remarkable, even beautiful for some observers, environment on the planet. Equally from a human use perspective the plants of the rainforest have provided the basis for many medicinal drugs and it is quite possible that further medicines could

**Table 9.2** Information currently collected regularly on the socioeconomic benefits from forests

| Type of indicator | FRA | Forest Europe (Criterion 6) | ITTO (Criterion 7) | Montréal process (Criterion 6) |
|---|---|---|---|---|
| Economic indicators | Value of forest product removals. Contribution of forestry to GDP | 6.2 Contribution of the forest sector to GDP6.3 Net revenue of forest enterprises 6.8 Imports and exports of wood and products derived from wood | 7.1 Contribution of the forest sector to GDP 7.2 Value of domestic production (products and services) | 6.1.a, b Value and volume of production 6.1.c Revenue from forest based environmental services 6.1f, g Value and volume of trade6.1h Export and import shares 6.2a, b Investment and expenditure (on various forest-related activities) |
| Labour indicators | Forestry employment | 6.5 Number of persons employed 6.6 Frequency of occupational accidents and diseases | 7.7 Training and labour development programmes 7.8 Existence and implementation of health and safety procedures | 6.3a Employment in the forest sector6.3b Wage rates, average income and injury rates |
| Consumption indicators | Wood removals. Area of forest removed for other land uses | 6.7 Consumption per head of wood and products derived from wood 6.9 Share of wood energy in total energy consumption, classified by origin of wood | 7.6 Number of people depending on forests for their livelihoods 7.9 Area of forests used for subsistence uses and traditional and customary lifestyles | 6.1d, e Consumption of wood and non-wood forest products6.3d Area and per cent of forests used for subsistence purposes |
| Other use indicators | Area of forest designated for social services | 6.10 Area where public has access rights for recreation and intensity of use 6.11 Number of sites having cultural or spiritual values | 7.10 Number and extent of forests available primarily for: research, education and recreation 7.11 Number of important archaeological, cultural and spiritual sites protected | 6.4a Area and per cent of forests available/managed for recreation 6.4b Number and type of forest visits and available facilities 6.5a Area of forests managed for cultural, social and spiritual values |
| Governance and participation indicators | Involvement of stakeholders in forestry policy. Involvement of stakeholders in forest management | | 7.4 Mechanisms for cost and benefit sharing 7.5 Conflict-resolution mechanisms 7.12 Tenure and use rights in public forests 7.14 Involvement of local people in forest management | 6.3e Distribution of revenues derived from forest management |

*Source*: adapted from FAO's *State of the World's Forests* (2014), page 9.

yet be discovered that would provide cures for some of the most widespread and lethal illnesses. Whichever position is taken, the rainforests represent one of the front lines of environmental destruction and conservation debates.

## Issues: reef systems

The world's reef systems have been described as the 'rainforests of the oceans'. This is a reference to their comparable levels of biodiversity, and also the fact that they are similarly under threat. The big difference of course is that the reefs are underwater and often subject to the old adage 'out of sight, out of mind'. Awareness of the importance of reef systems, and mangrove to a lesser extent, has grown in recent years but remains largely restricted to marine scientists, divers and those who rely directly on reefs for fishing resources. Reef systems are under pressure due to a number of factors. Unsustainable fishing methods, such as the use of explosives to stun fish, can damage reef systems but the greatest threat comes from pollution of coastal waters and the bleaching of coral due to fluctuations in water temperature. In another example of how environmental issues are connected, the end result of damage to reef can be traced back to issues as apparently unconnected as deforestation many miles from the sea or the use of nitrogen-rich fertilisers in agricultural production. Both of these processes have impacts on river systems that then drain into the sea carrying either silt that suffocates the reef, which is a living organism, or the nitrates from fertilisers that can over-stimulate marine growth, creating algae blooms that also damage the reef. Climate change and the warming of the oceans have also been cited as one of the main reasons why coral reefs lose their natural colourfulness and die. The implications of the loss of this habitat can also be far-reaching. Reef systems act as a nursery for many species of fish. If the reef dies and no longer offers this form of protection then a whole generation of fish species can be impacted upon. Fish stocks are under threat from more advanced fish-finding technologies and the use of drift nets and other methods that are non-selective in the fish that are caught. Again this can have a major impact on fish stocks if immature fish are caught before they have had the chance to spawn a following generation of fish.

## Issues: fisheries

There have been several cases of previously well-stocked fisheries being exploited to the point of collapse. One of the most infamous is the case of the northern Atlantic cod stock, which experienced a devastating collapse in the early 1990s. The Canadian government had been warned that it needed to reduce quotas for catches but refused to act to the level required because of the political consequences of the number of job losses that would result from such drastic measures. There was a further factor of long-distance trawlers operating outside Canada's 12-mile nautical jurisdiction, which also contributed to over-fishing in this region. Again we can see both domestic and international politics in action over this issue. Short-term policies were adopted when longer-term vision and strategies were required. A similar situation has occurred with regard to European Union fishing quotas and trying to balance the needs of local economies based on fishing and related industries and the sustainability of these stock for the longer term. The EU example has the added complication of a supranational body ruling on an issue that is highly emotive within certain regions of its member states. For example, the north-east and south-west of the UK both have long histories of fishing industries and the local economies there have struggled to adapt to

**Table 9.3** Numbers of threatened species by major groups of organisms 2010–2014

| | Estimated number of described species | Number of species evaluated by 2014 (IUCN Red List version 2014.2) | Number of threatened species in 2010 (IUCN Red List version 2010.4) | Number of threatened species in 2011 (IUCN Red List version 2011.2) | Number of threatened species in 2012 (IUCN Red List version 2012.2) | Number of threatened species in 2013 (IUCN Redspecies 2013.2) | Number of threatened species in 2014 (IUCN Red List version 2014.2) | Species evaluated in 2014, as % of species described |
|---|---|---|---|---|---|---|---|---|
| **VERTEBRATES** | | | | | | | | |
| Mammals | 5,513 | 5,513 | 1,131 | 1,138 | 1,139 | 1,143 | 1,199 | 100% |
| Birds | 10,425 | 10,425 | 1,240 | 1,253 | 1,313 | 1,308 | 1,373 | 100% |
| Reptiles | 9,952 | 4,256 | 594 | 772 | 807 | 879 | 902 | 43% |
| Amphibians | 7,286 | 6,410 | 1,898 | 1,917 | 1,933 | 1,950 | 1,961 | 88% |
| Fishes | 32,800 | 11,323 | 1,851 | 2,028 | 2,058 | 2,110 | 2,172 | 35% |
| **Subtotal** | **65,976** | **37,927** | **6,714** | **7,108** | **7,250** | **7,390** | **7,607** | **57%** |
| **INVERTEBRATES** | | | | | | | | |
| Insects | 1,000,000 | 4,980 | 733 | 741 | 829 | 896 | 954 | 0.5% |
| Molluscs | 85,000 | 7,109 | 1,288 | 1,673 | 1,857 | 1,898 | 1,929 | 8% |
| Crustaceans | 47,000 | 3,164 | 596 | 596 | 596 | 723 | 725 | 7% |
| Corals | 2,175 | 856 | 235 | 235 | 236 | 235 | 235 | 39% |
| Arachnids | 102,248 | 204 | 19 | 19 | 20 | 21 | 158 | 0.20% |
| Velvet Worms | 165 | 11 | 9 | 9 | 9 | 9 | 9 | 7% |
| Horseshoe Crabs | 4 | 4 | 0 | 0 | 0 | 0 | 0 | 100% |
| Others | 68,658 | 453 | 24 | 24 | 23 | 40 | 65 | 0.66% |
| **Subtotal** | **1,305,250** | **16,781** | **2,904** | **3,297** | **3,570** | **3,822** | **4,075** | **1%** |
| **PLANTS** | | | | | | | | |
| Mosses | 16,236 | 102 | 80 | 80 | 76 | 76 | 76 | 0.6% |
| Ferns and Allies | 12,000 | 359 | 148 | 163 | 167 | 187 | 194 | 3% |
| Gymnosperms | 1,052 | 1,010 | 371 | 377 | 374 | 399 | 400 | 96% |
| Flowering Plants | 268,000 | 17,838 | 8,116 | 8,527 | 8,764 | 9,394 | 9,806 | 7% |
| Green Algae | 4,242 | 13 | 0 | 0 | 0 | 0 | 0 | 0.3% |
| Red Algae | 6,144 | 58 | 9 | 9 | 9 | 9 | 9 | 0.9% |
| **Subtotal** | **307,674** | **19,380** | **8,724** | **9,156** | **9,390** | **10,065** | **10,485** | **6%** |
| **FUNGI and PROTISTS** | | | | | | | | |
| Lichens | 17,000 | 2 | 2 | 2 | 2 | 2 | 2 | 0.01% |
| Mushrooms | 31,496 | 1 | 1 | 1 | 1 | 1 | 1 | 0.003% |
| Brown Algae | 3,127 | 15 | 6 | 6 | 6 | 6 | 6 | 0.5% |
| **Subtotal** | **51,623** | **18** | **9** | **9** | **9** | **9** | **9** | **0.03%** |
| **TOTAL** | **1,730,523** | **74,106** | **18,351** | **19,570** | **20,219** | **21,286** | **22,176** | **4%** |

*Source: Adapted from IUCN Red List, http://cmsdocs.s3.amazonaws.com/summarystats/2014_2_Summary_StatsPage_Documents/2014_2_RL_Stats_Table1.pdf*

the decline in these industries. Again what makes good environmental sense with regard to conserving stocks may be for the longer-term benefit of this industry, but in the shorter term some difficult and unpopular policies may have to be introduced.

## Issues: energy security

Gaining popular support for environmentally friendly policies is always going to be a challenge for governments. This is mainly because they are going to be expensive, either in terms of direct taxation to raise funds for eco-projects, or in the costs of goods if a 'polluter pays' principle is adopted. As already indicated, most aspects of modern life have environmental costs associated with them, even if they are not always immediately apparent. Although the majority of people are likely to endorse conservation measures in principle this position could be severely tested if the true cost of goods and services were to be calculated in terms of environmental impacts. For example, energy security has come to dominate many aspects of domestic and international politics. There is a huge range of potential energy sources from fossil fuels to nuclear power to many variations of renewable energy. The political economy of energy production has numerous environmental aspects. Fossil fuels pollute and access to supply is not always guaranteed. Nuclear power has the advantage of not producing greenhouse gas emissions, but there remains no fully acceptable solution as to what to do with the radioactive waste that is produced during this process. There are also massive costs involved in safely decommissioning nuclear power stations at the end of their productive lifespan. Renewable energy sources, by definition, would appear to be an obvious solution to our energy needs, but even these are subject to political issues with regard to initial investment and where they should or should not be sited, and they also face active resistance from those with interests in maintaining the status quo in energy markets.

---

**EXAMPLE BOX**

### Energy production

The production of energy can be seen to be one of the most basic concerns in the contemporary world. Food security is obviously a major issue but many aspects of food production are reliant on secure and sustainable energy supplies. Energy security operates at all local levels but also informs the geo-strategic thinking and policies of the world's major powers. This is particularly the case in ensuring supplies of oil and gas. Arguably many of the military conflicts involving the major powers in recent years have, at least to some extent, been informed by energy supply considerations. By now it should be apparent that when looking at environmental issues it is extremely difficult to separate out the natural science of environmental degradation or conservation from the whole range of economic and political factors that inform domestic and international relations. A nomadic tribe on the edge of the Saharan desert may gather firewood for heating and cooking in what appears to be an act of local subsistence. It is, but it also feeds into a much bigger picture of advancing desertification, which in turn has climatic effects and can be related to major environmental negotiations and agreements such as the Kyoto Protocol or the UN Convention to Combat Desertification.

The key to understanding the impact of all of the environmental issues considered here is to recognise that none of them happen in isolation from each other. They are all interconnected, even though some of these connections may not be clear even to those most closely associated with each localised event. The following section looks at the political, economic and socio-cultural processes that relate to environmental issues.

# Processes

Fundamentally environmental conservation or degradation is a natural, physical process. Even before the emergence of Homo sapiens the natural world experienced significant changes in the natural environment, including waves of extinctions. Earth's ecosystems are dynamic and constantly changing, both within relatively discrete micro-habitats and in the interaction between these and the overall system. Humans are not the only species to disrupt the lives and habitats of other species, but we have 'advanced' to a stage where, unlike any other species, our combined actions are having impacts at the global level. Climate change scientists continue to debate their predictions on how such change will impact on the planet, and at what rate. However, there is now near universal agreement that climate change is happening, it is largely due to human activity and the consequences of changing climatic patterns are becoming increasingly severe.

The natural environment has its own dynamism but this can be modified by human actions in the political, economic and socio-cultural fields. Most IPE approaches highlight the interconnections between the realms of politics and economics. This position is not being challenged here but for the purposes of this analysis this section will begin by looking at the political processes relevant to environmental issues. These operate at national and international levels with some aspects of subnational politics to be considered, and also a number of standing intergovernmental agencies such as the IPCC, UN Environment Programme and UN Development Programme.

Table 9.4 illustrates the relationship between socio-economic processes and climate change-induced risk and vulnerability. This is clearly a very simplified model and one that would lead to a broad range of variability if applied to differing local environments and circumstances. That said, it does summarise the fundamental factors and characteristics of environmental change and the factors that may contribute to, or alleviate, such change.

## Earth Summit process

The UN Conference on Environment and Development took place in Rio de Janeiro, Brazil, 3–14 June 1992: 172 states attended with 108 of these represented at the head of government or head of state level. This was an unprecedented gathering of political leaders drawn together to discuss environmental issues. There was also a parallel NGO forum with representatives from 2,400 civil society groups. MNCs attended, but in a lobbying of governments capacity rather than a discrete conference mode. Resulting documentation included the Rio Declaration on Environment and Development, the Statement of Forest Principles, the United Nations Framework Convention on Climate Change and the United Nations Convention on Biological Diversity. Follow-up mechanisms were the Commission on Sustainable Development; Inter-agency Committee on Sustainable Development and the High-Level Advisory Board on Sustainable Development. This was

**Table 9.4** Socio-economic processes and climate change-induced risk and vulnerability

QA2 From the following list, please pick the five main environmental issues that you are worried about. (MAX. 5 ANSWERS)

| | Air pollution | Water pollution (seas, rivers, lakes and underground sources) | The growing amount of waste | The impact on our health of chemicals used in everyday products | Depletion of natural resources | Agricultural pollution (use of pesticides, fertilisers, etc.) | Shortage of drinking water | Loss or extinction of species and their habitats and of natural ecosystems (forests, fertile soils) | Our consumption habits | Urban problems (traffic jams, pollution, lack of green spaces, etc.) |
|---|---|---|---|---|---|---|---|---|---|---|
| Europe 28 | 56% | 50% | 43% | 43% | 36% | 29% | 27% | 26% | 24% | 23% |
| Belgium | 60% | 48% | 42% | 42% | 39% | 28% | 31% | 27% | 27% | 28% |
| Bulgaria | 62% | 51% | 42% | 40% | 28% | 37% | 18% | 15% | 18% | 28% |
| Czech Republic | 55% | 44% | 61% | 35% | 33% | 25% | 29% | 21% | 23% | 26% |
| Denmark | 57% | 57% | 41% | 53% | 40% | 30% | 45% | 29% | 30% | 24% |
| Germany | 49% | 54% | 45% | 51% | 40% | 35% | 22% | 37% | 30% | 19% |
| Estonia | 47% | 47% | 52% | 48% | 31% | 29% | 14% | 24% | 31% | 28% |
| Ireland | 47% | 57% | 53% | 44% | 28% | 24% | 31% | 19% | 18% | 27% |
| EL | 59% | 64% | 36% | 55% | 35% | 42% | 35% | 23% | 19% | 24% |
| Spain | 58% | 57% | 30% | 40% | 45% | 33% | 41% | 23% | 19% | 20% |
| France | 58% | 52% | 41% | 51% | 47% | 35% | 33% | 29% | 28% | 19% |
| Croatia | 58% | 48% | 55% | 39% | 29% | 35% | 37% | 12% | 26% | 14% |
| Italy | 56% | 51% | 40% | 41% | 33% | 31% | 19% | 18% | 25% | 29% |
| Cyprus | 61% | 58% | 34% | 58% | 31% | 36% | 55% | 23% | 19% | 28% |
| Latvia | 49% | 61% | 53% | 53% | 25% | 30% | 13% | 18% | 14% | 20% |
| Lithuania | 64% | 53% | 54% | 63% | 19% | 25% | 11% | 11% | 21% | 26% |
| Luxembourg | 57% | 56% | 41% | 42% | 40% | 26% | 35% | 23% | 24% | 22% |
| Hungary | 68% | 49% | 59% | 30% | 33% | 29% | 33% | 13% | 19% | 19% |
| Malta | 65% | 40% | 45% | 35% | 15% | 26% | 30% | 17% | 14% | 46% |
| Netherlands | 54% | 57% | 32% | 48% | 52% | 23% | 29% | 38% | 41% | 25% |
| Austria | 53% | 52% | 49% | 44% | 40% | 30% | 26% | 29% | 24% | 21% |
| Poland | 56% | 37% | 54% | 32% | 24% | 19% | 22% | 13% | 15% | 22% |
| Portugal | 66% | 51% | 48% | 26% | 36% | 22% | 48% | 14% | 15% | 14% |
| Romania | 60% | 45% | 37% | 33% | 24% | 24% | 26% | 14% | 18% | 17% |
| Slovenia | 60% | 49% | 49% | 42% | 27% | 40% | 39% | 17% | 23% | 12% |
| Slovakia | 53% | 48% | 55% | 41% | 30% | 23% | 47% | 19% | 20% | 20% |
| Finland | 66% | 67% | 57% | 38% | 46% | 16% | 24% | 20% | 31% | 20% |
| Sweden | 60% | 64% | 34% | 61% | 38% | 28% | 41% | 50% | 42% | 13% |
| United Kingdom | 52% | 39% | 48% | 34% | 29% | 19% | 18% | 30% | 16% | 31% |

Highest percentage per country
Highest percentage per item
Lowest percentage per country
Lowest percentage per item

*Source*: IPCC Climate Change 2014: Impacts, Adaptation and Vulnerability p. 3.

an important process as it established standing bodies and a rolling agenda to maintain discussion and policy-making forums to address international environmental issues. Several follow-up meetings have taken place with regard to the conference of the parties of the above convention plus five- and ten-year review conferences of the Earth Summit, held in New York and Johannesburg respectively. The 2002 ten-year review conference was notable because the developing states complained that the developed states had failed to fulfil many of the commitments they had pledged to at the Rio conference. It also occurred post-9/11. The era of the 'war against terror' has seen many states shift their focus away from environmental issues.

The Copenhagen Climate Change Conference of December 2009 was widely regarded as a failure as it did not produce a legally binding agreement to reduce greenhouse gas emissions. A partial agreement was reached between the major powers with a marked shift in the dynamic within the developing world as China, India and Brazil distanced themselves from the positions adopted by the smaller and more vulnerable states, such as Tuvalu. By the time of the Rio+20 meeting, held in Johannesburg in 2012, some critics suggested it should be known as Rio−20 as many of the environmental conservation indicators demonstrated that the situation was actually worse than it had been in 1992.

The main political unit in international relations remains the national government. With over 200 such bodies in the international system there is an understandable variance in how environmental issues are approached. Most of the more developed states have advanced governmental bureaucracies that include ministers with specific responsibilities for environmental issues. Their departments may be subdivided to sections dealing with specialised policies on energy, agriculture, transport, wildlife conservation and other aspects of the environment. Importantly, some of these posts will be 'mirrored' by government officials working in other sections of the administration. For example, an official in the department of transport would have a portfolio that related to those in the departments of both energy and environment. In some respects this should accommodate some coherent 'joined-up' policy prescriptions. While this may sometimes be the case it is also a recipe for conflicting bureaucratic politics to take place, especially if each department is competing for a slice of their government's overall budget. In addition to potential conflict over policy priorities within an administration, environmental issues have become something of a party political football with opposition parties routinely disagreeing with the standing government's policies in this area. In some respects this is no more than an extension on normal party politics within the regimes that allow for this. That said, it is noticeable that environmental issues have moved from being relatively marginalised in most parliamentary debates to becoming one of the central issues of political and popular debate.

The above point on departmental budgets immediately connects the political realm with the economic. Many government officials may have the best will in the world to adopt environmentally sustainable policies but do not have access to the material resources to do so. Very often, especially in the developing world but also in the most developed states, it is the drive for economic growth that is the root cause of the environmental problems that need to be addressed. The process of economic growth continues to hold a central position among most governments, and the majority of economic consultants and advisers. This is not to say that it is not possible to have economic growth without environmental degradation, but the dominant model of development currently reflects this trade-off between growth and sustainability. This is illustrative of the long-standing approach to development that argues for a top-down or 'trickle-down' approach where the political priority has to be growth first, then environmental conservation and, possibly, social justice. This approach has long been supported by MNCs, which obviously have a vested interest in promoting economic activity as a priority, and criticised by NGOs, which tend to favour more bottom-up, grassroots approaches.

The economic processes involved in environmental issues have two distinct aspects. One can be seen in terms of the degradation that is caused by undervaluing the environment in market calculations of the worth of a particular good or service. In contrast, the value of the environment is becoming increasingly realised in some quarters, including some MNCs. The process by which the environment is calculated into the private sector can take many forms. As noted above, it can be referred to as part of an MNC's publicity campaign in an attempt to bolster its CSR credibility, which may or may not be wholly genuine. Other examples can be where the natural environment itself becomes a commodity. This would concern nature reserves operated as profit-making businesses and a range of activities that would come under the broad heading of eco-tourism. An example of the latter is the relatively recent addition of Japan as a whale-watching destination. Japan continues to be one of the few nations in the world to undertake whaling, allegedly for scientific purposes although at least some of the meat is subsequently sold in commercial markets. There has been an awareness gained that you can only kill and sell a whale once, but you can profit repeatedly by selling whale-watching trips. Hence there is a financial incentive to conserve rather than deplete the whale population. Similar financial incentives can be found in other sectors. Deforestation was referred to above as a serious environmental issue; it is, but this is not to say that forest resources cannot be harvested in a sustainable manner. Clear felling often results in a one-off payment to local landowners and resulting environmental damage caused not only by the heavy machinery required to fell and transport the logs but also the loss of other forest resources accessed by local people, especially if they retain a subsistence lifestyle of hunting and gathering from the forest. A more appropriate method would be selective logging, which utilises timber resources but also maintains the surrounding ecosystem. This may be a slower process and income would be generated over a longer period, but a similar amount of income could be generated without the negative impacts that are almost always associated with industrial-scale logging practices.

The above examples demonstrate that the process of making a profit does not necessarily have to result in significant environmental degradation. MNCs, by their basic characteristic of economies of scale, do tend towards the larger and therefore more damaging practices. Moreover, as they rarely have a particular association to a piece of land, other than as a source of wealth creation, they are less likely to see 'value' in the land other than how profitable it can remain. Once its profitability has been maximised the MNC is free to move on to exploit new territories. On the other hand, local inhabitants are far more likely to have social, cultural and even spiritual connections to their natural environment. This is something that is difficult, if not impossible, to calculate in terms of a financial worth. There are examples of indigenous peoples accepting relocation packages from governments and MNCs in order for their traditional lands to be mined or flooded for a hydroelectric power scheme or some other sort of resource usage. There are, of course, many other examples where locals have been forcibly evicted and even killed to remove them from particular sites. Arguably in the former case there is, perhaps, a case to be made for a market price having been found to replace the feeling of identity associated with a particular piece of land. Yet this seems to be conflating two quite different worldviews of 'value' in the realms of the financial and the spiritual.

Considering socio-cultural aspects of the environment might appear out of place in a section looking at the processes that surround these issues. Yet in all of the above, whether it is with regard to governments, MNCs, NGOs or individuals, the common thread on the emergence of the environment as an agenda item is a process of consciousness and the raising of environmental awareness. NGOs explicitly aim to do this with the majority of their campaigns, which rely on

**Table 9.5** Chapter summary

| | Key actors | Key processes | Emphasis on political economy | What causes change? | Global institutions? | View of conflict in global relations? |
|---|---|---|---|---|---|---|
| Pro-environment | States pursuing Sustainable Development Goals, MNCs with corporate social responsibility agendas, environmental NGOs, individuals | Recognition that the Earth represents a finite set of resources that should not be over-exploited at non-renewable rates. International cooperation to minimise human impact on natural environment, such as the International Panel on Climate Change meetings and negotiations | Recognition of the relationship between political intervention (in relation to environmental protection and management) and the free-market economic forces that tend not to factor in environmental degradation when setting market prices for various goods and services | This can be caused at the level of government with new laws passed or a concerted effort to mainstream environmental issues as a core element of a broad range of policies. MNCs can choose to amend their business practices to become more 'environmentally friendly'. NGOs actively campaign to change public, business and civil society behaviour. In many respects individual behaviour is one of the most important aspects of promoting a pro-environment agenda | The United Nations is the main forum for dealing with environmental issues at the global level. This is implemented via bodies such as the UNEP, UNDP, the Earth Summit process and the promotion of the UN Sustainable Development Goals | Perhaps surprisingly, conflict can lead to pro-environment outcomes. For example, where several communities share a water catchment area. Although this can lead to conflict it can also become the common interest that brings competing parties together to manage the equitable division of use of a resource, with a pro-environment outcome |
| Anti-environment | States/MNCs favouring profit over sustainable use of resources, individuals | Unsustainable extraction and use of natural resources as represented by some government policies, business practices and individuals' patterns of consumption | The counter to the above where sustainability and renewable use of resources is inadequately factored into commodity chains and end-user patterns of consumption | Again, government policies, business practices and individual behaviour can all operate in a manner that is unsustainable in terms of change over time and the rate at which resources are consumed | Although anti-environmentalism is not institutionalised in the way normally thought of some Green campaigners would argue that bodies such as the World Trade Organization are necessarily anti-environmental as they promote a neo-liberal free-market agenda that, in the main, does not prioritise environmental protection over economic profit | Conflict can, of course, lead to environmental degradation. Resources might be exploited at non-sustainable rates in order to raise funds to continue an armed conflict. In areas that are armed conflict zones it will also be difficult for environmental NGOs to operate or for international monitoring and policing of the environment to take place |

mobilising popular support. MNCs do this, to some degree, in relation to their CSR campaigns. Governments also attempt to justify their policies, particularly those that are dependent on being re-elected. In each case awareness of environmental issues is a crucial factor. Added to this is the politicisation of these issues, as mentioned at the start of this chapter. Awareness suggests there is a single reality about the nature of environmental issues and how they might best be addressed. In outlining the range of actors, interests and agendas referred to above it is apparent that this is far from the case.

## Summary

This chapter has considered the wide variety of actors, issues and processes relevant to environmental issues. Each sector is complex in its own right so this is necessarily intensified as they interact. Neither governments, MNCs nor NGOs are homogeneous groups and each sector includes tremendous variances. Even if one were to adopt a very state-centric view towards environmental issues you could not look at the issues and agendas of the US and a small island state and say you were comparing like with like, although they may share some common interests. Similarly, some MNCs may be taking CSR very seriously, while others continue to be entirely profit-driven. NGOs are a wildly diverse sector in terms of the issue areas they campaign on and their size and capabilities.

The issues referred to above have only scratched the surface of what might be considered relevant to the environment. By definition everything is, so it has not been possible in the space allowed here to do more than highlight some of the key issues in the contemporary environmental agenda. The way in which environmental issues are reported in the media is clearly important in informing popular debate surrounding these issues. In this respect the media itself, especially when seen as an MNC, becomes an important actor in relation to these issues. How government policies, MNC activities and NGO campaigns are reported are important as part of the process of informing and shaping the environmental agenda.

Finally, the processes of environmental change can be seen as operating at two distinct levels. First, there is the 'real world' physical process of environmental change, which can either be towards degradation or sustainability. Second, consider the political processes that impact on these physical changes. These involve the myriad actors referred to in this chapter. Both sets of processes are constantly being played out and interrelating with each other.

## Reflective questions

1   What factors led to environmental issues coming on to the political agenda in the early 1970s?
2   What interests can you identify in relation to the various actors involved in the debates surrounding environmental issues?
3   What incentives and impediments are there with regard to addressing various environmental issues?
4   How has the Earth Summit process evolved since the Rio conference of 1992?
5   What role does the media play in highlighting environmental concerns?
6   How might individual lifestyle choices have an impact on global environmental issues?

# Suggestions for further reading

Berkhout, F., Leach, M. and Scoones, I. (2003) *Negotiating Environmental Change: New Perspectives from Social Science*, London: Edward Elgar.

Brundtland Commission (1980) *North–South: A Programme for Survival*, London: Macmillan.

Carter, N. (2007) *The Politics of the Environment: Ideas, Activism, Policy*, 2nd edn, Cambridge: Cambridge University Press.

Chape, S., Blyth, S., Fish, L., Fox, P. and Spalding, M. (compilers) (2003) *2003 United Nations List of Protected Areas*. Gland, Switzerland, and Cambridge, UK: UNEP-WCMC and WCPA. IUCN.

Clapp, J. (2005) *Paths to a Green World: The Political Economy of the Global Environment*, Cambridge, MA: MIT Press.

Connelly, J. and Smith, G. (2002) *Politics and the Environment: From Theory to Practice*, London: Routledge.

Dodds, F., Strauss, M. and Strong, M.F. (2012) *Only One Earth: The Long Road via Rio to Sustainable Development*, London: Earthscan.

Dodds, F., Howell, M., Onestini, M. and Strauss, M. (2007) *Negotiating and Implementing Multilateral Environmental Agreements*, New York: UNEP.

European Commission (2014) 'Attitudes of European citizens towards the environment', *Special Eurobarometer*, 416: 15.

Food and Agriculture Organization (2014) *State of the World's Forests 2014*, Rome: FAO.

Food and Agriculture Organization of the United Nations (2009) *State of the World's Forests 2009*, Rome: FAO.

Intergovernmental Panel on Climate Change (2008) *Climate Change 2007: Synthesis Report*, Geneva: IPCC, Figure 2.5, p. 40.

Intergovernmental Panel on Climate Change (2014) *Climate Change 2014: Impacts Adaptation and Vulnerability*, Geneva: IPCC.

World Wide Fund for Nature (2014) *Living Planet Report 2014*, Gland, Switzerland: WWF.

# 10 Technology in the global political economy

## Chapter learning outcomes

After reading this chapter, students should be able to:

- Engage in debate about the nature of technology and technology change and identify the ways in which technology can be identified in relation to both things and social and cultural patterns of behaviour.
- Identify the significance of the distinction between innovation as process change and innovation as new products or services.
- Understand and be able to explain how technology is used by large and small firms to compete effectively in their key markets, and to explain how failures of technology management can account for failures to survive of firms and sectors of national economies.
- Explain the significance of technology in shaping the emergence and possible future trajectories of change in the global division of labour.
- Be familiar with intellectual property rights (IPRs) and their significance for international economic activity.
- Offer interpretations of the nature of the individual and the influence of technology on the person as a subject.
- Relate discussion of technology and innovation to the theoretical debates discussed elsewhere in this book.

## Introduction

International political economy involves technology a great deal, and in many ways. Discussions of the relative power of leading multinational companies often hinge on their ability to use technologies to compete; discussions of the dangers of their activities often hinge on the threats their products and practices present. Technology also provides a vital resource for governments, but a focus on state-to-state relations is likely to simplify and underestimate the importance of technology as a factor in both international relations and the world economy. Much debate on environmental policy, and nearly all discussion of energy security, engage with questions of the merits (and problems) of present and future technologies. The same is true of food security and information security. Production technologies, communication technologies, technologies of surveillance and the self, technologies that can destroy the planet and those that can save humankind: the list of potential issues is very long. It touches on nearly every aspect of IPE, including 'classic' questions about states and markets and inequality, and emerging questions about the changing world order and the growing power of new actors – firms, networks and social movements – in world politics. But IPE, although it discusses all of this, does not always theorise these issues very well. It does not always have a very clear idea of how to conceptualise technology or technology change. And it fails quite often to think critically about them. With the exception of only a few studies (e.g. Skolnikoff, 1994; Stoneman, 1988'; Pavitt, 1999) technology as a set of structures and processes that shape IPE has tended to be underestimated as a key factor in understanding the field.

So in approaching this chapter, there is a great deal to discuss, but the intellectual resources to look critically at technology have to be found and clarified. Despite the importance of all the issues in the previous paragraph, most IPE texts do not even have a chapter on technology. However there are also writers in IPE who explore questions of innovation, technique, technological competition, techno-structure and the philosophy of technology. Very often, they draw on business studies or cultural studies. Together, they provide good starting points. And there is a rich literature in political economy as well as business case studies that scholars in IPE have learned to draw on (perhaps rather late), which provides a vital resource for understanding.

The most important thing here is probably not to dwell on the bigger questions too long, to get into a level of detail where we can offer more than tentative generalisations. Five questions get us into detailed discussion of the main issues here. They form the main structure of the chapter:

- What is technology here/what do we mean by 'technology'?
- How does it shape the ways firms behave and compete?
- How does technology change affect global conflict in IPE? (Obviously one could ask the same question of military security, but that is outside the brief here.)
- How does technology shape *individuals* and *groups of people* as *agents* in world economy, and how does it create capacities for the *state* as an *agent*?
- How can we best locate technology within theories of IPE so as to take account of it as seriously as we should (which of course implies a debate about how seriously we should take it)?

Here we will try to answer the problem of conceptualising technology in the first point. The problem about theory arises in all sections but especially the last. The issues about thinking critically will also arise in each section in turn.

## What is technology?

At first, our idea of technology might seem simple. We are surrounded by technology – mobile phones, the world wide web, downloading software, the systems that provide electricity, water and sewage management that we take for granted until they break down, logistical systems that fill supermarket shelves and the technologies of military power from the suicide bomber's belt to the advanced cruise missile. Isn't technology just the *stuff* we use? Are we (humankind, not just one culture or another) not 'man the toolmaker?' But these things, this 'kit' comes from somewhere. We learned to use it. Everything in this list requires infrastructure. Most of the things we use would not be manufactured at all if the cost of individual items reflected the cost of research and development directly. They can often today only be produced efficiently if, like mobile phones, they are produced in large numbers for a global market. How did that global market come about? Some technologies triumph over others – not all good ideas work commercially, and some technologies work so well, or are marketed so well, that others struggle to get noticed. The obvious example is the success of Microsoft's operating system MS-DOS, but there are innumerable others.

One example of a set of common assumptions about technology occurs right at the start of Stanley Kubrick's film *2001 – A Space Odyssey* (1968), in which a group of hominid apes seem to discover a technology – the use of basic tools, bones, as weapons to kill. Kubrick directly links these technologies to the advanced computer technologies that the film cuts to over the credits, which are directing a space mission, and where the computer eventually takes over from human operators and kills them, apparently to defend the mission it was programmed for. The film reflects a set of deeply embedded ideas not just about the threats of technologies, but also about the (alleged) fact that technologies are 'taking over', and that technologies have determined the fate of humankind in very strong ways throughout our history. Kubrick's view in the film is influenced by a then-prevailing set of attitudes about technological determinism – technology *determines* (i.e. is the sole principal cause of) social and economic systems, their behaviour and the outcomes that follow from their use. We find this notion in work that welcomes the power of technology, in communications and media technologies, in life sciences, in ideas of what drives economic progress and in images of everyday life, such as the dominance of the car and the capacity of ever-improving domestic tools to bring an end to housework, and perhaps to the end of all work. We find it as much in science fiction as in the self-images and self-understandings shared then by many (most?) natural scientists and science journalists. These attitudes were never unchallenged and have become less popular, much more nuanced, today. They are reflected in different ways in another very influential Kubrick film, the satirical masterpiece *Dr Strangelove* (1964), which is also shaped by technological determinism, but where the technologies of nuclear war drive decision makers who rapidly lose all control of the conflict they start. In both movies, technology is clearly very powerful, but it is also embedded in social institutions. Technology is as much a reflection of a set of values and social practices as it is a toolkit or body of practical knowledge.

So it is possible to say that a 'technology' is a thing or an artefact, but also that it is that *created thing in a social and economic context*. Technology is as much about organisation, management and competition as it is about producing things. And technology generally consists of a *set of things embedded in cultures and values* rather than a single object, however significant some individual objects may be. When we ask what managers do, what 'entrepreneurship' is, it certainly cannot be reduced to questions of technology, but it involves technology deeply – how work is organised, how businesses exploit technical advantages they have, logistics and information technologies, as well as productive systems. The complexity of managing these variables is a key part of the challenge of modern management. If you doubt this, look up online the biography of leading entrepreneurs such as Steve Jobs (Apple Computers), Marjorie Scardino (Pearson Group), Anne Mulcahy (Xerox) or Paul Ottelini (Intel). The very dated image of 'man the toolmaker' is not only gendered or perhaps ignorant of other species; it also mistakes the complexity of human relations with technology, where technologies are part of culture, something we perform and define and recreate, not merely something we make and use.

Furthermore, technologies *have and create meanings* that are often critical building blocks of a culture. The invention of the automobile involved basic underlying technologies ('metatechnologies') – the invention of the internal combustion engine, the electrical systems for instrumentation, the rubber processes to make tyres. It created a metal box where people, often on their own, travelled in long convoys on freeways in total separation from each other, in a kind of idealised individualism. Or, at least, until they had an accident, at which point individuals and social groups collided, something observed (in very different ways) in two films both called *Crash* (1996 and 2006). The culture of the car mapped a great deal of the world of the 1950s and 1960s – the Beach Boys sang about how 'we had fun, fun, fun, 'til her daddy took the T-bird away'. The Ford Thunderbird may have been *the* car North American males wanted to be seen in, but the song went round the world, and quite a lot of people who heard and danced to it must have had no idea at all what the girlfriend's father had done – one artefact, but many meanings in different cultures. The systems of meaning that surround all of our technologies, including the military ones and the production systems hidden within factories, are at least as complex, and change as rapidly, as the systems that produce them and keep them working.

Technology is, then, what? A thing, an artefact (a thing made by human ingenuity), a social system, a set of things embedded in a particular organisation, a set of cultural meanings, or a global structure of power capable of creating inequalities, winner and losers? It is not one of these rather than the others. It is *all* of the above. At the same time, although it may appear that technology so underpins everything in social and economic life that it is everything, this is not a very useful idea expressed in this way. If we say that technology affects nearly everything in our experience of the world, then that implies we can at least separate technology (cause) from 'nearly everything' (effect). But if technology and the world it changes are wholly embedded in each other, we need another strategy to make sense of it. Technology is, one can propose, all of the above, but it is important for the sake of clarity that we state which we mean at any one time. In saying this, we are admitting that technology cuts across the traditional boundaries of academic disciplines and that it touches on much more than traditional IR or IPE.

---

**CONCEPT BOX**

## Summary: what is technology?

Technology is stuff – machinery, equipment, kit. It is at least to a minimum effect made by people – artefacts used for a purpose, as an extension of human capabilities (but often these days an unimaginable development of human skills.

But technology is also a social system – it is used by groups of people or societies, and it has come to define the nature of those societies. Prehistoric societies are often defined by the tools or technologies they used, but so too are modern societies.

Technologies involve innovation – in new *products* and in new *processes*. Process innovation is a vital element of industrial research even though it may seem less glamorous than the creation of new products. Process innovations often facilitate the design and creation of new products. They also help firms to get costs down and to gain the potential learning effects of production. Technology change affects social and political relations; but social and political contexts also have powerful impact on technology and the production of economic change.

Innovation systems vary from one country to another, so some countries (notably Sweden and Finland) have highly effective innovation systems that sustain very active international companies (ABB, Nokia) even though they are relatively small countries. 'National innovation system' models are widely used to explain different patterns of innovation. But companies are mostly international, and have their own distinctive research cultures (e.g. 'the HP way' in Hewlett Packard), which cuts across national boundaries. Often, the study of individual sectors and individual companies will throw more light on the behaviour of KBIs than focus on state or country-based analysis.

Metatechnologies or 'base technologies' – technologies that form the basis of a whole economic system. Examples include the development of arms making and cotton-spinning machinery (both sectors used automated pattern-based machines) at the start of the industrial revolution, the internal combustion engine – the car engine, also of course used for aircraft – in the first half of the twentieth century, and the microchip. On each of these technologies, other industries and technologies were based, and they formed the basis for widespread growth and new forms of employment and skills.

# Technologies as a principal tool of global economic competition

Obviously, technologies change. The process of technology change –innovation – may involve either *product innovation*, the development of new products, or *process innovation*, the development of new techniques or new ways of making things. The more spectacular side of technical innovation, which gets on the top of news stories generally involves new products – new drugs to treat a dangerous disease, new technologies to save energy, new weapons systems, new capabilities on your mobile phone and so on. But process innovations are at least as important in business. They may take place step-by-step, so there are few obvious breakthrough moments. But they help firms to reduce costs, to become more efficient, to become more competitive. Some of the most important innovations in the automobile industry, for example, were those process improvements made by Japanese engineers that enabled them to produce cars with much more reliable engines and transmissions, with longer lasting systems that demanded less service time, and that enabled them to out-compete European and American firms in the 1970s and 1980s by producing cars that were more reliable and cheaper to run as well as cheaper to buy. In doing this, they were copying what Japanese firms had already achieved in textile machinery, machine tools and electronics. It was process engineering innovation that made possible much of Japan's global economic power in the 1980s and onwards.

Large firms in specialist areas such as pharmaceuticals, computing software and aerospace use technological innovation to compete in a wide variety of ways. Innovation is so important in some of these sectors that firms will spend huge amounts of money investing in research and development. Inevitably, some of this investment will produce no returns at all; but other investments may well produce not only large increases in income but also major gains in market share and the ability to dominate competitors and markets. For example, the major pharmaceutical companies, with a turnover in the several hundred billions of dollars a year, spend 12–15 per cent of turnover on research and development. Major electronics firms typically spend 5–10 per cent of income on research. Oil, gas and energy firms also spend around 5 per cent on research and development, a figure that excludes investment in exploration for new sources of supply, and that includes money spent on energy retrieval techniques and downstream technologies (in other words, investment in oil and gas processing or refining as well as pipeline technologies). Excepting relatively small firms, which may specialise entirely in particular aspects of research and spend most of their income on research activities, it is possible to analyse global competition in terms of the levels of spending on R & D. As this paragraph suggests, what emerges from such an analysis is a pattern where major firms in any individual sector commit roughly comparable amounts to research: if we study individual sectors, we find that they have common patterns in the way research impacts on business strategy and in the characteristics of major players as sources of knowledge as a factor in competitive behaviour. It follows from this that when scholars and analysts want to understand patterns of competition, looking at detail at performance within a specific sector, often trying to compare all the actors in that sector together, will provide very important tools. And investors selecting which firms to commit capital to will use similar kinds of analysis to make their decisions.

Small firms – sometimes very small firms – use product and process innovations in distinctive ways because they cannot spend very much on R & D, but they have to focus what they do very tightly. Many small firms fail; but those that are successful innovators may become larger very quickly. The availability of IT resources and the possibilities of developing online businesses have changed the profile of innovation. Twenty-five years ago, very few new graduates started their own businesses from scratch, although a few have always done so. Given the opportunities of e-business, some 15–20 per cent of British graduates will start a new business of their own within two years of graduating, a figure that masks quite a difference between different business sectors.

The figures are similar in the US and Canada, but rather lower in continental Europe. Many economists will point to the importance of having a pool of smaller challenging companies even in a sector where a few large firms predominate because they help to focus competition and they may create innovations that enable them to challenge in the future. For example, many small businesses have grown and collapse trying to produce and market mobile device apps. Those few that have succeeded have become very effective challengers of older and more established software firms.

It is also possible to compare innovation systems as a way of analysing patterns in the advanced technology industries. This kind of analysis originated in the 1980s in the analysis of national innovation systems, building in turn on the much earlier work of Alfred Marshall and Joseph Schumpeter. Some economies were observed to have advantages over others, which were not merely questions of size and economies of scale, including the successful innovating economies of Sweden and Finland, and the dynamic economies of some of the (then) newly industrialising world. This also applied to specific high-tech regions within countries, which had the capacity to help to lead the economy out of recession and to create new jobs and new patterns of working through technological strength. These included Silicon Valley in California, the 'M4 corridor' and the Scottish 'Silicon Glen' in the UK, Catalonia in Spain, and the Rhone-Alpes region of south-eastern France. In the 2000s, it has included more local 'regions' of major cities specialising in software, gaming, film animation, video and online businesses, including communities within Shanghai and the revived East End of London. Scholars of national innovation systems have also pointed to the dangers of countries with large primary product resources relying on those products for export success. Instead of relying on single products with unstable prices and demand, such as oil or cocoa, why not build a national innovation system that is capable of building the non-oil economy (in many cases) or the non-cocoa economy, which Ghana has partially succeeded in doing. National systems are primarily created by firms; but governments and city or state administrations can also make a difference here in promoting more balanced growth.

The national innovation systems literature has pointed towards two criticisms, which are both important in understanding international high technology activity. For in a globalised world, technical innovation is often not nationally based, and technological capabilities, although they are unevenly spread across the world system, are not easily confined by national boundaries. Cross border regional innovation systems may be important (most obviously between France, Switzerland and Germany, but there are plenty of other examples). The European Union has been important in encouraging these kinds of cross-border collaborations and mergers. International intra-firm innovation is also important. Large firms concentrate research capability in some countries rather than others for a mixture of reasons (which include tax advantages, access to university expertise, access to a pool of highly skilled labour and access to suppliers). But many firms, including most of the largest, have research centres in different countries (Hewlett Packard and Intel are good examples). These may be set up to compete with each other, on price or intellectual property ownership of their successful research; or they may cooperate in networks. Either way, trade within a single major company across international boundaries in intellectual property and components accounts for a significant proportion of all international trade, at least 12 per cent (estimates vary quite widely) (this kind of intra-firm and inter-firm collaborative networking has been discussed also in Chapter 3).

## Kondratieff cycles and major innovations

There is an important argument about the nature of technology and its role in economic development that originates in the work of a Russian economist, Kondratieff, in the 1920s, which was refined by Schumpeter in the 1940s, and that was developed by a range of scholars in the 1970s and 1980s (notably Christopher Freeman). This provides an important theoretical avenue to making sense of the role of technologies in IPE; it is also an argument that is contested.

Key scholars in this field argue that technology change forms a series of waves – sometimes innovation is more rapid, sometime there is a period of consolidation. Innovation is not a smooth, steady evolutionary pattern. It is a dynamic and sometimes strongly disruptive force. In order for new technologies and ideas – new intellectual capital – to develop, old technologies and old ideas have to be scrapped, a process Schumpeter labelled 'creative destruction'. The abandoning of intellectual capital is often difficult for people and social groups (such as a workforce) to bear –they have to give up on old assumptions and practices in order to adopt new ones. But technologies are not automatically adopted – they have to be diffused and accepted, and human resistance is also an important factor in the slower adaptation of firms, and this resistance may come from consumers or environmental concerns as well as from a workforce.

All the same, economists have tried to model innovation in a number of ways. One has been especially influential. Apart from a relatively short cycle of growth followed by recession – the business cycle, typically of five to seven years – which both liberal and Marxist economists had discussed throughout the nineteenth century, Kondratieff suggested that there was a longer term and more fundamental cycle of roughly twenty-five to thirty years, which was dominated by innovation patterns. Each wave – each Kondratieff cycle, or just 'Kondratieff' – is associated with a new technology that forms the basis of the new economy. It shapes the social and cultural changes of the day as well as the patterns of trade and production. It may also have an influence on the rise and fall of dominant powers, a view that Schumpeter held quite strongly, although more recent writers have tended to say only that changes in technology cycles are one factor among many in shaping patterns of world hegemony. Each Kondratieff has been associated with a deep recession – much more powerful and much more painful than those associated with a shorter trade cycle. These slumps have also had important political and cultural effects.

The first Kondratieff defined early industrial capitalism, and is associated with iron, factory production of cotton and wool products, and early automation to produce firearms. It also developed through the rapid adoption of steam and water power in new and more efficient forms. Its emblems are often said to be the cotton gin (in the US), the mass production of firearms with interchangeable parts (notably in the US and Britain). One symbol of this is the building of the first iron bridge over the gorge at Ironbridge in Shropshire, UK (late eighteenth century into the 1820s). Another is the rapid development of the steam rail system in the UK, US, France and Belgium.

The second Kondratieff is associated with early chemical engineering, large volume steel production, more sophisticated textile and machine tools production, and a much greater concentration of capital in the hands of large firms, many of which are either operating internationally or form parts of emerging international cartels – deals that firms use to undermine competition. The great railway boom starts in the first Kondratieff, but pretty much all of the companies in every country that start making railways in the 1830s go bust by the 1840s. There was a global recession in the 1840s, which saw the collapse of banks and agriculture as well as many industrial firms. But this also gives rise to a strong recovery in the 1850s, which lead into a period of rapid technologically based economic growth. That included the growth of worldwide trade on the back of innovations in shipping (iron steam ships; improved navigation) and growing demand in the new industrial cities across much of the world economy. It is the second Kondratieff that sees a steady increase in global economic activity and global economic power, not least in finance, reaching into China, Japan, most South American states, and many parts of Africa. This second wave also sees the invention and rapid spread of the early Morse telegraph system, which played an important part in the evolution of the railways, but also in warfare from the American Civil

War (1861–1865) onwards. While the British totally dominate the first Kondratieff, the second witnesses the rise of Germany, France and the US as rivals to the UK, and a diffusion of technology even as economic power seemed to become more concentrated.

The third Kondratieff (1890s–1930s) follows a slump in the 1890s, which was not as serious as that of the 1840s, except in world agriculture; but it was profoundly important in promoting greater industrial development, further increases in firm sizes, and a shift of population from the land to industrialised cities. It is associated with the concentration of power in the hands of industrialists, who Americans often called the 'robber barons' of the world economy, and the growth of major international (especially European) cartels – for example, in coal and steel. The third wave is usually associated with the development of new forms of power – electricity, oil and gas, and with the development of the internal combustion engine. It also witnesses more advanced communication technologies with more powerful social and cultural impacts, including radio and cinema. It evolves new forms of mass consumption (cinema, early vacuum cleaners and other domestic goods), as well as mass car production ('Fordism'). It includes the emergence of a capacity to produce standardised arms in enormous quantity, especially in the First World War. It takes mechanical engineering and machine tools to a very high level of sophistication. But is dependent on the organisation of the labour force in a hierarchy with a great emphasis on the role of the semi-skilled worker who assembles or builds products through a repetitive set of processes that are highly controlled – the control of the labour process is the most important key to making money in this Fordist, production line-based, form of economic system. The economy and the culture of mass production emerge at the same time, not just in its greatest capitalist exemplars (the US, but also the UK, France and Germany), but also in the rapidly industrialising power of the Soviet Union, which was quick to adapt modern production methods from the US for itself.

The fourth Kondratieff (late 1930s–1970s) is generally associated with more advanced electronics, the jet engine and space technologies, plastics, agricultural chemicals such as DDT and fertiliser production, penicillin and aspirin (and more advanced pharmaceuticals more generally), more sophisticated production techniques in many industries, a widening of education and skills across a larger workforce (including many women workers and managers). It is more research and development intensive. It is more knowledge intensive. It produces the first computer (for decoding purposes during the Second World War), the first microprocessor (in California in the late 1940s), the further extension of much that is associated with new production methods and ideologies (mass consumption spreads from the US to Europe in the 1950s and 1960s and extends to many other countries, for example, in east Asia), and so does the development of advanced factory production. The rate of technology change increases, and so does the wider public awareness of some of the (good *and* risky) implications of technology change.

Is there a fifth Kondratieff cycle, begun but not yet complete, associated with more flexible forms of working, more sophisticated uses of a wider range of technologies, with innovation leadership passing from the largest firms to the most agile (some, of course, having grown very large, but many also small but dynamic)? Is this fifth cycle characterised by new media applications as well as by software, by online trading in goods and services, and by new sources of energy as well as new forms of power? The limitations of the Kondratieff cycle analysis may become clearer if we ask these questions. Some scholars (Keith Pavitt, for example) have always maintained that this kind of argument was much too generalised, and that we need to look not at overall patterns of innovation, but at innovation in specific countries, specific sectors and specific firms. If, the critics suggested, there were patterns in innovation at all, they were to be found at a micro level after much more specific study. Much recent research has suggested that what drives changed patterns of innovation and technological success or failure is the way in which networks within and between firms are managed (an explanation taken up elsewhere in this text in Chapters 2 and 3). You may want to discuss the question of a fifth wave, whether it exists at all, and if it does what it consists of and what its social and economic effects are. However a fifth wave is characterised, it will involve among other things a more sophisticated structure of global supply chains, an extensive exploration of new media and communications and surveillance technologies (whose full potential is not yet clear), a powerful role for a much more complex and variegated system of finance and debt, and new genetic biotechnologies as well as new material sciences as well as computing power.

## Oligopoly competition in high-tech sectors: how multinational firms use technology to compete

Most high-tech ('knowledge-intensive' or 'knowledge-based industry' – KBI) sectors are dominated by a small number of producers that operate globally and compete intensively both for customers and for the attention of governments and international regulators. This is known as oligopoly competition – classic oligopolies or monopoly theory predicts that where only a few firms act in a market, they will collude in reducing competition, but contemporary economic and business theory suggest something different happens. In Chapter 3, we explained why oligopolies characterised much international business in general, but here we need to explain specifically why oligopolies are even more important in global high-technology business activity.

Why oligopolies at all? Five reasons: knowledge is key in advanced technology: (i) patents and intellectual property rules create barriers for new firms to enter, keeping new players out; (ii) research and development is expensive – only large, relatively established firms can afford to do it; (iii) existing large firms will take over successful 'rising star' firms to exploit their knowledge, skills and strength, deny them to others and so reduce competition; (iv) successful large firms are able to build big stocks of cash and the support of large shareholders, enabling them to use M & As aggressively to grow still larger, making them more immune to competition and creating important national champions that governments may often protect from the 'normal' rules of anti-trust and competition policy – what economists call 'rent-seeking behaviour'; (v) as the largest players address each other in competition, they naturally push each other to grow and succeed, but at the same time grow apart from 'the rest' – smaller firms in the sector.

To give one example that illustrates much of this, in June 2016, Microsoft paid just over $26 billion for the professional networking service Linkedin. Microsoft, had been founded in 1975. For a generation it almost completely dominated world markets in computer software, which was much more profitable than the more mature hardware sector. But since 2000, the software market had also become mature, profitability fell, customers moved to mobile devices, Samsung had become an increasingly powerful rival and Microsoft were slow getting into the new media market for apps. Linkedin, founded in the early 2000s, provided services that had become popular globally and that are now widely used not just to make contact but for business partnership and collaboration. HR officers will usually check someone's profile on Linkedin in assessing them for a post, and individuals use it to advertise themselves and their professional skills. Microsoft has piles of cash but is behind in the apps and social media race, so buying into what was seen as one of the best in the market looked like a strong move. Whether it proves to be so, and whether the very high price paid proves to be good value for Microsoft remains to be seen. But the takeover certainly shook the competition and grabbed the attention of commentators; it also points up the tendency of emerging business sectors to concentration and oligopoly as they start to mature.

The tendency to oligopoly is always increased when the major customers of producers are also large firms – where there is oligopsony as well as oligopoly. This is because the customers have established links with suppliers, and because there is a high degree of specialised knowledge on both sides of the market. Power systems, robotics and aircraft engine manufacture are good examples. As a result, KBIs tend to be characterised by a distinctive structure: a very small number of powerful lead actors, few or no convincing middle-sized competitors rising to challenge them and a very large number of small firms that provide services and specialist roles, including aspects of activity outsourced from the big firms and high-risk marginal research that the larger firms are reluctant to try until they see it works. The small firms often act as subcontractors for the majors, and may sometimes have been set up by teams of former staff at a major who have gone independent. If they succeed, the large firm will buy them back up, creating enormous instant wealth for the entrepreneurs who set them up – but inevitably most fail. However, it is also important to note that when more radical technology changes occur, old established oligopolies may break up or disappear as new producers better able to exploit the new ideas and techniques arise. One good example is the challenge to established automobile manufacturers posed by new electric car technologies, which are not only a threat to car makers but also to engine manufacturers, designers and conceptions of what a 'positive image' of a car might be in advertising. Electric transport technologies – even if the adoption of electric cars has been slower, many cities around the world now have electric powered buses, for example – also creative completely new opportunities, as in the emergence of new battery designs and technologies.

Examples of oligopolies are also discussed in Chapter 3, which you may want to go back to if you find any of these ideas difficult. But among many possible examples, we might list civil airline manufacture (Boeing and Airbus), the market for mobile phone hardware, computer chip making and pharmaceuticals, as well as automated factory systems included advanced robotics. In each of these examples, whatever differences there are between them, costs of entry into a market are very high, patent protection for market leading firms is strong and the cost of R & D serve in themselves as barriers to entry. Leading firms have established powerful positions involving both large percentage shares of given markets and brand loyalties and reputations for reliability. At the same time, these oligopoly sectors are highly competitive in many respects. But leading firms can slip behind and lose their position if they fail to innovate, if they take too many risks in innovation, or if their products damage their reputation (for example, by producing health, safety or environmental crises).

It follows from this discussion that technology and innovation are not merely issues to which firms and business respond passively. They use innovation all the time as key elements of a competitive array of instruments. Awareness of technology change is obviously most important in advanced technology industries, but it is also significant in every sector. Mature businesses in food processing or door and window manufacture need to be aware of changes that might reduce their costs or change the mix of labour and machinery that they deploy just as much as advanced aerospace or drug manufacture.

## Technology, work and patterns of global labour

Technology shapes patterns of work; it affects what people actually do at work day-to-day. The shift from home working in cottage industries to large factories in the nineteenth century is one example. The growth of more flexible working systems in the 1980s and since is another. Thus the use of robotics and computer control, as well as computer design, has reshaped manufacturing. People and automated systems work in teams to participate in a division of labour that has been repeatedly re-engineered, as we know from the language used to describe it: 'teamworking in a culture of continuous change', 'working together in a perpetual quest for quality' and so on. This kind of self-promotion by giant multinationals is not mere nonsense – it reflects an ideology of how competition works. Writers such as Mark Rupert have pointed to the direct connections between the culture of work, the culture of training, and the globalisation of the ways in which not just managements but also whole workforces think. Firms such as McDonald's and Pizza Hut are so influential across the global system because they train staff in service industries to adapt to very specific patterns of work linked to very specific technologies designed to deliver those services more effectively. Critics would say the language used by multinationals to sell themselves and at the same time train their workforces is a dangerous nonsense, but it is also a very powerful production of social relations. Continuous adjustments to the mix of what people, machines, software and control systems do have become the essence of technology in business. They also affect a range of other activities – how healthcare systems and universities work, for example.

This is clearly the case in manufacturing, and one can see it if on a visit to a manufacturing plant. It is equally clearly the case in service industries, although it may be harder to seethe underlying patterns of work in a shipping or insurance office. And it is true too of what happens at the top of a business. All boards of companies (especially all boards of holding companies) manage the sources of capital. The functions of senior managers and boards of directors have changed in so far as much more rapid information is available, and decisions need to be taken more rapidly, because of the information technology available to them providing that information. This also means that boards can often cut out layers of management that were previously created to organise information flows to the board, which IT now manages. This enables a wider variety of corporate structures than in the 1970s. It also helps smaller companies, which are able to use the technologies of management more effectively than large competitors to survive by being quick and aggressive in their markets. These kinds of management technologies have also been the main force shaping the development of complex global supply chains (networks that provide components or maintenance services or other expertise) or the global trade in skills (especially in buying in key managers or researchers and their knowledge), again often on a global level. Logistics management, the management of the supply chain as efficiently as possible in shipping and truck services, saves on the costs of transport and of holding stocks, and helps to drive competition. It is, of course, entirely dependent on sophisticated uses of information technology. This has been one reason for the emergence since the early 1980s of a *global division of labour* in which firms and their customers rely ever more on increasingly complex international exchanges of goods and services to meet their needs and demands. Note that the creation of an international/global division of labour was not a one-off event that occurred at a particular point.

The absence of innovation may have different impacts on work and workers. The UK economy has been characterised by relatively low levels of investment (excepting only some of the highest technology firms) by comparison with business in rivals including the US, Germany, Sweden and France. It is perhaps not surprising therefore that productivity (measured either as per unit of labour cost or measured per unit produced including all costs) in the UK is 25–30 per cent lower than in those countries. This is also reflected in poorer working conditions in the UK compared to other European economies (the US is more similar). These poorer conditions have included a very rapid growth in 'zero hours contracts' where workers are paid a minimum wage level, but are expected to be available without regular working hours at the call of employers with no predictable working hours, holiday hours or job security. This relative labour intensive system, for those firms that have adopted it forms an alternative to a capital intensive system where workers are paid substantially more, valued more and expected to have much higher levels of skill and expertise. The growth of this kind of firm partly explains lower productivity, and partly also explains the relatively slower rate of technological diffusion in many UK industrial sectors.

Changes in technologies inevitably pose challenges and threats to organised labour. Trades unions have a long history of resisting innovations for this reason. But new innovations have also been welcomed by workforces and their unions, especially where they have been introduced with some level of consultation. And innovations provide opportunities for the reduction of dangerous working conditions or the improvement of conditions at work, which unions have often welcomed. Technology change provides an important nexus of issues for workers and unions, which has been the subject of a range of studies (notably by researchers at Sussex University and Nottingham Trent University, both in the UK, and by German and French research teams) which goes beyond the scope of this text.

# Limitations on the role of technology

Whatever importance we attach to technology and innovation as key issues in changing patterns of IPE, there are important factors that limit the spread of innovations and that may reduce the rate of technological change and limit its social effects. After all, many technical innovations go unheeded, and even influential ones may take much longer than one might imagine to catch on. Factors limiting the diffusion of innovation include limitations on the availability of finance for investment and the degree to which managers and other financial decision makers are risk averse. Investment in riskier technologies is likely to be less in a recession, or in the period coming out of a recession, than in a boom, when investors are generally much more open to new ideas. Individuals, firms and social systems have different capacities to absorb technological innovations. India, with a surplus of graduates, and very different levels of education in different regions, found it had a relative advantage in developing an IT industry in and around Bangalore, which has become world class, even while much of the rest of the country has remained relatively disadvantaged in new technology. China, with a strongly centralised direction of education policy, has succeeded in developing a comparable leadership in creative media industries in the Shanghai region; but this has not necessarily helped other regions of the country's economic development as much as central government expected. The factors at work here are as much cultural as economic, although they also reflect institutional capacities. It is when we look at different patterns of technological change and their real results in economic and social change that we discover how much innovation patterns are *not* merely a result of market forces. To take another example, in 1958, Ghana and Malaysia both gained independence from the UK. At that time, they had comparable literacy rates, similar population numbers, and similar levels of GDP and of engagement in the world economy. Fifty years later, Ghana has achieved some respectable levels of growth by comparison with other countries in Africa, has a highly developed civil society and a democratic state (despite quite long periods of military rule in the past). Ghana also has a great deal more political stability than some other west African countries. But it has developed at a far slower rate than Malaysia, which now enjoys a GDP approximately ten times that of Ghana ($386 billion as against $34.4 billion). There are many explanations for this, some of which are complex and some of which make sense at a regional rather than a purely national level – Malaysia is carried along by a region of higher growth, but has also done its share of carrying neighbours, advantages Ghana has lacked. But technical innovation and education in technology are two of the most important factors in the difference. Malaysia made a series of decisions (very much state focussed rather than market focussed) to promote large oligopoly firms designed to compete within its region with South Korea, Taiwan and Hong Kong, to develop higher education, to develop technical education at all levels, and to attract capital in advanced technology industries. It also committed to the technical education of women as much as men, even though socially and in religion it remains a conservative Muslim society. The aim was to build a domestic technical capability through spin-offs from multinational firms and to build human capital across Malaysian society. Part of this was a political deal – ruling political elites offered goodies in the form of rapid and sustained economic development in exchange for little opposition and little questioning of how they did business. But at an economic and social level it worked, and at the same time most Malaysian commentators would say this has preserved social stability in a country that experienced a serious civil conflict in the 1950s before the British withdrew. High technology education and the skills that went with it have helped to make Malaysia a successful, if not a very open, society. But none of this would have happened if the state – what economists have called the 'competition state' – had not played a leading role in managing the transition.

This previous discussion also suggested that 'technology' *does not have a fixed meaning.* It means one thing in firms, usually the definition just used. It means another to the individual. The person who gets up, switches on her TV, runs a bath with clean water, takes her iPod to the gym before boarding the train to work, is very conscious of the systems she uses in some respects, and has a range of very sophisticated skills. But she is almost certainly not very aware of the systems that underpin what she does each day, and it is probably true that all of us have a 'horizon' of awareness of technologies beyond which quite a lot of important things happen or where systems operate that we have little understanding. The meanings of technology are *mediated* by social structures, ideas and ideologies, and they reflect choices made by individuals and groups, and most especially by powerful institutions. And as the concept of technology is not a simple given, so the effects of technology in IPE are not simply determined by either economy or science: they are affected by these, of course, but they are also political.

To check this, imagine you go to Baghdad as it is today (we wrote this paragraph in the first edition of this text; unfortunately what it describes is still as valid in the second edition). The failures of the US and its allies after the 2003 invasion to address the infrastructure needs of the city, to facilitate the provision of clean water and reliable electric power supply was a choice made for a combination of ideological and economic reasons as well as from sheer lack of thought. The city works, after a fashion, surprisingly well, because individuals, families and larger communities have adapted to conditions that people in the advanced economies would think were unbearable. But there is still little electricity, no reliably clean water, and dreadful failures of the sewage system make the Euphrates river dangerous and obnoxious. The land-based telephone system, never very good, has largely been abandoned. Instead, people use their own electricity generators, systems they can maintain themselves, which use diesel or petrol, at huge environmental cost. The relatively wealthy drink bottled water, the poor get ill with water-borne disease. The mobile phone system works relatively well, and has been the fastest growing business in a damaged economy. These failures also reflect choices made by the government, and by aid agencies. Continuing violence is surely a factor in this failure to rebuild; but it is certainly not the only one. For the peoples in the city, failures of basic technologies that many other people can take for granted shape their everyday experience, and naturally it also affects their political responses to an ongoing war. 'Technology' includes systems we use every day without thinking – unless they fail. One might make the same kinds of observations about the consequences of global climate change on vulnerable Pacific island communities. And climate change has produced acute problems for people in Europe and the US who have bought homes in flood plains that previous scientific advice held would flood only once every century, and who have now found themselves flooded out of their homes three or four times in the, last decade. But they cannot now get either insurance or government recompense for their plight (the government responsibility is for having granted permission to build on vulnerable land, not, of course, for the weather itself).

All those examples suggest that political and social choices are key factors in the diffusion and management of technologies, including the choices of major firms and their interaction with governments and regulators. There are many examples of this, but perhaps the most significant is that between the US FBI and the Apple Corporation in 2016 over the FBI's demand for Apple to create software that would enable the government to unscramble the content of messages on a terrorist's mobile phone. There are important rights on both sides, and the argument is specifically a US one in so far as it has evolved within the framework of law derived from the US constitution. But the more general issue of conflicts between the obligation on the state to protect individuals through being able to fight potential criminality including terrorism and the obligation on IT companies to protect their customers from intrusion on their privacy (which is guaranteed in most constitutions in some form or other) is a global issue that will not disappear. But the choices and arguments here are not really 'merely' legal; they are political in a profound sense, and they illustrate very well the significance of how the state and the citizen's rights and identities are changed within a global context as technology evolves. One resource to understand better how technology, culture and everyday life interact can be found in a wealth of literature, including science fiction and 'dystopias', narratives of undesired and feared possible technological outcomes that surround us.

---

**LITERATURE BOX**

## Frankenstein's legacy

Technology questions and arguments are often fiercely reflected in science fiction. The best science fiction draws on a solid understanding of contemporary science while making imaginative leaps into how technologies and advanced technology societies might evolve. Leading authors, including H.G. Wells, Jules Verne, Philip K. Dick, William Gibson, Ursula le Guin and others, debate questions about technology and its capacities to shape, improve or destroy lives that IPE also needs to consider. The origins of many of these debates can be found in Mary Shelley's *Frankenstein*. Shelley's novel is one of the most sophisticated tools for starting to think about the relationship between science, scientists, technology and society you can find. It does not try to tell us that all science is wrong, and it does not say that scientists should be ignored in favour of some naïve kind of romanticism. It does suggest that science without ethics is dangerous and that scientists – such as Dr Frankenstein himself – are most dangerous when they become powerful and arrogant. Rooted in a critique of *both* eighteenth-century scientific optimism *and* romantic suspicion of that optimism, Shelley's novel is a good deal more sophisticated than some popular representations of it in film have suggested. Put in contemporary terms, this is not an argument against science but an argument for having strong ethical restraints on scientists.

If we want to understand the impact of technology on IPE, we need to remember that – as elsewhere in this book – 'IPE' itself has an enlarged and critical definition. It is not just about firms and markets or regulation and states. Cultures of technology impact on political behaviour, but also constitute political behaviours. Asking questions about *Frankenstein* leads us to ask questions about the interaction of cultures and globalisation and business. It also leads us to ask about the value of Shelley's many successors in film and literature who explore questions of ethics, the culture of difference, the importance of valuing knowledge and using it wisely, in writing about science and technology in society. See, for example, the very varied work of the authors mentioned above, or that of Arthur C. Clarke, Donna Haraway and J.G. Ballard.

---

## Intellectual property and technology

Intellectual property is knowledge that can be bought and sold. It includes patents, copyrights and designs. The purpose of intellectual property rules is not to keep ideas and techniques secret, but to enable them to be traded in an orderly way. There is a balance of interests here – it is in the general public interest that firms should innovate, and that those innovations should be diffused around the economy as quickly as practically possible. This requires that individual inventors and firms that specialise in innovation should do research, develop new products and processes, test them for safety and efficiency and market them. It also needs firms to encourage others to buy their innovations and adopt them, since this produces greater competition and brings the price of the innovation down more quickly. But of course none of this is necessarily in the inventor's or innovating firm's interest. Benjamin Franklin is said to have encouraged innovation as one of the main qualities of the new republic of the US in the 1770s: 'make a better mousetrap and the world will make a path to your door!' But if you make a better mousetrap and do not have legal protection, the world may well leave your door alone and merely reverse engineer your product to copy it. Individual firms will only innovate if they know that they are going to be able to secure a good level of return on their investment. Patenting and intellectual property rights more generally are supposed to protect that.

Advanced technology sectors are dominated by concerns about how intellectual property rules work. Software is covered by copyright rather than patents – this changes the way the rules work, meaning that software producers get added protection for much longer. This provides an incentive to put computer power into the market in the form of software rather than embedded in hardware, a point that has shaped the development of the personal computer market. Pharmaceutical companies take longer than others to bring new products to market because of the extensive safety and testing requirements of new drugs. This justifies drug patents having a much longer life – so the companies can recover their investment in research and testing – than, say, engineering products. Research in industry is structured around the intellectual property rules that apply, and the legal and political control of intellectual property rights (IPRs) is of growing importance. This also means that specialist legal firms working in IPRs are kept very busy, as ongoing legal disputes between Samsung and Apple over mobile phone technology arguments demonstrate.

This is also reflected in international trade negotiations. Firms anxious to use their strengths in IPRs to compete in the marketplace push governments and international trade organisations and industry associations to adopt principles that support their own position and weaken those of rivals. As a result, negotiations such as those in the WTO Doha round, which are formally conducted by governments, are always surrounded by major firms and their representatives, pressing negotiators to move in particular ways. Most WTO trade disputes, again formally brought by governments, have trade associations on both sides pushing the case of individual firms. This can be seen as somehow illegitimate rent-seeking activity, but it is also a natural corollary of the nature of the negotiating process. The problem is that some actors, notably developing countries, are weakened in this kind of situation unless they are able to organise in similar ways to the well-resourced industry associations of developed countries. This they have started to do, and countries such as India and Brazil have similar patterns of organisation, and make similar use of specialist consultants, to the most effective developed negotiators. These lobbies, like those in 'developed' markets, tend also to favour larger firms and dominant interests – there are no 'level playing fields' here. The importance of lobbying by large firms and by trade organisations (typically representing all firms in a sector, but tending inevitably to give greater influence to the larger ones) cannot be over-stressed. A pure economic theorist would see such activity as running counter to effective competition, which it very often is: the classical economist Adam Smith was especially critical of the efforts of business leaders to get together to subvert competition when they got the chance. But disputes over IPRs are also an inevitable consequence of a system where technological innovation is so crucial to the development of profitability and the assurance of a growing share of a given market. It is not surprising that leading firms that spend so much on R & D also spend so much on corporate legal protection in legal disputes that may last for years. Nor is it surprising to discover that regulators – whether parts of the state or institutions charged by the state with establishing intellectual property regimes – are bombarded by interest groups wanting to shape the rules in favour of their members or clients.

## Technology, competition, and mergers and acquisitions

Firms engage in mergers and acquisitions (M & A) for a range of reasons, often primarily concerned with financial economies of scale. But they may also seek to buy up a rival in order to get access to its intellectual property or its research potential. More crudely, firms may buy up another not because they want its assets, so much as to deny them to a leading rival. Technology is a major resource, including the knowledge and know-how of a workforce. Technology, including intellectual property in all its forms, counts as s significant asset on the balance sheet of any company engaged in the global knowledge economy. But valuing 'know-how' is formidably difficult, and if the know-how a company owns is its principle asset, this makes for difficulties (especially in recession) in valuing not just companies but whole sectors of the economy. This is an important issue for accountants and auditors as well as for company directors. It may also become an important question in a democratic society for government and for citizens, not only because mergers and acquisitions among larger multinationals are likely to affect the efficiency of competition, but also because mergers are constructed (among other things) so as to minimise any tax liabilities that arise in the newly formed corporate structure. Tax avoidance schemes can be embedded into corporate structures as they reorganise, an important issue given other questions about carefully constructed corporate tax avoidance by the largest firms at the time of writing. The significance of merger and acquisition activity for technology change is a question to take further in a more advanced discussion – it may mask a failure by a cash rich firm to do its own innovation effectively as it provides rewards for smaller innovating firms that are the target of takeovers, and many, perhaps the majority, of mergers and takeovers in high-tech industries do not succeed in their primary objectives. In defence of widespread M & A activity, we should also note that many economists would point to the importance for all firms of competition not just in markets for products or processes, but also for capital. To manage a merger or takeover, a firm has to have the capital to afford the new business. If it has a pile of cash, it has to justify to shareholders this use of it; if it has to borrow more heavily (a heavily 'leveraged buy-out') to acquire the other company, it has to justify to lenders that use of their money. Since there are always plenty of calls on investment money, the planning and accounting necessary to succeed in getting the cash needed is part of a competitive process against others who are also trying to borrow the same money for their own purposes. Market competition in capital markets is at least as important in product markets in shaping the behaviour and success or failure of high tech business, not least because high tech is typically seen as more risky (but also potentially more rewarding) than investment in a 'mainstream' corporation.

## Technology and the individual person as subject in IPE

This section makes a sudden change of focus. IPE has not always tried to understand the position of individual women and men within the systems of global structures and power plays on which it often focussed. Traditional studies in international relations tend to neglect individuals except individual leaders or decision makers. IPE has often followed an IR agenda, as Chapter 1 noted, and so individual people and groups of individuals once found little role in the field because of its fundamental agenda. This fundamental shift in agenda puts the ontology of the approach (its 'theory of what exists') to IPE in question. As soon as this is acknowledged, the door is open to ontological critique: *why* do some actors seem to count for a great deal, and other people or institutions do not count, and do not count as 'actors'? Why should we *not* rethink the position of individuals in the study of IPE; for the purposes of this particular chapter, how does technology and innovation impact on the individual and their capacity for action and individual moral responsibility?

There are a number of leverage points for this critical argument. One, advocated in particular by Murphy and Tooze (1996), starts with a phenomenon that, they argue, IPE neglects and should not: poverty. If we ask why radical inequalities occur in global politics, there might be several answers. But if we are to investigate poverty, as they suggest, do we not need to also ask about the everyday experience of the poor? How do individual people experience, define and understand the world? If we ask that question, we cannot ask it only of 'the poor' for very long. These are after all individual people, with a diverse set of responses to their situation. And poverty may not in any case be experienced as *the same* in different cultures and contexts, although no doubt there are many similarities. Individuals use the available technologies, make choices and overcome difficulties or negotiate strategies to survive. People here are 'victims' of poverty, but that is not all they are or what they are essentially: they are also agents, initiators, survivors, witnesses and negotiators. They are both victims and perpetrators of the violence of poverty, as films such as the two great Brazilian films *City of God* (2002) and *Central Station* (2008) explore. Of course states, large and small, regional power systems and social and economic structures all shape the realities of poverty. But we cannot validly discuss its place in international political economy without also exploring and giving a central place to those individuals and groups who experience it.

Feminist political economists make similar kinds of arguments. They look to the experience of women in social and economic development, in people smuggling, in sweatshops, in migratory labour, in house and field work. In raising these questions, they may also look at women in large groups (for example, the class of working women). But they might equally well look at the micro-political economy of their chosen research topic, which leads directly to individual women as agents, negotiators witnesses, victims, decision makers, mothers, entrepreneurs and no doubt more. At the same time, feminist writing goes beyond offering a distinctive agenda of study of a distinctive ontology, a theory of what counts and what *ought* to count in the theory of IPE. Feminist scholars have also explored questions of how knowledge is constructed within IPE, and how that knowledge might be critiqued and developed. The epistemological critique opens the possibility of different forms of knowledge in the field, while questioning the privileging of *some* forms of knowledge over others. The newly established forms of knowledge include the work of those scholars who are investigating these questions, which other more traditional or orthodox IPE generally reflects. But this heterodox IPE also looks at the knowledge these women identify as previously excluded. This might use some kind of grounded theory or critical discourse analysis approach to explore the meanings people in particular institutions give to their lives, how they conceptualise and construct the world, how they use special language and distinctive social practices to do so and how they find *agency* in these experiences.

One particular issue here relates to women's indigenous knowledge. Women in particular communities hold special knowledge, which may be medical (knowledge of healing plants) or agricultural (knowledge of particular techniques that suit their own soil or seed or water supply), important when women do most of the teaching, all the midwifery and a disproportionate amount of the agricultural labour in many societies. This special knowledge has a recognised status within some societies, for example, in Amazonia, in India and among Arctic peoples. But it is significant also where it may not be recognised. In the Caribbean and Africa as in developed societies, women often take roles as heads of families and as key organisers of small businesses as well as their more 'traditional' work. This approach, often called 'standpoint feminism' (see also Chapter 2), suggests that specific groups of women have valuable knowledge: the kind of critique involved asks about the standpoint of women, but does not mean 'women in general' or all women, but emphasises that varied communities of women will have different and perhaps contrasting experiences and knowledges.

New technologies nearly always have at least one feature in common, which has often been noticed. They accelerate time, or, if you prefer, they seem to contract time. This new element of speed was actually first observed in the railway revolution of the mid-nineteenth century, where time seemed to contract and distances narrow. Other innovations, including the Morse telegraph and steamships, seemed to have the same effect. The spread of mobile phone technologies, satellite news and Internet applications that enable an intense range of human contacts from selling old clothes to sex intensify these relations. When Tomlinson (2007) wrote his interesting and important cultural study on speed, he anticipated further developments, which would go beyond what he could already see. He wrote before the 'new sharing economy' of Uber and Airbnb. He anticipated the shift from computer software to mobile apps, but not the increasing use of bots with the great variety of human contacts they would bring. These also present new business opportunities and the potential to restructure existing patterns of business as online grocery delivery and eBay have already transformed retailing. These changes potentially also shake up existing businesses – as the emergence of Uber transforms existing taxi services in many countries. How regulators respond to these kinds of innovation is also important: city authorities in Paris and Berlin have tried to outlaw both Uber and Airbnb, whereas in many other places they have been encouraged. It is not yet clear how the revolution in applications of mobile technologies might transform business and working experience in the longer run, and that is something that readers might like to reflect on. This acceleration of business, work and human potential also again raises questions about the nature of subjectivity and the ways in which individual identities might be challenged by innovative ways of living as well as doing business.

## Who has technology leadership?

Governments have worried about the loss of something they often call technological leadership. This has been a key element of debates about the decline of US hegemony or its rise to 'unipolarity' (single-state dominance) both in the US and elsewhere, a question particular asked by neo-realist theorists. But countries don't have technical leadership; firms, researchers and entrepreneurs do. The argument matters in IR theoretically as well as in policy terms, as part of a set of claims either that the US holds global hegemony (whether that is seen as very much a good thing or not) or that it has lost or is losing it. Of course, firms with strong records of patenting may appear to have technical leadership – but the majority of world patents are registered in the US for legal reasons, to get protection of the US courts, whether or not the research on which they are based was done in the US. Nonetheless, US science and technology does have obvious and very broad based strengths. Other countries with strong positions in technology markets and innovation include the obvious large states, but also some smaller but intellectually well-endowed actors such as Malaysia, Sweden, Switzerland, Finland and Canada. World leadership in one specific technology, wind energy generation, remains in Denmark. World leadership in thorium-based nuclear power generation, a potentially more environmentally friendly power source than uranium systems, lies between India and Canada. The UK retains strength and depth in specific technologies including graphine, first discovered in Manchester University and now the subject of a race to apply and patent the carbon-based material in a wide range of applications.

But working solely in a national framework is simply not the way in which global firms work. They are global operators. They may be based legally in one country or other, but they operate in many others. Many firms in Europe, but also elsewhere, may be based in one country, do their research in another, and pay their corporate taxes in a third. Where they are based is primarily a question of taxation and regulation. But firms that are 'based' in, say, California or Delaware in the US may have their research division based in Germany; they may also have research labs in a dozen other countries. Defining state leadership in many technological fields is thus very hard, although in defence it is usually easier to assess. US firms such as Boeing and General Electric are primarily based in the US and produce their knowledge there – but they are exceptions rather than the rule. And important research operations, including much 'hard' physics and heavy engineering, are so expensive that they are routinely done by multinational consortia of laboratories and countries, and not just in any single state. The European Large Hadron Collider is only one such example. This is true of non-military space research today, and of fundamental physics and astrophysics. But it is also the case in automotive engineering, advanced robotics and high voltage power systems, where many large and smaller firms are members of consortia that collaborate both on R & D and on getting new designs to market as quickly as they can. And in the 2000s, the US Congress questioned whether US security was threatened when up to 30 per cent of research students and postdoctoral fellows in US universities in biotechnology, pharmaceuticals and new materials technologies are either from China, Taiwan or South Korea. When Congress issued their warning report, universities and firms joined together in response to point out that without the pool of expertise this research created, they would be unable to do their research, even if a side effect was the rapid transfer of technology outside the US.

Having said that, it is clear that in some areas, European Union firms have a distinctly strong position, including bioengineering, pharmaceuticals and food processing. Japanese firms have particular strengths in biotechnology applications (especially marine biotechnology), anything connected with domestic electronics, and production systems (for example automation and robotics). US firms have strength across a wide range of fields but not in all. The US has particular strengths in defence-related research, because of the long-term impact of very high state funding, but also in software engineering and applications and in business systems. There are quite a number of fields where there is no clear leader, including advanced power systems and renewable energy resources other than wind power (where Denmark is a world leader). Other fields where there is no obvious leadership include chip manufacture, where the US, Japan and China all have strengths, advanced materials, where there are a range of countries with diverse strengths, and nuclear power, where France is the leading exporter, but where Sweden, Canada and the US all have technical strengths. China has an acknowledged strength in a range of existing technologies, but is also emerging as a world leader in electronic technologies (lithium batteries), media technologies and some software applications. We do not know so much about Chinese strengths in military applications of technology except that they recognised about ten years ago that they needed to accelerate investment in innovative technologies, and that they are doing whatever they can to catch the US in online technologies but also in new materials and in military applications of stealth technologies. We also know that Chinese firms are some of the world leaders in terms of their size (Chapter 3 shows the three largest firms in the world are now all Chinese banks); and that large Chinese firms in general have built up cash reserves that enable them to buy further new technologies, new IPRs and to invest in research not only in China but globally if they choose to do so. The short answer to the core question here is that no country has 'technological leadership'; but the firms that hold it are still based primarily in the US and a few other advanced economies. However some countries, and we should include Malaysia, India, Indonesia, Mexico and Turkey as well as the main European high-tech economies challenge that US strength. But we cannot generalise unless we look very carefully at sectors and individual firms rather than in the more sweeping terms often used by politicians.

**Table 10.1** Chapter summary

| | Technology as source of change? | Technology as a structure? | Technology and power? | Geopolitics? | Optimistic/pessimistic about technology? |
|---|---|---|---|---|---|
| Neo-realism | Technology is a key source of change although not the only one | Technology is *not* a separate structure, but part of a global structure of power and influence (balance of power) | Technology is an important element in state power and in competition between states for power and hegemony | Technology is a key source of power and technology change a source of changes in power and balance of power | Neither very optimistic nor pessimistic, but tends towards pessimism |
| Neo-liberalism | Technology is generally welcomed and seen as a 'natural' source of change; origins of technology questioned less often | Most neo-liberals do not emphasise any concept of structure, and in any case technology is not seen as a structure in itself | Technology has the power to reshape agendas and a source of power for states and non-state actors; firms that are better managers of technology most likely to compete effectively | Technology is an important factor in global trade and supply chains and economic competition; not a major factor in geopolitical competition | Generally very optimistic about possibilities of change for market dynamism and extending consumer choice, and also for opportunities for increased globalisation |
| Orthodox Marxist | Technology is a very important but not 'autonomous' source of change, which occurs at more fundamental level of 'relations of production' and economic structure | As neo-realism: technology is part of a global structure of power and empire not an autonomous structure of its own | Technology is an important source of potential change in the ways capitalism works but is not a source of fundamental change | Technological change likely to reinforce and deepen imperial competition between states under capitalism | Not very optimistic but tends to pessimism especially in short term |
| Gramscian | Technology is capable of being part of processes transforming political economy and culture and creating opportunities to move from 'war of position' to more dynamic 'war of movement' politics, but will not do so on its own | Technology is not autonomous but a significant factor in existing situation and possible changes. Hegemonic powers will also have strong technological advantages to reinforce their dominance | Technology is a source of power and a source of potential change but underlying class and cultural hegemonies remain compelling and entrenched | Geopolitics is a set of structures and behaviours rooted in relatively long-standing power relations | More optimistic about possible significant change than orthodox Marxists but hold all the same it is difficult, intractable and cannot be easily assumed. Resistance – movement towards emancipation – is possible but difficult in the face of this power. Cultural challenges are important alongside political and economic if resistance is to become effective |

| | | | | | |
|---|---|---|---|---|---|
| Feminist | Technology is likely to be a source of reinforcing patriarchy as of providing basis for change but can provide opportunities for change if they are seized | See 'Technology as a source of change?' entry | Technological change tends to reinforce power of individuals states and dominant structures (patriarchy) but can be used to challenge these forms of power by effective organisation and cooperation for resistance | See 'Technology and power' entry | Varies from one scholar to another. More Marxist feminists – see 'Marxist' above; more postmodern feminists see? 'Postmodernism' below. |
| Postmodernism | Technology is a vital source of change; but this change for many postmodernist scholars may not be more than superficial. Postmodernist authors may underestimate the unevenness of technology change but they do recognise its unpredictable impacts | 'Technostructure' is an important element of global power and global domination to be critiqued and its forms of knowledge are to be questioned for many (not all) postmodernist authors | For postmodernist scholars, power is diverse, fragmented, not centralised, but pervasive and powerful through discourse: technology changes reflect and reinforce this | Critique of technology helps to deconstruct power and geopolitical structures and tendencies. But the forms of power represented in geopolitics always need to be challenged | Varies from one scholar to another, but many postmodernist scholars are enthusiastic about technology change |
| Green theory | Technological change is suspected by most green theorists but can be seen as an important basis for social and economic reconstruction when done and managed at a small-scale level | Most green theorists would see technology as a structure or part of a structure of power | Technology is not autonomous of those firms and interests that manage it; technological innovation can potentially challenge state and dominant interests but is more likely to reinforce them | Geopolitics is an arena of conflict over the future of globalised and industrial models of society; most green theorists challenge this; most want to shift thinking and priorities to a more local and human scale level | 'Light' green theorists are more optimistic about potential for change; 'dark' green theorists are more suspicious and more dubious of the real impact of any technological change other than a move to specific non-industrial green technologies |

## Summary

It has been widely recognised that both 'orthodox' international relations theory and more conventional accounts of global political economy tend to underestimate the significance of technology and innovation. This can be verified by looking in most IPE textbooks. However there are exceptions. These include the text by Skolnikoff, his dated but still valuable *The Elusive Transformation* (1983). It also includes discussions of the knowledge structure, in which technology issues are important, in Susan Strange's *States and Markets* (1988), influenced by her earlier reading of Schumpeter. Several journals offer valuable articles, most regularly *Research Policy*, but also the *Review of International Political Economy* and *New Political Economy*, and some of the main business studies journals.

However, looking across the discussion in this chapter, it is possible to conclude that technology makes an enormously significant impact on international political economy. It shapes corporate strategies and patterns of trade and exchange. It shapes patterns and structures of competition, which have long-term effects on practice, on conflict and on outcomes in the world political economy. It tends, with exceptions, to promote or accelerate globalisation. It creates a world of intellectual property, which offers both opportunities and threats to key players. It shapes the distribution of power between states, not just because it affects defence capabilities, but also because it underpins many of the sources of economic and financial power. It shapes conflicts, but also provides frameworks within which a great deal of cooperation takes place. It is also crucial in shaping the everyday experience of life and labour for many millions of people, offering both liberation from difficult work such as manual drawing and carrying of water and at the same time new forms of oppression and control in the workplace. Perhaps most important, technical innovation offers a series of risks and calculations for investors and ordinary citizens about the future, against which decisions about education, investment, lifestyle, security but also mundane day-to-day choices, have to be made.

## Reflective questions

1  Explain why it is difficult to define what technology is before trying to understand its impact on IPE.
2  How does technology shape patterns and specifics of competition in international business?
3  What role does technology often play in mergers and acquisition activity?
4  Why are oligopolies, common in all international business, even more significant in knowledge-based industries (KBIs)?
5  What opportunities and threats do innovations pose for labour in developed and developing societies? You may want to answer first in general terms and then try to sophisticate your answer by looking at specific industries and specific countries.
6  How does technological change shape (reshape?) human subjectivities?
7  How might technical innovation be understood differently by: (i) a neo liberal writer; (ii) a feminist writer; (iii) a new institutional economics/network theorist; (iv) a Gramscian scholar?

## Suggestions for further reading

De La Mothe, J.R. (2001) *Science, Technology and Global Governance*, London: Routledge.

Dunning, J. and Lundan, S. (2008) *Multinational Enterprises and the Global Economy*, 2nd revised edn, London: Edward Elgar.

Freeman, C. (2008) *Systems of Innovation: Selected Essays in Evolutionary Economics*, Cheltenham: Edward Elgar.

Harris, P.G. (2009) *Climate Change and Foreign Policy*, London: Routledge.

Kofman, E. and Youngs, G. (eds) (2008) *Globalization: Theory and Practice*, 3rd edition, London: Continuum.

Moore, P. (2010) *The International Political Economy of Work and Employability*, Basingstoke: Palgrave Macmillan.

Pavitt, K. (1999) *Technology, Management and Systems of Innovation*, Cheltenham: Edward Elgar.

Skolnikoff, E.B. (1994) *The Elusive Transformation: Science, Technology and the Evolution of International Politics*, Princeton, NJ: Princeton University Press.

Stoneman, Paul (1988) *The Economic Analysis of Technology Policy*, Oxford: Oxford University Press.

Strange, Susan (1988) *States and Markets*, 2nd edn, London, Continuum.

Talalay, M., Farrands, C. and Tooze, R. (eds) (1997) *Technology Culture and Competitiveness in the Global Political Economy*, London: Routledge.

*The Economist* (especially its excellent quarterly reviews of technology issues).

Tomlinson, J. (2007) *The Culture of Speed: The Coming of Immediacy*, London: Sage.

Tooze, R. and Murphy, C.N. (1996) 'The epistemology of poverty and the poverty of epistemology in IPE: mystery, blindness, and invisibility', *Millennium Journal of International Studies*, December (25): 681–707.

Wajcman, J. (2013) *Feminism Confronts Technology*, Cambridge: Polity Press.

Company annual reports provide valuable resources for researching key technology businesses and debates.

# 11 Culture

## Chapter learning outcomes

After reading this chapter students should be able to:

- Engage in theoretical debates about the nature of culture, the impact that globalisation has on culture and how cultures can be in conflict.
- Explore the emergence of aspects of global culture.
- Understand and explain resistance to cultural globalisation and in particular the hegemony of Western culture.
- Understand and explain how social institutions shape cultures in a non-coercive manner.
- Recognise various aspects of the political economies of cultures and how they are impacted upon and evolve as a result of processes of globalisation.
- Relate discussion of culture to the theoretical debates discussed earlier in this book.

## Introduction

A significant factor in relation to globalisation is its impact on various cultures around the world. It has been suggested that the seeds of a global monoculture have already been sown. This chapter will consider this proposition in light of the issue areas discussed above and related theoretical debates. The potential impact of the spread of a dominant system of production, and the possibility that a common set of intrinsic values necessarily follows, will be critically presented. The emphasis here will be on the promotion of certain types of 'knowledge', values, norms and 'rights'. Huntington's 'clash of civilisations' thesis has attracted renewed attention with regard to competing value systems. The ongoing debate surrounding cultural relativism and/or universality will be reviewed.

The concept of 'cultural imperialism' suggests a monolithic expansion and dominance of a single form of political, economic and socio-cultural order. However, the process of globalisation is more diverse and complex than the imposition of colonial rule. One reason why the Roman Empire was able to expand so dramatically was the manner in which the invading forces adapted and absorbed elements of local cultures. Although this was supported by the military might of the legionnaires it was a more efficient and successful strategy to not wholly alienate and repress the colonised culture. While the dominant control was centralised and directed from Rome there was also a relatively tolerant attitude taken towards the local norms and practices that were not seen as being in direct opposition to Roman rule. In the contemporary global political economy it is worthwhile considering what aspects of cultural diversity may be viewed as being challenged, and possibly repressed, by processes of globalisation. Is there a sense in which some aspects of globalisation, notably the dominance of neo-liberal economics, are promoted and protected against alternative economic systems? Can multiculturalism be seen as a challenge to the current economic world order, or are economics and socio-cultural issues two distinct and separable areas of the processes of globalisation?

Many authors looking at the spread of neo-liberal economic policies seem to conflate this with the increasing 'reach' and influence of Western media. This may be in the form of music, television and radio programmes and the very active promotion of the teaching of English as a foreign language. The US Peace Corps volunteers of the 1960s onwards were instructed to not only teach English but also to be ambassadors for the American way of life. The fact that the English language was being increasingly taught to non-English speakers was the foundation for these new English speakers to be able to access and, probably, be influenced by wider cultural norms and values of the broadly defined 'English-speaking world'. More recently the shift in the balance of various languages has altered. The demographics of the US means that there is a relative decrease in English-only speaking Americans with a corresponding rise in those whose first language is Spanish. Similarly, an increasing number of non-Chinese are now studying Mandarin as China emerges as an increasingly important international power. Such issues should be borne in mind when considering alleged cultural dominance and expansion. There are examples of 'traditional' cultures being significantly challenged, to the point of extinction in the case of some indigenous languages. Important as this is for the preservation of cultural diversity there are relatively few examples of this in recent times with the more common pattern being the expansion of language skills and cultural awareness, rather than the wholesale erosion and replacement of one cultural form with another. The following section looks at the so-called 'triumph' of neo-liberalism as the dominant economic form in the contemporary world order, but also asks whether this dominance extends to the realm of cultural norms and values.

## Liberal triumphalism

There are a range of theoretical positions on the importance of culture in international relations, and the cultural impacts of globalisation. One of the most prominent in academic circles since the end of the Cold War in 1989 has been liberal triumphalism. This school of thought was founded very much on the work of Francis Fukuyama (see Chapter 2) and has remained quite popular even in the post-9/11 era. The main assumptions are that human history has been a constant process of movement from one human condition to another in the search for the most effective systems of political, economic and social governance. Fukuyama claimed that capitalism and Western-styled liberal democracy constitute one such form of human governance. Rival systems of organisation and governance have included fascism, radical nationalism and communism. All of these rivals have been defeated by liberalism over the past century and thus the liberal democratic and capitalist system has triumphed. Liberal triumphalists claim that the human pursuit of development and progress has resulted in this type of system or condition and that it is in fact the pinnacle of human civilisation. No other ideological form of organisation or governance can compete with it and as such all people now desire (or soon will) to adopt capitalism and Western-styled democracy. Liberalism has, in short, triumphed.

The implications of these assumptions for international relations are that processes of globalisation are encouraging the adoption of liberalism around the world. This, in effect, is creating a more homogeneous and cohesive human world in which peoples from different states are increasingly similar in their culture. This is termed cultural homogenisation. While there have always been cultural exchanges of some sort throughout human history these exchanges have tended to be limited in scope and have been relatively mutual. However, in the contemporary world, the combination of the triumph of liberalism with globalisation has meant that cultural exchanges are occurring at extremely rapid rates and at very deep levels. Also, these exchanges are not as mutual as in the past and seem to be dominated more by the export of Western, liberal culture to the rest of the world.

Liberal triumphalism points to examples such as the 'victory' of the West in the Cold War and the perceived defeat of communism as a rival ideology, to prove its thesis. There are, however, many critics of this theoretical approach. These criticisms can be divided into two broad approaches. One approach claims that liberalism has not triumphed and many different ideological and cultural approaches to organising human society still exist. The existence of communism as the national ideology of some states such as China and Cuba is said to undermine the claim that capitalism and Western democracy 'defeated communism' in the Cold War. Furthermore, the existence of Islamic-based ideologies and the prevalence of Islam in the socio-cultural, political and economic characteristics of many states is also used to discredit liberal triumphalism. The second critique of Fukuyama's thesis is based upon the perception of negative results of cultural homogenisation and the triumph of liberalism. This criticism does not refute that liberalism has triumphed and is leading to a homogeneous world culture. Rather, advocates of this critique agree that these processes are taking place but they argue that the cultural dominance of Western, liberal societies is not desirable. Radical groups such as Al-Qaeda are advocates of this second critique.

## Clash of civilisations

At the opposite end of the spectrum is the clash of civilisations thesis. This approach can be seen as the polar opposite of liberal triumphalism. Its main advocate was Samuel Huntington (see Chapter 2) who argued that international relations consisted of conflict between different and opposing cultural or civilisation groups. He claimed that globalisation was not leading to the homogenisation of cultures around the world. While it is true that some features of cultures, such as food, clothing and music, are being shared this does not constitute homogenisation. Instead, the sharing of cultural characteristics is something that has always taken place and does not necessarily represent the coming together of cultures to form one. Rather, it is argued that there are large groups of people who, broadly speaking, share the same culture. These groups are civilisations and Huntington argues that there are perhaps eight such groups in the world (see discussion in Chapter 2). Furthermore, these civilisations are inherently opposed to each other in many ways and retain their cultural distinctions through resistance to and conflict with others. There is no constant process of progress from one condition to another as is argued by liberal triumphalism and there will not be an emergence of a single global culture.

This position has also been criticised, not least of all by liberal triumphalists. Again we can identify two broad camps of critics here. The first claims that processes of globalisation have in fact led to greater cultural exchanges and the sharing of cultural characteristics now takes place at deep-rooted levels. In a sense the structure of cultures changes as the adoption of cultural practices, values, norms and so on, takes place. In this sense there are no insulated civilisation groups; instead there are multiple linkages between cultures, which are increasingly changing societies. At the same time, this critique suggests that even where cultures remain relatively static there is no reason to believe that different cultures are in fact opposed to each other. They simply have different characteristics. The second main critique of the clash of civilisations approach to understanding culture in international relations is subjective and normative. Critics here argue that defining societies as inherently different from each other and claiming that they are in conflict with each other can only lead to more radical interpretations of international relations. Indeed, people such as the late Osama Bin Laden would most likely have agreed with Huntington and advocated the same kind of perception of international relations.

## Binary opposition

Binary opposition is a term developed and used by critical theorists, usually structuralists, to analyse how humans construct meanings and definitions. It is claimed here that we define people, objects, processes and issues only by identifying opposites. In this sense people, for example, are defined as one thing because they are not another. Thus, an adherent of Islam is identified as a Muslim because he/she is not a Hindu and so on. Cultures are also defined in opposition to each other. 'Civilised' is found opposed by 'barbaric', 'developed' is opposed by 'undeveloped' and 'enlightened' opposes 'backward'.

In this sense, seeing cultures as binary opposites can be useful in identifying ways in which social barriers are constructed between people of different backgrounds. By constructing meanings through comparison, perceived differences between cultures are essentially maintained. This view contradicts the notion present in liberal triumphalism that people and cultures can and will all share many similarities and will not be 'opposed' to each other. Furthermore, perceiving cultures as opposite to each other can lead to confrontational attitudes or stereotypes, which would encourage a clash of civilisations. At the same time, the definition of binary opposites in a given context can also be seen to be culturally relative. Postmodernists could argue that there are no tautological claims and therefore there can be no binary opposite to such claims.

## Anti-globalisation/structuralist and green thought

A third main approach to understanding culture in contemporary international relations and in international political economy can be seen to be, on the whole, critical. This approach suggests that as the world integrates further as a result of globalisation and as people interact more with each other, cultures are changing. These cultural changes take place very rapidly and are quite overarching. This in itself is not seen as a negative development in human history and can be seen to have positive effects. These include the reduction of international conflict and greater cooperation. However, there is much concern about the type of cultural change that takes place and which culture is becoming dominant. This approach shares some of the assumptions present in liberal triumphalism, which relate to the unequal exchanges between cultures. Generally it is observed that Western, capitalistic culture is spreading around the world to much greater effect than other cultures. Western music, clothing styles, language (English is sometimes referred to as 'globalish' as a representation of its global usage), ideologies and institutions are more dominant around the world than any other.

The Marxian critique is that capitalistic culture is based on the concepts of competition and accumulation. The result of these conceptual foundations is the division of wealth, justice and opportunity between people. For example, some people in capitalistic societies will become wealthy and powerful but only at the expense of others who become poorer, weaker and have fewer opportunities for a good quality of life. Capitalistic cultures are, therefore, unequal and unfair. If this is the type of culture that is becoming dominant in the world then there is a risk that increasingly societies will become eschewed in this way. Surely, it is argued, this cannot be desirable.

Environmentalist critiques share this Marxian assumption that Western capitalist culture is dominating others on a global scale. The primary concern of this theoretical approach is not so much to do with the levels of exploitation and inequality between people as it is with the human impact on the environment. It is argued that capitalistic cultures express two key characteristics that relate to the environment. The first is the prevalence of consumerism. This means that people express a conceptual assumption that quality of life is based upon how much you consume in terms of resources, food, manufactured products, entertainment and so on. The desire to consume without inhibitions means that the planet's resources are increasingly used, leading to environmental degradation and pollution. It is important to note that the planet's resources are finite and, as such, consumption of resources is unequal between people. Some will consume more at the expense of others. The second key characteristic of capitalistic societies of relevance here is the dominant perception that the environment is there to be utilised to meet human demands. This is directly linked to consumerism and results in negative impacts on the environment. The dominance of capitalistic cultures is, therefore, seen to be a negative thing by environmentalists as it entails the encouragement of environmentally damaging practices.

# Global culture

In international relations new dynamics and processes that relate to culture are becoming increasingly important. With regard to more common issues of concern in IPE, such as trade, finance, globalisation and security concerns, culture issues are now seen to be important. This is in terms of the impact of cultural issues in determining the behaviour of state and non-state actors as well as how culture affects other issues such as environmental degradation. As cultural influences have increasingly spread, the interaction of cultures, as opposed to simply the interaction of individuals or groups of people, has become an important determinant of actor behaviour. As noted above, there are many indicators that certain cultures are becoming more dominant than others and the exchange of cultural features is becoming more uni-directional. Western culture can be seen to be imported by non-Western societies at the expense of existing cultures. This is usually termed 'cultural hegemony'.

The spread of cultural influences has been a combination of 'push and pull' factors. The push factors come from historical experience of imperial expansion and the imposition of institutional structures that require certain language skills and other cultural attributes and sensibilities. In order to progress in relation to a dominant, albeit imposed culture, the colonised population needs to assimilate and modify their behaviour to achieve success. To maintain control, imperial powers would often draw from local populations to fill administrative posts, albeit only up to a certain level of authority. It is worth noting that many of the leaders of former colonies had experience of the colonial power's education system, including periods of study at leading European private schools and universities. This facilitated a certain level of indoctrination into the norms and values of elite society of the imperial powers. That said, some of these leaders subsequently adopted harsh authoritarian models of governance. Furthermore, the export of cultures to other societies can be linked to processes of political and economic dominance. For example, English is a widely spoken second language in many parts of the Middle East and French is widely spoken as a second language in many parts of North Africa. The primary language of both of these regions is Arabic. British and French imperialism in the Middle East and North Africa respectively during the 1800s and early 1900s have encouraged the use of these foreign languages.

In terms of pull factors, the processes that lead to cultural hegemony can be related to domestic processes of modernisation and the wilful import of elements of other cultures. The popularity of the late Michael Jackson in many places such as South America and South East Asia is an example of this type of cultural import. Similarly, the growing global audience for football is altering patterns of entertainment consumption in various parts of the world, to the point that Japan and South Korea co-hosted the football World Cup Finals in 2002. American Football also has an increasingly global audience with the annual Super Bowl match receiving the second highest television audience for any sporting event after the football World Cup Final. As an example of a global brand name Manchester United is now recognised in most countries of the world. This is due to the availability of broadcasts, such as those via Sky Sports and also the proliferation of Manchester United merchandise, notably apparel such as T-shirts.

The expansion of the Internet has provided the platform for the spread of ideas and has fuelled the aspiration towards particular cultural forms. This extends well beyond the world of entertainment to the spread of individualism and calls for democratisation. Western democracies have long called for political reforms within more authoritarian regimes. However, the concept of sovereignty and non-intervention remains sacrosanct and the position taken tends to be that popular movements at the local level should drive democratic reform. The Internet has served the dual function of providing a window to the outside world, showing how civil society engages with the political process in liberal democratic systems. It has also facilitated the organisation of pro-democracy movements within non-democratic states. The spread of democracy has become synonymous with other processes of globalisation. Governments in China and Burma, for example, remain firmly non-democratic. Both of these governments heavily filter and censor Internet communications in an effort to maintain their sovereign control.

## Resistance to cultural hegemony

At the same time as there are numerous processes that have led to the emergence of a global culture, there are also differing responses to it. Broadly speaking there tends to be acceptance of or resistance to the exchange of cultures. In the first case, cultural exchanges are seen as positive developments and the emergence of a dominant culture is not necessarily a bad thing. Having similar cultural characteristics can help to develop greater communication, understanding and cooperation between cultures. In the second case, the increasing rates of cultural exchange and the emergence of a dominant culture are seen as undesirable developments. Here, the disruption of existing cultural practices and norms is viewed as damaging to the well-being of the society. Furthermore, there is quite simply a level of resistance to the dominance of other cultures because they are foreign.

Resistance to cultural hegemony is not exclusive to any one culture or society. Instead individuals or groups of individuals in any society may resist forms of cultural exchange or hegemony. Other individuals or groups of people within the same society will, at the same time, welcome cultural exchange. Those who do resist cultural hegemony often express this resistance in non-violent ways. Grassroots movements aimed at raising awareness, supporting existing cultural practices and norms, and 'educating' people on the negative impacts of cultural hegemony are commonplace. Other non-violent practices including the boycott of goods and services that are believed to be too culturally invasive are also evident. For example, the boycott of 'Barbie' dolls in many Islamic societies has come about because of the Western clothing and fashion styles that the dolls come with. These clothes are believed to be too immodest and encourage the import of Western clothing styles to these societies.

Language is often cited as the key indicator of a vibrant and distinct culture. The imposition of non-native languages has already been noted as a central characteristic of embedding colonial power. Many indigenous civil society groups are actively campaigning to reinforce and disseminate traditional cultural skills. For example, Native Languages of America is an NGO that is dedicated to the survival of native American languages. Its website holds a database of material relating to more than 800 such languages. In addition to language skills there are also attempts to preserve and pass on traditional methods of hunting, cooking and craftwork to future generations. Some of these may seem at odds with processes of modernisation and there is often a tension between modern and traditional practices. However, the value of traditional skills can be seen in terms of self-sufficiency and maintaining a distinct cultural identity. For all the benefits of modernisation, many indigenous populations have experienced negative impacts as a result of interaction with the outside world. Difficulties in moving from the traditional to the modern have resulted in social, economic and environmental disruption. Some individuals have assimilated more easily than others. Many indigenous communities have above average incidences of drug and alcohol abuse and high suicide rates among young adults. 'Traditional versus modern' does not have to be an either/or choice. The key issue appears to be one of personal identity and a sense of belonging to a particular community.

Processes of globalisation can be characterised by all manner of impacts on personal interactions. This can be via enhanced transport and communication systems through to the way in which worldviews have expanded as individuals have a greater sense of their place in the world. Sense of place and belonging to a particular piece of territory is an ancient concept harking back to the earliest forms of human civilisation. Even hunter–gatherer societies and nomadic peoples maintained a sense of territory and how far the range of their territories extended. Identity politics has become one of the central features of the study of international relations in recent years. There has been a long-standing focus on what constitutes national identity in relation to the post-Westphalian nation state system. It is now recognised that this is only one aspect of what can be multiple identities that exist simultaneously as part of each individual. Race, class and gender are the traditional aspects that sociologists have highlighted when looking at social structures. These aspects can be added to in terms of many other dimensions, ranging from political or religious beliefs to the neo-tribalism of modern societies that can extend to identifying oneself with a particular musical genre, such as those represented by punks or goths. The latter example may appear somewhat trivial but, for the individuals concerned, this can form an important aspect of self-identification.

As national governments are confronted with processes that appear to be lessening the level of control they command over certain aspects of their affairs, individuals are looking beyond the level of the nation state in terms of cultural identity. National pride can still be evoked at times of war or major international sporting events but beyond that national identity is now simply one of many, rather than the determining factor in forming and maintaining cultural identity. One interesting phenomenon in this regard is the development of the concept of global citizenship. This is a departure from the traditional understanding of citizenship, which would be associated with belonging to a particular national group. As worldviews have broadened there has been a resulting awareness that it is insufficient, even actively dangerous, to assume that the world consists of discrete political units with no conception of broader processes, such as global warming.

The cultural dimensions of global citizenship are extraordinarily complex. On the one hand they involve a recognition that humanity lives on a shared, finite planet and that cooperation is required to meet the common interest of environmental sustainability. Yet in addition to this awareness there is also a recognition that the world is divided by competing worldviews that, in some cases, appear wholly incompatible. This is one of the greatest challenges for conflict resolution. Disputes over territory can be mediated to some extent and political jurisdictions can generally be agreed upon, although some parts of the world do have long-term disputes of this nature. Cultural differences are more difficult to resolve unless one takes the position of cultural relativity and a fair degree of tolerance of counter-views. This generally works between governments where the concept of sovereignty still holds significant meaning and, although some practices may be criticised, there is unlikely to be intervention in the domestic affairs of another state, apart from rare and extreme examples such as the prevention of genocide. With growing multiculturalism within domestic jurisdictions it is in this arena that cultural issues are coming to the fore and presenting some potentially problematic issues.

Tolerance of minority belief systems and behaviours is a growing concern for many societies and their governments. The French government has taken a very direct approach to this issue with the suppression of certain religious and cultural symbolism. This can extend to forms of dress, notably for Muslim women. Ironically this is within a society that maintains a political right to free speech that allows a platform for extreme right-wing groups to present their views, which are often abhorrent to other sectors of French society. The ability to present controversial views is an aspect of the Western system of political freedoms that characterises political liberalism. Such a system can allow the election to the European Parliament of candidates that hold extreme nationalist views and are avowedly anti-EU. This illustrates the level of tolerance that such a system embodies, but it also highlights that tensions remain with various worldviews existing, often with cultural differences at the heart of these disagreements.

There are several other examples where cultural differences can be highlighted with reference to domestic legislation. Dignitas is a Swiss-based organisation that promotes the assistance of suicide for terminally ill patients. This would not be allowed within any of its European neighbours. The issue of abortion is highly charged with emotion and illustrates a rare example of diversity within EU law, for example. Different EU member states have varying laws with regard to this issue, such as the criteria by which an abortion may be legally undertaken and how far into pregnancy this procedure can be conducted. In the United States there is also variance between state legislations. Although not part of the due legal process, it is worth noting that in extreme cases people convicted of murdering doctors who have carried out abortion procedures have claimed a defence of 'justifiable homicide'. There is a marked inconsistency in the logic of a right-to-life campaigner taking a life. However, they would argue a utilitarian position of promoting the greater good by preventing what they would term as feticide. This position is often associated with deeply held religious beliefs.

Resistance to cultural hegemony can also take violent forms. Around the world the targeting and vandalising of symbols of Western culture, such as McDonald's fast food restaurants and Starbuck's cafes, as well as Western banks and shops, occurs during demonstrations or protests. The concept of counter-culture is usually associated with the protest actions of the 1960s: notably the student demonstrations in France, and elsewhere in Europe, and the alternative lifestyle developments of the west coast of the United States around this time. The so-called 'hippy culture' saw the rejection of establishment material consumerism. The stereotype image of this time is one of the promotion of peace and love. That said, this was also the time of more radical confrontational groups such as the Black Panthers and Nation of Islam. Counter-culture in contemporary times maintains some of the anti-establishment ethos but is now taking different forms of protest against different targets. In the 1960s the key targets were national governments and the assumption that 'success' was measured by one's socio-economic position in society. While some of these concerns still remain the protesters at G8 and G20 meetings are now more likely to be highlighting the broader negative consequences of the neo-liberal project. Government policies are still targeted but these are mainly in relation to the extent to which they promote neo-liberal economic policies.

There are also a range of non-state actors that are organised to resist cultural hegemony specifically through violent and armed means. Al-Qaeda is an example of a group that some would argue falls into this category as much of its founding ideology expresses a keen interest in resisting Western cultural dominance of Islamic societies, which some have termed cultural imperialism.

EXAMPLE BOX

## Al-Qaeda, *Charlie Hebdo* and freedom to offend

In January 2015 the Paris offices of the satirical magazine *Charlie Hebdo* were attacked by heavily armed gunmen killing twelve people. The attack was prompted by the publication of cartoons featuring depictions of the prophet Muhammad, which certain groups deemed to be blasphemous and the more extreme elements of these groups calling for violent retribution. This attack echoed the reaction to an earlier controversy in 2005 when the Danish newspaper *Jyllands-Posten* published similar cartoons.

Following these attacks several European heads of government joined a mass demonstration in Paris condemning the killings. The phrase *Je Suis Charlie* (I am Charlie) become the slogan of the protestors. Significantly the following edition of the magazine featured another representation of Muhammad on its cover, and the print run was massively increased from a normal 60,000 to 3 million copies, which were translated into several languages. This incident exemplifies the manner in which aspects of culture can become highly politicised. Reactions ranged from moderate inter-faith groups coming together to condemn the attacks to far-right groups seeking to capitalise on the incident and link it to their anti-immigration arguments. The broader debate related to the degree to which 'free speech' may be taken when various individuals and groups may take offence. It also highlighted a large variation, even within the supposedly largely homogenous Western world, when it comes to legislation that attempts to balance the protection of free speech against what might be considered as incitement to racial or religious intolerance.

## Non-coercive globalisation

The above examples have tended towards oppositional and potentially violent and confrontational dynamics of cultural expansion and resistance. The following examples highlight non-violent but no-less effective means of cultural dominance. These are often implicit rather than explicit forms of persuasion and control. In part they are evidenced in the dominant social norms and values of mainstream culture. Furthermore, these can be represented via various national and international institutions. Mainstream media is also significant in promoting particular cultural values.

Edward Said, drawing on the earlier work of Antonio Gramsci, highlights the significance of social institutions such as education, literature, art and media. Many education departments attempt to impose a national curriculum in schools that reflects a particular viewpoint, especially in relation to national historical narratives. The Textbook Authorisation and Research Council of the Japanese Ministry of Education has faced criticism, particularly from China and Korea, with regard to history textbooks used in Japanese schools which provide a sanitised version of Japan's role and actions during the Second World War. The teaching of one's history is a crucial dimension in identity formation and attitudes towards others. History lessons are important for both what they highlight, and also what they omit. Several countries promote an annual Black History Month to emphasise the particular experiences of the black population. This is important both for the self-awareness and empowerment of black communities as well as inter-race relations more generally. The African American academic Dr John Henrik Clarke (1993) said:

> History is a clock people use to tell their historical culture and political time of the day. It's a compass that people use to find themselves on the map of human geography. The history

tells them where they have been, where they are and what they are. But most importantly history tells a people where they still must go and what they still must be.

This quote applies to all peoples and their cultures. History is seen as a dynamic and unfolding narrative and experience. It is not just about the past but also the present and the future. This is important in the context of processes of globalisation, widespread migration and moves towards multiculturalism. Identity politics is a significant factor in community cohesion and/or conflict.

Both fictional and non-fictional literatures play a role in shaping cultural norms and values. Even novels can play a part in challenging and embedding cultural stereotypes and prejudices. Personal histories such as Maya Angelou's *I Know Why the Caged Bird Sings* or Edward Said's *Out of Place* use the format of autobiography to highlight and critique broader socio-economic and political events they have experienced. Many of these encompass the period of decolonisation and resulting changes in circumstances. Although these are the stories of individuals they tell a broader narrative of their times. These forms of literature represent the 'alternative' voices. They stand out precisely because they are new, critical and often dissenting narratives. They are the exceptions that prove the rule. Mainstream literature, by definition, continues to reinforce the majority view. In the fields of international relations and international political economy the majority of the world's university libraries continue to be stocked with texts written by European and American authors. Even in the field of development studies, authors such as the Egyptian economist Samir Amin are exceptional in representing an authoritative academic voice from the global South. The field of international economics continues to be dominated by traditional neo-liberal thinking and policy prescription.

The field of visual arts has been used for political purposes for centuries. Renaissance figures such as Michelangelo were commissioned by Popes to create works of art. The motivation for such commissions may have been justified in terms of illustrating the 'glory of God'. However, there was also an underlying aspect of self-promotion and legitimisation of the political position enjoyed by the Papacy. Similarly, numerous royal families have commissioned flattering portraits of themselves and their children in addition to grand architectural designs of castles and landscaped gardens, which also symbolise and reinforce their political position. Other examples include the explicit political art of former Soviet Russia and communist China as well as the wartime propaganda of both the Nazi government in Germany and the Allies during the Second World War. Anti-war art can also be cited with examples such as Picasso's *Guernica*. In the private sector nationalist symbolism has been used to promote particular products. A classic example of this is the frequent use of the Stars and Stripes and the American Bald Eagle in the advertising of Harley Davidson motorcycles. This is a form of subliminal advertising linking a product with aspects of patriotism. One of the company's advertising slogans is 'Free to Ride'. This can be read as symbolising the political freedoms enjoyed in the United States.

The role of the media is arguably the most influential factor in promoting aspects of cultural expansion in an implicit rather than actively explicit manner. Here the media is referred to in its broadest form including print, broadcast and Internet-based news services. In addition, music, film and television are all important conduits by which audiences receive various messages that either challenge or, more commonly, reinforce cultural stereotypes and resulting attitudes. The very act of news reporting, and the role of the editor, is crucial in determining what issues constitute 'news' and also the way in which stories are presented with emphasis placed on certain features that can slant a story in a particular way. News stories are often geared towards perceived audiences, usually along national lines. Editorial adages include 'sex sells' and 'if it bleeds, it leads'. This reflects either an accurate assessment of readers' and viewers' interests and tastes, or an active manipulation of the audience. If it is the latter then one might wonder what the motivation for this might be. Conspiracy theorists, and various neo-Marxists, would consider this as an example of a sinister plot to distract citizens from more pertinent stories about power structures and how they are maintained. For example, political demonstrations are often only covered if violence breaks out. Even then the angle taken on the story is one of disruption to law and order rather than whatever the protest was about.

Michael Moore's film *Bowling for Columbine* (2003) includes an insightful analysis of the role of the media from US rock singer Marilyn Manson:

> [T]hat's not the way the media wants to take it and spin it, and turn it into fear, because then you're watching television, you're watching the news, you're being pumped full of fear. There's floods, there's AIDS, there's murder, cut to commercial, buy the Acura, buy the Colgate, if you have bad breath they're not going to talk to you, if you have pimples, the girl's not going to fuck you, and it's just this campaign of fear, and consumption, and that's what I think it's all based on, the whole idea of 'keep everyone afraid, and they'll consume'.

Fear and consumption is certainly something that can be identified in the dominant culture of the recent past. The Western alliance has had a fear of the spread of communism followed by a perceived clash of civilisations and the so-called 'war on terror'. In each case the response has been to highlight consumerism as either an escape from this fear or as an example of the rightness of the 'Western way'. There are strong vested interests to promote this negative climate. In 1961 US President Dwight D. Eisenhower warned of what he described as the military–industrial complex. This referred to the self-serving agendas of both the armed services and the private sector. The media also plays a significant role in both reinforcing fears by emphasising bad news, and also providing a platform for the advertising industry. The entertainment industry plays a role in the evolution of popular culture, although there is an ongoing debate surrounding the extent to which behaviours may, or may not, be influenced by the consumption of images and text. This is particularly pertinent to the issue of violence in society. The 'flower power' era of the late 1960s referred to above was relatively short-lived and films, television and popular songs have generally gravitated towards the representation, possibly even promotion, of a more individualised and competitive culture and society.

When trends in globalisation are referred to they are usually couched in terms of the spread of mass consumerism. More specifically patterns of consumption are geared towards the personal acquisition of goods. Furthermore, these goods are rarely one-off lifetime purchases. Many manufacturers adopt an approach of built-in obsolescence whereby goods are deliberately designed to have a relatively short period of productive use. The incentive, of course, is that when the product breaks or simply wears out the consumer will need to make another purchase to replace it. In addition there is also the issue of what is considered fashionable at any given time, with perfectly functional items being discarded if they are no longer in vogue. Advertising campaigns can play a major role in shaping consumer choices but this does not mean that there will necessarily be a drive to persuade people to all buy the same products. Far from it, as diversifying markets, and even producing competition between consumers who may favour differing brand names for similar products, actually expands markets still further. The 'culture' of mass consumption does not necessarily mean that there are shared norms, values or preferred tastes. Great cultural diversity can exist within what might be termed the 'mega-culture' of neo-liberalism. The key elements of the arguments surrounding 'cultural imperialism' are more to do with lifestyle aspirations than political or religious ideologies or traditional cultural norms and values.

The so-called triumph of liberalism is normally referred to in terms of the rights of individuals to vote in a form of democracy and the apparent success of free-marketeering over interventionist command economies. The latter point is open to greater dispute following the overextension of credit facilities and the resulting downturn in the majority of the world's economies. Despite this caveat, the emphasis in both the political and economic fields is at the level of the individual rather than the wider community, and both are also more associated with short-term rather than longer-term perceptions. In the political case one is asked to vote for a politician for a relatively short term of office, perhaps four to five years. The assumption is that if one is not content with that person's performance they can be quickly replaced. There is also a temporal dimension to the economic sphere. Capitalism as a philosophy of economic accumulation can be seen to have longer-term goals, as in maintaining and ideally increasing the amount of available capital. Of course this is simply based on the artificial value given to particular currencies and commodities. The 'true' costs of goods, as in the social and environmental capital costs, are rarely calculated. This is one of the great concerns for many critics, especially green theorists, of the spread of mass consumerism and a culture of individual-based consumerist desires that do not take wider community and environmental costs into account and are, therefore, fundamentally non-sustainable.

## Summary

Post-Cold War, the so-called 'triumph' of liberalism has led to the spread of Western culture to virtually all parts of the world. This is not to say that it has been wholly embraced everywhere. As noted above, it is also resisted, in some cases violently. The Westminster model of democracy has been described as an inappropriate colonial imposition at odds with traditional decision-making processes, for example in Fiji where this argument was used as a partial justification for the over-throw of a democratically elected government in 1987. Western styles of dress and behaviour are considered immodest and actively offensive in many cultures, although trends continue to be towards growing Westernisation. The issue of culture has come to the fore in both the study and practice of international political economy. Traditional security concerns remain firmly on the international agenda, but security issues are increasingly being linked to factors that are cultural in origin.

This chapter has highlighted a broad range of cultural issues and the manner in which they influence the evolution of both domestic and international relations. The issue of multicultural-ism, by its very existence, questions the extent to which there is some sort of monolithic, hegem-onic global culture emerging. However, it is possible to identify some key attitudes and trends, which can be said to represent aspects of Western culture that are, at least, having impacts on other cultures around the world. Neo-liberalism has spread around the world, but with varying degrees of acceptance. China is the classic example of a state experiencing the impact of processes of glo-balisation, but attempting to manage this as far as possible on its own terms. It has largely accepted neo-liberal economic policies while maintaining a strong central political authority. It also retains a very keen sense of its own cultural heritage, as do many societies. Traditional cultural values can be very resilient. Some have even experienced a level of resurgence in the face of challenges from alternative norms and values.

The argument surrounding the possibility of a global monoculture tends to miss two crucial points. First is the strength and resilience of non-Western cultures to maintain a clear sense of their own cultural identity. Second is the fact that it is not that dominant cultural norms and values are being disseminated to other cultures that is the primary issue. Rather it is that the Western culture of individualism and mass consumerism is having an impact on the rest of the world due to depletion of resources, polluting impacts on a global scale and military actions to ensure access to overseas resources.

**Table 11.1** Chapter summary

| | Key actors | Key processes | Emphasis on political economy | What causes change? | Global institutions? | View of conflict in global relations? |
|---|---|---|---|---|---|---|
| Mono-culturalism | Potential influences from governments, religious groups and other bodies that promote a particular set of cultural beliefs and practices – and the restriction or exclusion of others | Monoculture may be maintained simply due to isolation and lack of interaction with other cultures, although processes of globalisation make this level of isolation increasingly rare. It is more likely to be a conscious choice of a culture to identify itself in opposition to other cultural influences and attempt to distance the members of its community from other, differing, sets of norms, values and practices | The level of political involvement in determining cultural issues varies considerably. Some states enact laws that require certain cultural traditions to be legally adhered to and other 'foreign' influences rejected. In economic terms this may lead to a more coherent and, arguably, more efficient society and economy. The counter argument to this is that such policies risk isolationism and missed opportunities to trade internationally | By definition monoculturalism tends to be relatively static and less dynamic and open to change. Change is more likely to arise due to external forces rather than from within such a culture | There are few institutions that can claim to be fully monocultural. Even something as dogmatic as the Roman Catholic church encompasses variations between different dioceses. Some institutions do have agreed rules that all members are expected to abide by, such as the UN or the World Trade Organization, but even here it is still possible to highlight differences between members | Monocultures necessarily identify themselves in relation to other cultures that do not share their views and practices. While that may appear to be a recipe for conflict this does not have to be the case. The concept of cultural relativism and a degree of tolerance towards other cultures can avoid such conflict. This is a very controversial issue though and there are constant debates on how far tolerance should extend before another's cultural practice is deemed unacceptable |

**Table 11.1** Continued

| | Key actors | Key processes | Emphasis on political economy | What causes change? | Global institutions? | View of conflict in global relations? |
|---|---|---|---|---|---|---|
| Multi-culturalism | Government policies can actively promote multiculturalism. It is also assisted by the movement and mixing of people, diaspora maintaining aspects of their culture in host communities and a general willingness of communities to engage with different literature, music, cuisine and other aspects of multiculturalism | Many processes lead to interactions between and the mixing of cultures. Sometimes this can be actively assisted and others it is a more natural process of mixing and hybridisation as various cultures evolve and draw on influences from other cultures | Multiculturalism tends to emerge as a result of 'natural' processes of migration and cross-fertilisation of cultures rather than via direct government intervention. However, governments can play a role in outlawing discrimination on the grounds of race, religious beliefs and other cultural practices. Economically multiculturalism fosters greater links to other countries and can facilitate increased levels of trading | In contrast to monoculturalism a more diverse cultural mix is likely to be in a state of constant evolution as different cultural influences and practices react to each other, mix and hybrid forms emerge | There is no single institution that would claim to represent multiculturalism. Some, and again the UN can be cited here, will say that despite having agreed rules and practices these can operate with respect for different cultural norms, beliefs and practices. UNESCO is an example of a body that actively promotes multiculturalism | The 'clash of civilisations' thesis suggests that current and future conflicts are more likely to be driven by cultural differences, rather than traditional border disputes or control of resources. Some commentators would still agree with this, citing conflicts at both the domestic and global levels. There has even been reference made to the 'failure of multiculturalism'. |

## Reflective questions

1   What role do cultural factors play in influencing and shaping processes of globalisation?
2   Outline what you understand by the term 'cultural imperialism'.
3   How do forms of resistance to cultural hegemony manifest themselves?
4   Does globalisation only relate to certain global 'brands', or can this also extend to personal behaviour?
5   How important are social media platforms in shaping cultural values and norms?

## Suggestions for further reading

Ali, T. (2002) *The Clash of Fundamentalisms: Crusades, Jihads and Modernity*, London: Verso.

Angelou, M. (1984) *I Know Why the Caged Bird Sings*, London: Virago Press.

Anheier, H. and Yudhishthir, R.I. (2007) *Conflicts and Tensions*, London: Sage.

Appadurai, A. (1996) *Modernity at Large: Cultural Dimensions of Globalization*, Minnesota, MN: University of Minneapolis Press.

Bhabha, H. (1994) *The Location of Culture*, London: Routledge.

Chabal, P. and Daloz, J.P. (2006) *Culture Troubles: Politics and the Interpretation of Meaning*, London: C. Hurst & Co.

Clarke, J.H. (1993) *African People in World History*, Baltimore, MD: Black Classic Press.

Mikula, M. (2008) *Key Concepts in Cultural Studies*, New York: Palgrave.

Moore, M. (2003) *Bowling for Columbine*, London: Momentum Pictures.

Mudimbe-Boyi, E. (2002) *Beyond Dichotomies: Histories, Identities, Cultures and the Challenge of Globalization*, Albany, NY: State University of New York Press.

Reeves, J. (2004) *Culture and International Relations: Narratives, Natives and Tourists*, London: Routledge.

Said, E. (1994) *Culture and Imperialism*, London: Vintage.

Said, E. (1999) *Out of Place: A Memoir*, London: Granta Publications.

Said, E. (2003) *Orientalism*, London: Penguin Books.

Tomlinson, J. (2001) *Cultural Imperialism*, London: Continuum.

Zank, W. (ed.) (2009) *Clash of Cooperation of Civilisations: Overlapping Integration and Identities*, Farnham: Ashgate.

# 12 Security

## Chapter learning outcomes

After reading this chapter students should be able to:

- Understand changes in security studies from a narrow agenda focused on inter-state war to a much broader range of issues.
- Understand and be able to explain the emergence of 'new' security issues in international relations and IPE in the latter half of the twentieth century including the emergence of nuclear weapons, environmental change and related issues, identity politics and the rising power of MNCs.
- Comprehend contemporary processes of change linked to globalisation that is leading to the emergence of more security issues including water, energy and food security, migration and demographic change, capital movements and financial crises, the revolution in military affairs and international terrorism.
- Explain how security issues are no longer simply state- and military-centric.
- Relate discussion of security to the theoretical debates discussed earlier in this book.

## Introduction

This chapter is designed to relate to the previous chapters in the context of a dynamic, contentious and evolving set of security agendas. Whereas many IR textbooks will focus on state- and military-centric security, the distinctive nature of IPE approaches, as opposed to IR, means that they tend to adopt a broader interpretation and analysis of security issues. This is the approach taken here. The discussion in this chapter demonstrates the evolution of the study of security issues from traditional analyses to much broader ones that consider both state and non-state actors as having security interests, and that take account of a range of issues. During the latter half of the twentieth century processes of globalisation, technological and industrial development, environmental change and demographic growth, among others, led to the emergence of critical security studies. This field of study has been characterised by a shift away from the dominance of the billiard-ball model of international relations. This model, as was discussed in Chapter 1, sees states as the only important unit of analysis in IR/IPE and power and military security as their primary concern. Furthermore, this model of understanding and explaining assumes that states are unitary and rational egoistic actors, meaning that, in effect, everything that goes on inside the state (the agency of individuals, MNCs, NGOs and so on) is irrelevant to security studies.

A different model to understanding security has come to dominate this area of IPE. This model has developed as a result of the emergence of critical security studies (Booth, 2004) and can be seen to offer a dramatically different approach to the billiard-ball model. While the state is still seen as a primary actor in international political economy and international relations, other actors are acknowledged. This is done in two ways: first, by acknowledging that non-state actors do have significant degrees of agency and, therefore, can impact upon security issues (whether these be traditional military security issues or others). Second, it is acknowledged that non-state actors themselves have legitimate security concerns and thus deserve attention. At the same time as critical security studies sees a plurality of actors as constituting a main element in security studies, the range of issues that are considered is much larger than the limited set of issues in traditional security studies. In short, what actually constitutes 'security' and what threats to this security there are has drastically changed. Critical security studies does not only see military security as being important. Instead, security has come to denote a vast range of issues, which still includes military security but also a range of other issues. The emergence of revised forms of security studies has been caused by developments in both the academic fields of IR and later IPE, as well as events and processes that have unfolded in the real world.

This chapter outlines some of these developments and explores some of the most important security issues in terms of international political economy. The following section thus explores processes following the Second World War and how they created 'new' security challenges for state and non-state actors. The second section deals with key issues in the contemporary era and how they relate to some of the topics discussed in earlier chapters. This is followed by a conclud-ing section that summarises the main points.

# The development of 'new' security issues

## The nuclear era

Towards the end of the Second World War the United States was able to develop and use nuclear technology in the form of atomic bombs. The scale of the destruction that these weapons brought has few equivalents in human history. The firebombing of Dresden during the Second World War is a comparable event. However, the ability to destroy entire cities with a single bomb changed the nature of warfare and the meaning of military security. One of the most significant ways in which nuclear weapons changed military security relates to the range of actors involved in any military security dynamic (Hough, 2013). As other states developed nuclear weapons and the technology itself advanced and more powerful weapons were created, military security for the vast majority of states throughout the world was altered. The context of the Cold War meant that there was a bipolar world system and the threat of conflict between the two poles and their allies could be felt practically everywhere. This was combined with the destructive power and damaging effects of nuclear weapons (which through the 1960s and 1970s were proliferating) to mean that military security interdependence on a global scale developed. The notion of mutually assured destruction (MAD) existed not just for the nuclear-armed belligerents of any conflict, but also for many states that may be impacted also. In Europe, for example, Germany, France and the UK would most likely have been the first states to have been hit with nuclear weapons in the event of a break-out of nuclear war between the United States and the USSR. Security studies had to evolve to take account of the changing intensity of military security and the rising levels of interdependence this created.

Since the late 1990s the issue of nuclear weapons proliferation has been at the forefront of much international relations (Buzan *et al.*, 2007). The UN Security Council, for example, has focused on this issue as one of the key threats to global instability. The 1998 detonation of a nuclear warhead as part of a test by India and the subsequent Pakistani detonation announced the arrival of the two South Asian rivals as nuclear-weapons-capable states (both tests were conducted underground). While nuclear weapons proliferation has been managed and controlled in most regions of the world, North Korea has been able to develop a nuclear weapons programme and has manufactured up to a dozen nuclear bombs. North Korea's capability was demonstrated in late 2006 with the successful underground detonation of a nuclear weapon. Iran's nuclear programme has been the focus of much scrutiny, with the International Atomic Energy Agency reporting that the programme appears to be for civilian use but also that some research and development into a weapons programme was taking place up until the early 2000s. There is much suspicion and mistrust between the international community and Iran over whether or not the latter is secretly pursuing nuclear weapons. Iran in turn seems to be demonstrating signs of greater insecurity as the West, led by the United States and Israel, put more pressure on the Iranian government to stop some of its nuclear activity. Whether or not some states are pursuing nuclear weapons programmes or will do so in the future, the security challenge of nuclear proliferation remains a key issue on the global security agenda.

International cooperation and coordination is evident, however, in seeking to manage existing nuclear weapons stockpiles and the ability of non-nuclear states to develop nuclear weapons (see Table 12.1). On 8 April 2010 US President Barak Obama and Russian President Dmitry Medvedev signed a new Strategic Arms Reduction Treaty (START) in Prague, Czech Republic. The treaty replaces the previous START II agreement, which expired at the end of 2009 and facilitates the reduction of both states' current nuclear weapons by one-third from approximately 2,600 for Russia and 2,126 for the United States to around 1,550 for both. The treaty also requires both states to reduce by one-third the long-range delivery systems (missiles) for nuclear weapons, allows for a vigorous inspection structure and mechanisms for further coordination in non-proliferation activities. The reductions in weapons will take up to seven years to implement and the treaty should be viewed as part of a broader process of reducing nuclear weapons stockpiles globally and preventing the development of nuclear weapon technology in other states. Just four days after the new START was signed, President Obama hosted a two-day summit on nuclear security in Washington in which forty-seven states were represented. The gathering was by far the most comprehensive international meeting on nuclear security held to date and was focused on the dual issues of reducing nuclear weapons and non-proliferation.

At the same time as nuclear technology was being used for the creation of weapons, this technology was being harnessed for energy production in many states. Use of nuclear technology to produce energy can be very cheap and efficient, making it desirable for national governments and private energy sectors. However, it also produces nuclear waste from spent radioactive fuel as well as polluted water and other material. Nuclear waste is highly radioactive and contaminated and it can take hundreds of thousands of years for the radiation to be reduced to safe levels. Nuclear

**Table 12.1**   2015 Estimated global nuclear warhead inventories

| Country | Warheads |
| --- | --- |
| USA | 7,100 |
| UK | 225 |
| France | 300 |
| Israel | 80 |
| Pakistan | 110 |
| India | 100 |
| Russia | 7,700 |
| China | 250 |
| North Korea | 10 |

*Source*: Arms Control Association Fact Sheet, October 2015, www.armscontrol.org/print/2566.

energy is generally quite safe as long as nuclear material, energy plants and so on are monitored and maintained constantly. However, nuclear energy production can lead to radiation leaks and environmental damage, which are harmful to humans. These facts have caused much concern for human and environmental security. In essence, the threat of nuclear contamination can often be just as significant to individuals and groups of people as, say, the threat of war.

## Global environmental agenda

As is discussed in Chapter 9, the environment has become a key area of consideration in IPE. In particular, environmental change and the impacts this has on the human condition have, for many scholars, become central to the study of international relations and international political economy. The environment emerged as an issue in the era after the Second World War as a result of two processes. The first was an intellectual and anthropocentric development. During the 1950s and 1960s intellectual debates in IR were still centred on military security, power and state relations. However, small spaces had begun to open up for debate on other issues relevant to the human world. The environment was one of the topics that benefited from this development. The second process was environmental. Two centuries of industrialisation in Europe and North America, as well as elsewhere, had begun to take its toll on the environment and impacts of human activity were beginning to be noticed. At the same time, demographic growth and urban sprawl meant that people around the world were being affected by the environment in different ways. Regardless, it was not until the 1970s that intellectual attention was really given to environmental issues. Many changes in the environment were being witnessed and recorded including deforestation, climate change, pollution and droughts, to mention just a few.

Studies conducted and conferences held (see Chapter 9) began to highlight that the planet's environment and resources were finite, that humans rely quite precariously on these and that the environment was changing significantly. For many, these realisations began to underpin other security issues such as military security and war. People and governments since the 1970s have had to consider environmental threats to their security and well-being. Climate change, for example, is taking place and has resulted in changes to the human condition for many. Perhaps one of the best examples is that of small island states in the Pacific Ocean, which have seen sea levels rise to the extent that their lands are being swallowed by the ocean. Security from invasion by another state is not a central concern when your very land is disappearing beneath the waves. IPE is essentially a discipline that is driven by intellectual debates and real world issues. Environmental change has become a major issue in the 'real world' and so has shaped intellectual debates. This has also contributed to the development of critical security studies and the relative shift away from state- and military-centric security studies.

## Identity politics

As is discussed in Chapter 4, the modern world has seen the intensification of processes of integration in the political, economic, security, environmental and socio-cultural realms. These processes combined are termed globalisation and have increased in pace quite significantly since the end of the Second World War. Perhaps an area that has begun to receive most attention since the end of the Cold War is integration in the socio-cultural sphere. Here, there are a number of processes taking place that are resulting in greater interaction, integration and conflict between different socio-cultural groups. In the first instance, the proliferation of forms of mass media and the domination of these mediums by Western, largely American, products is leading to what can be seen as cultural homogenisation. Western clothing, music, movies, sports and other forms of social expression can be found in practically every society and are fast becoming more popular than other cultures' counterparts. Second, the mass movement of people around the world in the form of temporary travel (for example, for business trips or holidays) as well as more permanent forms of migration are resulting in increased interaction between socio-cultural groups. The effects of these processes are sometimes to increase understanding, familiarity and diversity in societies, thus altering communal identities. On the other hand, cultural imports and migration can lead to friction between communities.

Advancements in technology for travel and communication as well as increases in availability of mass media since the 1970s have been coupled with increasing economic and political integration. The human world has, as a result, changed quite dramatically. Societies around the world are becoming eclectic and diverse, and now share common features with others. The impact on European societies, for example, has been quite dramatic as Europeans themselves have integrated with each other extensively and as immigration from Africa and Asia has rapidly increased. Questions of national and regional identity now feature very high on political agendas in European governments and in central EU institutions. Meanwhile, some communities have resisted (sometimes violently) Western cultural influences. Afghanistan under the Taliban during the 1990s and early 2000s would be a case in point here. Questions of Afghani or Islamic identity being eroded are often cited as key elements in the Taliban's ideology and as significant considerations in the motivations of groups such as Al-Qaeda and, more recently, Islamic State (ISIS). In much the same way as the emergence of nuclear technology and the occurrence of environmental change, issues of identity politics have had a direct impact on security studies, altering perceptions of what constitutes security, what threats there are to it and for which actors.

## The rise of MNCs

Multinational corporations have existed and operated in the global economy for quite some time. However, only in the last few decades have MNCs been major players in international political economy (Ohmae, 1999). The number of MNCs has increased extremely rapidly since the 1950s and the scale of their operations has also increased. MNCs operate in virtually every economic sector in the global economy and account for a very large percentage of global trade (some studies conclude that more than half of world trade is carried out by MNCs). Furthermore, many MNCs have become so large and prosperous that they have larger annual GDP turnovers than most states. Somewhere in the region of half of the largest economies in the world are actually MNCs, not states. The meteoric rise of the MNC in the last half century or so has affected many aspects of the global economy and of international relations. For example, MNCs are key components in the health of the global economy and are largely responsible for the maintenance of economic growth. Because many MNCs have become so large and important actors in their own right, intellectual debates have, since the 1970s, viewed MNCs as actors in their own right. More traditional approaches (especially realism) still view MNCs as merely elements of states. In either perception, MNCs are studied as important features of the modern world.

Yet MNCs are not only seen as economic actors engaged in business activities. They are also seen through the prism of security studies. In the first instance, the security of MNCs is increasingly considered in critical security studies – usually in terms of the economic well-being of companies and financial stability, but also in more traditional, physical security terms. Second, the influence MNCs have on other forms of security has become increasingly important. MNCs, for example, manufacture weapons and supply national militaries with services. This directly influences national military security. In other cases, MNCs actually engage in warfare themselves, either on behalf of states or in more controversial scenarios on behalf of themselves of other non-state actors. In terms of economic security, MNCs (whether seen in state-centric or pluralist ways) are important to other actors. National economies rely heavily on MNCs for investment, employment, economic activity, goods and services. The security of national economies, therefore, is directly related to MNCs. Governments are often willing to offer financial aid to MNCs that are struggling in order to safeguard the health of the wider economy. MNCs also directly impact environmental security as well, in both positive and negative ways. Pollution and environmental degradation are often caused by large MNCs and so they can be seen to have a major impact on environmental security. Through the development of cleaner technologies or problem-solving technologies, MNCs can also be seen to be remedying environmental problems and so providing environmental security. Critical security studies has been deeply influenced by debates on MNCs and the actual agency of such entities in international political economy.

## Emerging issues

### Water, energy and food security

Over the past century the global human population has seen very rapid growth, from approximately 1.6 billion in 1900 to over 7 billion in 2015. The rapid expansion in population has placed increasing pressures on energy and food requirements (Homer-Dixon, 2001). The dual processes of urbanisation and industrialisation, which have been seen most dramatically in Europe, North America and South East Asia but that have also taken place to some extent in virtually all states, have also led to greater need for both energy and food. Furthermore, advancements in healthcare and medicine now mean that most societies around the world have longer life expectancies than they did at the start of the twentieth century. Combined, rapid demographic growth, industrialisation, urbanisation and longer life expectancies have meant that demand for energy and food has often exceeded supply in some areas. On a global scale, there is no overall shortage of either energy or food; however, the political economy of both of these sectors has led to chronic shortages as a result of unequal distribution of resources.

During the 1970s the two oil shocks of 1973–1974 and 1979–1980 resulted in fuel shortages in much of North America and Western Europe, as well as elsewhere. The 1973–1974 period was the first time in the modern era that the industrialised world's overall demand for fuel was not met by available supplies. This was followed by fuel shortages in less-developed states also. In the early 2000s fossil fuel production in the form of oil, gas and coal has steadily increased as new sources have been discovered and developed and as facilities have been upgraded. For example, oil production totalled roughly 45 million barrels per day in the 1960s and 1970s whereas current production totals around 80 million barrels per day. Similar increases in the production of gas and coal have also been seen. Thus, supply of fossil fuels has increased quite significantly since the 1970s. However, demand for energy has soared at an even faster rate. The rise of South East Asian economies, rapid and expansive industrialisation in China and India and economic development in South America, the Middle East and Africa have led to increases in demand for energy. As demand increases, so does competition for the limited amount of energy resources available.

One result has been increases in the international price of oil, gas and coal. A second result has been greater energy insecurity and the creation of national policies to combat this. Many states are now seeking to invest in new sources of energy such as large-scale oil and gas exploration in the Caspian Sea region, the Arctic and the Gulf of Mexico. Other policies aimed at energy security include the development of new technologies and renewable energy sources. Increasingly, states are developing wind power farms, solar power fields and hydroelectricity infrastructure in order to meet energy shortfalls. European Union states, for example, have begun to really harness wind power. Spain and Germany now each generate somewhere in the region of 5,000 MW of wind power annually, which represents approximately 12 and 8 per cent of total electricity supply respectively. The EU as a whole now gets around 4 per cent of its energy needs from wind power and a recent report suggests Europe's wind power potential could fuel the Union several times over. Meanwhile, states in the oil- and gas-rich Middle East are expanding solar power capabilities. Even Saudi Arabia, which possesses the world's largest reserves of crude oil, is beginning to consider expanding its solar power infrastructure. Importantly, Saudi Arabia, along with other Arabian Peninsula states, receives as much solar energy in a single year as all the energy value of all the known reserves of oil, gas and coal in the world – harnessing this energy would provide much energy security for many states. Nuclear energy is also being developed as an alternative or in addition to fossil fuels.

During 2007–2008 world food prices rapidly increased, causing a global food crisis that negatively hit both developed and developing states alike. There were a number of causes of the price increases including rises in oil prices, multiple severe droughts around the world, increased demand due to demographic growth and expanding dietary demands due to increased wealth (Garrison *et al.*, 2009). Whatever the causes of the crisis, its impact was to highlight issues of food security for most societies. Unrest and instability spread throughout many states as people protested against high food prices and limited food stocks. However, there was little national governments could do in the short term. Policies have been created and implemented to secure food supplies by some more prosperous states. Rich states are buying millions of acres of arable land in poorer states, mostly in Africa, central Asia and Eastern Europe, and using the produce exclusively for their own domestic consumption. This has led to fears that as some states secure land in others to ensure their own food security, the food security of the states in which the land and rights to the produce are bought will be hurt. This is especially the case with regard to African states, which already have difficulty in feeding their own populations but that need the economic investment.

---

**EXAMPLE BOX**

## The GCC and international farm purchases

The Gulf Cooperation Council (GCC) states (Bahrain, Kuwait, Oman, Qatar, Saudi Arabia and the United Arab Emirates (UAE)) have witnessed growing food insecurity. Due to the lack of water and arable land these states have to purchase the vast majority of their food supplies from abroad. The food price crisis of 2007–2008 resulted in huge increases in the GCC's food bill, which topped $20 billion in 2008. In response, these states have purchased agricultural land and food production rights around the world. The UAE, for example, has invested heavily in Sudan, and Saudi Arabia has invested in Ethiopia. Future investments are sought in the Philippines, Madagascar and Kazakhstan to name a few.

These purchases have raised concerns in the food producing states that domestic food supplies will be reduced and concerns in the GCC states that their food security is reliant on the security of farms thousands of miles away. However, in the majority of cases, as has happened in Sudan, the GCC investment is to bring online new arable land and not to simply purchase the rights to existing farms.

Access to fresh water has also become a major global security issue. Fresh water sources are decreasing overall because of a number of factors. Pollution of river and lake systems, growing demand from larger populations and industrialisation, and climate change have led to major water shortages. In many states access to fresh water has never been guaranteed for the entire population due to a lack of infrastructure and limited supplies. In others, fresh water supplies are often disrupted and are not reliable. Yet even in states that have traditionally had plenty of fresh water due to climatic conditions, shortages in recent years have been witnessed. Thomas Homer-Dixon suggests that conflict over fresh water shortages will be the primary cause of international conflict in the twenty-first century. Indeed, conflicts over water sources have already been seen in arid regions across Africa and Asia. The issue of fresh water rights in the West Bank and Jordan Valley have complicated the Palestinian–Israeli conflict and contributed to the failure to achieve a lasting peace there.

It is certainly the case that energy and food security have become national and global issues of great importance. The threat to the security of states and peoples of not having enough energy and/or food has increased significantly in recent decades and policy making has reflected this. It also seems that in many circumstances energy and food insecurity is a zero-sum game where one state's security comes at the expense of another in the competition for limited energy and food resources.

## Migration

In the modern world the migration of people from one state to another and from one region to another has taken place at increasingly high rates (Castle, 2013). The international movement of people in the early twenty-first century far surpasses previous trends. Demographic growth has meant that populations have become so large that people have often had to migrate to another part of the planet in order to secure resources for survival. This also happened on a large scale during the eighteenth and nineteenth centuries when European expansion and colonialism relieved some of the population pressures on resources in Europe. A more contemporary example can be found in Sudan where nomadic and settled communities in the western province of Darfur have come into conflict over territory as their populations grow.

At the same time as demographic pressures are causing more migration, advancements in transport technology have encouraged and facilitated the mass movement of people. The development and proliferation of air travel has drastically reduced travelling times and costs around the world. It is now possible to travel via airplane to the other side of the planet in a little over a day and at relatively cheap prices. Several decades ago long-distance international travel was mostly limited to sea transports and to the segments of society that could afford quite high costs. This helped limit the movement of people around the planet. However, air transport allows people to move quite quickly and cheaply, meaning that travel is open to broader sections of society and not just the elite. At the same time, developments in rail and vehicular transport have provided the means for people to travel internationally. In the case of the former, the creation of large international rail networks has facilitated migration. Furthermore, new technologies such as the magnetic levitation rail allow for trains to travel at relatively fast speeds of up to 550 km per hour and with the potential to travel at faster speeds than commercial aircraft. With regard to vehicular transport, the proliferation of car ownership in most societies has increased mobility.

The technological developments that have allowed for greater movement of people have been utilised for both temporary and more permanent migration. People from different states and societies increasingly travel abroad on short business or holiday trips. This form of migration can be very profitable for many tourism markets and is largely encouraged. However, tensions between societies do arise as a result of this form of migration. Very few states now have entirely homogeneous populations and most populations possess minorities, which have formed out of immigration. Hispanic immigration into the United States, for example, since the Second World War has resulted in a significant part of the US population (around 15 per cent).

While many of us will likely agree that diversity and cosmopolitanism in our societies has many positive benefits, there are many who would highlight the problems that can arise from rapid migration. For many societies cultural homogeneity is key to communal identity. The Taliban-led government in Afghanistan during the 1990s, for example, formulated a set of laws that prohibited the use of television sets, radios and published media. The purpose of these laws was to limit the influence of Western and other non-Islamic/Afghani cultures on Afghan society. Likewise, the immigration of people that were not Muslims into Afghanistan was discouraged and limited. Even in states that are seen to be culturally diverse and accepting there can be many tensions between citizens and immigrants. Racially motivated crimes are of concern in the UK and other EU states.

Another impact of contemporary processes and patterns of migration is related to illegal activities. Policing and regulation of societies and law enforcement are often complicated and made more difficult by the mobility of individuals. Managing the movement of criminals, contraband and so on has become a major challenge for national governments and international institutions. A crime may be committed in one state and the perpetrators travel to another quite easily. Illegal activities of all kinds, but especially the movement of contraband such as drugs, weaponry and stolen property, are no longer restricted by time and space to small areas. Poppy seeds used to produce opium can be grown in the mountains of Afghanistan, transported through Iran and on to Europe, North America and elsewhere at low cost and in short periods of time. Stopping these operations is very difficult. A major concern of the United States is preventing 'terrorists' from entering the country with weaponry and carrying out attacks.

## Financial crises and capital movements

A salient feature of the modern global economic system is the liberalised and dynamic movement of capital from one market to another and from one investment to another. Capital (as in money supplies) has become truly global and no longer restricted to single markets. A capital investor based in one state may wish to invest the capital in practically any market in the world and for almost any endeavour. Most national governments, international institutions and even private sector actors do not now possess the ability to control capital entirely and in many circumstances they have no control at all. The owners of capital, of course, do possess such abilities. As the capitalist global economy intensifies and becomes even more embedded and as trade in goods and services continues to be further liberalised, capital becomes even more mobile. Many observers see the free movement of capital from one market to another as a very positive and healthy characteristic of the global economy. After all, classical liberal economic thinking (which in many ways forms the basis of the structure of the global economy) claims that the purpose of capital is to generate profits, and even more capital. In order to maximise profits, capital will seek the most efficient and productive use for it, therefore rewarding sound economic endeavours and generating greater economic growth and prosperity. By removing governmental controls on where and when capital can be invested or removed, capital is allowed to be as useful and profitable as it can be.

There are also those observers who do not advocate classical liberal economic theory and who see the liberalisation of capital movement as a very negative and damaging aspect of the global economic system. In this view, if capital is allowed to be invested for any economic purpose (as long as it is legal) and in any market, this can lead to economic growth. However, capital investment may also harm the local community and environment, for example, in the creation of factories and polluting industry. At the same time, if capital can just as easily be removed as it is invested then this detracts from economic security in the market in which it is invested. Furthermore, this freedom of movement allows capital to, in a sense, instigate a 'race to the bottom' as markets compete with each other for the capital investment. Markets will make themselves seem as desirable and profitable as possible to the owners of capital in order to out-bid their competitors. Providing capital investors with tax breaks, exemption from labour and environmental protection laws, and other forms of preferential treatment in order to attract it can lead to damaging effects for the people and environment. Even once the capital investment is secured, the threat of the capital moving to another market at any time is constant.

One of the clearest examples of such fears being realised is the Asian financial crisis of 1997–1998. On 2 July 1997 Thailand's baht began to rapidly devalue. The Thai currency suffered an almost 20 per cent devaluation over a two-month period after Thailand started to suffer from large speculative attacks and the bankruptcy of its largest finance company, Finance One. The first devaluation of the Thai baht was soon followed by devaluations of the Indonesian rupiah, the Philippine peso, the Malaysian ringgit and, to a lesser extent, the Singaporean dollar. By early November 1997 Hong Kong's stock market had collapsed, suffering a 40 per cent loss in October of that year. These financial and asset price crises set the stage for a second round of large currency depreciations. This time, not only the currencies of Thailand, Malaysia, Indonesia, the Philippines and Singapore were affected, but those of South Korea and Taiwan also suffered. The result of this crisis was massive negative growth in overall GDPs. Indonesia was worst hit as its economy shrank by approximately 80 per cent during the crisis, while the other states hit by the crisis saw their economies shrink by around 30 to 40 per cent.

In essence, the crisis was caused by fears of lower profits and economic recession in the newly developing states of South East Asia. The owners of capital feared that their investments in these states would not return suitable profits or would even lose money and so capital began to move out of these economies very rapidly (capital flight). As there were limited governmental controls on the movement of capital there was nothing anyone could do to stop the exodus. In short, fears of economic crisis became a self-fulfilling prophecy as the initial withdrawals of capital led other capital investors to fear the worst and withdrew their capital. The free movement of capital had helped these economies grow very rapidly since the 1970s as it flowed into their economies unhindered. But it just as easily flowed out unhindered. This has become a common fear of many governments and people around the world. Capital has become so privileged and controls on capital movement largely removed that states and markets now have to contend with each other and hope that capital comes in and stays in their economies. The threat of capital flight is ever-present and so capital mobility has become a key security issue in the twenty-first century.

At the same time as capital flight has become a major issue in contemporary international political economy, so too have financial crises caused by capital *immobility*. The global financial crisis that began in August 2007 with the sub-prime mortgage crisis in the US market has become the greatest economic crisis since the Great Depression of 1929 (Bellamy-Foster and Magdoff, 2009). Practically every state has been hit with recession and the failure of private sector actors. Banks as well as other major economic entities have closed down very rapidly and in large numbers as they have gone bankrupt. Countless projects have been cancelled or put on hold around the world as funding has dried up. The crisis has demonstrated the incredibly high level of interdependence in the global economy and the lack of security against capital forces and trends shared by most states. The crisis has been caused by the slowing down of capital flows around the global economy as capital owners shy away from investing in markets and lending to each other. In effect capital is not moving around the world in large enough quantities and at a fast enough pace to satisfy all demands. Recession and decreased economic activity has followed and will only be replaced with economic growth and dynamic activity once capital begins to move faster again. Again, there are only so many means states and non-state actors have at their disposal to combat problems of capital movement. As has clearly been demonstrated by the economic collapse of Iceland (previously thought to be one of the most stable and healthy economies in the world), security threats are no longer simply about military action.

## The revolution in military affairs

There are many phenomena that have shaped contemporary critical security studies and altered the security agenda in IPE. There has undoubtedly been a shift away from considering security as only pertaining to states as actors and military issues. Yet we cannot ignore military security or state security interests if we are going to consider security in IPE. Indeed, developments in the military sphere compel us to consider military security as being perhaps more important than ever before. As discussed above, the advent of nuclear weapons and the systems used to deliver them helped to reshape military affairs in the twentieth century and continue to do so today. At the same time, the nature of military interdependence was highlighted due to the possibility of large-scale destruction. In addition to nuclear weapons, new military technologies have emerged, which have transformed the nature of modern warfare. These technologies have made war far more destructive, far more costly in financial terms and more efficient. Modern military technologies are sometimes said to be less costly in terms of civilian casualties as they are more 'accurate'. However, in reality military–industry complexes around the world continue to find more ways of killing and destroying – accuracy is often not sufficient or a matter of consideration.

The revolution in military affairs (RMA) that has taken place since the 1980s has altered the effects time and space have on military warfare. As a result military security has truly become a globalised issue (Benbow, 2004). Previously, states had to consider their immediate surroundings when assessing their military security. Stability and the lack of military threat from one's neighbours or near abroad used to be sufficient to ensure one's own security. In the contemporary world, states must consider military threats from states much further away. The United States now has to think about states as far away as North Korea and even Iran when it considers the military security of not only overseas assets but the actual mainland US as well (in the same manner, practically every other state in the world must consider the United States' military capabilities in their security assessments). The development of intercontinental ballistic missiles (ICBMs), long-range stealth aircraft, fully automated machines and weapons of mass destruction (WMDs) all mean that the military reach of many states now exceeds their near abroad.

This reorientation of how space impacts warfare also means that some states can engage in conflict from a long distance away while others do not possess the same projection capabilities. For example, unmanned US Air Force and Navy drones are increasingly being used in Afghanistan and Pakistan (even though the use of them in the airspace of the latter is a highly contentious issue) to combat the Taliban. These drones are able to act as intelligence-gathering spy planes as well as platforms to launch highly destructive missiles. While these drones are launched from bases in the region and not very far from the theatre of operations, they are often 'piloted' by personnel back in the United States using satellite links. Others are programmed and, in effect, pilot themselves. Developments of unmanned drones and other technologies that allow one party to fight battles from far away are encouraging next-generation arms races. The ability of one state to possess these types of capabilities adds to its security yet detracts from the security of others and often renders existing military capabilities obsolete – even defensive ones. The twenty-first century may see many next-generation arms races and the realignment of security concerns.

## Invisible military forces(?)

By 2008 scientists at the University of California at Berkeley in the United States had managed to engineer material that bends visible light around objects. The project is funded by the US military and the material has obvious military applications. By using molecular engineering, the Berkeley scientists have been able to create material that has electromagnetic properties. These properties absorb electromagnetic radiation in the form of visible light and direct it around the material. The result is, in effect, the ability to cloak an object in the material and bend light around it. The observer looking at the object would actually see the reflection of light from behind the object, therefore making the object invisible to the naked eye.

The 'invisibility' material could be used to coat military equipment such as tanks, aircraft, ships and other weaponry, which would make them appear invisible to the enemy. Coupled with existing 'stealth' technology, which makes objects invisible to radar and other detection methods (but not to direct visual observation), this new technology could mean that future battlefields house entirely invisible and undetectable forces. Suits for combat soldiers may also use the light-bending material to render soldiers invisible on the battlefield. Fears have been raised that this technology has already been used by military forces on individual soldiers in intelligence-gathering operations. However, the US military and the scientists at Berkeley claim that the technology is not that advanced yet and large quantities of the new material cannot be manufactured at this stage.

Clearly the development and application of 'invisibility' technology by military forces (and exclusively the US military at this point) would severely reduce the deterrent capabilities of other states. This would reduce their military security and so could cause further arms races.

The militarisation of space also has become an area to note. Space remains largely demilitarised but the use of satellites for military purposes and plans to develop military material for use in space may change this. Satellites orbiting the planet have long been employed by militaries for gathering information, communication and coordination. Current-generation missile technology uses satellite systems for guidance and targeting. Newer technologies include such things as anti-satellite missiles and space-based missile launch systems. The latter could be developed as part of an international missile defence system planned by the United States and some of its allies. One of the elements of this system would be missile-launching platforms orbiting the planet. Again, these developments would significantly alter existing notions of security and make the current military capabilities of most states entirely obsolete, thus leading these states to rearm themselves with more advanced technologies.

One of the more recent developments in modern warfare has been termed cyber warfare. As use of modern technologies linked to the Internet by governments and non-state actors increases, a new sphere for conflict has arisen. In most states, and especially in the most developed states in Europe, North America and South East Asia, the Internet and related technologies are used very widely. Governments, for example, now utilise the Internet for most of their functions. Military forces also widely use the Internet in some form or another (usually involving complex cyber security systems). Since the late 1990s developments in methods of conflict either using the Internet or targeting online capabilities have been seen. Cyber attacks on government and business targets that use the Internet can severely disrupt communications and standard operations. The advent of cyber attacks has created another form of security issue for both state and non-state actors. This has added to the reinterpretation of security as a concept in the contemporary world system.

An example of this form of security threat can be found in the experiences of the United States. In 1999 the email systems of several US government departments were overwhelmed by a massive surge in incoming spam-like emails, which caused the systems to crash. The backlog of incoming illegitimate emails delayed and crowded out legitimate incoming emails and hindered outgoing messages. The disruption to communications and the functioning of various agencies was unprecedented and lasted several days. While never proven or admitted, the events of 1999 have been seen by some as a cyber attack on the United States originating from China. It is suggested that this (supposed) attack was in retaliation for the May 1999 bombing of the Chinese embassy in Belgrade, Serbia, by NATO forces during the Kosovo War.

## International terrorism

Acts of terrorism are not something that are particularly new to international relations (no matter how one defines such an act or, indeed, what a 'terrorist' is). But the events in New York, Maryland and Pennsylvania on 11 September 2001 ushered in a new era of international relations characterised by the heightened importance of international terrorism (Halliday, 2001). The terrorist attacks on the United States in 2001 were largely unpredicted, at least with regard to the scope that they took place, even though intelligence services had predicted that an attack on the United States mainland was possible/being attempted. The response of the United States and many parts of the international community to these attacks was to engage (perhaps it is more appropriate to say 're-engage') with an effort to combat terrorist networks (and terrorism itself as a concept) around the world. The initial phase of this 'war on terrorism' was the 2001 invasion of Afghanistan to remove the Taliban from government there and to defeat Al-Qaeda and apprehend its members deemed guilty of orchestrating the 2001 attacks. This phase remains incomplete as the Taliban are at the current time resurgent in Afghanistan and to an extent in Pakistan, and Al-Qaeda remains operational. Other elements of this war on terrorism have included changes in the roles and limitations of state institutions domestically (such as the suspension of some freedoms of speech, association and judicial processes) as well as greater freedom of action at the international level for some states and less for others.

A number of states around the world have utilised the war on terrorism as a pretext for pursuing domestic and foreign policy interests. In the mid-2000s Russia stepped up its campaigns against Chechen and other separatists in the Caucasus while Israel reoccupied parts of the West Bank that had been handed over to the Palestinian Authority as part of the peace process there as well as invading Lebanon to stop attacks by Hezbollah, a group considered by many to be a terrorist organisation. Many authoritarian governments (such as Syria, Egypt, China and Uzbekistan) tightened their grips on power under the pretext of combating terrorists within their borders. Even in Western Europe and the United States civil freedoms have been reduced to some extent, as under the US Patriot Act. Meanwhile, terrorist organisations, and other organisations classed by some as terrorist, have been increasingly active. Many terrorist activities are targeted at the domestic level but there has been a significant increase in the scope of these types of activity and many acts of terrorism are now international in nature. As an introductory explanation, terrorist activities include acts of violence such as bombings (delivered using technology such as cars and telecommunication equipment; and people, as in suicide bombings), assassinations, sabotage and kidnappings, as well as the logistical, training and financing operations that support violent acts.

One of the key problems in international relations with regard to terrorism is the analysis of what causes people to engage in terrorism, how we define what is classed as a terrorist act and therefore who is a terrorist, and the impact of the war on terrorism on these things. In many cases the motivations of terrorists are clear and can be easily understood as relating to poverty, lack of political and economic opportunity, responses to policies and actions taken by some states, which negatively impact on others and so on. In other cases, though, terrorism is motivated by criminal activity and is intertwined with broader processes of crime. It can be argued that international cooperation in law enforcement can be effective in combating terrorist groups. There has been a vast increase in the level of international cooperation in this field. At the same time, however, analysis suggests that, often, actions taken as part of the war on terrorism simply cause more terrorism. The US-led invasion and occupation of Iraq since 2003, for example, was founded upon a number of foreign policy goals, which included combating terrorism. The conflict ultimately acted as a boon for terrorist organisations as well as legitimate resistance movements, both of which experienced rapid rises in numbers of recruits. As Iraq descended into less stability and order, terrorist groups such as Al-Qaeda were able not only to be based and operate in Iraq, but also to carry out attacks internationally. Until the root causes of the poverty and disillusionment that encourage people to turn to 'terrorism' are studied and addressed, the threat of international terrorism and the war against it will continue.

## Summary

The nature of security studies is such that as processes in the 'real world' take place and international relations change over time, the field of study also changes. This chapter has discussed some of the key developments that have led to a more comprehensive and critical approach to studying security issues. The emergence of nuclear weapons, environmental issues, identity politics and non-state actors (most notably the MNC) following the Second World War helped to transform how we define security, whose security we should consider and what security challenges are faced in the modern world. Critical security studies entails the consideration of state and non-state actors as well as individuals. Furthermore, in contemporary study security is no longer defined simply as military security but it is also defined as things like environmental, identity and financial security. There are now many issues that challenge our security. Some of these are still related to military security, especially in light of the RMA, which is yielding ever more destructive weaponry and means to employ them. But we are also faced with challenges over the maintenance of our energy and food supplies, as well as the preservation of cultural identities. As has been shown by global financial crises, the interdependence and dynamic nature of the global economy has become extremely important to the economic security and well-being of individuals as well as states as a whole. As the human world develops and becomes ever more complex, so do the security challenges we face.

## Reflective questions

1    Traditionally, 'security' has been seen as state- and military-centric. Is this still the case in the twenty-first century?
2    Which processes can you identify that have altered perceptions of security since the 1960s?
3    Why should we consider non-state actors when defining and discussing security issues?
4    In your opinion, which are the most significant security challenges in the contemporary world?

**Table 12.2** Chapter summary

| | Key actors | Key processes | Emphasis on political economy | What causes change? | Global institutions? | View of conflict in global relations? |
|---|---|---|---|---|---|---|
| Security | Ideally provided by the state, with some degree of personal citizen responsibility for the welfare of themselves and their families | Military forces to protect borders and, as deemed necessary, oversea strategic interests. Domestic legislature combined with civilian police investigation/enforcement | Security may be inherited by being born to a privileged elite group. Or it may be worked for in a more meritocratic society. Either way security is more likely to be found in the 'core' of a socio-economic order rather than on its margins | Challenges to an existing order. This may take the form of armed rebellion or more subtle challenges over time where the powerbase of ruling elites is more gradually eroded | The United Nations Security Council is not a world government but does have a degree of legitimacy to intervene within national borders as the need arises. It also plays a significant role via its specialised agencies such as the World Health Organization. Proponents of the neo-liberal agenda would argue the World Trade Organization, World Bank. IMF, etc. also promote growth and stability – thereby increasing security for all | Conflict may be seen from a 'just war' perspective, whereby the ends justify the means. An armed conflict might be considered legitimate to depose a regime deemed to be undertaking a form of genocide within its borders. This is a very state-centric view and various aspects of security are no longer so 'easily' resolved in terms of deposing a government. Global issues such as energy, food and water security are likely to become increasing linked to future conflicts, which will not be resolved by overthrowing regimes |
| Insecurity | In some cases governments may actively persecute some of their own citizens. Insecurity is also an issue for those considered stateless, refugees and asylum seekers | Insecurity can arise as a result of natural disasters or marginalisation and potential prejudice based on race, religion, sexual orientation or similar characteristics leading to discrimination | Insecurity can occur among elite groups if these are successfully challenged. However, it is more easily identifiable among peripheral, marginalised groups that have less access to material wealth or the means to pursue it | Insecurity may come suddenly in the form of an unexpected shock, be it a natural disaster, stock market crash or outbreak of violence or disease. More common is the ongoing, lingering insecurity of disadvantage – political, economic, sociocultural | Opponents of the neo-liberal model argue that although some benefit from economic growth this is often at the disadvantage of others in an exploitative manner, which does not factor in the true social and environmental costs associated with this model – thereby increasing insecurity | Arguably any form of conflict leads to insecurity, at least for one of the parties involved. From a critical security perspective conflict is now much more complex than state-to-state rivalry. Insecurities can arise as a result of competition over resources, both within and across national borders, over identity issues and clashes or, increasingly, due to insecurities where there is no easily definable enemy (such as climate change) |

5    In what ways do increasing global energy and food demands, and dwindling supplies threaten your security?
6    How does the 2007–2009 global financial crisis demonstrate how economic interdependence can be a security threat?

## Suggestions for further reading

Bellamy-Foster, J. and Magdoff, F. (2009) *The Great Financial Crisis: Causes and Consequences*, New York: Monthly Review Press.

Benbow, T. (2004) *The Magic Bullet? Understanding the Revolution in Military Affairs*, London: Chrysalis Books.

Booth, K. (2004) *Critical Security Studies and World Politics*, Boulder, CO: Lynne Rienner.

Buzan, B., Ware, A. and Hoffmann-Martinot, V. (2007) *People, States and Fear: An Agenda for International Security Studies in the Post-Cold War Period*, 2nd edn, Colchester: ECPR Press.

Castle, S. (2013) *The Age of Migration: International Population Movements in the Modern World*, 5th edn, Basingstoke: Palgrave Macmillan.

Collins, J. and Futter, A (eds) (2015) *Reassessing the Revolution in Military Affairs: Transformation, Evolution and Lessons Learnt*, Basingstoke: Palgrave Macmillan

Garrison, N., Homer-Dixon, T. and Wright, R. (2009) *Carbon Shift: How the Twin Crises of Oil Depletion and Climate Change Will Define the Future*, New York: Random House.

Halliday, F. (2001) *Two Hours That Shook the World; September 11th 2001*, London: Saqi Books.

Homer-Dixon, T. (2001) *Environment, Scarcity and Violence*, Princeton, NJ: Princeton University Press.

Hough, P. (2013) *Understanding Global Security*, 3rd edn, New York: Routledge.

Ohmae, K. (1999) *The Borderless World: Power and Strategy in the Interlinked Economy*, London: Harper Paperbacks.

UN Department of Economic and Social Affairs: Population Division (2014) *The World Population Situation in 2014*, New York: United Nations.

# 13 Migration and labour

## Chapter learning outcomes

After reading this chapter students should be able to:

- Engage with academic debates on the causes and impacts of migration on the contemporary global political economy and individual societies.
- Understand the roots of migration at the regional level and be able to explain how this process of movement developed into migration at the global level after the Second World War.
- Explain the relationship between economic, political and physical security and migration.
- Understand migration as a key driver of globalisation but also as a result of other processes of integration.
- Comprehend contemporary processes of labour demand and supply, and the ways in which migration is a result of the global division of labour.
- Critically analyse the human rights considerations of national migration policies.

## Introduction

Migration is a term that refers to both the temporary and more permanent movement of people both within and across national borders. Migration has been a key feature of the human experience throughout our history. Indeed, for most of human history migrating has been the norm, while living as settled communities in one place is a somewhat recent feature of human experience (only several thousand years out of tens of thousands or even hundreds of thousands of years). Human societies emerged as small hunter-gatherer communities that relied on near constant migration to find and/or follow sources of food (and freshwater). The discovery and development of agriculture and animal husbandry, in particular, altered the dynamics of human survival allowing communities to settle and live in one place for long periods of time (rarely indefinitely though). Still, a myriad of reasons continued to encourage people to move from one place to another. At times some factors 'push' people away, for example, due to lack of food, environmental insecurity, conflict, and political disputes; and at others, people move because factors 'pull' them to relocate to another area. These 'pull' factors can include abundant food supplies, economic opportunities and welfare, environmental security, and peace and stability.

The UN's Department of Economic and Social Affairs and the International Organization for Migration (IOM) both estimate that there are over 230 million migrants worldwide – up from an estimated 150 million in 1990. In the contemporary era, settled communities remain the central feature of the human world with urbanisation constantly progressing and urban populations growing while rural populations decline. Only very small numbers of people still maintain a truly nomadic or migratory way of life. Yet, while cities continue to grow and new ones emerge, and states embed further as the means by which people are organised into communities, migration has again become one of the most important and evident characteristics of the human world. The rapid development of transportation and communication technologies as well as the global triumph of capitalistic patterns of production, exchange and consumption, make migration necessary. This chapter explores the drivers behind migration; the impacts that global migration has on the economic, social and political nature of societies; and responses to migration. The first section of the chapter offers a discussion of how we define and interpret migration. This is followed by an analysis of the relationship between migration and multiculturalism, economic development, and labour. Two final sections consider the human rights implications of migration, and governmental responses.

# Understanding migration

The movement of people can have a number of causes (both push and pull factors) and consequences. Before a more critical discussion of migration can be developed it is important to note that the movement of people, whether for shorter or longer periods of time, can be either voluntary or involuntary. Generally, involuntary migration is the result of intense push factors, for example, dramatic changes in environmental conditions leading to the inability of the natural environment to support human settlement. Here one can consider the impact of long periods of drought and the desertification of a previously liveable environment. The resultant decline in food and freshwater supplies can mean that people are no longer able to survive if they remain in the same place. They are pushed away from their land, homes, and possessions as they search for sources of sustenance. Conflicts can also drive people away from a place where they may have lived for a period of time (from just a few years to many centuries). Here the threat of physical insecurity, or perhaps even the certainty of death, if they remain is more than sufficient to force people to move elsewhere to seek safe refuge. Involuntary migration also tends to be more problematic for those who are moving (the migrants) and the societies to which these people move (the host societies). This form of migration usually emerges relatively rapidly as conflicts, economic collapse, environmental catastrophes and so on either take place over short periods of time, perhaps a few years or even months, and escalate to reach a 'breaking' point very quickly. This makes planning for such scenarios difficult, exacerbating the human crisis that tends to accompany this type of migration. This is discussed in more detail in the following pages.

Voluntary migration tends to be far less traumatic an experience than involuntary migration. Here, people identify better opportunities elsewhere and plan (although 'planning' should be understood quite loosely here) to move from one place to another. These opportunities may relate to environmental factors, but are more likely to relate to human conditions. For example, a person might choose to become a migrant by moving to another country to pursue a better education (assuming, of course, that the country being left has a poorer and/or more expensive education system than the destination country). Another reason may be to seek better employment in terms of higher salaries, more rapid promotion, better working conditions and so on. People who migrate for this type of reason are generally called 'economic migrants'. Something that needs to be understood here is that globalisation has progressed the emergence of a global division of labour.

**AUTHOR BOX**

## Caroline Brettell and James Hollifield (eds) (2014) *Migration Theory: Talking Across Disciplines*

Migration has not been considered a particularly important issue in IPE and has been largely excluded from the mainstream IPE research agenda. Most IPE textbooks will only deal with migration as a feature of other issues such as environmental change, conflict and globalisation. Few textbooks, for example, will have a detailed discussion on migration let alone an entire chapter dedicated to it. However, migration is increasingly being researched in-depth and from a range of theoretical and disciplinary perspectives. Brettell and Hollifield's (2014) *Migration Theory: Talking Across Disciplines* offers a good next step for the student of IPE who wishes to gain a greater insight into the nature of migration and its causes and effects. Brettell and Hollifield also offer the reader a very useful review of existing approaches and analyses. This edited collection contains chapters on the history of migration, different theoretical and methodological approaches to analysing migration, which include political, economic, sociological, geographical and anthropological studies. Policy responses and the role of governments are also considered. The range of actors discussed in this text demonstrates the multifaceted, and multi-stakeholder nature of contemporary migration and is an essential read for students wishing to develop their understanding of migration.

As discussed in Chapter 4, economic integration is dividing up areas of the global economy into zones of production and consumption. Some of these zones are characterised by higher value-added and capital-intensive modes of production, while others are characterised by lower value-added and labour-intensive production. Different forms of work can be found in all countries and all areas of the world, of course, but to some extent we are witnessing the concentration of wealth and opportunities in developed areas of the world. This attracts people from less-developed states, and less-developed areas of developed states, towards what can be seen as the economic centres. Here migration (both legal and illegal) from Africa and Asia to Europe is an example of economic migrants being pulled towards an area that offers greater prospects. We should also note that economic migrants can be highly skilled and educated, as well as those with few skills and limited or no education. It is quite common in contemporary political discourse in Europe, for example, for the term migrant to be understood as something rather negative. This is quite misleading and is based more on the assumption that migrants have little to offer the economies that host them. This can be true in the case of the migration of what may often be the best and brightest of developing societies, which has a positive effect on the host economy and a very detrimental effect on the home economy – this is called the 'brain drain' effect (see below).

**EXAMPLE BOX**

## 1915–1918: The Armenian Genocide and forced migration

April 2015 marked the centenary of the systematic expulsion and extermination of between 800,000 and 1.5 million ethnic Armenians from what would become the modern Republic of Turkey. During the First World War the Ottoman Empire was opposed to the Allied Powers and found itself under attack from the British, French and Russian Empires. Defeat on the battlefield was accompanied by dissent and turmoil at home. The Ottoman response was to promote a nationalist ideology that saw Ottoman citizens of Turkish ethnicity as the 'nation' while other ethnic groups were excluded, often being distrusted, exiled and/ or killed. Ethnic Armenians were perhaps the single most persecuted group because of their emerging alignment with the Russian Empire, their Christian faith, and their own emerging form of nationalism that was incompatible with the Turkish nationalist goal of inhabiting and ruling over all of Anatolia (most of modern day Turkey). On 24 April 1915 over 250 Armenian intellectuals and community leaders were arrested and subsequently executed in the Ottoman capital, Constantinople (later renamed Istanbul). This is seen as the start of a period of several years in which Armenians were targeted. Those who survived migrated in different directions, some moving eastwards into what would become the modern state of Armenia, others moved farther afield to different countries in Europe, Asia and the Americas. Today, more Armenians (approximately 5 million) live in the 'diaspora', than those (approximately 3 million) who live in Armenia itself. Their migration was, of course, an example of a forced or involuntary migration caused by conflict and specific governmental policies.

It is important to note that the term 'Genocide' is not universally applied to the case of the experiences of the Armenians during and after the First World War. The Turkish government, for example, still refuses to recognise it as genocide, highlighting instead that outside of the initial events in Constantinople on 24 April 1915, Armenians were only killed or forced to migrate in 'Western Armenia' (parts of the east of modern-day Turkey), which was at the time a theatre of war. The Russian Empire had invaded this part of the Ottoman Empire and ethnic Armenians were seen to have sided with the invading Russian armies. This does not justify the killing and forced migration of entire communities. Yet again the Turkish government highlights that the Allied Powers attacked the Ottoman Empire forcing millions of Muslim civilians to migrate into the remnants of the Ottoman Empire, and several hundred thousands more were killed. Acknowledgment of these atrocities and the impacts the resulting migrations had would be welcomed by the government in Ankara as a condition for acknowledging the experiences of the Armenians. Nonetheless, in April 2015 events around the world that included Turkish governmental involvement commemorated the Armenian experience.

# Economic migration

The economic impact of migrants is often seen to be a controversial issue for a number of reasons. First, debates about migration can become highly politicised and can be understood not as a distinct phenomenon but part of broader value-laden political discourse. Perceptions of the impact of migration on economic well-being for both the home and host countries are very influential here and can often portray migrants inaccurately. This is perhaps more important in host countries where managing migration to promote the perceived benefits while minimising the perceived losses has become a key demand on governments. Second, despite a wealth of academic and specialist knowledge on the matter, general conclusions about the economic impact of migration tend to be wildly inaccurate and misleading. A key problem here is that immediate impacts for some sectors of society (in both home and host countries) are considered as reflective of the overall effect on entire economies and generalisations emerge that are applied as standard across different cases. It is difficult, for example, for members of an individual town or suburb in a host country like the UK to remove themselves from the consideration of migration as they may witness or experience a change in their situation or local community that they attribute to migration (whether this is perceived to be a positive or negative change).

Finally, evidence of the economic effects of migration is not that easy to establish as there are a great many other factors that might have an impact as well. For example, if we simply considered economic growth rates over a period of time and contrasted that to immigration (and emigration) over the same period of time we may see that both increase. Yet this does not mean that economic growth increased because of migration. It may even mean that migration was a result of economic growth and not a contributing factor to it. At the same time, there may be little or no correlation whatsoever, or other factors, such as new technologies, industrialisation, urbanisation, trade liberalisation and so on may be the real drivers behind growth rates and migration could be just a feature of demographic change. It all really depends on the specific country and period of time one examines.

Another issue to understand is the difference between unskilled versus skilled economic migrants. Unskilled migrants can provide labour for low-value-added economic activity such as manual labour, cleaning services, and agriculture. In host countries it is often assumed that because migrants seek to leave their own countries due to poverty, unemployment and/or insecurity they will be unskilled and uneducated (or else they would not be in poverty). In this way migrants can be seen as undesirable and unhelpful to the host economy. This is of course, not accurate. Most migrants are actually rather skilled and educated and migrate to seek greater rewards for their advanced capabilities. This type of migrant can contribute significantly to the strength of a host economy. This can come at the expense, however, of the strength of the country they leave. The loss of labour with technical skills, advanced knowledge and research and development skills (the cornerstone of a modern economy) is a phenomenon referred to as a 'brain drain'. Here, the rewards can be greater in more developed economies and so skilled labour will migrate to gain the best opportunities. In general economic terms this makes perfect sense and should be encouraged in a capitalist system where efficiency, productivity and profitability are promoted. The loss of skills and knowledge, however, may have as significant an effect as a lack of what economists call 'factor endowments', or in other words the factors (such as natural resources, labour, capital and so on) that are used to produce goods and provide services. Labour is a key component of economic productivity and welfare and losing the most skilled workers reduces the factor endowments available. Critical theorists and Marxists would argue that migration simply promotes greater inequality between richer and poorer societies and reinforces the dependency of the latter on the former.

At the same time, however, we should not discount the beneficial impacts of economic migration for home countries. There are two key economic benefits for home countries: remittances and the reducing pressure for job creation at home. Remittance is wealth earned abroad by migrant labour that is transferred back to their home country. In 2014 the World Bank estimated that global remittance flows totalled over $580 billion, with approximately $435 billion going from developed to developing states. It is important to note that remittances are not all about money flowing from richer to poorer economies, demonstrating that migration is not a one-way street from poorer to richer societies. Large developing states like India ($c.$\$70 billion$) and China ($c.$\$64 billion$) receive the most remittances, but smaller developing states like Jordan ($c.$\$4 billion$/$c.$10 per cent of GDP) also rely quite significantly on remittances to balance economic accounts. Economic migration from developing to developed states also acts as an outlet or 'pressure valve' to relieve some of the stress caused by high demographic growth rates and low job growth rates in the poorer societies. The UN estimates that over half of the world's population is under 30 years old, with over two-thirds of populations in developing countries being under 30 years old. The combination of large youthful populations, relatively rapid growth rates, high unemployment and low job growth rates means that developing societies face immense pressures. Poverty, instability, crime/violence and extremism can grow rapidly under these conditions. The ability of at least a proportion of the 'excess' or unemployed labour from these societies to migrate to more affluent markets to find jobs is essential in many cases.

---

**CONCEPT BOX**

## Migrants or expatriates?

It is common to refer to migrants when talking about people moving from poorer societies to richer ones, and to refer to expatriates when talking about people moving from richer societies to poorer ones. This is a misleading distinction as anyone who migrates to another country for work or other legitimate reasons is a 'migrant', but at the same time could be referred to as an expatriate, or 'expat' for short. Distinguishing between migrants and expats is somewhat discriminatory and something that is found in Western discourse quite often. If you moved from your country to another to work, would you class yourself as a migrant or expat?

---

In addition to the direct positive effects of migration, the movement of people, whether temporary (for example, for trips to another country for tourism, education exchanges or short-term work) or more permanent, can have other benefits. In particular, migration can help to promote interaction between peoples, which can result in greater understanding, dialogue and collaboration in international relations. Issues of cultural diversity that can result from migration are discussed in more detail below. However, it is useful to note here that multiculturalism and the economic effects of migration are often seen to be one and the same. When multiculturalism, for example, is seen as unsuccessful, as has happened in the UK and Germany in recent years, this is seen as an indictment of the economic effects of migration too.

## Technology and migration

The advancement of communications and transport technologies have facilitated the movement of people at the global level. Technological developments have perhaps as much to do with migration as any economic, environmental or political factors. By the late 1700s and early 1800s the development of ocean-going sea vessels and railway systems allowed people to move farther, more quickly and cheaply than ever before in human history. The ability to move across greater distances helped to open up new spaces for people to migrate to. At the same time, the speed at which people could move from one place to another encouraged more rapid flows of not only goods, services and money, but also ideas, knowledge and the awareness that shorter-term migrations were possible. This coupled with affordable (at least for some) costs of travel meant that more people were interested in migrating and were able to do so. Through the twentieth century the further development of land and sea travel was joined by air travel, advanced road networks and vehicle ownership. Knowledge of the world through education and mass media also began to facilitate understanding of where one could migrate to and raised interest in moving to what could be seen as a better place. Over the past few decades, and especially since the 1970s, short- and long-distance travel has become far more accessible to the masses in both the developed and developing worlds. The lower costs and increased efficiency of travel are extremely important here. More people are now able to travel to more locations and in a shorter time than in the past. People are now far more likely to be able to travel multiple times (perhaps quite regularly throughout their lives) and this makes migrating a less daunting and less permanent phenomenon.

In addition to these technological revolutions in the means of travel, migration is also caused by changes in the global political economy that relate to production, exchange and consumption. As a result of the globalisation of the economic system we now have a world that is characterised by very high levels of integration between markets. This has, in turn, led to increased competition between markets all over the world and increased opportunities that encourage economic migration. The contemporary global division of labour is driven by technological progress and market forces that respond to the supply and demand of different types of labour. High-technology manufacturing and research and design, for example, increasingly are concentrated in advanced economies meaning a more concentrated demand for highly skilled and educated labour, while low-technology and labour intensive activities like mining, agriculture, and low-value-added manufacturing are concentrated in poorer economies, thus concentrating the demand for this type of labour. People with different skill sets, therefore, may find the need/desire and the opportunities to migrate to specific economies to seek employment.

## Labour in the twenty-first century

Labour refers to the input of human energy, knowledge, skills, time and activity that is invested in the production and/or provision of goods and/or services such as food, clothing, cars, education, banking and so on, and their exchange and consumption. For several decades IPE scholars have been interested in the division of labour – initially within societies and regions, and more recently at the global level. IPE has also been interested in the ways in which value is placed upon various forms of labour and how demand is met by supply through migration and relocation. Of course, in the case of the latter it is the business enterprise that relocates productive operations to where the labour can be found cheapest and most productive. We also need to consider the impact that different forms of labour and changes in how people are educated and trained (or not) have on societies and international relations. In early mercantilist and realist thought, labour was seen as a key element determining the wealth and power of individual states. Of particular importance was the ability of governments to organise and utilise labour to produce military and industrial resources. As an extension of this concern with the wealth of nations, the use of labour to produce goods and services that can be exported to increase national income and a trade surplus was also central to analyses of labour. In the contemporary era, however, labour needs to be understood not as something that states can possess and harness, but as a factor endowment that corporations (especially MNCs) and individuals themselves can possess and use to pursue profits and welfare.

Marxists and structuralists argue that labour is essential for human existence and production (to ensure basic human needs and some *wants* are met). However, they also argue that the labour of the masses is exploited by the economic and political elites of societies around the world (in both developed and developing states) in order to accumulate resources, wealth and power. The inherent competition and pursuit of accumulation found in capitalism, has resulted in global divisions of labour in different industries. Here the value given to distinct forms of labour and their produce differs. Historical sociologists have highlighted that historical processes of labour efficiency and specialisation facilitated the development of knowledge and technology. This is a key component of the contemporary global political economy and the role of labour, including migratory labour, is essential for market-driven economic growth.

As globalisation has rapidly integrated previously separate labour markets into one single global labour market, capitalists, MNCs and states have gained access to sources of labour from around the world. Even though the exact economic impact of this modern experience is debated (as discussed above in the section on economic migration) it has been suggested that this can lead to greater prosperity for all. Certainly in macroeconomic terms, the ability of labour to migrate to where it can be used most efficiently is something to be encouraged, and at the micro-level tens of millions of people around the world benefit by being able to 'sell' their labour in far flung markets.

# Migration and multiculturalism

As people move around the world they take with them various aspects of their identities and knowledge. Languages, beliefs (religious and secular), customs, fashions, ideologies and so on, migrate along with people. In the era of globalisation different cultures increasingly interact with each other through various processes of economic, social and political integration. These include the trade of goods and services, mass media and migration. But as cultures interact they do not assimilate with each other and become identical – or at least not in the short- to medium-term. People often remain somewhat distinct from each other in at least some areas of their lives, whether this be in the language(s) they speak, the religious beliefs they adhere to, or their traditions. When people with at least some distinct cultural characteristics exist in the same society together we can refer to that society as being multicultural (i.e. it is characterised by multiculturalism). As discussed in the technologies section of this chapter migration is not always a permanent process. Because the technologies exist that allow people to migrate quickly, relatively cheaply and over greater distances than in previous eras, migration is increasingly a temporary moment in the lives of migrants. Short-term visits to other countries, for example, to pursue a university education, or even just for a holiday are quite common now. Some argue that when migration is a permanent condition, migrants are more likely to assimilate into the host society. Certainly there is a relatively high chance that the descendants of a relative who migrated and settled in another society will share more with others in that society. But when migration is seen as a temporary move there is less motivation to 'fit in' with the host society.

Within political science and social sciences more generally, there are varying arguments and theoretical positions on the prospects, and support, for multiculturalism. On the one hand, there are positions quite broadly linked to liberal scholars who accept migration and, therefore, multiculturalism as a healthy feature of modern, globalised human relations. On the other hand are more critical or postmodern arguments that question the desirability of multiculturalism in modern developed societies. Whichever perspective is adopted, however, multiculturalism is acknowledged as a component of the contemporary global political economy and as a by-product of global level migration. As you will see below, governmental responses to migration are largely driven by considerations of whether or not multiculturalism can work and/or is desirable. Indeed, governmental policy on migration is perhaps driven as much by these considerations as it is by economic concerns, and is certainly informed more by discussions of multiculturalism than humanitarian concerns. We must also remember at this point, that most developed societies are multicultural to some extent, with different ethnicities, religions, languages, and traditions present. The experience of these societies can vary, however, with multiculturalism working well for long periods of time in some places (perhaps the UK and to an extent the USA) and leading to tensions in others (for example, France).

Of course, not all societies can be classed as multicultural. There is far more of an impetus for migrants to move to relatively prosperous and stable areas within their own countries, or other countries entirely. This means that the poorest societies in the world do not experience much immigration. This is reinforced by the global division of labour where people will migrate to seek employment where it is needed, which is not likely to be in the least developed countries. Yet, at the same time even some of the most advanced societies are not multicultural either. Australia and Japan have traditionally been good examples of rich countries with largely homogenous populations. While this has begun to change somewhat, Japan in particular remains largely monocultural. The dynamics leading to multiculturalism have a lasting effect. Middle-income developing countries like Russia and China are multicultural in some areas within their borders not because of mass immigration of people moving from poorer countries looking for employment and a better life, but because of historical processes of imperial expansion and ethnic diversity. Former colonial powers like Britain, France and the Netherlands, are culturally diverse as a result of their positions in the global economy, which continues to shape migration. British, French and Dutch citizens continue to emigrate to other parts of the world, especially former colonies, while citizens from former colonies immigrate into these countries.

Multiculturalism is a problematic term in both theory and practice. Some commentators use the term as a negative experience – claiming that multiculturalism 'has failed' or 'never works'. Increasingly we see the emergence of mainstream public discourse in EU member states, for example, that emphasises a supposed lack of integration of migrants into their host societies. Chapter 11 on culture touches more on these concerns and resistance to cultural interactions. This view of multiculturalism tends to be rather nationalist and right wing in terms of political discourse, but also stems from those who do not resist migration but who promote integration (in that migrants should adopt significant elements of the host society's culture). Similarly, a leftist argument here is that migrants (and minority groups who may not have immigrated) are exploited economically and then isolated by the broader host society. This ghettoisation of migrants can create a hostile environment for collaboration and further hinder integration. Multiculturalism should, in theory, acknowledge cultural differences and promote respect for the 'other'. But much controversy remains around the extent to which tolerance can (and should) be promoted. The section below on governmental responses furthers this discussion. Thus controversy surrounds how far such tolerance should be extended. In addition to these considerations, questions have arisen in regard to rights and responsibilities before the law. Here, the equality of all citizens and residents is of importance with some advocating differentiation before the law on the grounds of specific beliefs and values. One example from the UK is the question of to what extent civil laws regulating marriage, divorce and inheritance should reflect religious laws for Muslim and other minority communities.

## Human security, human rights and migration

On 10 December 1948 the UN General Assembly adopted the Universal Declaration of Human Rights. This declaration is binding on all UN member states and established the international community's commitment to acknowledging and protecting human rights. The declaration consists of a significant number of articles and principles and is, as can be expected from such a significant document, quite complex. But at its core is the establishment of a number of human rights and laws to protect them. These rights include: the right to life; the prohibition of slavery; freedom of association, conscience, thought and religion; the right to work; the right to physical security; and freedom of movement. All of these rights have implications for our discussion of migration, but of course this latter is of most concern.

The UN Development Programme's 1994 Human Development Report was the first time human security has been articulated and explored in a structured and coherent manner. In this report human security was identified as one of the key challenges facing humanity. The report defines human security as the 'legitimate concerns of ordinary people who sought security in their daily lives' (UNDP, 1994, p. 22). The report goes on to elaborate on this definition citing seven key aspects that need to be considered and promoted. These are: economic security (e.g. freedom from poverty); food security (e.g. access to sufficient food); health security (e.g. access to health-care and protection from diseases); environmental security (e.g. protection from such dangers as environmental pollution and climate change); personal security (e.g. physical safety from such things as torture, war, criminal attacks, domestic violence and drug use); community security (e.g. the survival of traditional cultures and ethnic groups); and political security (e.g. enjoyment of civil and political rights and freedom from oppression). Undoubtedly all of these aspects of human security, along with the universal rights outlined above, have implications for migration and how we respond to the movement of people around the world. If we are to uphold and protect human rights and promote human security, and if we have the rights and responsibilities to protect these even for people in different countries, then migration can be seen as a natural, legal and positive aspect of human civilisation.

Today, many migrants that are classed as illegal (what we can regard as involuntary in many circumstances) are compelled to migrate to other places both within their own countries and to other areas of the world. They are compelled to leave places like Syria (where up to one-third of all illegal immigrants trying to enter the EU have come from in recent years) because of the very real and imminent threat to their lives. Their security, well-being and freedoms are violated and one would be correct to highlight that the international community has the responsibility to act in order to protect these inalienable rights. This is, of course, a controversial issue and one that is not easy for governments to discuss and come to agreement on, but it must be acknowledged that the violation of human rights and the lack of human security is a key driver behind migration – and often involuntary migration.

## Governmental and non-governmental policy responses to migration

Here it is important to note that different actors can have different views of the costs and benefits of migration. They can also, therefore, have differing policy responses to it. Furthermore, policies of individual actors can vary over time. For example, policies of migration can be state-driven, as was the case in the colonial era when European governments in particular promoted the move-ment of people for the purpose of colonial settlement. As discussed above the movement of refu-gees and asylum seekers are also groups that national governments try to control. While migration has been a feature of international relations for a very long time, in the twenty-first century it has become more complicated and its impacts have become more varied. Governmental discourse and coordination on migration is difficult and informs other areas of inter-state relations. This is also true of the policy responses of non-state actors and IGOs like the International Organization for Migration (see example box below). Migration can sometimes be caused by push factors such as dwindling environmental resources like fresh water, agricultural land and energy resources, but the potential for these problems to emerge in places where migrants move to is also possible. Migration increases population sizes and demands on resources. Governments, therefore, have to consider this possibility and in this way migration becomes a policy concern for decision makers. Migration can complicate inter-state relations as a result of these concerns and can even become a 'securitised' issue. Decision makers in EU countries, for example, have increasingly talked about the 'threat' posed by large influxes of migrants from Asia and Africa. How well founded these concerns are is debatable, but what is clear is that at least elements of governments and societies in Europe do now see migration as an economic and political security issue and one that needs to be responded to.

Concerns about resources becoming scarce are magnified by climate change. Our understanding of how this process impacts on human well-being, in particular through changes in the resource endowment of almost everywhere on the planet are coupled with increasing awareness of migration. Together these issues reinforce each other in policy-making discussions and in inter-governmental forums like the UN General Assembly the two are often dealt with at the same time. There is increasing appreciation in the UN and elsewhere that environmental changes are pushing people to move away from their traditional homes in search of more suitable living conditions. It is quite common to find that responses to migration focus on solving problems such as fresh water scarcity in the societies where migrants originate from. This is particularly the case when climate change has extreme effects causing 'environmental refugees' who, much like refugees fleeing from conflict zones, are pushed into migrating and who have very little to sustain themselves on.

---

**EXAMPLE BOX**

# Operation Triton (EU Mediterranean Illegal Migration Control)

In 2011 the Arab Spring revolution spread to Libya and led to an eight-month long civil war. The immediate result of this conflict was the overthrow (and murder) of former leader Muammer Ghaddafi. However, in the aftermath of the conflict armed militias and factions competed for control of Libya and its vast natural resources (primarily hydrocarbons). A state of conflict lasted from 2011 through 2016 (the time of writing) and the lack of governmental authority over its borders has meant that Libya is unable (or unwilling) to control the flow of illegal migration from its Mediterranean coastline to southern EU states, in particular Italy and Malta. The EU's border agency, Frontex, has reported a year on year increase in illegal immigration into the EU from 2012 onwards with approximately 200,000 illegal immigrants crossing the Mediterranean and landing in Italy in 2014 alone. The pressure placed on EU member states has been growing in recent years largely due to civil wars, environmental catastrophes and growing poverty in the Middle East and Africa. These illegal migrants add to the labour force in the EU (although if they are employed it will most likely be in the informal sector), add to demand on services like housing, education and healthcare, and add to the demand for resources like energy and food. This has led some in the EU to view this issue as a security challenge, while other see it as a humanitarian problem.

To add to the concerns about the impact of illegal immigration in the EU, the migration routes across African and the Mediterranean Sea, and the means by which migrants travel them, are notoriously dangerous. In the first four months of 2015 Frontex reported that over 1,700 people had lost their lives while trying to cross the Mediterranean, with over 800 feared dead in one single accident. The boats used by illegal migrants are often little more than small lifeboats or similar crafts with limited capacity to hold people and travel the open sea. Yet, hundreds of people are crammed onto these boats by human traffickers (who the migrants have to pay, often many thousands of dollars) and are unsafe. Concern for the loss of life as well as the challenge of managing migration led the EU to implement Operation Triton to try to control the flow of illegal migrants and save lives. This operation involves sixteen European states (from within the EU and non-EU states) and has a budget of 120 million Euros per year. The remit of the operation is to intercept migrants crossing the sea, take them to Lampedusa (an Italian island in the Mediterranean) and process them. By using naval and air capabilities it is hoped that Operation Triton can not only reduce the number of migrant deaths but also take control of this form of migration to the EU.

Since the 1990s migration has become a significant focus of international collaboration and coordination between governments, as well as non-state actors. In particular, there has been pressure from within developed states, which have largely been the recipients of migrants to regulate migration. Managing migration, however, also relies heavily on cooperation between governments (and other actors) from around the world. Migration is truly a global phenomenon and the process of moving from one place to another is not as straightforward as travelling from a home country to the host country. There are often a number of states that need to be traversed/ moved through along the way – especially when considering illegal migration, and many forms of involuntary migration involving asylum seekers, refugees and displaced persons. Contemporary patterns of migration are among the most complex and complicated phenomena in today's world, thus requiring highly structured and costly responses that are difficult to implement. See the example box below, which details the highly sensitive and multifaceted EU response to illegal migration from North Africa, especially Libya, to southern Europe, especially Malta and Italy, via the Mediterranean Sea.

Policy responses to migration have sought to both facilitate and promote the legal and equitable movement of people across borders in a similar way to efforts to facilitate the movement of goods and capital, and the provision of services. It is important to note that when IPE scholars discuss policy responses to migration, the issue is not only seen as one of resistance or security. This might be the assumption one could make after perusing mass media outlets for coverage of migration, but the reality of governmental and nongovernmental migration policies is far more balanced. Both state and non-state actors have developed mechanisms by which migration is monitored, facilitated, controlled and/or prevented. These range from domestic and international laws, aid and support mechanisms (for example, studies of human rights, economics, security and migration), and coordination through international institutions like the UN High Commission on Refugees.

# The International Organization for Migration (IOM)

**Headquarters:** Geneva, Switzerland

The IOM was founded in 1951 and like many IGOs has its headquarters in Geneva, Switzerland. At the time of writing it has 157 member states and 10 observer states along with over 80 IGOs with observer status. Even though the IOM has a global remit and is perhaps the most significant international body whose work focuses on migration, it has a rather modest budget of approximately $1.68 billion (which in comparison to many IGO budgets, is significant, but compared to national defence budgets, for example, is very small). As stated on its website the IOM is 'committed to the principle that humane and orderly migration benefits both migrants and society'. It works with governments, migrants and other non-state partners 'to provide humane responses to the growing migration challenges of today'. At the core of the IOM's mission is the belief that everyone should have the right of freedom of movement, and it recognises that migration is a complex phenomenon and a multifaceted issue with links to economic, social, political and developmental causes and effects.

With offices in over 100 countries the IOM plays a key role in working with national governments to promote international dialogue and cooperation on migration issues. It is important to note that its approach is not simply to facilitate migration or to prevent it. Rather the IOM's work with governments focuses on understanding the issues facing migrants and the societies they move to alike, and working to find political and economic solutions to help people before they become migrants (through reducing 'push' factors); helping migrants to move safely and legally, and supporting them once they have migrated to a new society/country; and helping host countries and societies absorb migrants effectively.

Despite its attempts to promote well-being, the IOM has been criticised by a range of actors from different positions. For example, some have criticised the IOM as an institution that simply seeks to control migration in the interest of national governments (usually host governments that are seen as wanting to limit immigration). Others have argued that it has been used as a mechanism by which governments evade international human rights laws and that it supports governments in upgrading control over their borders and constructing centres for migrants that are little more than prisons. Perhaps the most damning criticism is levelled at the very ideological position the IOM is founded upon, with some claiming that it adheres to a nationalist ideology that focuses on the concept of 'homelands'. In response to criticisms, the IOM presents itself as an organisation that is concerned with human well-being above all else and one that works towards this goal within the constraints of a global system dominated by states pursuing their interests.

*Source*: http://unitedkingdom.iom.int/

## Summary

The movement of people around the planet is a key component of the contemporary global political economy and is an increasingly important issue in international relations. This chapter has outlined the characteristics of migration and discussed the key economic, political, social, and environmental causes and effects. It is important to remember that migration can be a voluntary process whereby people seek to move from one place to another in order to pursue better living conditions, environmental resources, employment opportunities, access to education, access to healthcare, to secure their human rights and so on. Here a conscious decision is taken to migrate because conditions are perceived to be better elsewhere – what we can term pull factors. At the same time, however, migration may be an involuntary process whereby people are compelled to move from one place, perhaps their traditional homeland, to another location because conditions have deteriorated to the extent that staying put is either not possible or highly damaging. Wars, persecution (for example, religious, ethnic or gender-based), environmental disasters, resource scarcity, poverty and so on can act as push factors that force people to migrate to better conditions out of necessity. The nature of the global economic system in many ways creates the conditions for labour migration (more often seen as a voluntary form of migration, but that can very clearly also result in involuntary migration). The global division of labour that has accompanied the

**Table 13.1** Chapter summary

| | Key actors | Key processes | Emphasis on political economy | What causes change? | Global institutions? | View of conflict in global relations? |
|---|---|---|---|---|---|---|
| Economic migration | MNCs; individuals; NGOs; national governments | Processes and structures related to the global division of labour, technological change, development/ underdevelopment, urbanisation, industrialisation, climate change, political/ institutional integration | Economic well-being and development as the key drivers (push and pull factors), while political processes regulate (facilitate or hinder) the movement of people | Urbanisation; demographic growth; climate change; conflict; development; education | Can be seen as highly important in managing economic migration | Can hinder economic migration through restricting the economic and political opportunities to migrate; but can also encourage people to migrate to seek better economic conditions |
| Political migration | National governments; individuals; NGOs | War; conflict; authoritarianisation/ political repression; institutionalisation | Importance of the economics of political repression, insecurity and instability | War; conflict; climate change; insecurity; persecution; ideological affinity/difference; human rights violations | Can be seen as highly important in managing political migration | Often a key push factor encouraging the migration of people seeking to escape conflict, insecurity and/or persecution |

expansion of the capitalist system of production and consumption reinforces market forces that regulate labour supply and demand. What has emerged is a concentration of high-paying jobs that require highly skilled and educated workers in some areas, for example, in cities around the world, as well as within the more affluent economies in general. Furthermore, lower paying jobs that require manual, often unskilled labour have also become more concentrated in poorer societies around the world. Labour often, therefore, has to migrate to where the demand is located.

Migration is also an important social and political issue. There are many competing perceptions of migration and arguments that support the right of people to move around the world are countered by arguments that suggest there are damaging effects of migration on both home and host societies. There is no clear-cut answer to which school of thought is correct, but we can conclude that migration has become an important issue that governments and non-state actors around the world are increasingly concerned with. In particular, in host societies where migrants move to (the USA and EU countries are good examples here) the last decade or so has seen increasing public sentiment against large-scale immigration. A key factor in this discourse is the concern with cultural assimilation and multiculturalism. When migrants move to new countries they take with them many of their own customs, beliefs and languages. Host societies have become sensitive to the ways in which this phenomenon can change/has already changed their communities and a definite backlash is evident. We must remember, however, that migration has been a feature of the human experience throughout our history and migration takes place from developed countries to developing countries as well. Much like trade and capital flows, people are also increasingly moving around the world at ever greater rates as a result of globalisation and this is only likely to increase as global integration deepens.

## Reflective questions

1  In what ways has IPE analysed migration as a feature of the contemporary global political economy?
2  Why have scholars in IPE and other fields such as international relations and global studies only recently begun to study migration and labour?
3  What impact does migration have on cultural homogeneity/diversity in developed states? And does it have the same impact in developing states also?
4  It could be argued that migration is the feature of globalisation that states can exert the most control over (in contrast to capital flows, for example). Is this claim accurate? Why/why not?
5  What are the most important factors that lead to global-level migration (for example, are economic or security concerns more important)?
6  How can global-level migration best be managed to promote welfare, equality and stability?
7  Why has migration become a key political issue? And how does discourse on migration vary between richer and poorer states, and between democratic and authoritarian states?

## Suggestions for further reading

Boas, I. (2015) *Climate Migration and Security: Securitisation as a Strategy in Climate Change Politics*, London: Routledge.
Brettell, C.B. and Hollifield, J. (eds) (2014) *Migration Theory: Talking Across Disciplines*, 3rd edn, London: Routledge.

Brickner, R.K. (ed.) (2013) *Migration, Globalization, and the State*, Basingstoke: Palgrave Macmillan.

Castles, S., de Haas, H. and Miller, M.J. (2013) *The Age of Migration: International Population Movements in the Modern World*, 5th edn, Basingstoke: Palgrave Macmillan.

Dahlstedt, M. and Neergaard, A. (eds) (2015) *International Migration and Ethnic Relations: Critical Perspectives*, London: Routledge.

de Guchteneire, P., Pecoud, A. and Cholewinski, R. (eds) (2009) *Migration and Human Rights: The United Nations Convention on Migrant Workers' Rights*, Cambridge: Cambridge University Press.

Faist, T., Fauser, M. and Reisenauer, E. (2013) *Transnational Migration*, Cambridge: Polity Press.

Hollifield, J., Martin, P. and Orrenious, P. (eds) (2014) *Controlling Immigration: A Global Perspective*, 3rd edn, Stanford, CA: Stanford University Press.

Koser, K. (2007) *International Migration: A Very Short Introduction*, Oxford: Oxford University Press.

Messina, A.M. and Lahav, G. (eds) (2005) *The Migration Reader: Exploring Politics and Policies*, Boulder, CO: Lynne Rienner.

Quayson, A. and Arhin, A. (eds) (2012) *Labour Migration, Human Trafficking and Multinational Corporations*, London: Routledge.

Schierup, C., Munck, R., Likic-Brboric, B. and Neergard, A. (eds) (2015) *Migration, Precarity, and Global Governance: Challenges and Opportunities for Labour*, Oxford: Oxford University Press.

Schiller, N.G. and Faist, T. (eds) (2010) *Migration, Development, and Transationalization: A Critical Stance*, Oxford: Berghahn Books.

Timmerman, C., Martiniello, M., Rea, A. and Wets, J. (eds) (2015) *New Dynamics in Female Migration and Integration*, London: Routledge.

UNDP (1994) *Human Development Report*, New York: United Nations.

# 14 Health

## Chapter learning outcomes

After reading this chapter students should be able to:

- Understand and explain the demographic shifts leading to the so-called 'health transition'.
- Explore the emergence of lifestyle-related non-communicable diseases.
- Critically reflect on the role of the World Health Organization in promoting health.
- Recognise the impact of large pharmaceutical companies in relation to health issues.
- Reflect on the role of individuals in taking responsibility for their own health.

## Introduction

The political economy of health encompasses every aspect of human life, literally from 'cradle to grave'. Levels of healthcare provision can determine survival rates of both newborns and their mothers. In parts of the developing world naming ceremonies do not take place until a full year after birth, reflecting the relatively low survival rates of many infants in particularly impoverished communities. Life expectancy at birth ranges from nearly ninety in Monaco down to under fifty in Chad (CIA World Factbook 2014 estimates). Although the global average for life expectancy continues to rise there are huge variations regarding both access to healthcare and how aging populations are perceived and cared for. The factors influencing an individual's health during their lifetime are a mix of that person's patterns of behaviour combined with what level of government intervention and assistance there is in the healthcare sector. While some health determinants may be genetically inherited the manner in which one's life is led is playing an increasingly significant role in terms of both longevity and also quality of life. Moreover, broader aspects of the global economy, from patterns of trade and consumption to the manner in which foodstuffs are labelled and marketed, are also crucial elements in determining both an individual's options as well as choices in relation to their health.

This chapter takes a very broad and inclusive approach to the issue of health recognising that many factors and forces are at play with regard to structural determinants at local, national and up to the global level. Environmental factors such as access to potable water or levels of air pollution are clearly influential at the immediate local level. How the relevant local authorities and national governments respond to such issues, possibly with overseas development assistance is also a major factor. Broader economic issues come into play as access to healthcare is increasingly privatised and the ability to enjoy a healthy lifestyle, for example, being able to live in a relatively clean and safe neighbourhood or afford to buy healthy food, is dependent on individuals and households having sufficient disposable income to adopt such lifestyles. Other factors may be more cultural in nature. With greater levels of internal and international migration, plus intergenerational changes in outlook, attitudes and practices, how healthcare is perceived (by both patients and clinicians) is also important. What is clear is that there is no 'one size fits all' approach to health and healthcare. The following sections outline key trends in health and healthcare provision, and responses to these trends.

# The health transition

When looking at changing patterns of health it should first be noted that these changes are happening within the broader context of a global demographic transition with progress being made on reducing the rates of infant mortality and many people experiencing increased lifespan. The latter being a result of a combination of better health education, enhanced levels of medical interventions and generally improved living standards in all but the poorest parts of the world or zones of armed conflict. Advances in medical science and major international initiatives such as the Millennium Development Goals/Sustainable Development Goals have also contributed to a longer-living population.

While health professionals are in the business of maximising people's lifespan there has been an unintended consequence in that although people are living longer many are increasingly adopting relatively unhealthy lifestyles. The health transition is most simply described as a shift from the dominant cause of illness and morbidity moving away from communicable to lifestyle-related non-communicable diseases (NCDs), such as heart disease and diabetes. As countries modernise and become more 'developed' there is a tendency for birth rates to fall and the average age of the population to rise. This is partly due to more women entering paid employment, rather than focusing on home life and child-rearing. Broader shifts away from subsistence and agrarian-based economies to predominantly urban living and cash-based economies have also impacted on family size. One consequence of a lower birth rate and an aging population is that over time there will be fewer among younger generations relative to older generations as the latter group increases in number and is also likely to manifest multiple chronic and debilitating illnesses and diseases, thereby requiring ever-greater resources needing to be directed towards care for the elderly.

Several issues arise as a consequence of the health transition. First among these is that it raises questions regarding the extent to which individuals are responsible for their own lifestyle and the health-related consequences of that lifestyle. This is also partly an ideological question about the appropriate level of intervention, or some might say interference of the state into the affairs of individual citizens. Although it is well known that smoking, excessive drinking and some other forms of drug use can have long-term health impacts many people would argue that it is up to them how they behave and where, when and how they take their pleasures. That is a perfectly defendable libertarian position to take. However, this becomes more complex when later healthcare costs are taken into account. Should the wider community foot the bill for what are, arguably, self-inflicted illness and diseases? This has become a more intense topic for debate in societies where austerity measures have led to cuts in public services and serious questions have to be asked regarding which patients should receive priority treatment. Such questions are asked at the national level where public healthcare provision is usually linked to some form of direct taxation to support a range of public services. At the international level health concerns are addressed via various means, sometimes targeting specific issues such as tackling the spread of HIV/AIDS or combating malaria or tuberculosis. While many states have aspects of such projects integrated into their bilateral overseas aid programmes, the key UN agency aimed at the coordination of such measures is the World Health Organization.

## The World Health Organization

As the leading inter-governmental agency working in the field of international public health, WHO acts as the main body for coordinating the reporting of and action on identified health issues. Based in Geneva this organisation employs over 8,000 staff working at the main Secretariat and across a number of regional offices. It also works with more than 700 collaborative partners, mainly research institutions. This approach to cooperative networking with other bodies has been at the heart of the WHO approach to health since its conception. The first collaborative project was the link to the World Influenza Centre, based in London, in 1947. The experience of the Spanish Flu pandemic following the First World War demonstrated the potential for infectious diseases to spread very quickly and with devastating consequences. In addition to pandemic awareness and rapid reaction response mechanisms, the WHO has also developed collaborative research projects for a wide range of health strategies.

The complex nature of health issues means that the WHO is required to take a broad multi-sectoral view towards both preventative and curative approaches to health. Governance is also an issue as WHO must work in partnership with national governments, multinationals operating businesses in the health sector, relevant civil society stakeholder groups and individuals. It also needs to be able to respond to the immediate health-related impacts of major natural disasters such as earthquakes, tsunamis, cyclones and related events, plus the more mundane but no less important agenda of ongoing health awareness-raising, education and health promotion. In addition the WHO plays a crucial role in reviewing and disseminating medical scientific research in order to better understand both the causes and range of treatments available to tackle health risks. In an effort to raise awareness about specific health issues the WHO has instigated certain days of the year to promote action. For example, there is an HIV/AIDS day, a tuberculosis day, a breast cancer awareness day, etc. There is also an annual World Health Day with a different theme each year. In 2015 the theme was food safety. There are also regular conferences held to discuss and address recognised issues, such as disaster risk reduction. March 2015 saw the first Ministerial Conference on Global Action Against Dementia. This is a reflection of how the international health agenda is very fluid and evolves over time in response to emerging threats and priorities.

Despite the central role played by the WHO, it is not without its critics. Few would challenge the overarching goals of the organisation, but there are some dissenting voices when it comes to how these goals might best be achieved. In particular there are a number of civil society groups that question the manner in which large pharmaceutical companies interact with the WHO, with the suggestion being that this type of lobbying is designed to further the interests and profits of these companies rather than directly addressing global health priorities. Foremost among these civil society activist groups is the People's Health Movement, who monitor the WHO via the WHO-Watch project and also produce a regular alternative world health report, Global Health Watch.

## People's Health Movement (PHM)

The roots of the PHM can be traced back to the Alma-Ata conference in 1978 where the health ministers of 134 countries, under the auspices of the WHO and UNICEF, set a target to achieve 'Health for All' by the year 2000. The failure to have reached this goal led to a coordinated response by civil society groups with approximately 1,500 delegates from over 90 countries meeting in Bangladesh in 2000 for the first People's Health Assembly. This led to the creation of the PHM and a subsequent People's Charter for Health. Since then PHM has developed into a number of regional networks coordinated by a global steering council. So-called 'country circles' have been created, but with a high level of autonomy as the steering council recognises that local groups will wish to organise themselves as they see fit and will identify their own campaigning priorities based on local circumstances, needs and capabilities. An example of this is the PHM-UK 'circle', which was launched at Nottingham Trent University in 2012. This event was timed to coincide with the Third People's Health Assembly being held in Cape Town, South Africa. While it was intended to highlight many of the global health issues surrounding the meeting of basic needs, particularly in the developing world, it was also an opportunity for relevant stakeholders to meet and discuss health priorities in a UK context. The 2012 meeting was initially driven by a small number of UK-based academics and clinicians, with additional input from civil society groups focusing on particular health concerns, such as asthma and diabetes. This group has continued to act as the main conduit for information sharing and coordination of joint actions across the various national groups. That said the combination of government austerity measures and increased pressure to privatise large parts of the UK health sector has meant that the highest profile campaigning has coalesced around groups such as Keep our National Health Service Public and the European-wide opposition to trade deals such as the Trans-Atlantic Trade and Investment Partnership (TTIP). The latter campaign is concerned about the encroachment of a neo-liberal agenda into public services beyond healthcare, but the potential impact of health services has drawn intense criticism from a large number of clinicians, administrators, health workers' unions and patient groups.

The agendas of the WHO and the PHM movement clearly overlap in terms of their focus on health and healthcare and their shared desire to promote healthy living, extend lifespan and generally improve life chances in relation to aspects of health. That said there are still some striking differences between the two. Although the WHO has a global remit, it is reliant on contributions from member states' governments for funding. This does therefore to some extent have a bearing on what resources are available for what projects and initiatives. PHM operations are largely based on voluntary contributions and work being undertaken by the employees of health sectors NGOs. This allows for a greater level of flexibility with regard for the type of issues to be prioritised and also how they might best be addressed. In addition to the public and civil society sectors there is also a further dynamic created when one considers the role and influence of the private sector. The pharmaceutical industry is one of the world's most profitable businesses and the manner in which it decides how to target its research and development strategies, in terms of which diseases/ markets these companies see as the most profitable, has a huge knock-on impact with regard to patterns of health treatment.

## 'Big Pharma'

As noted above, while average lifespan is increasing there is also a corresponding rise in illness and disease, with a disproportional amount of medication being prescribed to older patients – notably among more affluent communities. Coupled with a growing trend of privatisation in the health sector this creates a 'driver' towards pharmaceutical companies targeting those illnesses and diseases that are most prevalent among the wealthier percentile of the global population. This is a strategy that PHM and other civil society groups have criticised as, they argue, it does not marshal resources in a manner that will do the greatest good for the greatest number. Rather it increases inequality and disadvantages poorer communities and individuals who are unable to afford often costly medications. In addition to the marginalisation of such groups from accessing adequate healthcare provision this strategy also means that certain illnesses and disease, such as tackling malaria or tuberculosis, are sidelined in favour of more profitable treatments for anti-depressants or medication to treat high blood pressure. Without government intervention to address this trend the market-led strategy of these multinationals will be, understandably, to focus on the healthcare treatments that generate the most profit.

Pfizer, Roche, Johnson and Johnson and GlaxoSmithKline (GSK) are among the largest pharmaceutical companies, each with annual turnovers worth billions of dollars (see Table 14.1).

It is worth noting that most multinationals do not operate wholly within a single commodity market but are often a conglomeration of companies with investments in several cycles of manufacturing and product promotion. For example, while AstraZeneca are predominantly known for their work in the health sector they also work in other areas such as research into the genetic modification of crops. Similarly Johnson and Johnson produce a range of skincare items that would be more accurately described as beauty products than healthcare treatments. Pfizer owns subsidiary companies that manufacture household cleaning products. These companies' websites highlight the medical aspects of their operations, generally portraying themselves as working towards the improvement of human health. At a certain level this is undeniably true given the range of healthcare items they produce. However, they are first and foremost profit-making companies and there are potential controversies surrounding the extent to which they may put profit ahead of the 'greater good'.

One of the more notable issues surrounding the pricing of medications was during the late 1990s and into 2000/2001 when significant inroads were being made in producing anti-retroviral (ARV) drugs as a treatment for HIV/AIDS. The efficacy of these treatments was being demonstrated in the more developed parts of the world, yet the cost of these drugs made them unaffordable in the parts of the world where the quantitative demand was greatest. This issue came to a head when the South African government attempted to make use of generic drugs the production of which was, arguably, in breach of the intellectual property rights of the original manufacturers of these drugs. While the patent holders had a strong case for protecting their intellectual property, by attempting to control this they faced a public relations crisis as it appeared they were, in a sense, holding developing nations' governments to ransom by demanding high prices for life-saving medication. Ultimately the major ARV drug manufacturers had to reduce their demands, or risk alienating their customers with potentially very damaging impacts on their balance sheets. The issue of the pricing of medication remains contentious. In the UK in early 2015 the availability of a vaccine to fight meningitis B was delayed while the government negotiated what it considered to be an affordable price for this treatment. The charity Meningitis Now campaigned against unaccept-

**Table 14.1**   Annual turnover of largest pharmaceutical companies 2012–2013

| # | Company | 2013 ($m) | 2012 ($m) | Growth ($m) | Growth (%) |
|---|---|---|---|---|---|
| 1 | Pfizer | 47878 | 51214 | −3336 | −7 |
| 2 | Novartis | 47468 | 46732 | 736 | 2 |
| 3 | Roche | 39163 | 38006 | 1156 | 3 |
| 4 | Merck & Co. | 37437 | 40601 | −3164 | −8 |
| 5 | Sanofi | 37124 | 39511 | −2387 | −6 |
| 6 | GlaxoSmithKline | 33330 | 33335 | −5 | 0 |
| 7 | Johnson & Johnson | 28125 | 25351 | 2774 | 10 |
| 8 | AstraZeneca | 25711 | 27925 | −2214 | −9 |
| 9 | Lilly | 20962 | 20567 | 395 | 2 |
| 10 | AbbVie | 18790 | 18380 | 410 | 2 |

*Source*: Global Data (2015) at www.pmlive.com/top_pharma_list/global_revenues.

able delays in making treatments available, which could have prevented deaths and disabilities as a direct result of price negotiations. As with the ARV treatment example above, the political economy of the healthcare sector does raise questions as to whether or not the companies working in this field are qualitatively different to those producing, for example, televisions sets or toys. From their perspective, and that of their shareholders, they need to produce a profit. Not least to enable them to reinvest in the research and development that will allow them to work towards the next generation of improved treatments. Where this becomes problematic is when these companies are perceived to be profiteering from ill health.

Another aspect of the prescribing of drugs is when they are seen to be provided too readily. Just as there can be difficulties with a lack of affordability for certain medications, others have been criticised for becoming too widely prescribed. One aspect of modern life appears to be a marked increase in the number of anti-depressant medications being offered to patients. Although there is certainly a case for the treatment of chemical imbalances in the brain being offered there is also a concern that general practitioners may see writing a prescription as a relative 'quick fix' as opposed to alternative support and therapy that deals with the root causes of many people's anxieties and depression. Similarly, the sharp rise among children, and increasingly adults, being diagnosed with attention deficit hyperactivity disorder (ADHD) has led to what some might describe as a knee-jerk reaction to prescribe medication as the first rather than last resort for treatment. Arguably the pharmaceutical companies may simply be responding to a market demand by massively increasing the production of the range of brand name prescription drugs available to treat psychological and behavioural issues. One does not have to suggest there is a conspiracy between drug manufacturers and the medical profession to raise concerns about potential over-prescribing and medication dependency. One area where medics are questioning the validity of potential over-prescription relates to the use of antibiotics. While the initial introduction of antibiotics, such as penicillin, represented a remarkable breakthrough in treating bacterial infection, recent years have seen a marked increase in antibiotic resistance. Again the fault does not necessarily lie with the producers of these drugs. Yet there are concerns regarding the apparent focus on the production of 'goods' to cure illness and disease rather than focus more on the preventative aspects of leading healthier lifestyles in healthier environments.

## Determinants of health

The pharmaceutical industry tends to focus more on curative treatments rather that the promotion of preventative behaviour. An exception to this is in relation to dental health and the promotion of toothpastes and mouthwash products to reduce oral bacteria and tooth decay. The broader medical profession takes a more holistic approach to health with increasing awareness and proactive strategies to promote healthy eating and exercise regimes to enhance good health. Governments are also recognising that there are significant financial savings to be made by maintaining a healthy population. This is in terms of both maximising the productive days of the working age population and also attempting to minimise the growing costs of responding to ill health among all ages of the population. However, in order to make meaningful assessments of how to promote good health, it is first necessary to gain an understanding of what factors play a role in determining aspects of both good and ill health.

Several models have been developed to illustrate key factors that impact on the health chances of individuals and communities. Many of these are derived from the work of Dahlgren and Whitehead (2007) and their illustration of the factors leading to inequalities in health. Figure 14.1 is an adaptation of their concept explored further by Barton and Grant (2006).

**Figure 14.1** Factors impacting on the health chances of individuals

*Source*: Barton, H. and Grant, M. (2006) 'A health map for the local human habitat', *The Journal of the Royal Society for the Promotion of Health*, 126: 252–253.

    With people being central to this model, attention is drawn to the complex matrix of factors leading to both their inherent health chances, largely based on genetic factors and personal metabolism, through to external factors such as how 'healthy' the local environment is. Although the above model does not highlight the manner in which 'global forces' are playing an ever-greater role in determining local conditions these are factors that are growing in importance. What determines both a person's quantity (longevity) and quality of health is a mix of individual attributes and behaviours and how these interrelate with both local environmental conditions and national or even global structures and processes that, in turn, impact upon this local environment. For example, the dominance of the neo-liberal economic system has implications for both wealth creation and patterns of poverty, with resulting limitations and restriction to healthcare provision. What determines an individual or community's health may have political, social, economic, environmental and even cultural dimensions.

    As already indicated many aspects of health and healthcare have a political dimension to them. Political parties with different ideologies exhibit varying attitudes towards the level of engagement and intervention that they believe should take place with regard to engaging with and promoting the health of their citizens. This can be illustrated by the amount of government investment in public health services as opposed to expecting individuals to be more directly responsible for their own health, possibly via the purchase of health insurance. The United States provides an example of how divisive this issue can be in relation to the initiative that has become known as ObamaCare. Despite being one of the world's most 'developed' countries, until fairly recently many Americans were unable to afford adequate healthcare insurance. In 2010 the Obama administration signed into law a bill, the Affordable Care Act, which extended healthcare provisions to in excess of 50 million US citizens that had previously been outside of this system. While there was an initial investment cost in introducing this system, which opponents of this bill very vocally criticised, the eventual enactment of this legislation was a combination of hard-nosed business sense in ensuring a healthy and therefore productive working population, plus the more compassionate driver of it being 'the right thing to do'.

The ObamaCare example illustrates how the political and economic spheres are so closely interconnected. Although much of the controversy surrounding the proposed introduction of this bill, which was one of the central platforms of Barack Obama's Presidential campaign strategy, focused on the affordability of the plan to the US economy, it was largely disputed across the Democrat/Republican divide. There was a blurring with wider issues related to personal responsibility, accountability and freedom from state 'control'. It is often difficult to separate out individual aspects of health and healthcare without referencing the predominant context of the political economy of neo-liberalism. The erstwhile command economies of China and the former Soviet Union have now moved much closer to the free market model, even in relation to healthcare. Cuba is exceptional in the manner in which healthcare has remained a key element of what the government provides for its citizens. In relation to ophthalmology, Cuban surgeons have internationally renowned reputations and matching facilities. Given the economic sanctions imposed on Cuba by the US it is a measure of the Cuban government's commitment to this aspect of healthcare that they have been able to develop such a high level of expertise in this field. Of course there are other aspects of Cuban policies, such as the restriction of certain social and political freedoms, which are less impressive. As a determinant of health one does not necessarily have to experience a trade-off between personal freedom and a supportive public healthcare system. That said, there does appear to be an ever-closer relationship between the level of government intervention and the likelihood of people experiencing good health. In part this is a reflection of broad processes of modernisation and globalisation where there has been a marked shift away from subsistence to cash-based economies, away from predominantly rural to urban settlement and changing patterns of lifestyle with relevance to both exercise and diet.

Just as the so-called 'triumph of liberalism' has led to increased marketisation of formerly public services, with resulting impacts on healthcare, there have been other processes that also have, presumably unintended, consequences on health. Medical research and knowledge now enables a much greater understanding of what factors influence and potentially determine levels of health. Some of this knowledge resides largely within the world of medical scientists and clinicians. However, there is also a growing popular awareness of what constitutes a healthy or unhealthy lifestyle. Of course knowledge of longer-term consequences will not necessarily alter short-term attitudes and behaviours. Most people will be aware that excessive drinking, smoking, lack of exercise and diets high in fat, sugar and salt are likely to lead to relatively poor health, if not immediately then over time. Some people manage these ill health factors via periods of 'detox', shedding weight and building muscle tone only to subsequently slide back into poor eating habits and exercise avoidance. As noted above though health determinants are only partially to do with individuals' lifestyle choices. Although these are very important they also need to be seen in the context of what options are available, from which such choices can be made. For example, if you live on a remote low-lying atoll in the Pacific and sea-level rise and storm surges have destroyed your locally grown crops you have little choice other than to rely on imported foodstuffs, at least until such time as local production recovers. By necessity the imported foodstuffs are unlikely to include fresh fruit and vegetables but will be predominantly tinned and processed food, which will probably have high fat, sugar and salt content.

In addition to knowledge about how lifestyle impacts upon health there are other psychological dimensions to understanding the relationship between lifestyle and health. Continuing with the Pacific islands example, this is a region that has one of the highest rates of obesity and related health issues, in particular diabetes, in the world. Of the ten countries in the world with the highest rates of obesity nine of them are Pacific island territories. The shift from locally grown to imported food is a partial explanation for this prevalence. However, for some Pacific islanders there is also a self-perception that they are genetically predisposed to carrying a lot of weight. While it is true that many Samoans, Tongans and Nauruans are heavier than the global average this is more readily explained by lifestyle rather than genetics.

It is the case that some ethnic groups are born with certain health-related characteristics. Some Australian aborigines and First Nation native Americans are understood to have particular sensitivity and intolerance to alcohol. Allegedly, although this point remains disputed, Mohawks were hired to work on the construction of New York's skyscraper buildings because they did not suffer from vertigo. This is debatable as there are alternative explanations for the predominance of Mohawks among these workers. They may have had limited alternative work opportunities, they may have still suffered from a fear of heights but worked to overcome this as part of a cultural need to demonstrate their bravery. Much the same as Pacific islanders may believe they are born to carry a lot of body weight, once such a belief has started to circulate it may have been reinforced both among the Mohawk community and those who preferred to employ them for this construction work. As a determinant of health, cultural beliefs can be a very important factor.

Perception of 'ideal' body image is a topic fraught with difficulties and controversy. Eating disorders range from anorexia to bulimia and there is a certain level of subjectivity involved in what constitutes a 'normal' or 'attractive' body shape. That said, many medical authorities do now adopt a body mass index (BMI) criteria for measuring when an individual might be considered underweight or overweight. Both ends of the weight spectrum have aroused debates that question the validity of such measurements and how they might be understood and applied. Several feminist scholars have questioned the manner in which females, young girls in particular, are portrayed in fashion magazines with the 'norm' appearing to be an unhealthy thinness. Several European governments have recently intervened in this debate by enacting legislation requiring models to have a body mass index of at least eighteen or face prosecution. Yet simultaneously there is a risk that a potential backlash to this overly thin body 'ideal' may be contributing to what is a growing level of overweight and obesity among children. This latter trend is most prevalent in the Western world, but increasingly identifiable worldwide as the process of modernisation impacts on all communities. Another dimension to this issue is the extent to which parents acknowledge whether or not their children have weight issues to be concerned about. In the UK in March 2015 the London School of Hygiene and Tropical Medicine and the Institute of Child Health published the findings of a study looking into how parents perceived the weight of their children. Out of a group of nearly 3,000 parents only 4 identified their children as being overweight. In fact, based on BMI criteria, this figure should have been closer to 1,000 with a third of the parents taking part in the study seriously misperceiving the health of their children. Interestingly the study also found that there were significant determining factors based on ethnic origin with families from black and Asian backgrounds more likely to underestimate their children's weight in relation to health guidelines. This again reinforces the point that cultural factors can play a significant role in determining how health issues are perceived and reacted to.

The above section has looked at how a broad range of factors can significantly determine health outcomes. Some are genetically inherited, but the majority of these factors are external to individuals' personal physiognomy. Levels of state intervention, including legislation, can play a role. The manner in which the private sector prioritises certain research and development of treatments can also have health implications. Deep-rooted cultural beliefs, attitudes and practices will undoubtedly influence how aspects of health are perceived and responded to. It is virtually impossible to group all of these myriad factors together to make meaningful statements about common trends in the evolution of human health in the twenty-first century. That said, there are some factors that can be seen to be shared across various demographics in terms of age, race, class, gender or which part of the world a person happens to reside. The following sections make a distinction between the health experiences in the less-developed world and in the so-called 'developed' world.

# Health in the developing world

As noted in Chapter 8 on development this is a contentious term and one with many critics and various interpretations of not only what development might entail but, even when there is agreement on what this represents, how these goals might be achieved. One of the key indicators surrounding development that is largely agreed upon is the promotion of individual and community-based health and healthcare. This chapter began by drawing attention to the wide disparities between countries in terms of rates of infant mortality and the average lifespan depending on where one is born. Of the eight Millennium Development Goals, three were explicitly dedicated to aspects of health. One on reducing infant mortality, a related goal on promoting maternal health and a third broader goal to tackle HIV/AIDS, malaria, tuberculosis and a range of other diseases. The subsequent Sustainable Development Goals are far less specific with a more generalised goal of aiming to 'ensure healthy lives and promote well-being for all of all ages'. This is an undeniably well-meaning goal, but its relative vagueness masks some serious health deficiencies, particularly in the developing world, that need to be addressed as a matter of urgency.

The WHO's 2014 World Health Statistics report indicated that the risk of a child born in Africa dying before their fifth birthday was eight times higher than that of a child born in Europe. Nearly 800 women die every day as a result of complications during childbirth, with the vast majority of these fatalities occurring in less-developed countries. In the WHO African region 70 per cent of fatalities are due to maternal and neonatal causes, infectious diseases and nutritional causes. This is compared to only 8 per cent in high-income countries. Despite the rhetoric of processes of modernisation leading to a more homogenous 'global village' there remain clear indicators that health and associated life chances are markedly different depending on one's place of birth and access to adequate healthcare facilities. The health transition referred to above does represent a broad shift towards a predominance of lifestyle-related NCDs, but there remain distinct areas where development strategies have yet to eradicate the more 'traditional' vectors of ill health. Numerous determinants can explain this ongoing disparity between developing and developed states' experience of health and healthcare. Quite how this is explained may vary depending on the theoretical or ideological position one takes. From a neo-Marxist position there are structural aspects to who gets what, when, where and how that have a bearing on health. Others may focus much more on individual behaviours and be less sympathetic to what they might see as unhealthy lifestyle choices. Regardless of the ideological position taken with regard to individuals' personal responsibility for their health it is undeniable that some communities, predominantly in the developing world, face a range of disadvantages in relation to the options open to them to make healthy lifestyle choices. Understandably many of these communities have aspirations to follow the lifestyle they perceive to represent the benefits of development as enjoyed in higher-income countries. However, as with the old adage of needing to be careful what one might wish for, all that appears to glitter in the developed world may not be as positive and beneficial as it seems to be. While there are definite advantages to be had in higher income countries, if one has a high income, there are also serious health issues and health risks underlying life in the developed world.

## Health in the developed world

Although there is no single pattern or trend of moving from what might be broadly considered as a state of being 'undeveloped' to 'developed' there are certain traits of modernised life that can be linked to aspects of health. With growth in inequality being a notable characteristic of development it is possible to distinguish between health issues connected to both poverty and to wealth and related over-consumption. It is no longer the case that a fairly straightforward narrative can be put forward showing a preponderance of ill health associated with poverty, although clearly some correlations do still exist. In most developed economies basic infrastructure developments means that the incidence of water-borne illness and diseases are now extremely low. Whereas diarrhoea and related dehydration remain a leading cause of infant death in many developing countries, this is no longer the case in the developed world. Similarly illnesses such as rickets, which had previously been much more prevalent, have reduced dramatically. The introduction of routine and standardised vaccination programmes for children has also vastly reduced several previously common complaints. Yet there are still higher incidences of some forms of ill health among lower-income groups. Taking London as an example of one of the leading financial centres and capital of a highly developed state there are some striking inequalities that emerge when comparing income and health. In 2010 The Trust for London and the New Policy Institute produce a report profiling poverty in the city. In the section on poverty and health it was found that infant deaths are 50 per cent more common in lower-income households; death rates for various forms of cancer and heart disease are twice as high for people with manual rather than non-manual employment; people in the poorest fifth of incomes are at much higher risk of mental illness than those in the richest fifth. This differentiation doubles for women at 24 per cent and 12 per cent respectively, with an even higher ratio for men at 22 per cent and 7 per cent. Of adults in the age range 45–64, 40 per cent with below average incomes were found to have long-term illness, more than twice the number of adults in the above average income sector. It is perhaps unsurprising that a correlation can be found between low income and ill health. However, there are also health-related issues associated with non-manual workers and higher-income earners.

Although the above figures indicate a higher proportion of some illness and disease among manual workers and lower-income groups there are a different set of issues becoming prevalent among office workers and those with higher incomes. A survey of 2,000 British office workers conducted by the British Heart Foundation in 2015 found that 37 per cent of men and 45 per cent of women spend less than thirty minutes on their feet during their working day. More than half of these workers regularly ate their lunch at their desk. This is a reflection of modern work practices with an increasing amount of work being conducted electronically while seated at a computer workstation. A feature of modern life is that it is increasingly sedentary. This applies beyond the workplace with people tending to take some form of motorised transport as opposed to cycling or walking, even for relatively short distances. Although a minority of people do take regular exercise either via running, gym membership or playing some form of sport, this is not the norm. Much was made of the supposed impact London hosting the 2012 Olympic Games would have on the health of the nation. Despite an initial rise in active participation in sports when the winning bid was announced and in the run up to the games, Sport England has since reported that the number of people playing sports has actually declined significantly over subsequent years. While the games may have raised the profile of certain sports and increased their audience, the vast majority of people are not participants but passive viewers watching from the comfort of their armchairs and sofas, quite possibly simultaneously enjoying an unhealthy snack.

Another aspect of modern life that is only recently being more fully recognised and partially addressed is that of mental health. A growing number of potentially stress-inducing factors are combining to create new and diverse mental health risks, some of which also manifest themselves with related physical symptoms. If there is a predominant aspect of life in a modern, developed society it is that of change. Although this may sometimes be a change for the better the underlying scenario and socio-economic culture is one of uncertainty and, in many cases, anxiety. This is not simply confined to the workplace. Divorce rates and the reformulation of households are increasingly common. In Belgium marriages have only a 1 in 3 chance of not ending in divorce. This is not to say that all family members who are involved in family breakdown are likely to suffer anxiety and/or some form of mental illness. Far from it, as some marriages and family relationships may actually be the cause of stress and anxiety. The point here is that where there had formally been a higher level of stability, in both people's professional and personal lives, this is now less certain. Fear of losing one's partner or fear of losing one's job and related income are potentially significant stress factors with resulting health implications. More generally some people may feel pressurised to conform to certain types of appearance or behaviour to 'fit in' with the dominant culture. This relates to the earlier point on body image and potential eating disorders. Another factor in this type of peer pressure is the phenomenal increase in the use of social media, particularly among children and young adults. One in four people worldwide, with a growing number in the developing world as interconnectivity spreads, are now using social media platforms such as Facebook or Twitter. As with any technology the crucial factor is not what it does but how it is used. For every example of cyber-bullying there will be another more positive example of the support that can be offered by friends and family, or even complete strangers, via this medium.

Patterns of stress, and subsequent stress-management, vary between individuals. There are some who would say that they thrive in stressful situations and that change and competitiveness are what drives them to succeed. Yet such individuals are, almost by definition, unusual. The University College London's Stress and Health Study (also known as Whitehall II) is a large-scale, long-term study of over 10,000 participants that began in 1985 and is ongoing. It is unusual both in terms of the nature of its core research focus and also the insights it has been able to provide by following such a large number of participants over so many years. After a period of thirty years 70 per cent of those who originally agreed to take part in the study are still alive. One of the key findings of the study has been that the group are not exhibiting common signs of aging and ill health. Of course it is very difficult to work out exactly what the causal connections might be between how and why the various participants appears to be aging differently. What is clear is that the vectors for maintaining good health and succumbing to poor health are extremely varied, not just between the developing and developed world but also within each of them. Patterns of modernisation and globalisation illustrate the types of factors and characteristics of shifting from less developed to more developed. While there are major benefits to be had from improved basic healthcare the modernised world also presents a number of differing health risks and challenges. The final section of this chapter looks at aspects of technological innovation that have implications for the political economy of health.

# Technology and health

Medical science has made remarkable inroads in dealing with all manner of illness and disease. We now know more about what factors are likely to lead to ill health and what are the most appropriate treatments, both curative and preventative, than at any time in human history. Obviously there are certain resource constraints in that having this level of knowledge does not necessarily mean it will be applied to all people in all places. This is the nature of the political economy of human interaction and most aspects of healthcare provision remain subject to market forces and other aspects of political and related vested interests.

Technology does not have to be equated with 'hi-tech' to be able to make a significant impact. The NGO Practical Action was formerly known as Intermediate Technology and their development work has largely focused on the digging of wells, the building of sand dams and other forms of water collection and irrigation to enhance water and food security, mainly but not exclusively in arid sub-Saharan African communities. The health implications of this are obvious as local food production is enhanced with resulting nutritional benefits. Similar fairly 'low-tech' solutions have been found to harness wind and solar power in remote communities to ensure refrigeration units in medical dispensaries can store vaccines safely, plus supply electricity for lighting and other uses. These and similar projects are harnessing renewable energy systems on a basic but far-reaching scale to make a significant impact where a fairly modest level of intervention can make a huge difference to very basic life chances. The lack of immunisation or a shortage of water treatment facilities are matters of life and death in many communities, despite much of the world taking such items and resources more or less for granted.

One of the more controversial aspects of technology is genetic modification of crops. There is a marked difference of approach to this technology around the world. Whereas the US has largely embraced it and rolled out industrial scale agricultural initiatives based on this technology, the European Union states have tended to adopt a more cautious approach, although recently there does appear to be a shift among some EU member states on this with an acknowledgement that with appropriate oversight and controls some GM crop utilisation might be adopted. Adopting a precautionary principle is certainly prudent. That said, there are potentially significant health benefits to be explored in relation to the use of GM crops and other foodstuff applications. In the developing world climate change and other factors provide a demand for drought-resistant crops. In areas where storm surges flood growing areas, as noted above in relation to the low-lying atolls of the Pacific, crops that can grow in heavily salinated soil would be advantages. Other strains of crops can be designed to be resistant to specific pests or to be especially high in certain vitamins and other nutrients. The possibilities of such technologies, if not endless, are certainly rich with the promise of addressing a broad range of food security issues with resulting benefits to health.

Just as the EU is cautious about unleashing new forms of technology there are also concerns with regard to genome mapping. The Human Genome Project (HGP) represents one of the largest international collaborative scientific endeavours ever undertaken. Briefly it has enabled the identification of specific human cells that are associated with certain hereditary illness and disease, such as cystic fibrosis and muscular dystrophy. The potential application for such knowledge could be incredibly far-reaching with the potential to identify and address cell markers associated with a much broader range of ill health, including various cancers, diabetes and even some psychological disorders. The scale of this project and the manner in which it has been adopted was demonstrated in 2015 when it was announced that the whole of the Icelandic population were now part of a genetic database that could provide information on hereditary health risks. As with GM technology this is both a remarkable scientific achievement, yet also raises some concerns. With this level of health 'profiling' it would be possible to possibly discriminate against certain groups.

This might be in terms of employment opportunities or possibly raising insurance premiums for those perceived to be at high risk of future illness or disability. In theory there is supposed to be a degree of anonymity associated with such databases. Although clearly individuals would need to be identified if they were to be offered treatment. Data protection is becoming more of an issue as an ever greater amount of personal information is now stored and could be shared. This may be for profit in terms of marketing various goods and services, or in some more dystopian scenarios even more sinister purposes. Again, the technology is impressive. How it is monitored, controlled and applied is a major challenge for the future – in terms of healthcare and many other aspects of the world's political economy.

## Summary

This chapter has only been able to highlight some of the key points surrounding the political economy of health. Each section could be expanded into a whole book. For example, the technology section makes no reference to the application of what is known as e-health and the scope for remote diagnosis and prescribing that is making use of information and communication technologies to develop healthcare in regions where it is difficult for highly trained clinicians to be permanently based. Although the post-First World War Spanish flu pandemic was briefly referred to there is scope to discuss more recent outbreaks, such as the cases of Ebola identified in West Africa in early 2015. Cultural factors were mentioned and it would be possible to look at issues such as female genital mutilation in relation to specific cultural beliefs, attitudes and practices. There are clear health implications in zones of conflict, both open warfare and more low-level aspects of attrition. Climate change and related aspects of environmental degradation have health implications. What this tells us is that the political economy of health is not something that can be simply reduced to a person's ill health and corresponding diagnosis and treatment. There are a great number of factors that impact on health, not just at the level of an individual's physiognomy but also the environment that they inhabit and also aspects of their personal lifestyle options and choices.

## Reflective questions

1   What is the significance of the health transition for healthcare systems?
2   Why have lifestyle-related NCDs increased in recent years?
3   What level of personal responsibility should individuals take with regard to their health?
4   In what ways does the World Health Organization attempt to promote 'Health for All'?
5   How does the global People's Health Movement differ from the WHO in its approach to health?

## Suggestions for further reading

Barton, H. and Grant, M. (2006) 'A health map for the local human habitat', *The Journal of the Royal Society for the Promotion of Health*, 126: 252–253.
Biswas, A., Oh, P.I, Faulkner, G.E., Bajaj, R.R., Silver, M.A., Mitchel, M.S. and Alter D.A. (2015)

**Table 14.2** Chapter summary

| | Key actors | Key processes | Emphasis on political economy | What causes change? | Global institutions? | View of conflict in global relations? |
|---|---|---|---|---|---|---|
| Positive determinants of health | Governments Medical professionals Individuals Arguably pharmaceutical companies, although they have also faced criticism for concentrating on some medical conditions seen as more profitable and not tackling others adequately, such as malaria | Environmental factors Government legislation Health education programmes | The level of government intervention to promote individuals' health is controversial with many feeling that people need to take responsibility for many aspects of their health. In economic terms having a healthy workforce is clearly a benefit for any national economy. This has to be balanced with how much is invested in public health services | Health education is obviously important but is not always wholly successful. For example, cigarette packets can be labelled with 'Smoking Kills' messages yet people will still choose to smoke | The World Health Organization is the key global institution. The broader UN is also relevant with many of its development goals focusing on health issues | Conflict is rarely going to be positive for health promotion. On occasion there may be an argument for conflict to be necessary to overthrow a regime to improve the health of communities disadvantaged by the current government |
| Negative determinants of health | Governments can both promote health but also undermine health provision if they prioritise other areas of spending at the expense of health services The food and drink industries have been heavily | Ill health can be as a result of genetic predisposition towards certain illnesses or, more often, as a result of government support for health services and people's ability to access them. Individuals need to | The distribution of wealth is also often an indicator for the distribution of heath. As such the interface between government policies and the economics of health is crucial in determining both positive and negative aspects of health, | Health can be negatively impacted for a great many reasons. Political instability may lead to conflict and less emphasis on health services. Economic issues may be a factor in societies where medical services | There is no global institution that seeks to promote ill health, although some might argue that the World Trade Organization and a global economic system that puts profit before the health of individuals, and the | Armed conflict is clearly a negative determinant of health, and increasingly for non-combatants caught up in these conflicts |

**Table 14.2** Continued

| Key actors | Key processes | Emphasis on political economy | What causes change? | Global institutions? | View of conflict in global relations? |
|---|---|---|---|---|---|
| criticised for some of the products they sell, as has the advertising industry for the manner in which these products are promoted. Individual behaviour is also a key element here so the lifestyle choices people make are key, although it should be recognised that some people do not always have healthy options available to them | have the option to choose a healthy lifestyle before we can begin to discuss whether or not they choose to do so | but is often most clearly identifiable when explaining why ill health occurs | are predominantly offered by the private sector and, therefore, unaffordable to some people Deteriorating environmental conditions can also negatively impact on quality of health | global ecosystem more generally, is a negative determinant for many people's health | |

'Sedentary time and its association with risk for disease incidence, mortality, and hospitalisation in adults: a systematic review and meta-analysis', *Annals of Internal Medicine*, 162(2): 123–132.

Central Intelligence Agency (2014), *World Factbook 2014*, New York: Skyhorse.

Dahlgren, G. and Whitehead, M. (2007) *Policies and Strategies to Promote Social Equity in Health, 1991* Stockholm: Institute for Policy Studies.

Gudbjartsson, D.F. *et al.* (2015) 'Large-scale whole-genome sequencing of the Icelandic population', *Nature Genetics*, online publication available at www.nature.com/ng/journal/vaop/ncurrent/full/ng.3247.html (accessed 9 February 2016).

Smith, R. and McMurray, C. (2001) *Diseases of Globalisation: Socioeconomic Transitions and Health*, London: Earthscan.

The Trust for London and the New Policy Institute (2010) *London's Poverty Profile*, London: New Policy Institute.

WHO (2008) *Closing the Gap in a Generation: Health Equity Through Action on the Social Determinants of Health*, Geneva: WHO.

WHO (2014) *World Health Statistics 2014*, Geneva: WHO. www.ucl.ac.uk/whitehallII/publications/2015_ publication (accessed 14 October 2016).

# **15** Concluding thoughts and remarks

This book can be used as an interpretive guide to actual events in the 'real world', but also to differing positions that interpret and describe these events. Of course, there are going to be differing views/perspectives on all issues and phenomena, but having read this book you should now be able to assess these in a more informed and critical manner.

One might assume that theoretical positions are relatively fixed, given their key concepts and assumptions. While this is true to some extent, all theories are constantly open to challenge and critique. As is demonstrated in Chapter 1, on the theoretical foundations of IPE and mainstream contemporary approaches, each school of thought has a particular worldview, which is increasingly subject to challenge as global systems and structures evolve. Some theorists may interpret these changes as reinforcing their core beliefs. Others may struggle to rationalise their theoretical position in relation to emerging processes and their consequences. The alternative approaches discussed in Chapter 2 are necessarily more in tune with processes of globalisation given their relatively recent evolution. Nevertheless, even some of these approaches can include some quite dogmatic and fixed positions and opinions. Chapter 3 focuses on business theories and global business behaviours, and explains how the complexity of multinational enterprise behaviour and strategies contribute to the complexity of the IPE.

The debate surrounding the extent and significance of processes of globalisation continues. There is no clear consensus on this with actively competing views between the hyperglobalists and the sceptics. Even the transformationalists remain far from being a homogeneous group, with differing protagonists emphasising differing aspects of globalisation as being significant. Regardless of one's position within the globalisation debate, even arch sceptics, it is undeniable that the world is experiencing some significant changes. For example, the national security agenda of the twenty-first century is different to that of the eighteenth, nineteenth or twentieth centuries. Basic principles of sovereignty, citizenship and self-determination may be ongoing concepts but how each of these are understood and promoted has changed. Similarly, the issues covered in the above chapters have also undergone elements of transformation both in terms of the actual phenomena and their relative position on national and international agendas.

The jigsaw analogy referred to at the start of this book can be applied in relation to the various issues under consideration here. However, depending on which approach you are taking you may have a different set of 'jigsaw pieces' compared to someone who favours a differing theoretical approach. For example, classical realists only deal with states and how they relate to each other. They do not have 'pieces' that represent individuals or other species. The liberal approach would be more complex as it would include 'pieces' for numerous non-state actors. At the same time, green theorists would wish to consider the whole spectrum of biological and environmental interactions. Some of these approaches are clearly more complex in their approach than others, yet each is able to construct a worldview with its own internal logic and rationale.

All of the issues that have been discussed in this book overlap and interrelate to some extent. Governance, for example, can be seen in relation to international/global finance and trade via the Bretton Woods institutions. Issues of environment and development are closely related to finance and trade, but are generally dealt with in alternative forums. There is, therefore, a certain tension and potential conflict between the actors and agendas in these two discrete but related areas. Cultural issues have not normally been part of traditional security agendas. However, in recent years the security agenda has evolved to include many more non-military issues. This is reflected in the culture, environment, development and technology chapters. As such, it is clear that the division of issue areas in IPE is increasingly difficult to maintain given the close connections between them. Furthermore, some issues that are of importance to IPE such as health and media, while not being addressed in individual chapters in this book are still relevant and have been included in discussions regarding other issues.

As a practical guide this book should have provided you with an insight into the range of issues that form part of the study of IPE. You will have seen differing interpretations and emphasis placed on certain aspects of international political economy. As you continue with your studies you should be able to return to this book and read it afresh in light of your growing understanding of the subject area. In particular you will find the further reading lists in each chapter a useful starting point for extending your awareness and understanding of IPE.

# Glossary

**absolute advantage**   A position developed by Adam Smith representing the ability of one state to produce a good more efficiently and cheaply than other states. When a state has absolute advantage it benefits from trading with others through specialisation in this good(s) and the importation of goods for which the production costs are lower abroad.

**alienation**   The concept created by Karl Marx denoting the effects of class conflict and materialism on the identities and associations of the individual. Through the competition for material possessions and wealth individuals are separated from each other, and in particular across class boundaries, in an atmosphere of mistrust and belligerency.

**anarchy**   The absence of a centralised authority that governs the behaviour of actors within any given theatre of relations. At the global level of analysis this equates to the absence of a global government that creates and enforces rules of behaviour for states and multinational/transnational actors.

**autarky**   The concept of being self-sufficient and self-reliant. An actor possesses this ability if it can survive in its form and function without relying on interactions with other actors such as trade for the import of goods and services or export for raising revenues.

**balance of payments**   An accounting system used to calculate and record a state's international financial transactions related to the import and export of goods, services and capital. Ideally the inward flow of financial resources should equal the outward flow to ensure a balance.

**balance of trade**   The net worth of a state's exports and imports of goods and services. Higher exports than imports will result in a trade surplus while higher imports will lead to a trade deficit. The balance of trade often does not remain constant and (short-term) surpluses or deficits are common.

**banks**   Financial institutions that act as repositories for capital deposits and sources of borrowed capital. Banks take in deposits and lend a large amount of them to other actors as investments for interest returns. In this way they act as mechanisms that direct capital supplies to areas of demand (from depositors to borrowers).

**bilateralism**   Form of policy making and action that involves interaction between two actors. This type of relationship is largely characterised by communication and coordination between the two actors resulting in agreement on a course of mutual action.

**bonds**   Credit instruments that are issued by governments or corporations in exchange for capital to cover expenditures that cannot be covered by existing resources. These are usually long-term instruments that can be traded on international markets and have variable values depending on interest rates and the ability of the issuer to generate capital.

**Bretton Woods**   Post-Second World War global system of political and economic organisation based on liberal ideologies. It is named after the New Hampshire, USA, town that hosted the 1944 conference between the Allied powers that would go on to win the war and create the post-war organisations and regimes that would seek to regulate international relations for much of the twentieth century. The system consisted of the three core organisations and related regimes: the IMF, the World Bank and the GATT/WTO. The system is seen to have ended in its original form with the 1971 end of the dollar–gold conversion mechanism. But the regimes and the structure that it established remain in most ways.

**capital**   A term that has a number of meanings in different theoretical contexts but that is most commonly used in classical/neo-classical economics to refer to man-made physical resources used to generate goods and services as well as financial resources. In order to generate the former the latter needs to be available and invested where market demands arise. Other traditions see the term as also referring to labour and natural resources that go into productive processes.

**capital accounts**   Part of the balance of payments between states. This is the existing amount of capital within a state and the amount of capital being exchanged with others. If there are fewer capital resources in one state compared to the demand for capital then imports of capital are required. Where there is a surplus of capital in one state's account then capital may be invested abroad (exported).

**capital markets**   The sources of excess or under-utilised capital resources that can be accessed by actors or markets with capital shortages. These markets rely on intermediary institutions, which act as mechanisms to connect capital supply (savings) with capital demand (borrowers). Largely characterised by high fluidity, these markets are central to the well-being of the contemporary global economy.

**capitalism/capitalist production**   A system of organising human activity and production, which largely relies on competition between actors for the accumulation of productive capabilities, resources, wealth and power. According to liberal triumphalists this is the highest form of human development and the last stage in the movement from the original human condition to its final condition. Market forces determine production and other human activity through supply and demand mechanisms.

**civil society**   Sub-state collective of individuals into directly or indirectly associated groups with similar motivations and interests. Often seen as acting as a key entity occupying the space between state apparatus and the masses. This can be local/domestic, national, international or even global in scope as well as focused on private or public sector issues.

**class**   Seen as the main way in which people are grouped together in the capitalist world system. An individual's role in, and relationship to, the means of production and capital formation and movement determines which class one is associated with. For Marxists, the labourers that operate in production are seen as the proletariat, while the owners of the means of production and those that facilitate the allocation of capital are the bourgeoisie. In the modern/postmodern era the classes are seen as being in conflict due to the maintenance of the position of each by the other.

**climate change**   The result of a set of environmental processes that are, at of the time of writing, not universally accepted or understood. Characterised by rapid changes in climatic conditions and in particular the raising of global temperatures and changing environmental patterns that seem to be linked to human agency (industrialisation and the burning of fossil fuels). Sea-level rises, desertification, drought and decreasing fresh water supplies are linked to climate change and are negatively impacting the human condition for many around the world.

**common market**  Level of regional integration between states characterised by the establishment of a customs union or its equivalent, as well as the unrestricted movement of capital and labour. Member states will negotiate the deregulation of common borders and markets to ensure a high level of economic integration and the accompanying regime(s). This is classed as the final stage of regional integration.

**comparative advantage**  David Ricardo's development of the concept of absolute advantage, which addresses the limitations of the latter in a global economy. A state has a comparative advantage in the production of a certain good if it produces it at a lower cost than other goods it produces. This is an important neo-liberal assumption that supports arguments for specialisation and free trade.

**conditionality**  Notion employed by one actor towards another when the former is approached for assistance by the latter. Most commonly used to refer to the terms governing the supply of financial support by the IMF to member states. Here the provider of support will request certain changes in policy or behaviour by the borrowing state in exchange for its support. It can also apply to bilateral and multilateral relations between states.

**corporation**  A business entity that can be created with various productive functions supplying goods, services or capital to consumer markets. This type of actor has an undetermined lifetime, raises capital through shared ownership with private shareholders but has limited liability and is unlimited in potential size. The 'bottom line' of corporations is to maximise profits and grow in size.

**current account**  The key element in calculating balance of payments, measuring a state's net flows of imports and exports of goods, services and capital.

**debt**  The total amount of capital resources an actor has borrowed in the past and owes to another actor (the creditor). Global access to capital markets means that debt is no longer held by one actor to another in the same state/market but can be owed to an actor almost anywhere else in the global system.

**debt crisis**  The name given to the global phenomenon that emerged in the early 1980s when many states around the world, but primarily in the developing world, defaulted on debt previously taken from other governments and private sector actors. During the oil boom years of the 1970s petrodollars were readily available as capital deposits and were used to lend to states that were seen as being unable to 'go bust'. Variable and very high interest rates coupled with economic stagnation resulted in wide-ranging governmental defaults and the inability to service long-term debts. The problem continues at the start of the twenty-first century.

**debt relief**  As a result of the debt crisis many states have sought the cancellation or rearranging of debt owed to external actors. Bilateral and multilateral agreements have resulted in some rescheduling and cancelling of some developing states' debts but interest rates and repayments remain unmanageable by many.

**decentralisation**   A term used to describe the devolution of governance from a central authority to peripheral authorities. This usually relates to the deregulation of human activity by state governments to local governments but can also refer to more widespread deregulation where private sector actors assume the role of (limited) governance.

**deficit**   The condition that emerges when expenditures exceed the available revenues over a period of time. This is most commonly a term used when discussing governmental budgets over a fiscal year or the budgets of corporations.

**deindustrialisation**   Term referring to the reduction of productive capacity within an economy. States may pursue this course of action and replace the lost manufactured goods through imports while specialising in knowledge-based sectors. Also a policy suggested by some environmentalists in order to protect the environment.

**democratisation**   The process of reform of instruments of governance, which leads to representative and accountable government. It is often a slow process that relies upon the emergence of a strong middle class and private sector.

**dependency theory**   Approach largely developed by Andre Gunder Frank, which suggests that international relations between states are characterised by asymmetric integration. One state relies upon another to a large extent for essential products and services such as technology, manufactured goods, capital and security. These types of relationships are structural in nature and are fixed. Most commonly used to explain the relationship between rich and poor states and the reason for underdevelopment.

**depression**   An economic condition characterised by significantly declining levels of income, production, investment and employment. Can be restricted to individual states but in the globalised economic system depressions usually affect many states at any one time.

**derivatives**   Financial products whose value is derived from that of other products or processes. Using some version or other of mathematic models for calculating the price or expected change in price of a package of investment products, derivatives are established. These emerged in the 1990s as important investment vehicles. By the 2000s, they had taken so many varied forms that it had become impossible to define very accurately what a derivative is or was. Those selling derivatives had to understand both the mathematics and the markets they were dealing with if they were to succeed without simply engaging in a dressed-up gamble.

**development**   This is a term that can be used in many different settings. In contemporary IPE development usually means economic growth and modern industrialisation measured primarily by GDP and per capita incomes. However, alternative approaches to IPE can view development as being measured in different ways, such as the meeting of basic needs for all, access to education and health services, democracy, human security and environmental sustainability, among others.

**developmental state**   Type of government policy employed over long periods of time by developing states as they pursue greater economic growth and industrialisation. This relies on government support of domestic industries (especially infant and high-value-added industries) and the maintenance of external barriers to imports. Many newly industrialised economies such as the East Asian Tiger Economies adopted this type of policy to develop but the notion of a 'developmental state' is counter to the Washington Consensus and the neo-liberalism of the global economic system.

**economies of scale**   These can emerge as a result of improvements in the production process of a good. The main characteristic is the reducing of unit production costs as a result of increases in the number of units produced, which derives from greater investment and increasing efficiency of production. Of course economies of scale can only emerge when the demand for the good being produced is sufficiently high; states with small domestic markets must access foreign markets to develop economies of scale.

**efficiency**   The efficient production of a good or service is measured by the combination of the natural resources, labour and capital that are used in the production process as well as its duration. Fewer inputs and shorter time taken to produce a good or service results in higher efficiency.

**exchange rate system**   The system by which national currencies are exchanged in global markets. This system is founded on certain rules that specify the ways in which appreciation and depreciation of currencies can take place. Fixed exchange rate systems require governments to control the amount of currency movements to limit variations in exchange rates to a narrow rate. In a floating exchange rate system governments can allow currency movements to whatever rate they want.

**factor endowment**   An actor's (most commonly used to refer to states) endowment of labour, land, capital and natural resources – known as factor endowments.

**fair trade**   System of international trade that requires a greater level of government and civil society involvement to influence or control the exchange of goods and services. This is a more recent phenomenon in IPE, which has been used or desired to help developing states to get a fair price for their products and to get fair access to more developed markets. Regulation in some areas is needed, such as the governmental certification that goods are produced using suitable labour and resources.

**false consciousness**   One of Karl Marx's core assumptions about modern human society. The masses are burdened with false consciousness as a result of their alienation from each other and the means of production as well as hegemonic forms of knowledge and materialism. This is characterised by the inability to understand the origins of their condition and the ability for change.

**fiscal policy**   A strategy used by governments to influence domestic demand through tax and spending policies. By expanding government spending and/or reducing taxes governments can help to encourage domestic economic demand and output. By reducing spending and/or raising taxes governments can discourage economic demand and output.

**foreign aid**   Official or private sector financial support given by one actor to another. This is usually given by developed states to developing states to assist in development projects or to deal with sudden and significant burdens. Foreign aid can come with some conditionality but often only requires some form of guarantee as to where the support is being utilised. Bilateral and multilateral agreements on foreign aid are quite common in the contemporary era but are criticised for not doing enough to help developing societies.

**foreign direct investment**   The financial and resource investment in one state by an actor in another state. Usually a corporation or group of individuals based in one state builds or purchases productive capabilities in another state in the pursuit of maximising profits.

**foreign exchange**   The purchasing of an amount of capital in one currency by using an equal amount in value terms of another currency. Exchange rates rarely remain constant unless the relevant governments have pursued a policy of pegging currencies to each other.

**free trade**   The deregulation of international trade through the removal of governmental barriers to trade, including taxes, tariffs and quotas on imports and exports. The removal of official barriers to trade is seen in neo-classical economics to facilitate international trade and investment, thus encouraging development and integration. Much criticism has been levelled at the notion of free trade by developing states as it removes protection for domestic infant and sensitive industries (which are seen by many as the keys to industrialisation).

**free trade agreement**   A bilateral or multilateral agreement engaged in by governments to facilitate trade in goods, services and capital between them by removing barriers to trade such as taxes, tariffs and quota limits. Some free trade agreements cover the liberalisation of all trade while others only cover trade in certain products and services. Most will require a number of years for full implementation as barriers are reduced to zero in stages. Free trade agreements are key components of the Washington Consensus.

**genocide**   A term used to categorise the organised and intentional killing of a large number of people over a defined period of time (usually a relatively brief period). The term is especially used to refer to the killing of people who have been identified as a single group based on their ethnicity or nationality.

**globalisation**   Name given to represent processes of integration between states/markets/ peoples at the global level of analysis. Through these processes actors in one part of the world can become interdependent with others in geographically distant places.

**gross domestic product (GDP)**   The total monetary value of goods and services produced in an economy in one year. In IPE this measure is primarily used to measure the production value of national economies but can also be used to measure the production values of common markets, regional groupings and the global economy as a whole.

**hegemonic stability**   Most famously developed and articulated by Charles Kindleberger in the early 1970s. It argues that a dominant state is needed to enforce rules of interaction between states in order to avoid the security dilemmas and instability associated with a system that lacks the oversight of such a power.

**hierarchy**   The ranking of actors in any given arena according to their power, wealth, influence and productive capabilities. For example, if a state's capabilities are greater compared to others, this state will sit atop the hierarchy.

**historical materialism**   An approach to understanding and explaining human relations by analysing modes of production and the relationship of individuals to these as well as looking at how the changes in production affect society. This is a core Marxist approach, which sees the human condition as being determined by the historical drive for greater productive capabilities.

**human security**   refers to the human condition pertaining to the well-being and security of individuals (as opposed to communities and/or states). Consideration is given to the following: economic, food, health, environmental, personal, community and political security as experienced by individuals.

**hyperinflation**   Rapid inflation within a state over a period of time, which results in rapid and catastrophic falls in the value of its currency.

**imperialism**   The political, economic and in some ways cultural domination by one state over others. The imperial state will use its greater power and productive capabilities to dominate others and alter the patterns of production and economic exchange to its benefit. Imperialism is largely characterised by the monopolisation of international relations by the imperial power while other states are isolated from each other. Imperialism is seen as a thing of the past, most often equated with the European imperialism of the 1600s to mid-1900s.

**import substitution**   A strategy used by developing states or states pursuing greater levels of self-reliance. This entails governmental support of targeted domestic industries that produce goods or services that would normally be obtained from foreign sources. It is often costly and directs resources to activities that are less efficient than others but raises independence from external actors and can lead to efficiency over time.

**Industrial Revolution**   The process of economic transformation, which began in the UK and north-western Europe in the mid-1700s. This revolution was founded on technological developments that allowed for the use of fossil fuels as sources of power and machinery in production. The result was the rapid increase in productivity and efficiency, which led to significantly greater economic wealth and productive capabilities.

**inflation**   A constant increase in the absolute consumer price of goods and services due to an inability of supply to meet demand; or the constant decline in the purchasing power of money due to an increase in the amount of money circulating in the economy, which is not met by a corresponding increase in available goods or services.

**intellectual property rights (IPRs)**   Legal recognition of the exclusive ownership rights of the creator for new creations or production processes. The tools for ensuring protection of this recognition include patents, trademarks, copyright and trade secrets.

**interest rates**   The payment made to savers for gaining access to the capital resources they make available. This is usually facilitated by banks and is a tool that encourages savers to make the funds available for investment elsewhere. It is usually determined by a percentage or rate that may or may not be fixed depending on the agreement established at the time capital is made available.

**interdependence**   Dependence as described by Robert Keohane and Joseph Nye is a state of existence that is determined or affected by external forces. Interdependence, therefore, is quite simply a condition where mutual dependence exists between two or more actors. In a situation of asymmetric interdependence two or more actors are dependent on each other but to varying degrees. In a system of complex interdependence the use of military force or other forms of violent confrontation will be counter-productive and irrational due to the reliance of actors on each other.

**invisible hand**   Also referred to as the invisible hand of the market: a term used to identify the self-regulating nature of the free market. The term was coined by Adam Smith and includes the key processes of supply, demand, competition and efficiency as ways in which resources are allocated to further production and development. State regulation or involvement in the market is seen as preventing the work of the invisible hand.

**labour**   The contribution that individuals collectively make to the production of a good or service.

*laissez-faire*   A French term meaning 'to let be' or 'to allow'; this idea is synonymous with free-trade policies. The *laissez-faire* school of thought holds a pure capitalist or free market view that capitalism is best left to its own devices. The basic idea is that less governmental interference in private economic matters, such as pricing, production and distribution, makes for a better system.

**letters of credit**   A binding commercial document that is usually issued by a bank or other financial institution, which obliges the applicant to make a payment of a fixed amount to a beneficiary at a future date. This tool is normally applied in international trade of substantial value and/or where the applicant and the beneficiary are in separate states.

**liquid assets**   Things that can be used in a crisis to pay demands for money, which include cash reserves, short-term debt and gold and other precious metals.

**macroeconomics**   The consideration of overall economic processes and characteristics. This area of political economy explores issues at the macro level such as overall production, consumption, supply and demand, GDP, employment levels, debt, trade, fiscal policy and capital accounts.

**market**   A term with varying meanings but that in contemporary IPE means the way in which the economic activity of societies is organised for production and consumption of goods and services. This is in effect the 'place', albeit in abstract form, and ways in which goods and services are produced and purchased.

**migration**   is the movement of people from one community to another both within and across borders. This movement can be either temporary or permanent, and can be driven by economic, political, environmental and social factors.

**Marshall Plan**   A broad-ranging foreign policy strategy employed by the Truman Administration in the United States following the Second World War. This policy provided vast amounts of financial and productive aid to Western European states as they sought to rebuild after the war as a means of promoting markets for US goods and services and as a bulwark against the growth of communist movements in Europe.

**means of production**   In the modern global economic system these are things that are usually owned by private corporations but can be communally owned in some states/systems. These are the actual structures and equipment used in the production of goods and services.

**medium of exchange**   This is a key function of money but does not exclusively refer to money alone. In order to purchase a certain good or service something needs to be given in return but rather than relying on a system of pure bartering an object of a given value can be used in multiple transactions. This is most commonly now money but can be other things such as metals.

**mercantilism**  Central concern within realist strands of thought with the security of the state. The security of a state was seen as directly related to its power in relation to other states. This security can be enhanced not just by the creation of a large and well-equipped army but also by the acquisition of wealth. At the domestic level this leads to policies designed to maximise tax revenues and at the international level to pursue an overall trade surplus.

**monetary policy**  A governmental strategy used to influence the economic activity that takes place in a given economy by controlling the supply of money available. This may take two forms: either expanding the money supply to stimulate economic activity in a depression or restricting it to discourage inflation in an economic upturn.

**monopoly**  A condition where a single actor dominates the production of a certain good or service in a market and so can control the supply and cost of these commodities.

**most-favoured nation status (MFN)**  A WTO rule that requires that any preferential treatment between two WTO member states in terms of the framework governing trade between them must be given to all other members and reciprocated. If two states agree to bilaterally lower barriers to trade with each other, they must also give the same treatment to all other WTO member states.

**multiculturalism**  describes a condition within a given community (usually defined as a single jurisdiction) where the existence and acceptance of multiple cultural traditions is evident. Often this term is used to refer to cultures associated with different ethnicities and/or nationalities.

**multilateralism**  Form of policy making and action that involves interaction between three or more actors. This type of relationship is largely characterised by communication and coordination between the group of actors resulting in agreement on a course of mutual action.

**multinational corporation (MNC)**  A corporation that has commercial activities, including production of goods and/or services as well as capital investments, in more than one state. In the contemporary global economy such entities tend to be very large and are usually headquartered in one state while having operations in a large number of others.

**mutually assured destruction (MAD)**  During the Cold War, with the proliferation of nuclear weapons between the United States and the USSR, this term arose to represent the effects of a nuclear conflict. Once each side had reached what they saw as an effective first-strike capability, the need arose to develop a second-strike capability, which would allow them to launch a devastating attack even after sustaining a full assault from the other side. Even with their first strikes both states would still be hit with the rival's second-strike capabilities and thus be destroyed.

**neo-classical economics**  This is the dominant school of economic thought in the capitalist system. Its fundamental focus is on the deregulation of economic activity and the acceptance of purely market forces to determine production, prices, employment and so on. It is based on the belief that unhindered competition in the market will lead to maximum efficiency, productivity and self-regulation. In policy terms, neo-classical economics manifests in free trade, open markets and *laissez-faire* economics.

**neo-imperialism** The term given to the modern exploitation and domination of poorer socie-ties/states by richer ones. Here, military conquest and direct political control are no longer seen as the requisites for imperialism. Rather, it is structures that promote economic relationships, which are similar to those evident in the era of European imperialism and that result in devel-oping states being dependent on the wealthier and more powerful states. Furthermore, these structures are only alterable by the developed states that create them.

**neo-liberalism** In the contemporary global system this term represents the marked shift away from the pursuit of governmental involvement in the economy and towards placing greater responsibility for economic processes on the market itself. This type of change is favoured and actively pursued by many governments in the West but also, importantly, by the large interna-tional institutions established as part of the Bretton Woods System.

**oligopoly** A condition where a small number of actors dominate the production of a certain good or service in a market and so can coordinate with each other to control the supply and cost of these commodities.

**open markets** Markets that are fully liberalised, having no barriers to external trade in prod-ucts, services and capital as well as fewer restrictions on the movement of labour.

**per capita income** The amount each person earns if the total national income is divided equally across the population.

**power** Most commonly defined as the ability of one actor to make a second behave/not behave in a way that it would not/would normally act. This can be reliant on a number of categories of capability or a combination of them. For example, wealth, military power and political influence.

**prisoners' dilemma** Game theory model where two prisoners are held in isolation from each other and the release, or non-release, of each is determined by the action of the other. Crucially, which outcome is arrived at is determined by each prisoner assessing the probability of how the other prisoner responds to questioning. It is commonly used to predict behaviour and policy directions by focusing on the likelihood of cooperation or cheating.

**protectionism** Governmental policy that aims to protect domestic industries (usually infant or sensitive industries) from external competition. Tools available include taxes, quotas and other tariffs on imports as well as subsidies on exports.

**purchasing power parity (PPP)** An economics method used to determine the rela-tive capabilities of individuals in different states to purchase goods and services. Using per capita GDP methods does not accurately portray the comparative living standards of people in different states because the costs of goods and services may differ from one state to another. By comparing consumer prices of produce and adjusting relative capabilities to pur-chase, a clearer picture can be established of the comparative wealth of individuals in different states.

**real interest rates** When trying to accurately compare interest rates in different states it is essential to take account of differing national inflation rates. Real interest rates are determined by deducting the rate of inflation from the actual or nominal rate of interest.

**regimes**   These are the combination of procedures, rules/laws, values, ideas, norms and traditions in order to form a way of organising specific forms of international relationships such as trade. States that join such a regime will find their behaviour and expectations influenced accordingly/to some extent. Regimes can be described as collections of non-tangible institutions that are supported by organisations: so the WTO supports the global trading regime.

**regionalism**   Can operate within a national boundary or, more commonly, within the context of international political economy, across several nation states. Some regions are identified by their geographical location, such as the tropics or temperate regions. Others are known by their economic interactions, such as the North American Free Trade Area. The most advanced form of regionalism to date is the European Union, which has elements of a common currency, integrated military units and a degree of supranationality with some legislation taking precedence over national parliaments.

**regulation**   A government or intergovernmental policy to control aspects of a 'free' market. This may be on the grounds of common public good, such as health and safety regulations, to avoid monopolies forming or to reduce the risk of market failure.

**rentier**   Can be an individual whose income is predominantly derived from rents. A rentier state is one where its income comes from the export of its natural resources such as oil or timber. Renting out part of the state's sovereign territory to allow another power to develop military bases there may also generate external income.

**savings**   An important part of both personal and governmental economic strategies. They are the difference between disposable income and expenditure. There are marked differences between attitudes towards saving for either a specific purchase or as a precaution against unforeseen expenditures and the counter-position of not only avoiding savings but actually exceeding affordable expenditure, funded by taking out secured loans.

**scarcity**   A fundamental aspect of the international political economy as it drives market demand and pricing of commodities. The more widely a product is available, the greater the opportunity for competition between providers, unless a monopoly of provision applies, and this is likely to drive costs down. The model of supply and demand therefore suggests that as a commodity's scarcity increases, a rise in its value will follow.

**securitisation**   A process by which assets, such as mortgaged property, are treated as commodities that can be bought and sold. If a borrower defaults on a repayment that has been 'secured' in relation to property or some other tangible good then the lender can repossess whatever has been offered as security for the loan.

**self-interest**   Refers to any policy or action taken that is in the interest of the actor initiating such action, or possibly reaction to the acts of others.

**self-regulation**   A concept that can be applied to a range of activities. In the context of international political economy it is mainly associated with the private sector and the attempts by multinational corporations to monitor and control their actions in the absence of international authority to do so.

**socialism**  A system of social organisation whereby the ownership and control of the means of production and distribution of capital and other goods rests with the community as a whole. In Marxist theory socialism is seen as the stage following capitalism in the transition to a fully communal society.

**sovereignty**  A key element of the modern state system. The concept of there being no higher authority above the sovereign state underpins the majority of international relations. This remains the case despite many processes of globalisation that appear to be making national boundaries more open to external influence. These include growing economic interdependence, trans-boundary pollution and electronic communications that bypass governmental controls.

**stocks**  Stocks and shares are tradable commodities that are the basis of business at various stock exchanges around the world. Investors and speculators will buy stock, or a share, of certain commodities or businesses in the hope that over time the value of this stock will rise, thereby producing a profit should the relevant stocks or shares be sold on. Of course these values can also decline so there can be a lot of volatility in certain markets. Traders try to follow patterns in the fluctuation of stock and share prices in order to judge when to buy or sell in order to maximise profit.

**structure**  Structure can take many forms. This may be in the political, economic or even socio-cultural fields. Structures are not always easily identifiable. Johan Galtung's theory of 'structural violence' highlights how particular aspects of structures within which they operate can disadvantage certain individuals. For example, women living in a patriarchy are likely to face a range of gender-based disadvantages and discriminations.

**surplus value**  The difference between what a product costs to produce and what it is actually sold for. In other words it is the profit margin. Neo-Marxists and structuralists pay particular attention to this value as it is often closely tied to the role of labour and the way in which this is undervalued under capitalism.

**sustainable development**  A term that has become something of a 'catch all' phrase, which is open to many varied interpretations and has, therefore, lost much of its original substance. In essence it refers to a type of development where the needs of the current generation are met without compromising the ability of future generations to meet their own needs. This definition still holds true but is clearly compromised to some extent when there is a lack of consensus on how to define 'development'.

**tariffs**  Imposed by governments as a form of import duty. In addition to raising revenue for the national exchequer this is also a method by which domestic industries can be 'protected' from cheap imports. Despite the rhetoric of the majority of the world's governments and economists that embrace and promote free market economic policies there remains considerable evidence of the imposition of tariffs and other barriers to trade, particularly in relation to agricultural produce exported from the global South to the global North.

**technology**  Can often be thought of in terms of 'hi-tech' applications to weaponry, communications, health sciences or a range of other applications. However, it can also be relatively 'low' levels of technological development that can prove to be decisive. The invention of the stirrup, for example, created a cavalry force that proved superior to infantry forces. Similarly, it is low or intermediate technology such as solar cookers or small-scale hydropower projects that is at the forefront of meeting the basic needs of the world's poorest people.

**Third World**  A term that has its origins in the time of the French Revolution and the so-called 'third estate'. More recently it has come to be associated with the developing countries of the global South. In this scenario the US, Western Europe and similarly 'developed' states were seen as the First World, with the communist bloc states the Second World in the bipolar world order of the Cold War. Third World is less commonly used to describe the developing states as it has gained a rather negative association of backwardness and helplessness. Full consensus has yet to be achieved on a suitable alternative epithet.

**trade**  The range and diversity of traded goods in the contemporary global economy is immense. This is based on a system of exchange that can be traced back to the earliest human communities and their interactions. The exchange of goods and services may be based on raw materials, manufactured products and a range of services to facilitate this trade.

**transaction costs**  The costs incurred as a result of a particular exchange of goods or services. These may be in connection to the respective values of what is exchanged in terms of which buyer or seller makes the most profit or loss. Alternatively costs may be of a more abstract nature with regard to issues related to but not directly associated with a particular exchange. Trading with one partner may alienate other potential partners if they disapprove of this transaction. Other costs could include the use of intermediaries or some form of payment made to facilitate a transaction, such as the commission charged when buying or selling different currencies.

**unilateralism**  A policy or other action that is taken by a single actor, or single representative of a collection of actors, which is not part of an agreement with other actors. An example of this could be a unilateral declaration of independence, rather than a managed and agreed timetable towards independence.

**veto**  A position taken that effectively prevents the implementation of a proposal or action. For example, on the UN Security Council the five permanent members have the power of veto, which enables any one of them to block resolutions put before the Council.

**Washington Consensus**  The post-Second World War agreement between the major powers that established the Bretton Woods international financial institutions and agreed the criteria by which the post-war international economic system would be coordinated and managed.

**Westphalian system**  The Treaty of Westphalia (1648) marked the end of the Thirty Years' War in Europe. It is also often referred to as the start of the modern nation state system. This system places national sovereignty as its central guiding principle. There is no international authority higher than national government, with an ethos of self-help and non-intervention between sovereign states.

**world-system theory**  A view of the world that takes into account relatively long periods of history with a particular emphasis on the expansion of European empires and resulting patterns of trade. As wealth flowed from the colonies to the centre of power of each empire this maintained and reinforced the 'core/periphery' relationship between the colonisers and their subjugated territories. Importantly, this underlying relationship has continued to impact upon the relative division of power in the international system well beyond the period in formal decolonisation.

**zero-sum game**   The result of a competition or exchange where there is a finite and balanced amount of profit or loss. For example, an equal division would be a 50/50 split, or there may be a variation of 49/51 or 1/99, but whatever is gained from one actor in a relationship is necessarily lost by another, with the total value of the resources under dispute remaining the same. In contrast, a non-zero-sum game can see both win–win and lose–lose outcomes.

# Index